Illustrator Foundations

The Art of Vector Graphics and Design in Illustrator

Illustrator Foundations

The Art of Vector Graphics and Design in Illustrator

Rafiq Elmansy

Focal Press
Taylor & Francis Group
NEW YORK AND LONDON

Please visit the book's companion website at www.illustratorfoundations.com

First published 2013
by Focal Press
70 Blanchard Road Suite 402, Burlington, MA 01803

Simultaneously published in the UK
by Focal Press
2 Park Square, Milton Park, Abingdon, Oxon OX14 4RN

Focal Press is an imprint of the Taylor & Francis Group, an Informa business.

Notices

Knowledge and best practice in this field are constantly changing. As new research and experience broaden our understanding, changes in research methods, professional practices, or medical treatment may become necessary.

Practitioners and researchers must always rely on their own experience and knowledge in evaluating and using any information, methods, compounds, or experiments described herein. In using such information or methods, they should be mindful of their own safety and the safety of others, including parties for whom they have a professional responsibility.

Product or corporate names may be trademarks or registered trademarks, and are used only for identification and explanation without intent to infringe.

Library of Congress Cataloging in Publication Data

Elmansy, Rafiq.

Illustrator foundations: the art of vector graphics and design in illustrator/Rafiq Elmansy.

p. cm.

1. Computer animation. 2. Adobe Illustrator (Computer file) I. Title.

TR897.7.E355 2013

777'.7—dc23

2012021513

ISBN: 978-0-240-52593-8 (pbk)
ISBN: 978-0-240-52596-9 (ebk)

Printed in the United States of America by Courier, Kendallville, Indiana.

Typeset in Myriad Pro
Project Managed and Typeset by: diacriTech

This book is dedicated to my parents who have discovered my love for art and design, my beloved wife who supported me through every step of my life and career, and my two daughters for brightening my life.

Contents

Acknowledgments xiii

Chapter 1: Introducing Adobe Illustrator CS6 1

Scope of the Book 3

Is This Book for You? 4

How This Book Is Organized 4

What's New in Illustrator CS6 5

New Modern User Interface 5

64-bit Support 6

Pattern Creation 6

Gradient on Stroke 7

Image Trace 7

Illustrator CS6 Workspace 8

Managing Panel 10

Customize Your Own Workspace 11

Illustrator Preferences 13

Plug-ins and Scratch Disks 13

User Interface 14

Illustrator Shortcuts 14

Managing Resources with Adobe Bridge 16

Top Menus and Panel 17

Folders and Favorites Panels 18

Filters Panel 18

Collections Panel 18

Export Panel 19

Content Panel 19

Metadata and Keywords Panels 20

Compact Mode 20

Batch Rename 21

Output Images as PDF and Web Gallery 21

Chapter 2: Managing Documents in Adobe Illustrator 23

Working with New Documents 24

Working with Templates 27

Working with Artboards 28

Artboard Panel 31
Saving Artboards 31
Saving Illustrator Documents........ 32
Working with Rulers........ 33
Ruler Measurements........ 34
Video Rulers 35
Working with Guides........ 35
Convert Path to a Guide........ 36
Smart Guides 36
Grids........ 37
Guides and Grid Preferences 37
Working with XMP Metadata 38

Chapter 3: Drawing in Illustrator 41
Drawing with the Pen Tool 41
Free Drawing with the Pencil Tool 44
Closed Path Primitives 47
Rectangle Tool........ 47
Rounded Rectangle Tool........ 48
Ellipse Tool 49
Polygon Tool........ 49
Star Tool 50
Flare Tool 50
Open Paths Primitives........ 51
Line Segment Tool........ 51
Arc Tool 51
Spiral Tool 52
Rectangular Grid Tool........ 53
Polar Grid Tool 54
Modifying Paths 55
Path Eraser Tool........ 55
Eraser Tool........ 55
Join and Average Points 56
Simplify Paths 57
Clean Up 59

Chapter 4: Working with Color 61
Changing Artwork Colors 64

Color Panel 64
Control Panel 65
Color Swatches 66
Color Guide 72

Chapter 5: Working with the Gradient Tool **75**
Gradient Panel 76
How to Create Gradient 78
Applying Gradient to Stroke 79
Gradient Tool 81
Linear Gradient 82
Radial Gradient 83
Working with Meshes 86

Chapter 6: Working with Patterns **91**
Understanding Pattern Design 91
Converting Artwork into a Pattern 93
Working with the Pattern Options Panel 96

Chapter 7: Editing Artwork **101**
Working with Compound Paths 101
Working with Pathfinder 103
Shape Builder Tool 112
Splitting Objects into Grids 115
Transform Artwork 116
Move Objects 116
Rotate Objects 117
Reflect Objects 118
Scale Objects 119
Shear Objects 120
Free Transform 121

Chapter 8: Brushes **123**
Brushes Panel 124
Brush Types 126
Calligraphic Brush 127
Scatter Brush 131
Art Brush 133
Bristle Brush 134

Pattern Brushes.......... 138
Blob Brush.......... 140

Chapter 9: Working with Type.......... 143
Placing Text into an Illustrator File.......... 144
Text Properties.......... 148
Make with Warp.......... 149
Make with Mesh.......... 150
Working with Paragraph.......... 152
Area Text Options.......... 152
Text Area Threading.......... 154
Working with Text and Paths.......... 157
Convert Text into Path.......... 160

Chapter 10: Masks, Blends, and Blending Modes.......... 161
Working with Masks.......... 162
The Mask Concept.......... 162
Applying Mask to Artwork.......... 162
Applying Mask to Images.......... 165
Working with Opacity Mask.......... 167
Blends.......... 171

Chapter 11: Working with Images and Image Trace.......... 177
Links Panel.......... 179
Image Trace.......... 184
Image Trace Panel.......... 186

Chapter 12: Symbols and Graphs.......... 193
Working with Symbols.......... 193
Converting Artwork to Symbols.......... 194
Modifying Symbols.......... 197
Working with Graphs.......... 199
Switching between Graph Types.......... 202
Changing the Color of the Graph.......... 203
Add Artwork to Graph.......... 205

Chapter 13: 3D and Drawing in Perspective.......... 207
3D Perspective Grid.......... 208
3D Effects.......... 216
3D Extrude & Bevel.......... 216

Position 217
Extrude and Bevel 218
Surface 218
3D Revolve 223
3D Rotation 226

Chapter 14: Working with Effects 231
Appearance Panel 232
Live Effect 235
Illustrator Effects 237
3D Effects 237
Convert to Shape 237
Crop Marks 238
Distort and Transform 238
Path and Pathfinder Effects 240
Rasterize 240
Stylize 240
SVG Filters 241
Warp 241
Photoshop Effects 242
Object Distortion Tools 242
Blending Modes 245

Chapter 15: Arranging and Saving Artwork 247
Working with Groups 248
Lock Artwork 249
Hide Artwork 250
Arranging Objects 251
Working with Layers 252
Saving an Illustrator Document 255
Save Document as Template 255
Save Document as PDF 256
Save Document as JPG 256
Save Document as PNG 257
Save Documents as Photoshop PSD 258

Chapter 16: Illustrator for Web 261
Preparing Illustrator Documents for Web 262
Anti-aliasing 264

Optimizing Web Graphics 266
Saving for Web as GIF 269
Saving for Web as JPG 272
Saving for Web as PNG 273
Using Web Slices 274

Chapter 17: Printing 277
New Document Settings 278
Converting Text to Outline 279
Working with Bleeds 281
Setting Up Trim Marks 283
Working with Colors 284
Separations Preview 285
Printing Options 286
General Settings 287
Marks and Bleeds 288
Output 289
Graphics 289
Color Management 290
Advanced and Summary 291

Chapter 18: Integration with Adobe CS6 Applications 293
Integration with Photoshop 294
Export Artwork as Flattened Image 294
Export Artwork as Photoshop PSD Format 294
Copy and Paste 296
Integration with Flash 300
Integration with After Effects 303

Index 307

For more information and examples, and to get a full understanding of Adobe Illustrator and its tools, visit: www.illustratorfoundations.com.

Acknowledgments

As a visual and design artist, I have always been passionate about Adobe Illustrator and this book represents this passion. This book has come to life through the collective effort and hard work of a great team that has taken it from a draft idea to a final source of information in your hands.

First of all, I would like to thank everyone who worked and assisted me with this book project and helped me to successfully complete it. As you may know, during the writing of this book the Taylor & Francis Group acquired Focal Press. So I would like to thank the teams of both of these publishers.

Big thanks to Katy Spencer, the product manager, who has taken care of the book proposal in its first stage as a draft thought and initiated the project. She has helped me so much in the first stage of the project as a product manager, and later as a friend and mentor after she had moved from Focal Press.

During the second stage of the book, the responsibilities of the book product manager have moved to a very special person, David Bevans. I would like to thank him for all his support and help to complete this book and providing all the necessary support and resources to turn this idea into a successful book project in his hands.

Also, I would like to give special thanks to Jean-Claude Tremblay, Adobe Illustrator expert and instructor, for his amazing help in tech editing the book. Jean-Claude does not only provide tech editing, but he also gave suggestions and ideas for improving the book title and delivering it in the best shape.

I would like to thank project manager Dennis Troutman for the great help and support in the production process of the book. Also, I would like to thank Denise Power and Gail Newton.

I would like to thank the Adobe Illustrator beta program team for the great opportunity to join the prerelease program, especially Harpreet Singh, Chris Kitchener and Pallab Jyotee. And in the Adobe ME Prerelease program, I would like to thank Ahmed Gaballah, Avinash Singh Kotwal, Iouri Tchernoousko and Ashish Saxena.

Also, I would like to give special thanks and appreciation to the Adobe user group program manager and Adobe community professional managers Liz Frederick, Aaron Houston and Rachael Luxemburg.

At the end, I would like to give extraordinary thanks to my wife, Radwa, and my two children, Malk and Hala, for inspiring me and giving me the power to complete this book.

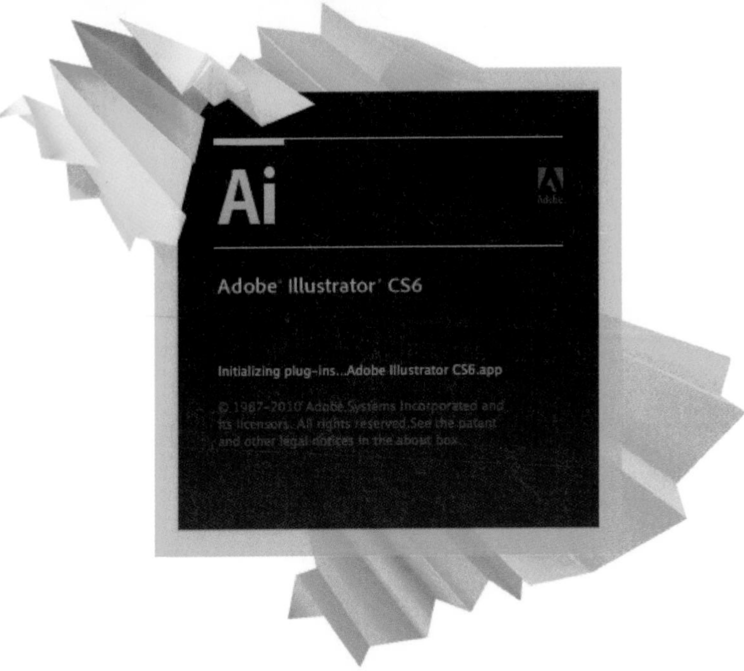

Introducing Adobe Illustrator CS6

When I first worked with Adobe Illustrator years ago, I felt that I was in front of artist's tools, similar to brushes and pencils. This is due to my traditional art background; however, applications in the digital world of design and art have replaced the traditional artist tools.

Adobe Illustrator is one of those applications that most designers and artists depend on to create illustrations, designs, and more using the creative features and capabilities that the designer can apply to visualize creative ideas. Through the years, Illustrator has developed to include more features and provide more options to artists and designers.

I know that many of you would like to skip this silly introduction and move directly to the features, interesting tips, and how-to examples. But I must say that these few pages are very important to setting up the concepts and ideas that you need to know while reading this book, as well as to using Illustrator more efficiently and professionally. It is important to understand some basic information before digging into the real-life tricks and techniques; this will make your learning process much easier and help you understand the concept of how to use Illustrator more efficiently and professionally.

Behind Adobe Illustrator and other graphic applications, there are two types of digital images or formats that construct the images and artwork that you see and use in your design or animation. These are bitmaps and vectors. Identifying the difference between these types is very important for any designer in order to know the difference between various image formats. Also, learning about the difference between bitmaps and vectors can help you understand how Adobe Illustrator creates artwork and how it is different from other application such as Adobe Photoshop.

Bitmap images or raster images are images based on arrays of bits that consist of pixels. These bits arrange next to each other to construct the whole image. This array of bits and pixels includes image information such as the colors, lines, and other required data that brings the image to your screen as you see it. One of the easy ways you can identify the bitmap images is to open the image in any graphic application and zoom in to the image many times until you see the image pixels; this means that the image you are viewing is a bitmap.

FIG 1-1 Bitmap and vector images

Bitmap images have many formats, such as JPG, PNG, BMP, and GIF. These formats are used in different digital graphic designs such as web design, application designs, and video sequence images. There is an important difference between the design source format and the final image format. The source formats are the file extensions that you use to save your design or image while working in it. For example, the source file extensions for Photoshop files are PSD and TIFF. These formats can include information such as the layers, effects, and masks.

In many cases, the source files are not very helpful as the final output format for the design; in order to use your design in web, user interface, and other design tasks, you need to save your design in one of the final image formats as above. The final image format does not include the design layers, effects, or masks—it makes the design flat by default. Thus, the final images are smaller in size than the source files.

The second type of format is vector graphics. Unlike bitmap images, vector images consist of linear paths that create the image and hold information about the image points. However, vector images result from calculations that lead to the final artwork. When you zoom in on the edges of a vector graphic and try to compare it with a bitmap graphic, you will notice that the vector graphic has much sharper and cleaner edges because it does not consist of pixels like the bitmap images do. Vector images are also resolution-independent, because the resolution represents the number of pixels that each inch or point in the image includes, while vector images do not include any pixels. This makes vector images easy to edit and scale.

Vector graphics have many formats, such as AI, CDR, and EPS. The difference between bitmap formats and vector formats is that the vector formats are source files that include the artwork source, layers, and effects. You cannot use these formats to upload images to the web or as a format for your final design images. The vector format needs to be converted into one of the bitmap formats, such as JPG, PNG, BMP, or GIF, in order to be able to use it in projects such as building websites.

While most of the graphic design applications can handle both image types in one way or another, some applications focus more on one format than the other. For example, Adobe Photoshop and PaintShop are more specialized in raster images and bitmap image editing. On the other hand, applications such as CorelDraw and Adobe Illustrator focus on vector images and give you huge capabilities to create and handle them.

Scope of the Book

In this Adobe Illustrator book, we will try to provide a full tutorial guide for you in order to cover all the required features and how to use the program tools and effects to create artwork. Each chapter will cover a specific part of the program and the features associated with it. Usually, we will start with discovering each feature and tool options and capabilities; then, we will move to a practical example to learn how each of the program tools and features work in real life. While many people like to go directly into the examples, trying to discover each tool before starting the practical examples will help you to understand its options and abilities. Subsequently, you can use the tool descriptions and examples in this book to visualize your artwork and ideas.

There any many advanced Illustrator books on the market that require previous knowledge of Illustrator. This book begins at the first step in the Illustrator world. Also, you will notice that this book is different from the other beginner's books because it does not limit the discussion to just describing the tools and their properties—it extends to provide practical examples to help you understand each tool and the feature's abilities.

The book is meant to prepare you to be a professional Illustrator user. While going through the different program options, we will try to discuss how each feature is used in real design projects and the benefits of using each feature. This will provide a wider scope of learning and help you to extend the practical tips and skills to real life. Along with the feature descriptions and examples, you will find side notes that include extra information related to each feature, which can add more value to the information included in the main content. You will also find notes that describe the common shortcuts associated with each feature.

Is This Book for You?

Are you graphic designer, web designer, animator, or video expert? Adobe Illustrator is one of the applications that is widely used in many design fields. Illustrator is involved in these fields at different levels. Some design and video projects are done in applications such as Photoshop or After Effects, and Illustrator is used to create assistant resources such as icons, illustrations, and artwork. While Illustrator can be an assistant application, it can also be used as the main design application for designs such as logos, printing materials, web designs, and mobile user interfaces or games. You can use Adobe Illustrator to build the whole design from A to Z, making Adobe Illustrator the main application in your design project.

Using Illustrator at any level makes it part of your different design projects. Thus, if you are working in any of the design fields above and would like to learn about a new tool to help you in your work, then this book is for you and can be your first step to excel in an essential design program like Illustrator. For students who would like to learn about graphic design and digital drawing, Adobe Illustrator is one of the main tools that you should learn about, and this book provides a beginner's guide to help you learn about this great program.

How This Book Is Organized

The book includes 18 chapters that gradually introduce you to each of Adobe Illustrator's features and tools. The first chapters are a basic introduction that provide basic information that can help you navigate the program features more easily, such as the program workspace and managing resources with Adobe Bridge, one of the efficient applications that allows you to preview, navigate, and arrange files.

After covering the basic features, the last chapters will discuss practical topics such as the integration between Illustrator and other Adobe Suite applications such as Photoshop, Flash, and After Effects. We will also cover how to create web designs in Illustrator and export content in HTML5 and mobile-friendly formats.

Each chapter covers a specific feature or part of Illustrator and discusses it and the features associated with it. Usually, this discussion starts with a description of the feature and its options; then we move to practical examples that help better explain each tool and feature. Along with the book, there is a companion website at http://www.illustratorfoundations.com that includes the practical examples with files that you can use to follow each example.

What's New in Illustrator CS6

Since Adobe Illustrator was first developed by Adobe in 1986, it has been revised through the years and turned from a basic typesetting and vector graphic tool into a complex application that supports creating content for web and mobile and adds 3D effects to artwork. Adobe Illustrator CS6 is the latest version and is bundled in the Adobe Creative Suite 6; you can also order it as an individual application. Before we can go into the rest of the book, let us overview the new features that have been added to Adobe Illustrator CS6.

New Modern User Interface

One of the remarkable features in the Adobe Creative Suite is that the applications share the same user interface style and theme. This makes it easy for the user to quickly become familiar with the application. For example, if you are using Photoshop and would like to learn about Illustrator, the unified interface will help you easily familiarize yourself with Illustrator.

FIG 1-2 Adobe Illustrator CS6 new interface

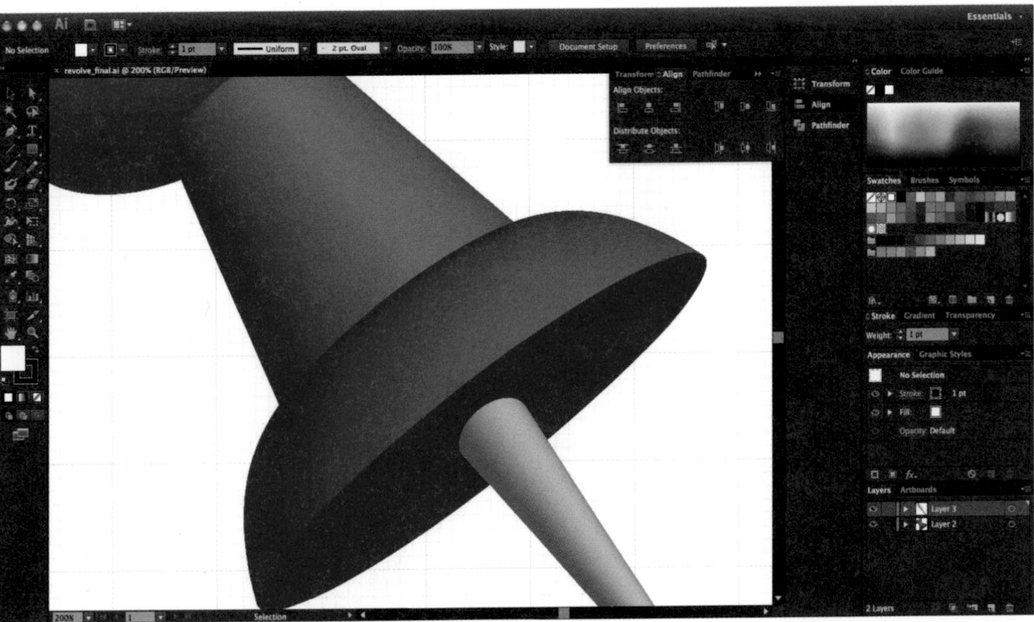

The new version of Illustrator has a unified new interface similar to Photoshop and some other Adobe CS6 products. When you install Adobe Illustrator CS6, you will notice the interface has changed to a dark theme similar to the one in Photoshop. The new version of Illustrator gives you the option to choose from four degrees of darkness and brightness for the user interface. You have the option to choose from the Illustrator Preferences dialog box the best theme style that fits with your taste.

64-bit Support

Most graphic applications love to consume computer resources, and good application performance depends on your computer hardware. The new version of Adobe Illustrator supports 64-bit; this support improves Illustrator performance, makes it faster, and helps you to work more efficiently.

Pattern Creation

Patterns are one of the important artwork elements because they help you to create repeated artwork from simple shapes and drawings such as backgrounds. However, patterns have not always been easy to use. Creating and defining patterns has been one of the more complicated processes in Adobe Illustrator. In the new version of Adobe Illustrator, this process becomes much easier using the new pattern creation features that allow you to create a pattern and define it with a preview of the final results, as we will discuss in Chapter 6.

FIG 1-3 Pattern creation panel

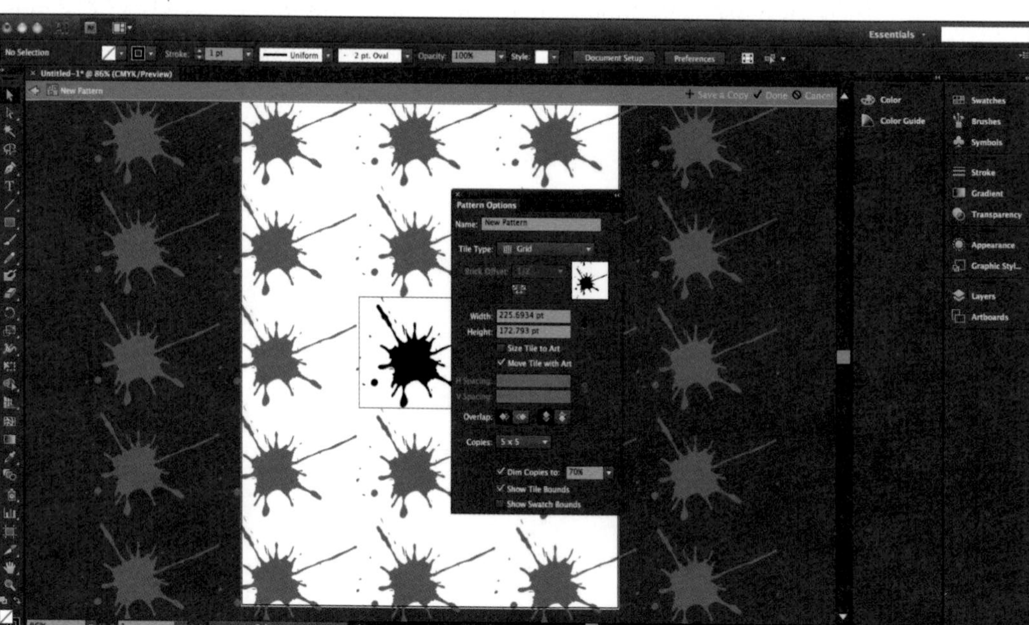

Gradient on Stroke

Objects in Adobe Illustrator can be filled with different types of colors, gradients, and patterns. In the previous versions, it was not easy to add gradient to strokes, because we had to convert them to outline with a normal fill in order to be able to add gradient. Now, the process is much easier because you can add gradient directly to strokes without extra steps, and you can do this while keeping the object editable.

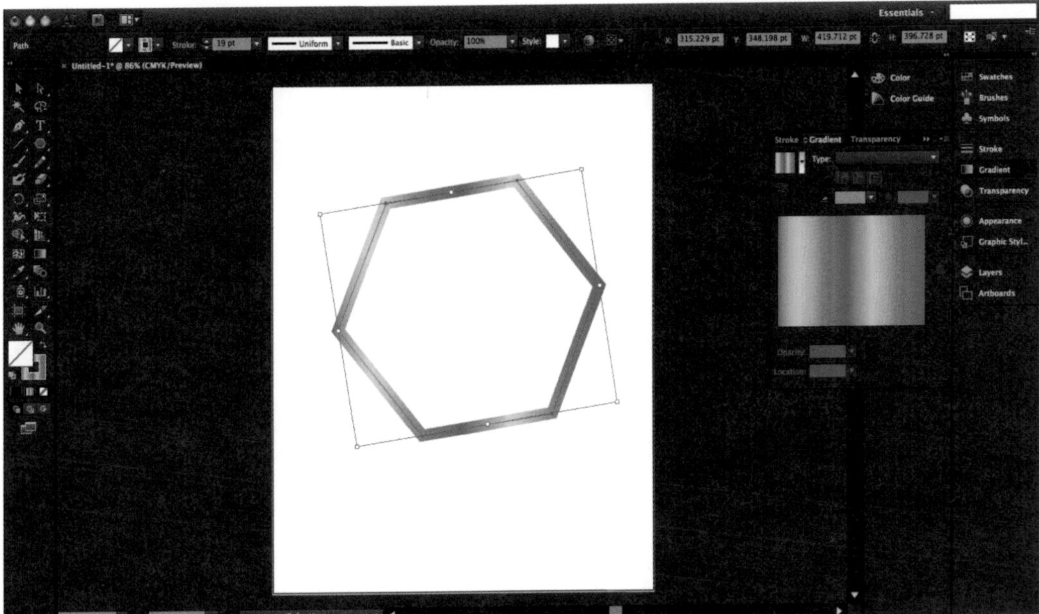

FIG 1-4 Add gradient to strokes

Image Trace

One of the amazing added features in the previous version was the ability to convert raster or bitmap images into vector paths, which gives you the ability to edit scale and give the bitmap image a more artistic or hand-drawn look. As we will see in Chapter 11 on working with bitmaps, Illustrator CS6 has an improved image tracer feature. We will also cover other features and tools such as the smart effects and Gaussian blur bitmap effect.

After this introduction to the book and Adobe Illustrator's new features that make it different from the previous versions, let us move forward to delve a little deeper into the Adobe Illustrator interface and essential sections such as the Preferences dialog box, which lets you set up your Illustrator options properly, and the Shortcut dialog box, which lets you customize the shortcuts of each feature to make your work faster and easier. Later in this chapter, we will cover how to manage Illustrator

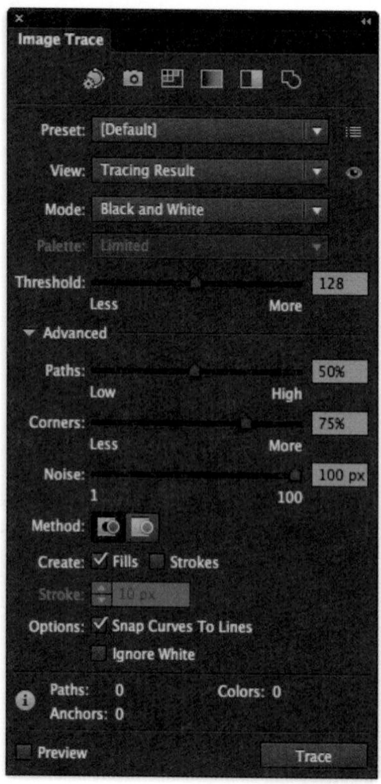

FIG 1-5 The image trace feature in Illustrator CS6

resources using Adobe Bridge, one of the companions of Adobe Illustrator, and other Adobe products. You can use Adobe Bridge to navigate, preview, arrange, and manage your files.

Illustrator CS6 Workspace

Since the production of the Adobe Creative Suite package, Adobe CS products have shared a similar interface and workspace concept. You will notice this when you open multiple Adobe products. Almost all of the products share the same user interface concept, such as the floating panels and the top menus structure.

While each application has different tools and functions based on its use, most of them share general functions such as the program Preferences and Shortcut dialog boxes. This is one of the reasons that it is easy for the novice user to understand the application user interface when he or she has previous experience with any of Adobe's products. This is one of the advantages of using integrated Adobe products in the design workflow. For example, you can share the files and jump between Adobe applications more easily than when using different unintegrated products. Also, using applications with the same user interface structure helps you to feel like you are in one place and not jumping between different interface concepts.

Adobe Illustrator is one of those applications that includes many panels, and when you work with these panels open, the workspace becomes busy and takes up much of the working area. This is one of the problems that we used to face in older versions of Illustrator. The current floating panel structure helps you to save more space for your working area and complete your work more professionally.

Understanding the structure of Adobe Illustrator can help you to find the features you want more easily than searching for them through the program. In this part of the book, we will focus on the anatomy of the Illustrator interface and how to customize the workspace to fit with your needs and work style.

FIG 1-6 The anatomy of Illustrator CS6 workspace

The Illustrator interface anatomy consists of following main sections:

- The top menu section is similar to many applications, and there you can find all the application options and features. While many features have special panels, these features still have representative commands in the top menus.
- When you choose an object on the stage, you can find this specific object's properties listed in the top bar of the Control panel. You can also find the Application bar, where there are icons that let you access assistant products such as Adobe Bridge and the Workspace menu, which lets you manage the workspace appearance.

- On the left side of the Illustrator interface is the Tools panel, the most important panel in the product because you use it in creating your designs and artwork.
- The workspace is in the middle of the product interface. You can open multiple files in tab order and display each file by clicking on its tab in the top of the workspace.
- On the right side of the application you will find floating panels that include some other important functions and options, such as the Color Swatch, Layers, and Appearance panels.
- On the bottom of the document window, you can find the Zoom list and the artboard navigator—we will talk about artboards in Illustrator in the second chapter. Next to the artboard navigator, Adobe Illustrator displays document-related information such as the active tool, the number of undos, the artboard name, and so on.

Note

The Application Frame command is available only on Mac, as Windows always shows the application in a framed user interface.

Managing Panel

Adobe Illustrator gives you the flexibility to handle a panel's size and position. The panels in Adobe products are called floating panels because you can easily move and arrange them in the workspace, gather them in tabs, or dock them in one of the workspace sides.

Note

The Window menu is where you can open panels. Just open the Window menu and check the panel to open it, or uncheck it to hide it.

To drag the panel or change its position, you can click and hold the top bar of the panel to start dragging it. When the panel is collapsed in the dock, you can select and drag the panel tab to move it. You can also attach the panel to any of the workspace panels by dragging it to this part. You will notice a blue highlight to show the place where the panel will be attached.

To collapse the panel, click the arrow icon in the top right of each panel. Close it by clicking the X icon in the top left. To maximize or minimize the panel, you can double-click the top panel's name and double-click it again to expand the panel content, or click on the up/down arrow to the left of the panel name. For some of the panels, you can click the panel handlers in the bottom and bottom corners to expand the panel to reveal more content.

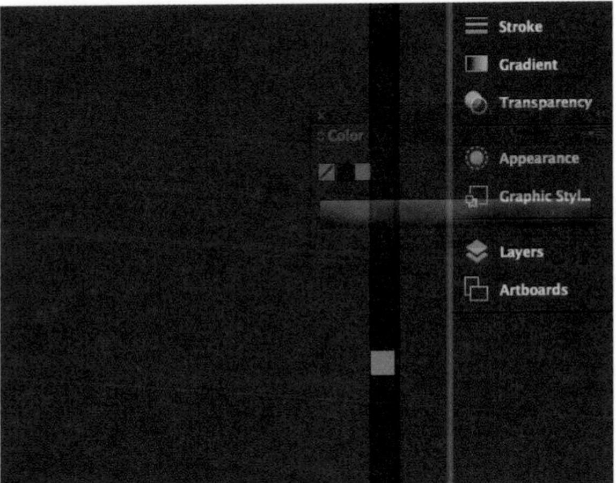

FIG 1-7 Changing the panel position in Illustrator

When you first install Illustrator, the panels appear on the right side as icons with the name of the panel—this is the collapsed status of the panels. You can drag the left edge of the panels' area to increase or reduce the width of the panels. When you decrease the width, you will notice that the panel names disappear. When you reduce the size, the panels are represented with icons only to save more space.

Customize Your Own Workspace

Because Adobe Illustrator is a multipurpose application that can be used to produce various types of designs, with each usage you have specific panels that are used more than others. This is why Illustrator gives you the option to create your own customized workspace that meets your needs.

Before we talk about how workspace customization works, let us explain two ways the Illustrator workspace appears on your screen. The first is similar to how panels appear on Mac computers, where the panels and workspace elements appear floating on the screen. The second way is the Application Frame, which is similar to the Windows method to display the application's elements. You can switch between both display methods through the Window > Application Frame command, which allows you to activate or deactivate the framed panels' appearance. This command is not available in the Windows version, as mentioned earlier.

At the top right of the Illustrator application, there is a drop-down list where you can manage workspaces, create a new workspace, or activate one of the previously created workspaces. The default workspace is the Essential Workspace, and you can find more workspace options such as web, layout, painting, and more. The workspace is a customized option that is based on your needs and the panels that you use more frequently.

Follow the below example to learn how to customize your workspace based on your needs:

1. Open Adobe Illustrator and start to change the position of the panels, open new panels, and set the workspace based on your needs.
2. From the top right drop-down list, choose New Workspace.
3. Name the new workspace "My Illustrator."
4. Choose the Essential Workspace and notice that the panel positions change back to the Essential Workspace look.
5. Choose the "My Illustrator" workspace to return back to your customized workspace.

Note

When you select a workspace and change the panel position, the new changes are saved automatically to the existing workspace. To reset the changes you did in one workspace, click the Reset command in the Workspace drop-down menu.

You can also manage the currently created workspaces through the Manage Workspace command from the drop-down list. The dialog box lets you do the following:

- Create a workspace from the New icon.
- Delete a workspace from the Delete icon.
- Rename a workspace by selecting it and adding a new name in the name field.

Illustrator Preferences

One of the most important parts of Illustrator is the Preferences dialog box, which you can reach from Illustrator > Preferences (Edit > Preferences in Windows). Through this dialog box, you can set the program tools and feature properties, such as the measurement units, user interface brightness setting, and more.

> **Shortcut**
>
> You can access the Preferences by pressing the Cmd+K (Ctrl+K in Windows).

The Preferences dialog box allows you to modify the settings of the following:

- General: Change the general settings of the application.
- Selection & Anchor Display: Set how the anchors and selection appear.
- Type: Set the setting of the text, such as the font measurement setting.
- Units: Determine the units used in the application document.
- Guides & Grid: Set the options of the guides and the grids in the document.
- Smart Guides: Control the options of the smart guides.
- Slice: Set the options for preparing your document for web use.
- Dictionary & Hyphenation: Set the language options and the dictionary options.
- Plug-ins & Scratch Disks: Set the plug-ins and disk amount assigned to Illustrator as RAM memory.
- User Interface: Choose the interface brightness from a range of selections through a slider bar. It also lets you set how multiple files open in either tabs or separated files.
- File Handling & Clipboard: Set how the system handles the copied files.
- Appearance of Black: Set how Illustrator handles black color on screen and print.

We will cover each of these settings when we reach its related chapter of this book. First, we will talk about two settings that are more related to the default application and when you first use the program.

Plug-ins and Scratch Disks

The first option of this item lets you set additional folders you can use as a place for the program plug-ins. The second option lets you set the scratch disks. When you create large and complex files, the application consumes the computer RAM to save the process while you are working with the files; this is the idea behind scratch disks. When the RAM memory finishes, the application uses parts of your hard disk as a scratch disk or extension for the RAM to save more information about the currently opened files.

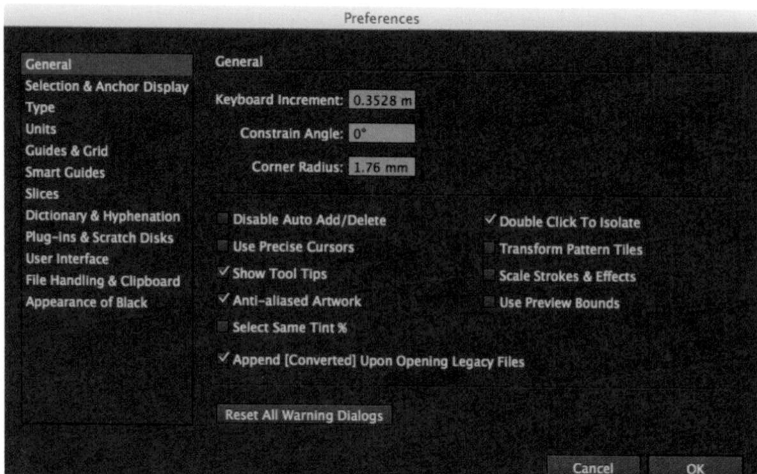

FIG 1-8 The Plug-ins & Scratch Disks option in the Preferences dialog box

The Scratch option lets you set which partition of your hard disk will be used as the primary scratch disk that will be used first and the secondary scratch disk that will be used after the first one runs out of space.

User Interface

The User Interface options in the Preferences dialog box include the following:

- The Brightness Level option lets you choose between four brightness levels: dark, medium dark, medium light, and light.
- The Canvas Color option lets you choose the color of the area that appears around the document. It can be white or simulate the brightness level that you chose in the previous option.
- The Auto-Collapse Iconic Panels option enables the panels that appear in icon style to collapse once you click outside the panel.
- The Open Documents as Tabs option enables the documents to open as tabs, so you can see the opened files' names as tabs at the top of the workspace.

Illustrator Shortcuts

Creating artwork in Illustrator requires a wide variety of tools and features frequently to create different results. However, using shortcuts in Illustrator is essential to be able to create artwork faster and more efficiently. Similar to other Adobe applications, there is a default shortcut set you can use in your work, but you can also customize the shortcuts to meet your needs and preferred keyboard keys. Thus, the shortcuts in Illustrator are set using the Keyboard Shortcuts dialog box in the Edit menu, Cmd+Opt+Shift+K (Mac); Ctrl+Alt+Shift+K (Windows).

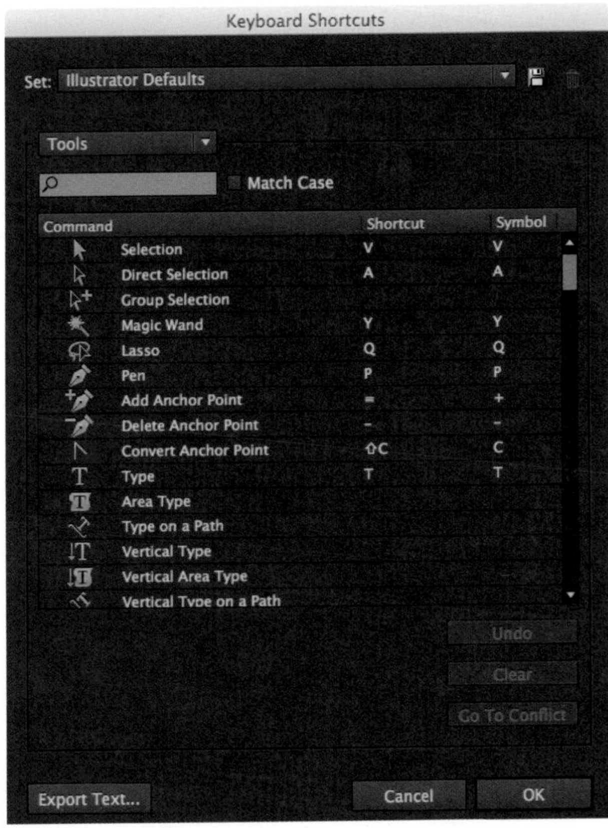

FIG 1-9 The Keyboard Shortcuts dialog box

First, let us overview the different options in the Keyboard Shortcuts dialog box and then see how to create your own shortcut list:

Note

The shortcut should be unique and not used in other tools or commands.

- The Set drop-down list let you choose the shortcut setting and create and delete specific shortcut sets. Default is the main choice, and to create a new customized shortcut, click on the Save icon to create a new set.

- You can choose between the Tools or Menu commands to change the shortcut for the commands in each of them. The Tools command represents the Tools panel, and the Menu command refers to the commands that you can find in the top menus.
- The search field lets you search for specific commands or tools.
- The tools and commands navigator lets you choose the tool or command to which you would like to assign the shortcut. It includes the name of the command or tool, the shortcut, and the symbol, which is usually the letter or the number, included in the shortcut combination.
- The Undo button lets you revert to the previous shortcut.
- The Clear button lets you remove the shortcut.
- The Go to Conflict button lets you go the shortcut that has the conflict.

Managing Resources with Adobe Bridge

Digital media has developed enormously and includes more file formats, applications, and resources than ever before. A smart designer or artist uses all these resources to help visualize ideas and create rich creative work. Years ago, it was a difficult and frustrating process to transfer files across different applications and formats in order to privilege the effects and features in each application. Thanks to new technology, these days have gone! There is now easy integration between applications and flexible handling of file formats.

Adobe Bridge is one of the companion applications that comes with Adobe products and allows you navigate, handle, and modify different resources such as images, videos, vector graphics, and so on. Using Adobe Bridge along with Adobe Illustrator can afford better resource management, as we will try to show. With Adobe Bridge, you can do the following:

- Easily view, search, label, rate, arrange, and sort images, as well as open files in their associated applications.
- View files' metadata information for the images and edit it through the File Info command.
- With the integration between Adobe Bridge and Adobe Device Central, you can easily test your images for output on mobile devices; you can also choose the device template on which you would like to test your content.
- Apply batch processes to certain images or folders, such as applying batch rename or applying commands such as Image Processor in Photoshop and Live Trace in Illustrator.
- Create PDF files from image files and edit the output PDF properties through the Output PDF & Web Gallery workspace.
- Create a web gallery for your images and upload it to your website.

The Adobe Bridge interface is similar to the other Adobe products, and it includes the following parts:

FIG 1-10 Adobe Bridge CS6 interface

Top Menus and Panel

Similar to other Adobe products, the top menu in Illustrator includes the important commands in the Adobe Bridge, such as the File, Edit, View, Stack, Label and Tools menus. The Stack menu lets you group the images in stacks for easy reach and navigation. The Label menu lets you rate and label images and folders. The Tools menu allows you to apply batch actions such as Batch Rename and Illustrator automation.

In addition to the top menus, the top panel includes important features and functions to help you while working in Adobe Bridge. The below points outline the basic icons and features that are located in this panel:

- The navigation arrows are used to go forward and backward while navigating for images. You can click the Arrow drop-down menu next to the navigation arrow to see the folders in the opened path.
- The Watch drop-down menu chooses the recent files opened in any of the installed Adobe products, such as Photoshop.
- The Camera icon allows you to download photos directly from your camera.
- The Refine icon lets you set the review mode for images, the batch rename, and the file information.
- The Open in Camera RAW option opens RAW files generated with digital cameras that support the RAW extension in the Camera RAW dialog box.
- The Output icon opens the Output panel that allows you to publish images as an image gallery or export them as a PDF document.

- On the right side of the panel you can find the workspace presets that allow you to set the workspace view that fits with your needs; you can also save your own custom workspace.
- Next to the workspace preset, you can search for content through the search field box.
- The Compact Mode icon converts between the full Bridge view that shows all the panels and functions and the compact view that shows only the necessary content that allows you to navigate and open files.
- Under the navigation arrows, you can find the navigation path of the current opened file.
- Next to the path, you can find image browsing options where you can choose the quality of the images while browsing and generate previews.
- The Rating Start icon lets you rate the content and label images.
- The rotation arrows let you rotate image previews either clockwise or counterclockwise.
- You can also open recent files, create a new folder, or delete images through the icons on the far right of the panel.

Folders and Favorites Panels

These two panels are located on the left side of the Bridge interface and let you navigate files on you local disk drive. You can also drag any specific resource or folder to the Favorites panel to save it for later use without the need to navigate it again.

Filters Panel

Under the Folders and Favorite panels, there are three panels in tabs: the Filters, Collections, and Export panels. The Filter panel lets you filter the resources based on specific terms such as the file type, keywords, date created, and so on. This menu is useful when you are searching specific resources that have specific criteria that make it easier to reach the resources.

Collections Panel

One of the most useful panels in Adobe Bridge, the Collections panel can help you arrange your related resources as collections even when they are in different locations on your computer. This way, you can reach a specific set of resources or files by opening its collection folder.

You can create a new collection by clicking the New Collection button in the bottom of the panel and then dragging the files into this new collection. There is also a smart collection that lets you add resources with specific criteria; for example, you can add files that are less than 10,000K and the collection will look for these images in the current folder and collect them.

Export Panel

The Export panel is new to Adobe Bridge CS6 and allows you to add sets of images and apply a specific modification to the queued images. Then, you can export these images with the modification applied to this bulk export. It is similar to bulk actions.

FIG 1-11 Export Add Preset dialog box

In this panel, you can create a specific preset from the bottom icon. In this preset, you define the export location and the modifications that will be applied to the exported images. Drag the images that you would like to export to the export preset, and click the Export arrow next to the preset name to open the Export dialog box and export the images.

Content Panel

The Content panel is the main menu in the application, where you can view the files and navigate the folders. When you select an image, you can see its preview in the Preview panel in the right side of the Content panel. At the bottom of the Content panel, there are the following icons:

- The thumbnail size slider allows you to resize the thumbnail in the Content panel. Click the right icon in the slider or drag the arrow to the right to increase the thumbnail size or to the left to reduce the thumbnail size.
- In the grid view, you can display the icons using grid lines between them.
- The Thumbnail View icon displays the thumbnails with the default view of the content thumbnails arranged together.

- The View Content as Details icon shows the content as thumbnails; next to each content is detailed information about it as well as the color profile assigned to it.
- The View Content as List icon displays the content in a list that includes small thumbnails for the content and information about the file size, format, and creation date.

When you right-click on any image or resource, you will find most of the features and commands related to each image in the contextual menu.

Metadata and Keywords Panels

In these panels, you can set for each image metadata and keywords that you can use for better organization for the image, such as adding information for each image and adding keywords for image search results. The metadata is information about the file that is saved in XML data format.

Compact Mode

Compact mode is a smaller version of Adobe Bridge with fewer icons, as it is a lighter version that includes only the necessary features, with fewer complications. You can switch between compact mode and normal mode by clicking on the icons at the top right next to the search box.

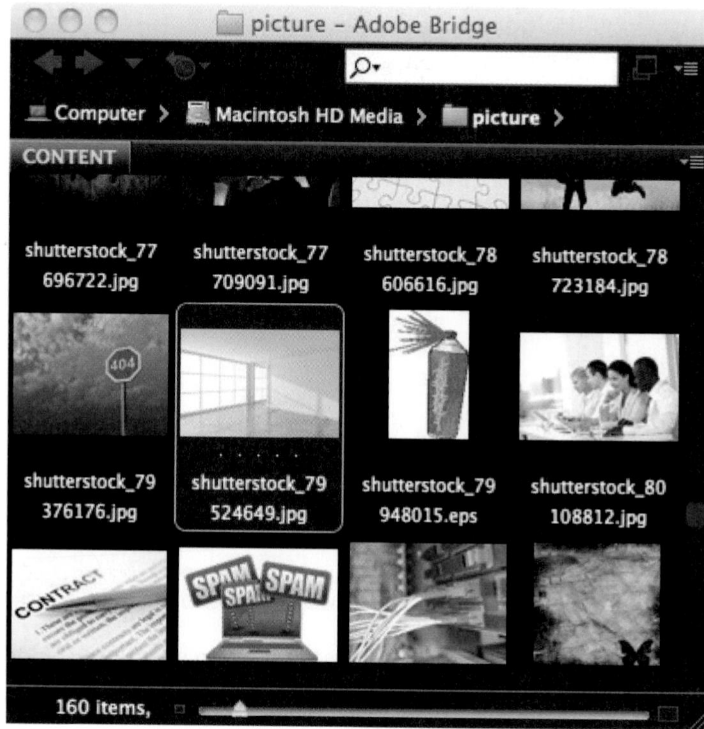

FIG 1-12 Adobe bridge compact mode

Batch Rename

Renaming files and images is a daily task for any designer, and sometimes you need to rename large sets of images, such as sequence images. The Batch Rename feature allows you to rename multiple images with specific renaming criteria. To rename a group of images, follow the steps below:

1. Select the images, right-click, and choose Batch Rename, or choose Batch Rename from the Tools menu.
2. The Batch Rename dialog box appears to add the renaming conditions.
3. Choose OK to start the rename.

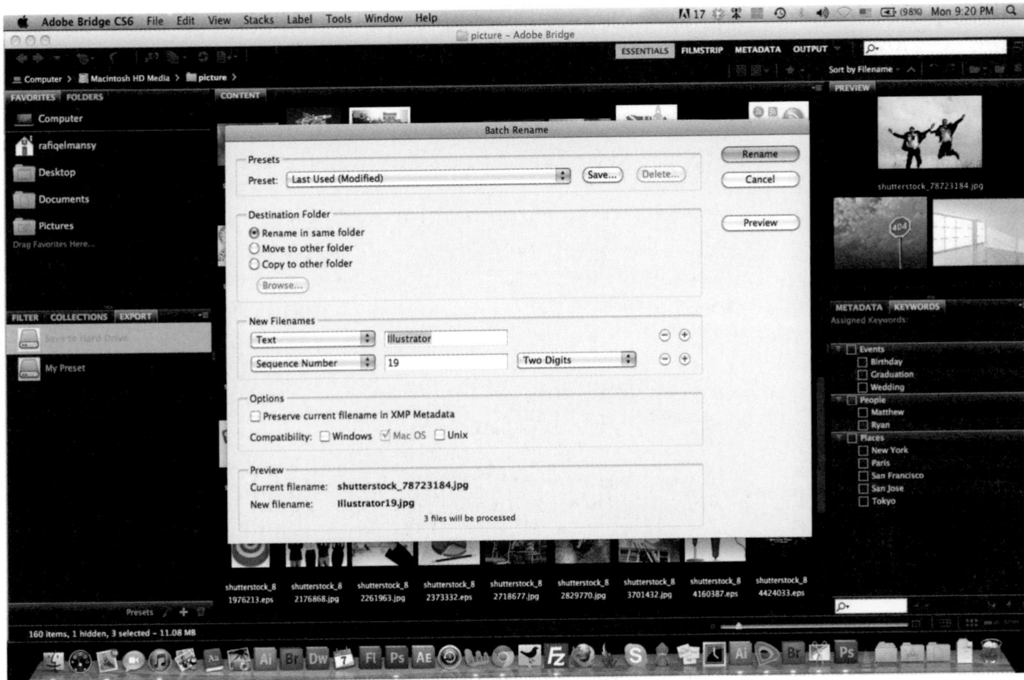

FIG 1-13 Batch Rename dialog box

Output Images as PDF and Web Gallery

When you click the Output for Web or PDF icon in the top properties panel, the Output panel appears in the right side of the Content panel. The Output panel includes two options: either PDF to export files as a PDF, or web gallery. Each tab includes the required options to create either a PDF or a web gallery from groups of images in the content panel.

At this stage, we have covered the basic information and knowledge that you will need for better understanding of Adobe Illustrator. While this chapter does not include many practical examples, it is helpful to show you how to handle files and prepare your Illustrator for your first tasks. Some users prefer to skip this part, but I believe it is important to overview before jumping to the next chapter, where you will learn about Illustrator documents and workspace.

For examples pertaining to this chapter, visit www.illustratorfoundations.com.

CHAPTER 2

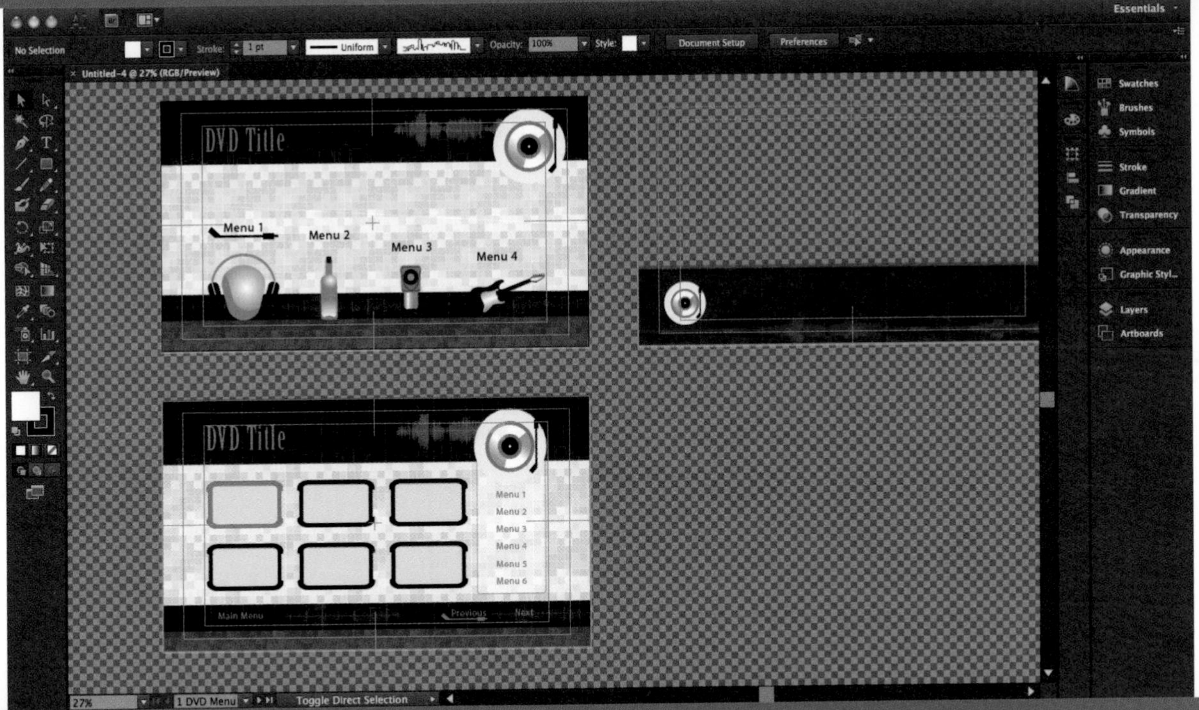

Managing Documents in Adobe Illustrator

In the first chapter, we introduced you to the Adobe Illustrator CS6 interface and anatomy and explained how you can find essential commands and options. We also described how you can customize the workspace to fit your needs and workflow. Let us move forward to the second chapter, where we will learn more about how to work with Illustrator documents and understanding the basic information required to handle files in Illustrator. We will also learn about the different saving options and how to work with the document artboards, rulers, guides, and grids.

Adobe Illustrator supports a wide range of both vector and bitmap files, and you can open any file in Illustrator using the Open command or the Place command. The difference is that the Open command opens the file and it appears in a new tab; the Place command places the file that you would like to open in a currently opened file, which means it allows you to place a file inside another one. When you open an Illustrator native document such as an AI or EPS file, you can see the artwork working layers and effects, with the ability to edit the file.

Working with New Documents

Creating a new file in Illustrator is an easy as choosing File > New from the top menu. When you choose the New Document command, the dialog box appears to let you set the document properties, such as the name dimensions and so on.

> **Shortcut**
>
> You can use the shortcut Cmd+N (Ctr+N in Windows) to open a new file. You can use the shortcut Cmd+O (Ctrl+O in Windows) to open an existing document.

Let us go through the New Document dialog box properties to understand each option as follows:

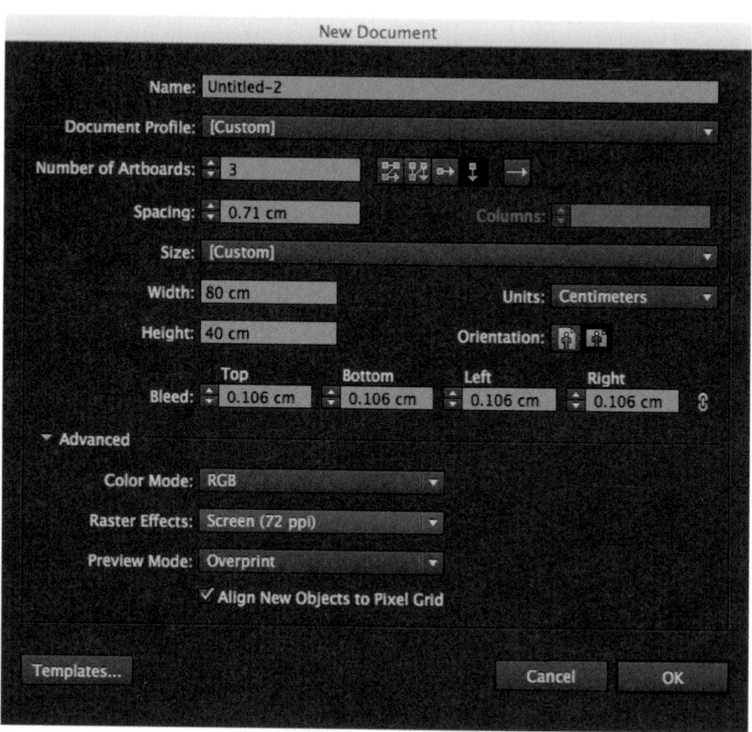

FIG 2-1 New Document dialog box

The name field lets you add the name of your document. If you do not set the name at this stage, this is fine, because you can still rename the document when you save it using any of the Save commands in the File menu.

Document Profile is one of the very useful commands because there are different document standards for web, video, or printing projects. Each of these standards has unique dimensions. Previously, it was very hard to remember all the different dimensions, such as different standard sizes for the web and different printing paper sizes. With the increasing number of media devices and the increasing range of screens dimensions, it becomes more difficult to remember all these standards.

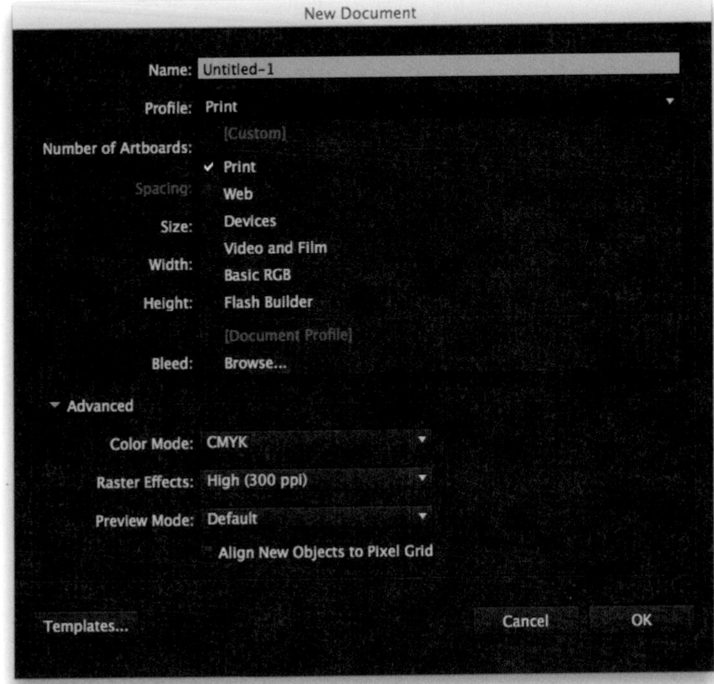

FIG 2-2 The New Document Profile setting box

When you choose a project or profile from the drop-down list, you can see that the Size drop-down list displays the different sizes that are associated with the specific project. The drop-down menu includes different project screens and documents dimensions, such as the following:

- Custom represents the dimensions that you add manually and does not refer to any standard from the list.
- Print displays the different sizes that can be used in printing projects, such as the paper sizes: A4, A3, A2, and so on.
- Web includes the different website standard sizes and computer screen sizes, such as 800 × 600 px and 1024 × 768 px.
- Device displays the presets that show the different mobile screen sizes, such as 176 × 208 px and 208 × 320 px.
- Video and Film displays the standards associated with video and animation dimensions that can allow you to create projects for different broadcasting and video projects.

- Basic CMYK shows the document dimensions that can be used for printing purposes in the CMYK color system. We will talk more about color formation later in Chapter 17.
- Basic RGB allow you to choose different dimensions in the RGB color format.
- Flash Catalyst allows you to add interaction to your Illustrator design and convert it to a Flash website or Flash interactive content. This application was released before the CS6 update.
- Browse lets you choose one of the files in your local computer as a reference for your new document's attributes.

The artboard is one of the very useful features in Illustrator that allows you to create multiple working areas in one document. It is similar in concept to pages in other applications. You can use the artboard to create and handle multiple artwork areas, such as web pages or printing papers.

In the Number of Artboards section, you can set the number you will need in one document. You can use the four icons to change the flow of the artboard, so you can choose the arrangement Grid by Row, Grid by Column, Arrange by Row, or Arrange by Column. The Change Left-to-Right Layout icon sets the flow of the artboard grid from right to left or vice versa. Next to the Number of Artboards section, you can use the spacing to set the space between artboards and the rows or columns to set how multiple artboards are arranged.

The Size drop-down list is related to the document profile we discussed before and shows the different dimensions associated with each profile. If you'd like to use custom dimensions, you can add these in the height and width.

The Units drop-down list lets you choose the measurement units you would like to use in your document. It can be through pixels, centimeters, millimeters, inches, and so on. Under the Units list, there are two icons for orientation, which sets the document orientation to be either horizontal or vertical.

The Bleeds list allows you to define a printing bleeds area (red guides) around the four sides of the document. The bleeds are applied to each artboard separately. You can check or uncheck the linkage icon on the right to link the bleeding values together. Thus you can change one value, and the other values will change based on it.

These are the main values in the New Document dialog box. At the end of the dialog box, you can find the Advanced options, which you can reveal by clicking the arrows next to Advanced. Here you can find more options. The first option in the advanced mode lets you choose the color mode for your document. It can be either RGB or CMYK. RGB is usually used on digital projects such as websites and video elements, because it uses a combination of the three colors red, green, and blue to generate the wide variety of colors you can view on your computer screen.

CMYK is mostly used in printing materials. Most printing machines use a combination of cyan, magenta, yellow, and black to mix and create your design. There is a slight difference between RGB and CMYK colors. When you choose the CMYK option, the file shows the colors as they will look in the printing materials. The Raster Effect option sets the default raster effect resolution setting that will be used for artwork that contains bitmap image effects.

The preview mode lets you modify how the artwork will look in the working environment. This option is for preview and does not affect the final artwork. The Preview Mode drop-down list includes the following three options:

1. Default: Shows the artwork in vector format with full colors and quality. It is the default setting when working in Illustrator.
2. Pixels: Shows the artwork in a pixel look. It does not affect the real vector nature of the artwork; it just shows the artwork in vector to let you preview the artwork in bitmap format.
3. Overprint: Displays the artwork in ink preview to show how the artwork will look in the color-separation papers.

The Align New Object to Pixel Grid option is one of the useful features that aligns the objects when you are creating artworks and need them to align to a grid. This feature can be used when you create a web design and want to eliminate some possible anti-aliasing problems.

Working with Templates

Templates are Illustrator files that you save as a reference for a design or artwork. Thus, when you need to create similar project such as similar webpage structure or brochure layout, you do not need to create everything in your design from scratch again. All you need to do is to open the template file.

Illustrator templates are saved in AIT format and are located in the Template folder in the Adobe Illustrator directory. You can save templates in any custom location in your local machine. When you choose the Template button in the New Document dialog box or use the New from Template command in the File menu, this opens your local drive to choose the template you would like to use. There are a variety of templates that are installed with Illustrator by default.

When you choose a template, Illustrator does not open the template itself for you to work on. Instead, it opens a copy of the template as a new document with the same content and properties. This way, you can base your work on the template without overwriting its content. Also, the template properties will overwrite any values you added in the New Document dialog box. Follow the steps below to open a new template:

1. Open Illustrator, and from the File menu choose New Document.
2. Click the Template button.

3. Navigate in the Illustrator installation folders to the Templates folder and choose any of the listed templates. Click OK to choose it.
4. A copy of the template document will open with an untitled name.

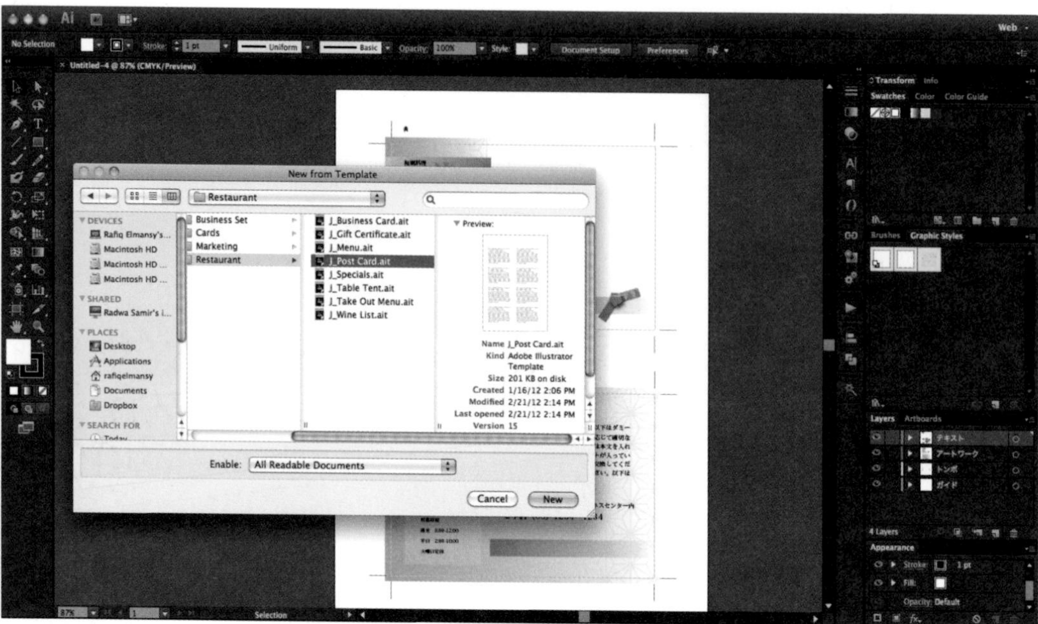

FIG 2-3 The new document with the template applied

You can save your document as a template simply by choosing Save as Template from the File menu and saving the file as an AIT document.

Working with Artboards

As we mentioned earlier, artboards are a great feature because they allow you to have multiple working areas in one Illustrator document. You can use the artboards to create multiple page designs such as brochures, flyers, or web pages. You can handle the different page designs more easily without the need to create a new Illustrator file for each page.

While artboards are used frequently, you can still have the chance to edit the artboard after creating it using the Artboard option in the New Document dialog box. Follow the below steps:

1. From the File menu choose New.
2. In the New Document dialog box, set the Number of Artboards to three and click the Arrange by Column icon to arrange the artboards vertically.
3. Click OK.

Notice that the new document is created and the artboards are arranged vertically. You can edit these artboards by clicking the Document Setup button on the Control panel at the top of the Adobe Illustrator interface.

Note

You can click the Artboard tool from the Tools panel to directly access the artboard editing mode.

The Document Setup dialog box lets you set up the document options as we saw above. Click on the Edit Artboard option to access the editing mode that allows you to edit the artboards. Once you click Edit Artboard, the dialog is closed and the Artboard tool is automatically selected (you can manually select the tool using Shift+O instead of the document dialog). You will find a transform rectangle appears around the active artboard. You can choose the artboard you would like to edit by clicking on it.

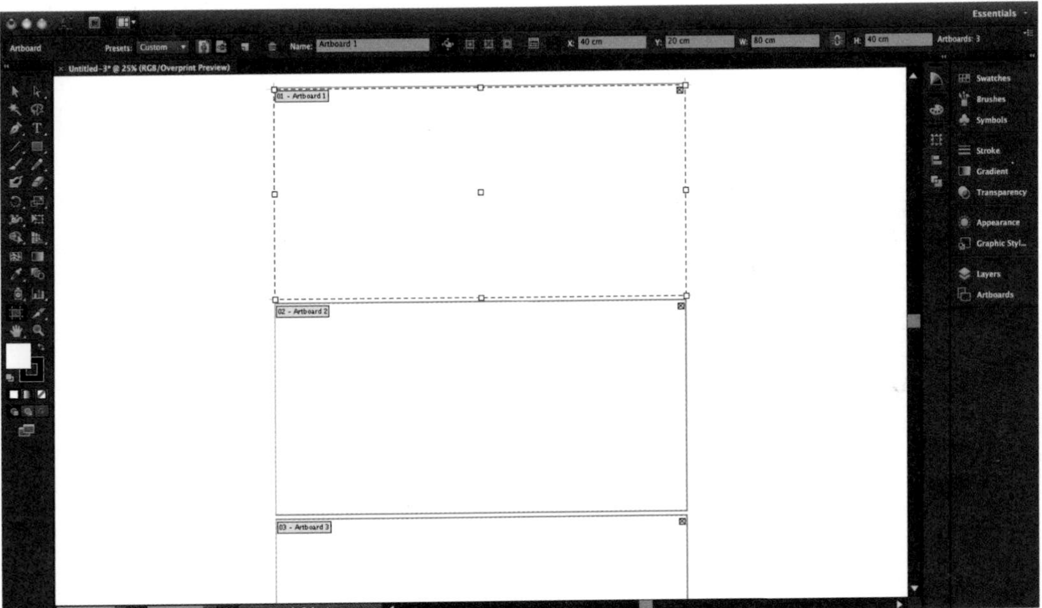

FIG 2-4 The artboard editing mode & the Artboard tool selected

You can edit the artboard using the transform rectangle, the values in the Control panel, or the Artboard Options dialog box that you open by clicking the icon in the control panel or double-clicking the Artboard tool. Let us see how to modify the artboard using the transform rectangle, then move to the Control panel values.

When you roll over any one of the rectangle sides, you will notice it turns green to identify that you can edit this part or drag the sides to change the size of the artboard. You can also click and drag any of the rectangles to resize it. You can click on the middle of the artboard area to drag it and change its position compared to the other artboards. In the top right of the transform rectangle, you will find a small X icon that you can click to delete the artboard.

Now, let us move to the Control panel and see the values that we can use to edit the artboard. The values from right to left are as follows. The Presets drop-down list lets you change the artboard size based on one of the standard sizes listed. Also, you can change the orientation between horizontal and vertical.

The next two icons allow you to create a new artboard or delete the selected artboard. The name field allows you to change the artboard name to make it more representative to the artworks that are included in it or to follow your project workflow naming conventions. Move/Copy Artwork with Artboard allows you to move or copy the artboard along with its content. If you activate this icon, you can move the artboard with its content, but if you deselect it, the artboard will be removed independently from the content inside it.

The Show Center Mark option displays the center mark to show the center of the artboard. Show Cross Hairs shows a crosshair in the four sides of the artboard. Show Video Safe Areas is helpful in video productions because it will show the safe area that you can use to create video artwork inside the artwork.

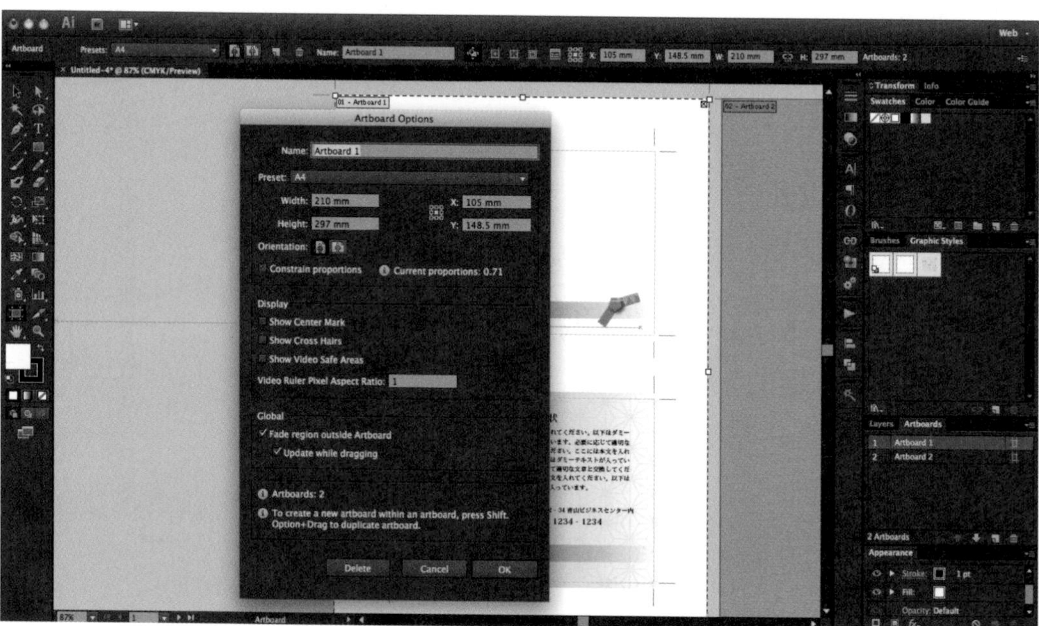

FIG 2-5 The Artboard Options dialog box

The Artboard Options icons open the Artboard dialog box, which includes similar options as those you see in the Control panel. You can also open the Artboard Options dialog box by double-clicking the Artboard tool from the Tools panel.

Next to the Artboard Options icons is the Reference Point icon. This icon includes very small boxes; when you select one of the boxes, Illustrator use this point location from the artboard position to display the X and Y measurement value. The X and Y values represent the position of the artboard.

You can change the position of the artboard using the transform rectangle we discussed earlier or by adding the numerical values in the X and Y values. The advantage of using the values is that it provides more accuracy compared to the manual method of adjusting them.

The Width and Height options change the size of the artboard. You can click the Linkage icon between them to ensure relative resize in both the width and the height values. You can exit the artboard editing mode by clicking the Esc button in the keyboard or choosing any of the tools from the Tools panel.

Artboard Panel

You can open the Artboard panel from the Window menu. The Artboard panel gives you the tools to easily handle artboards. The artboards are arranged at the bottom of the panel, and you can easily change the order by dragging the artboard layers to rearrange them or using the up and down arrows at the bottom of the panel.

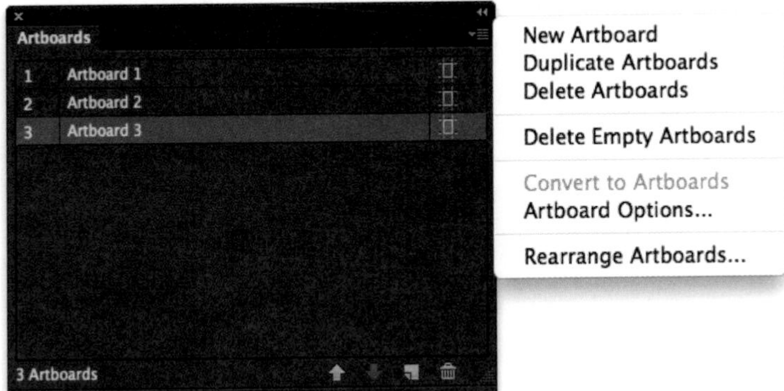

FIG 2-6 The Artboards panel

You can also edit the artboard by clicking the icon on the right of each artboard layer and opening the Artboard Options dialog box. You can delete the artboard by clicking the Delete button, or create a new artboard by clicking the New icon or dragging an artboard to it to duplicate. You'll find these commands in the panel context menu.

Saving Artboards

Saving Adobe Illustrator files that include multiple artboards is slightly different from saving a single artboard document, because multiple-artboard files include more than one defined area, and each one can include different designs that you save separately in any format. When you choose Save from the File menu, the Save dialog box appears, and in the bottom of the dialog box, you can open the drop-down list to choose one of the formats available. When you choose formats such as EPS or PDF, you will notice that the Use

Artboards option is selected. You can choose to save all the artboards or a specific range of the artboards in the new format.

Saving Illustrator Documents

When you save any document in Illustrator using any of the Save, Save As, or Save a Copy options from the File menu, the Illustrator Options dialog box appears to let you choose the different settings for the saved document, as follows:

- Version lets you choose the version of Illustrator for the saved document. Note that using versions older than the current Illustrator release may lead to losing some of the document functions that are not supported in older versions.
- The Fonts option lets you set the font embedding properties.
- The Options section includes creating a PDF-compatible file, embedding the ICC profile, using compression, and saving each artwork in a separate document.

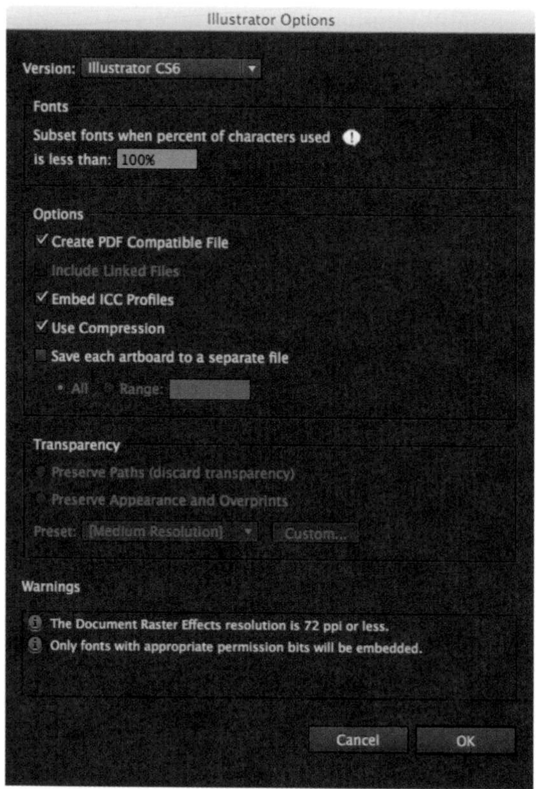

FIG 2-7 The saving Illustrator Options dialog box

At the end of the dialog box, you will see the Warnings section, which shows any errors and issues about the versions and compatibilities between the saved versions.

Note

You can open Illustrator files that are created in old versions in the new version, while you cannot open the new Illustrator files in any version older than the one used to create it.

There are many other saving options, such as saving an Illustrator file as a template for future usage and exporting the document to various types of formats using the Export command, as we will see in Chapter 15.

Working with Rulers

Rulers, grids, and guides are very important in your Illustrator project, because you will depend on them to create accurate artwork or designs and will use them frequently, especially when creating complex artwork. When you activate the ruler from the View > Rulers > Show Rulers option in the top menu, the rulers appear on the top and left side of the window or the artboard.

Shortcut

To show or hide rulers, press Cmd+R (Ctrl+R in Windows).

There are two types of rulers in Illustrator. The global ruler is not related to the document artboards arrangements. Thus, you can find that the origin or the point zero is fixed on the top left of the document and the ruler does not change when you move from one artboard to another. The second type is the artboard ruler (this is the default except for the video profile). This type of ruler has an origin zero point dependent on the active artboard position. Thus, you will see that the position of the origin point changes when you move from one artboard to another. The default location is at the top left corner of each artboard. You can switch between the two type of rulers from View > Rulers, and switch between the Change to Artboard Rulers or Change to Global Rulers options.

Shortcut

To switch between the artboard rulers and global rulers, press Alt+Cmd+R (Art+Ctrl_R in Windows).

To understand the difference between both types of rulers, follow the below steps:

1. Create a Print New document with multiple artboards.
2. From the View menu choose Rulers > Show Rulers or press Cmd+R (Ctrl+R in Windows).

3. Notice that when you click any of the artboards, the ruler origin (zero point) changes. This means that the artboard ruler is currently selected.
4. Now, from the View menu, choose Rulers > Switch to Global Rulers.
5. Notice that when you activate any of the document artboards, the ruler's origin or zero point doesn't change to identify the horizontal and vertical start point of the artboard.

Ruler Measurements

Adobe Illustrator provides different types of measurements to set your ruler. You can set these measurements from the New Document dialog box when you are creating a new dialog. You can choose between points, picas, inches, centimeters, millimeters, and pixels. For example, if you are creating web artwork or a web page, you can set your rulers to pixels, which is the standard measurement for the web. Also, you can set the measurements to inches, centimeters, or millimeters when you are creating printing materials.

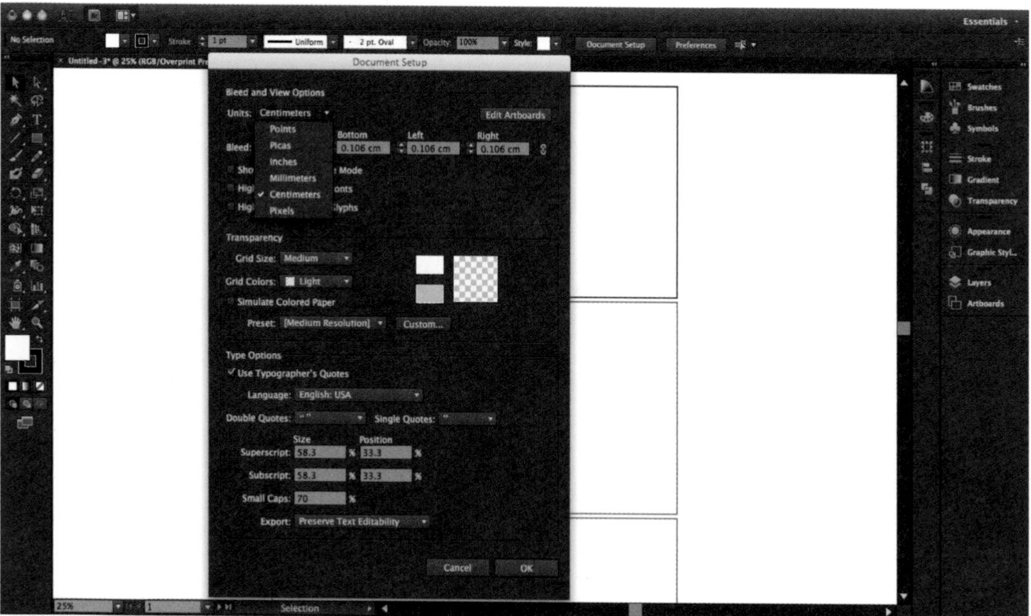

FIG 2-8 The unit measurements in the Document Setup dialog box

Note

After creating the document, you can change the measurement unit through the Document Setup dialog box, which you can reach by clicking the Document Setup button in the top Control panel.

> **Shortcut**
>
> Toggle between available measurement units using the Cmd+Options+Shift+U (Ctrl+Alt+Shift+U in Windows).

Video Rulers

The video rulers are artboard-dependent rulers that appear in a green color around the artboard. They reflect the video measurement for the artboard. The video rulers change based on the video preset you specify for the document from the New Document dialog box or for the artboard when you edit it through the Document Setup dialog box.

Working with Guides

When you create artwork in Illustrator, it is important to figure out the relationship between your design elements, lines, and objects. You can create guides to ensure more accurate positioning for your design. To create a guide, you must have the ruler enabled; click on the ruler and drag over the document content to create either horizontal or vertical guides. You can show or hide guides from the View menu by choosing Guides > Show Guides or Hide Guides. When you show guides, you can select the guide and change its position, unless you lock it using View > Guides > Lock Guides.

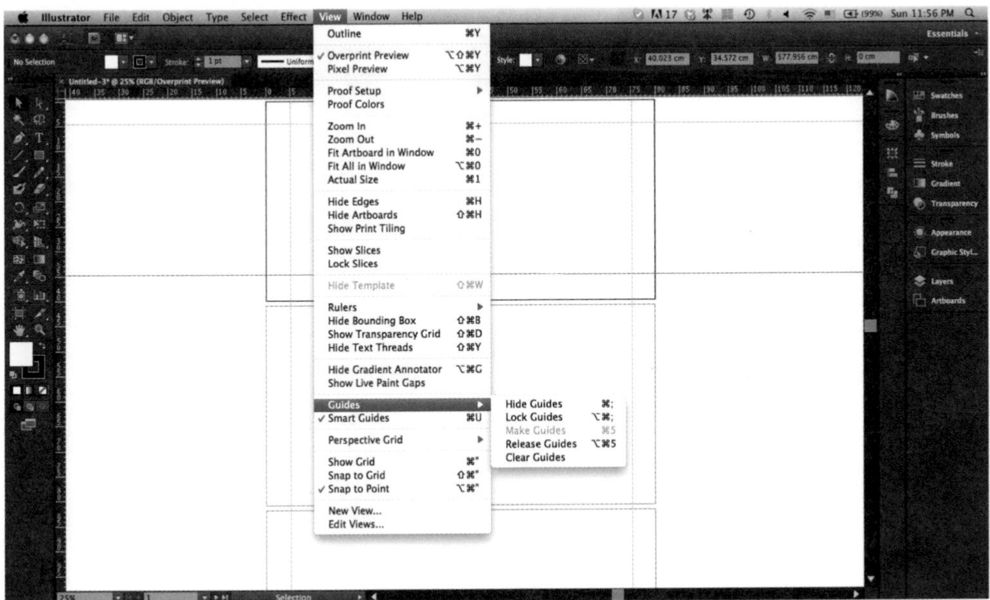

FIG 2-9 Show or hide guides from the View menu

One of the helpful options when you are working with guides, since they are unlocked by default, is that Illustrator allows you to modify the guide and transform it. This gives you greater ability to create more accurate guides for your work. To rotate a guide, follow the steps below:

1. Select the guide.
2. From the Object menu, choose Transform > Rotate.
3. The Rotate dialog box appears; enter 45-degree in the angle value.
4. Make sure that the Preview checkbox is selected to see the updated change in the guide position.

Convert Path to a Guide

In some cases, you need to create very customized guides, or rectangles to act like a guide in your design. Illustrator provides you an amazing option to convert any paths into guides and interact with them. You can convert paths into guides as follows:

1. Open the file Guide.ai from the companion website. This file includes a circle that we will convert into a guide.
2. Select the circle.
3. From the View menu choose Guides > Make Guide.
4. Notice that the circle converts to a guide in your workspace.
5. You can convert the circle back into a shape by choosing Guides > Release Guide.

Smart Guides

Smart guides appear when you drag the objects in the workspace to give you a fast preview of the alignment of the objects together. You can show or hide

FIG 2-10 The smart guides in green color while creating rectangles

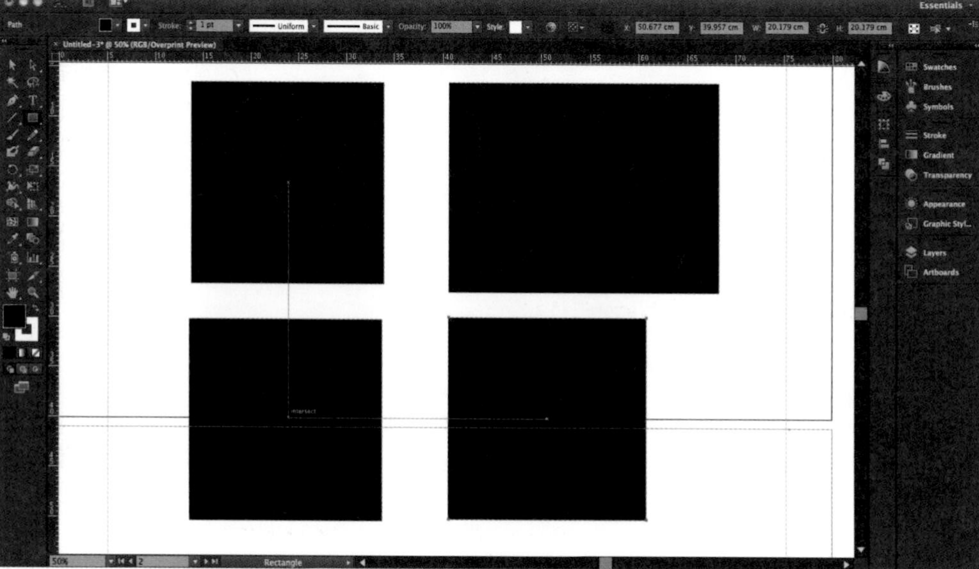

it from the View menu by checking Smart Guides to display it or unchecking it to hide it, or, use the shortcut Cmd+U (Ctrl+U Windows). The display options and behavior of smart guides can be found and customized in the preferences.

Grids

This is another way to ensure an accurate position for your design, as it adds grids in your workspace to guide you while you build your artwork. You can show or hide the grid from the View menu by choosing Show Grid. Also, you can set your objects to snap to the grid by choosing the Snap to Grid option from the View menu. When you activate the Snap to Grid option, your object will automatically snap to the nearest grid while you are drawing it.

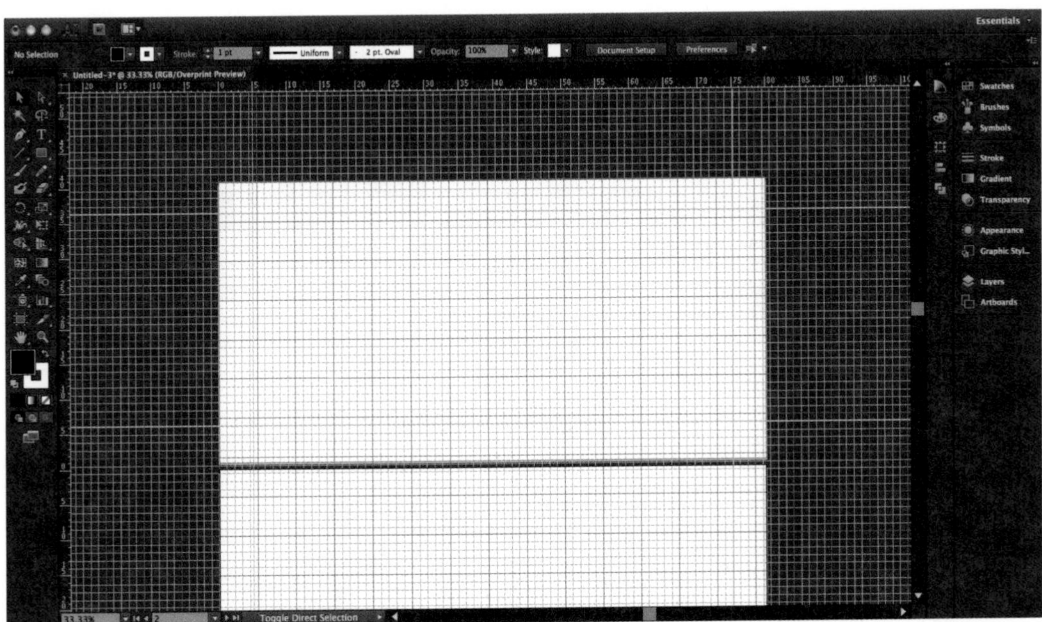

FIG 2-11 Grids are enabled in the workspace

Guides and Grid Preferences

You can change the options of both guides and grids from the Preferences dialog box. You can find the preferences in the Illustrator menu in Mac or Edit > Preferences in Windows. The Guides and Grid options in the Preferences dialog box include the following options:

You can set the color and the style of the guides to be either lines or dots. Dots are less visible, which is helpful if the lines coming across your workspace cause distortion, especially when you create many guides. You can set the

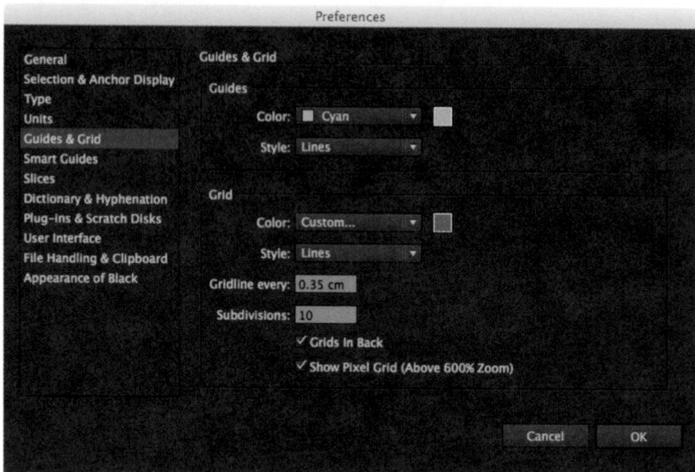

FIG 2-12 Guides & Grid in the Preferences dialog box

color and the style of the grids. You can also set the spacing between grids, set whether the grids will appear in the back of the document, and set whether they will appear when you zoom above 600%.

Working with XMP Metadata

After setting up your document properties, you may need to add more information about the document. This information is known as the XMP metadata. It is defined as XML-based information that is attached to the document so you can know more about it, such as the creation date, the copyright information, and other information. You can get information about the document from the File menu by choosing File Info. The dialog box appears, to show you the file information, and you can edit this information based on the document properties.

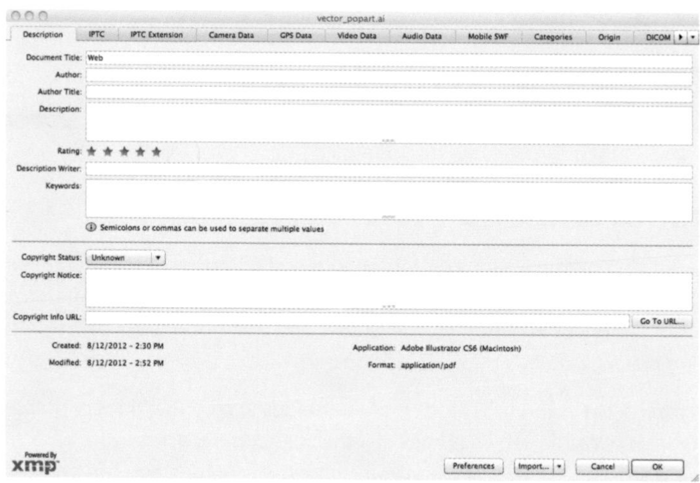

FIG 2-13 File Info dialog box

In this chapter, we have learned some of the basics that are very important to understand before getting into using the Illustrator tools. Such knowledge is essential when setting up your Illustrator document. Also, it can help you to create artwork more easily and improve your workflow in Illustrator. In the remaining chapters, we will use these options and features frequently while working in the examples.

For examples pertaining to this chapter, visit www.illustratorfoundations.com.

Drawing in Illustrator

We mentioned in Chapter 1 that Adobe Illustrator is considered a vector program that depends on paths to create objects and artwork, and the shape of each path is calculated through mathematical equations. Many of you may not enjoy this theoretical definition for the Illustrator artwork, especially the mathematical part.

In this chapter, we will shed light on how to create artwork in Illustrator using paths and shapes. Also, we will learn how to work with paths and modify them using the Illustrator tools. This chapter provides essential training to understand how to create artwork in Adobe Illustrator using paths and shapes.

Drawing with the Pen Tool

Let us start the drawing with the Pen tool because it is the most commonly used drawing tool in Adobe Illustrator. Learning how to use the pen tool will ensure you gain understanding of the paths and the anchor points concept.

But first, what is the path? The path is a line that defines your artwork. When it is filled with a stroke colors it becomes lines in your artwork. If the path is closed or open, it can be filled with a fill color, as we will see in Chapter 4, on color. You can easily identify the path of the object by selecting it or rolling over it using the Selection tool or the Direct Selection tool. It looks like outlines for the object.

The line of the path is actually the distance between the path points, known as anchor points. The anchor points determine the shape of the path and each anchor point has two handlers that help control the shape of the path to the right and left of the anchor.

The Pen tool uses paths to create the object. Follow the steps below to create a path:

1. Select the Pen tool from the Tools panel.
2. Click inside your document once to create the first anchor point.
3. Click on another place to create the second anchor point; notice that the first path, a straight line, appears between the points.
4. Click on a third place. This time keep clicking and drag to see that the path turns into a curve.
5. Click on a fourth place on the stage and notice how the created path takes a different curve shape.

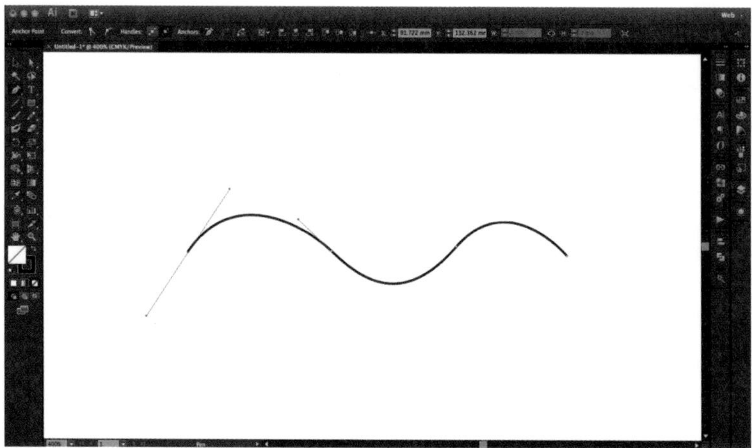

FIG 3-1 The path line with the anchor points

What is the difference between each anchor point and why does the path take a different look each time? Select the Direct Selection tool from the Tools panel. This tool lets you select the path anchor points individually. Select the first anchor point and notice that it does not have the anchor point handlers like the third anchor point does. This is because there are two types of anchor points:

1. The corner anchor point and the first point create a sharp corner in the path and do not have handlers because the paths on both sides are straight lines.

2. The smooth anchor point has two anchor handlers and the paths on its both its sides are curved. You can use the Direct Selection tool to modify these handlers, which affects the path curve.

Note

You can select a specific anchor point using the Direct Selection tool and drag to change its position or to modify the handlers.

FIG 3-2 The corner anchor point and the smooth anchor point

Follow the steps below to use both the corner anchor points and the smooth anchor points to create an outline for an image:

1. Open the file Image_outline.ai. This file includes a guide image, above which you will be creating your path.
2. In the Tools panel, check the color area. Make sure that the fill color is set to none (has a red line cross the thumbnail) and the stroke color is set to black. We will cover everything related to colors in Chapter 4.
3. Select the Pen tool and start clicking on the shape outline to create the first anchor point.
4. Start creating more anchor points with both corner and curve style to create an outline around the guide image.
5. You can click the Alt (Option) on the anchor point to convert it to a corner anchor point.
6. To close the path, just click on the first path anchor point, and Illustrator will understand that you would like to close this path. You will notice that when you click on the first anchor point, the mouse curser changes to display a circle next to the pen shape to indicate that by clicking over this point, you can close this path.

Shortcut

While the Pen tool is selected, you can switch between it and the Direct Selection tool by clicking Cmd (Ctrl in Windows).

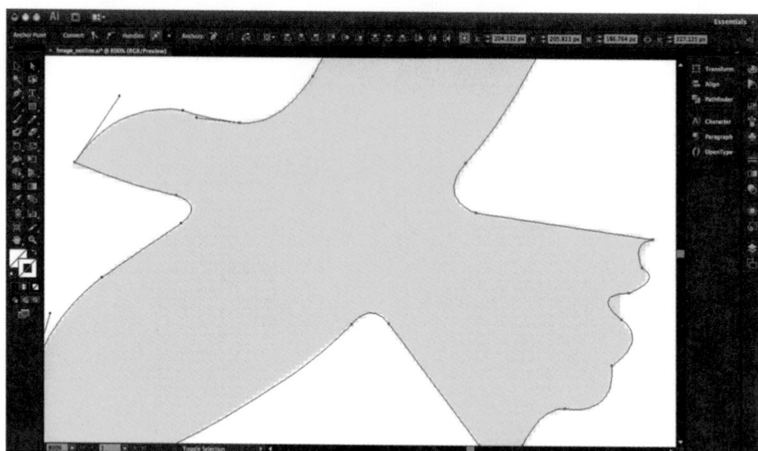

FIG 3-3 The path outline on the guide image

> **Shortcut**
>
> You can click the Shift key while creating a path to force it to generate either full vertical or horizontal.

When you click and hold on the Pen tool in the Tools panel, it expands to reveal more tools to add an anchor point to a created path, delete a specific anchor point, or change the anchor point status between smooth and corner anchor point. Each tool works as follows:

- To add an anchor point, select the Add Anchor Point tool and click on any place over a path to add an anchor point at that location.
- To delete an existing anchor point, select the Delete Anchor Point tool and click on the anchor point that you would like to remove.
- To change the status for the anchor point from corner to smooth, use the Convert Anchor Point tool; you can easily identify the difference between the two points, as the smooth anchor point includes handlers to affect the path shape, while the corner anchor point does not include any handlers.

> **Shortcut**
>
> You can click the minus and plus signs on the keyboard to switch between the Add Anchor Point and Delete Anchor Point tools. Also, you can switch between them by clicking the Alt (Option) key.

Free Drawing with the Pencil Tool

While the Pen tool does not really mimic a freehand pen, the Pencil tool allows you to draw in a freehand, and Illustrator will create the path and anchor point while you are drawing. Honestly, the mouse is not a suitable device with which to draw, especially using the Pencil tool, because it will lack accuracy and most likely frustrate you. Although you can draw using the mouse by setting up the Tool options such as fidelity and smoothness, the best method to draw with this tool and in Illustrator is with a tablet pen, because it simulates the real pen-on-paper drawing style with better accuracy than the mouse does. Wacom Intous is one of the most well-known and commonly used tablets. It is a must-have piece in your workplace or office.

The best way to understand the difference between the Pen and Pencil tools is to select the Pencil tool from the Tools panel and begin to try it and see how it is a better fit for freehand drawing.

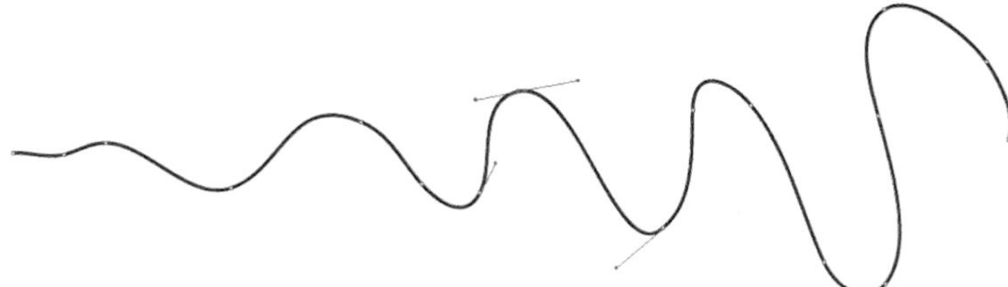

FIG 3-4 Drawing with the pencil tool

One of the impressive options in the Pencil tool is that you can easily edit your selected path while you draw your artwork; let us try it:

1. Open a new document.
2. Select the Pencil tool.
3. Start drawing a line.
4. While the line is selected, draw again over parts of the line. Notice that the line is modified with the new update.
5. While the line is selected, try to draw a line just near it; notice that the first line is removed and replaced with the new line.

The modifier keys plays an essential role while working with the Pencil tool, because they give you more control over your lines, as explained next. When you try to create closed-line artwork, it will be hard to point your Pencil tool to the first point of your drawing to create a closed path, and in many cases you end up with an open path. But you can click the Alt (Option) key while you draw, and the icon next to the Pencil tool curser will turn into a circle into identify that the created path will be closed. You can do this using the following steps:

1. Select the Pencil tool.
2. Start drawing your artwork line.
3. Before releasing the mouse, click the Alt (Option) key. Notice that the curser icon shows a small circle shape.
4. Release the mouse or the tablet pen to see the path connecting to the starting point and closing the path.

In some cases, you might like to draw a line and complete it after finishing your drawing. You can do this as explained next. You can set up the line options and how to interact with your modifications from the Pencil Tool options, which you can access by double-clicking on the tool in the Tools panel. The options include the following.

Fidelity controls the precision and number of anchor points that are added automatically while you draw with the mouse or the tablet pen. A lower number means that the path will have more anchor points and will be more complicated. A higher number means that the curve will have a low number of anchor points and a smoother look. (If you are using the mouse, use a higher value to make the result less jagged.)

Smoothness controls the smoothness of the path—a higher value means the created path is more smooth. Fill New Pencil Stroke applies a fill color to the created paths. So if you already have a fill color set to a color, this color will be applied to the path if this option is selected. Keep Selected keeps the line selected until you draw another one. When you activate Edit Selected Path option, you can edit the path by drawing next to it. Using the Within slider, you can tell Illustrator how near the new line should be from the old one in order to modify or replace it. Note: modifying the selected path requires that both the Keep Selected option and the Edit Selected Path option be checked.

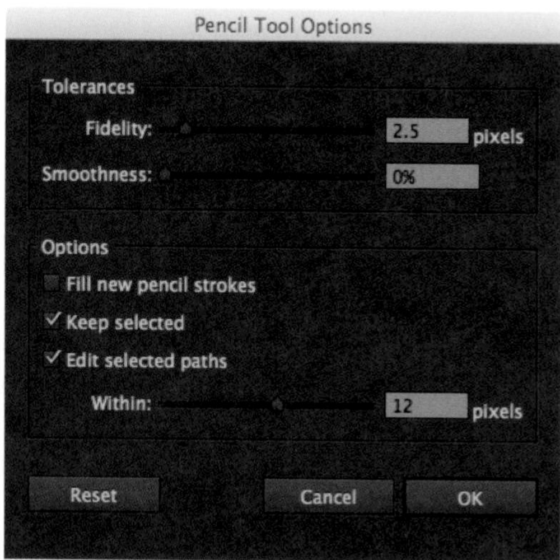

FIG 3-5 The Pencil Tool Options dialog box

Let us see how it works by following the below steps:

1. Select the Pencil tool.
2. Create a line and release the mouse or the tablet pen.
3. After drawing the first line, click Cmd (Ctrl in Windows) and start dragging from the last point of the previously created line. Notice that the lines are connected with each other.

Closed Path Primitives

Closed path primitives are actually shapes with a closed path and can be created using the Rectangle, Round Rectangle, Ellipse, Polygon, and Star tools in the Tools panel. These shapes can be used separately or as part of more complex artwork. Understanding how to create closed path primitives and their different options can help you in creating your artwork.

Before we start creating shapes, let us learn about the modifier keys, because they are used commonly not only in this task but also in many places in Adobe Illustrator. The modifier keys are assistant keys on your keyboard that are used to perform specific actions while creating the shapes in Illustrator. These keys are Shift, Alt (Option), Cmd (Ctrl in Windows), the space bar, and the arrows.

Rectangle Tool

As the name implies, you can use this tool to create a rectangle by simply selecting the tool and dragging over the stage to start creating your first rectangle:

1. Create a new Adobe Illustrator document.
2. Select the Rectangle tool from the Tools panel.
3. Click and start dragging while you are clicking on the mouse.
4. While clicking, you can press the Shift key in your keyboard to create a square with equal width and height.

While this is a rapid way to create a rectangle, you can use the Rectangle dialog box to create a more accurate shape with specific numerical width and height values:

1. Create a new Adobe Illustrator document.
2. Select the Rectangle tool from the Tools panel.
3. Click once to open the Rectangle dialog box.
4. Enter the width and height dimensions of the rectangle. For example, add 200 px width and 400 px height. Click OK.

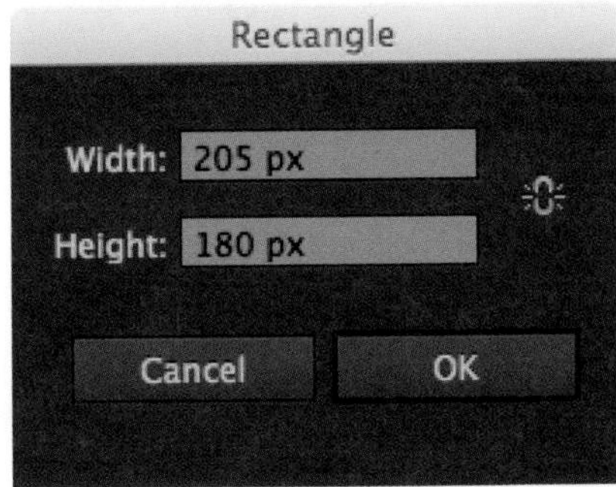

FIG 3-6 The Rectangle dialog box

In the dialog box, you will notice a linkage icon that you can use to create a linked ratio between both width and height. For example, when you have a width value 100 px and a height value 200 px, this means that the dimension of the width is half the height dimension. Thus, clicking the linkage icon maintains this aspect ratio when you change any of the width or the height values, as the following example shows:

1. While the Rectangle dialog box is open, add the value 100 px in the width value and 200px in the height value.
2. Click the linkage icon.
3. Change the width to 200 px. Notice that the height changes to 400 px.

When you click in the document to create the rectangle through the dialog box, you will notice that the registration point or the point you click represents the top left edge of the rectangle. You can set the point to be the center of the rectangle by holding the Alt (Option) key while clicking. When you hold the Alt (Option) key, you will see that the mouse curser shape changes to represent a registration point, and this point represents the center point of the created rectangle. This is true for all the shape primitives.

Rounded Rectangle Tool

This tool acts in a similar way to the previous Rectangle tool. The only difference is that it creates rounded edges for the rectangle; you can set the radius of the corner as follows:

1. Select the Rounded Rectangle tool from the Tools panel.
2. Click once on your document to open the Rounded Rectangle dialog box.
3. Set the width and the height to 205 px.
4. You can change the radius of the rectangle edges by changing the corner radius value. For example, change it to 20 px. Click OK.

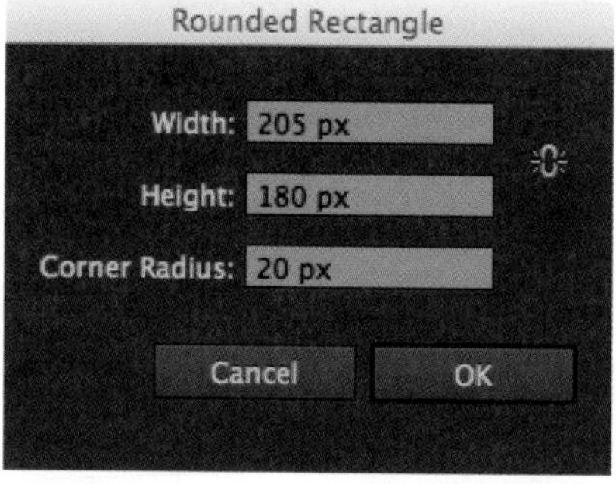

FIG 3-7 The Rounded Rectangle dialog box

Note

While dragging to create the rounded rectangle, you can click the up and down arrow keys to increase or decrease the radius of the corners by 1 pt.

Ellipse Tool

This tool lets you create a rounded ellipse similar to the above two features. You can click the Shift key while dragging within the document to create a full circle. When you select the Ellipse tool and click, the Ellipse dialog box appears to let you set the width and height of the ellipse using the same steps as the above tools.

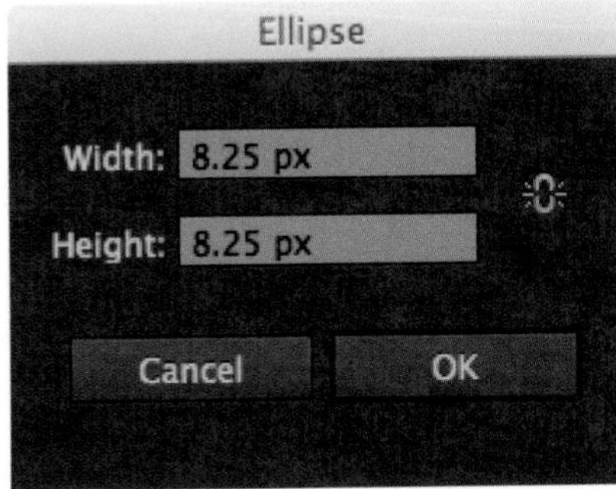

FIG 3-8 The Ellipse dialog box

Polygon Tool

When you select the Polygon tool and click within the document, the Polygon dialog box appears with slightly different options. The dialog box allows you to set the radius of the polygon and the number of the sides. When you click to create the polygon shape, the up and down arrow keys have other functions here than with the Rounded Rectangle tool. When you click the up and down keys, it increases or decreases the number of the polygon sides.

FIG 3-9 The Polygon dialog box

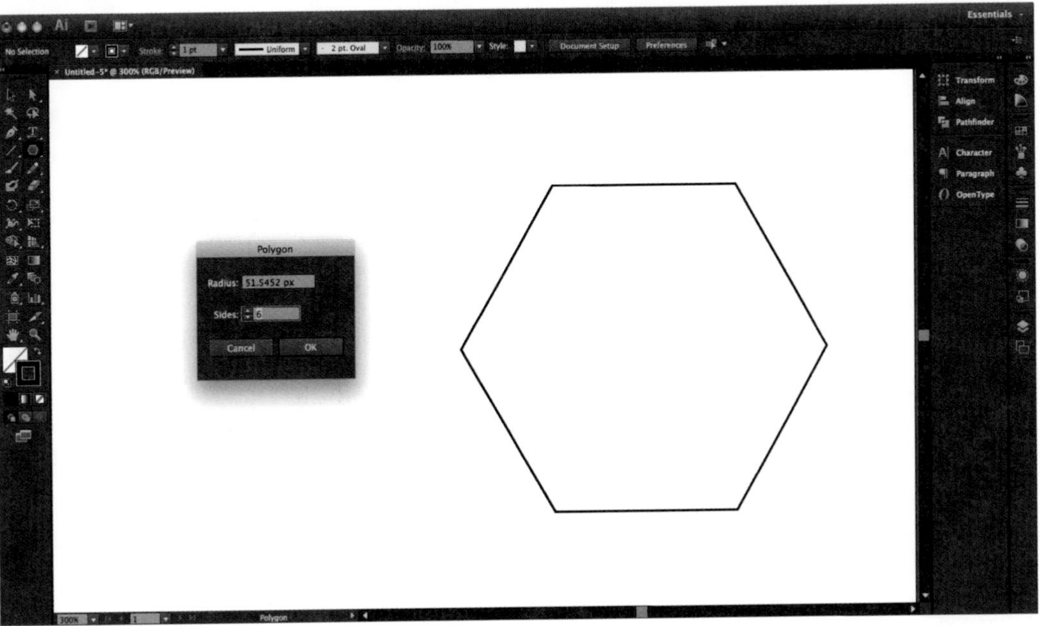

The least number of the polygon sides is three, which is a triangle. Thus, this can be an easy way to create a triangle in Illustrator. You can create a triangle by creating a polygon with three sides.

Star Tool

In addition to your ability to use the star by clicking and dragging inside your document, the Star dialog box includes the following options:

- Radius 1 indicates the outer radius for the star.
- Radius 2 indicates the inner radius for the star.
- Points show how many points the star will include. The least number of points is three points.

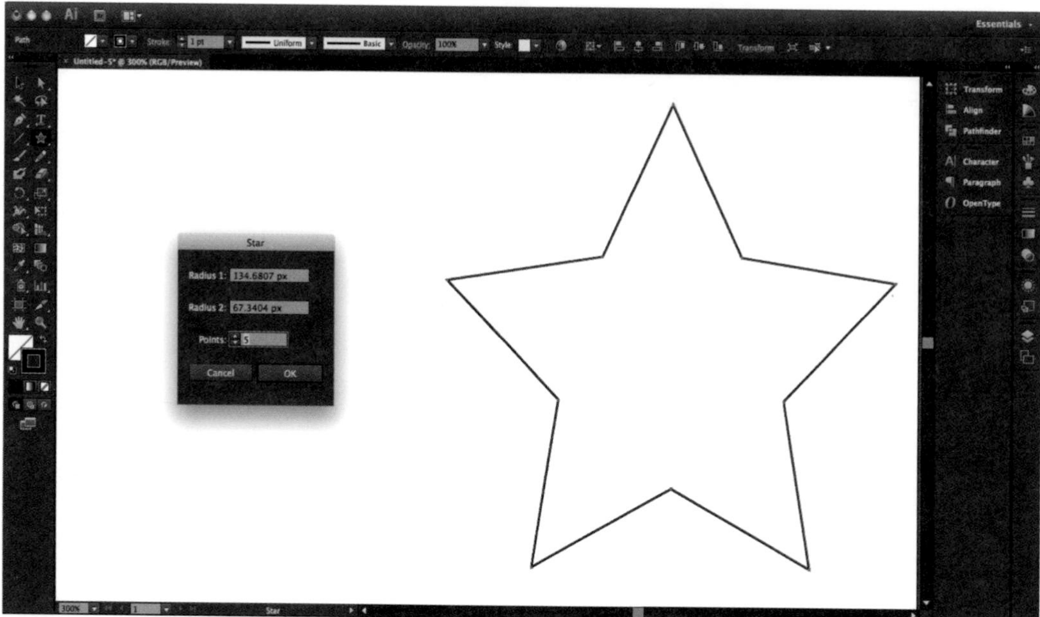

FIG 3-10 The Star dialog box

When you click and drag to create a star shape, the modifier keys affect the star as follows:

- Clicking the up and down arrows increase or decrease the star points.
- Clicking Cmd (Ctrl in Windows) lets you control the outer radius of the star points.
- Clicking the Alt (Option) aligns the star edges with each other.
- The Shift key aligns the star position in the document.

Flare Tool

This tool lets you create a light flare effect on the stage. It does not have many options, but it can be used to create an easy flare effect over objects.

Open Paths Primitives

Open paths primitives refer to shapes that include open paths; these shapes can contain only open paths or both closed and open paths. Let us overview each of these tools and see its different options.

Line Segment Tool

This tool allows you to create a straight line by simply choosing it from the Tools panel and clicking and dragging to create a line. Click once in your document to open the Line Segment dialog box, and you will find the following options:

- The length of the line
- The angle of the line
- Whether or not the line will include fill color

When you click the Shift key while dragging to create a line, the line is drawn with specific 45-degree angle constraints.

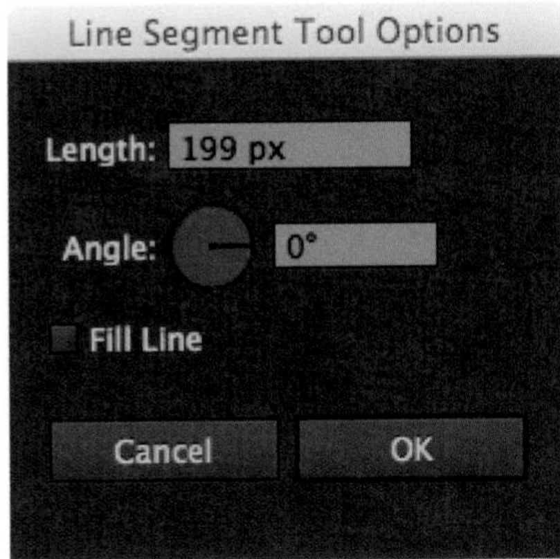

FIG 3-11 The Line Segment Tool Options dialog box

You will notice that the drawn line takes the point you click as the start point for the line. If you click the Alt (Option) key while creating the line, the point at which you start your drawing represents the center point of line.

Arc Tool

You can create an arc by dragging within your document or through the Arc dialog box by clicking once on the stage. The Arc dialog box includes the following options:

- Length X-Axis sets the length of the part of the arc in the X direction.
- Length Y-Axis sets the length of the part of the arc in the Y direction.

- Type chooses if the arc will be open or closed.
- Base Long sets the base of the arc to be the X or the Y side.
- Slope sets the curve of the arc, which ranges from −100 to +100.
- Fill Arc adds a fill color to the arc.

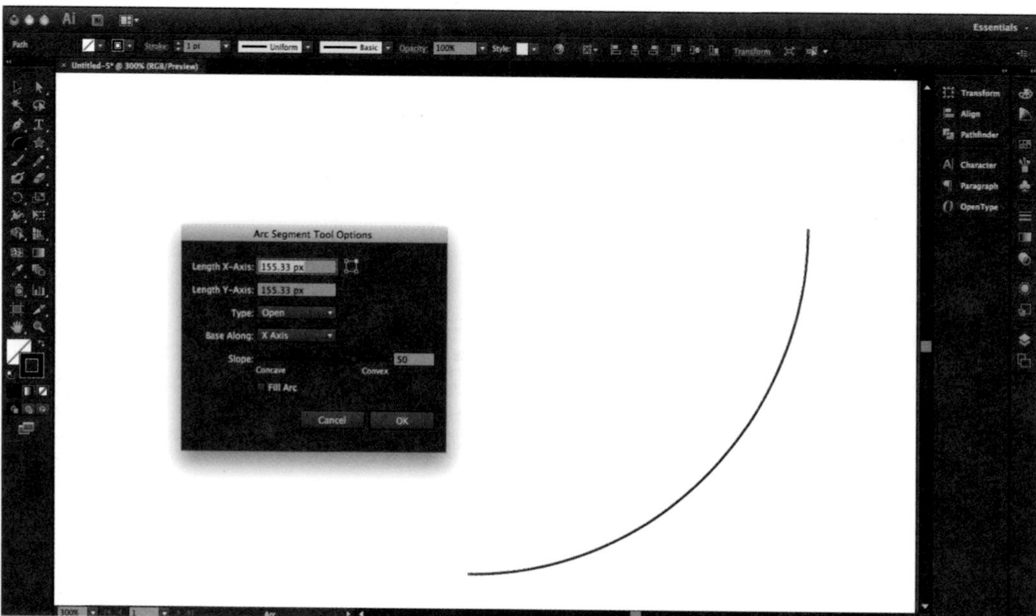

FIG 3-12 The Arc Segment Tool Options dialog box

When you click and drag to create an arc, you can press the Shift key to create an equal arc with both X and Y the same length. Also, you can click the Alt (Option) key to draw the arc from the center where you have clicked.

> **Shortcut**
>
> You can increase or decrease the slope value using the up and down keys.

Spiral Tool

You can choose this tool and click and drag to create a spiral that increases in size while you are dragging. You can also just click to open the dialog box, which includes the following options:

- Radius indicates the size of the spiral.
- Decay determines how each curve in the spiral will decrease in relation with the previous one. The 100% option creates full circle and 0% creates an arc.

- Segments set the number of points on each curve.
- Style sets the spiral curve direction.

Note

Clicking Cmd (Ctrl in Windows) while drawing the spiral modifies the decay value.

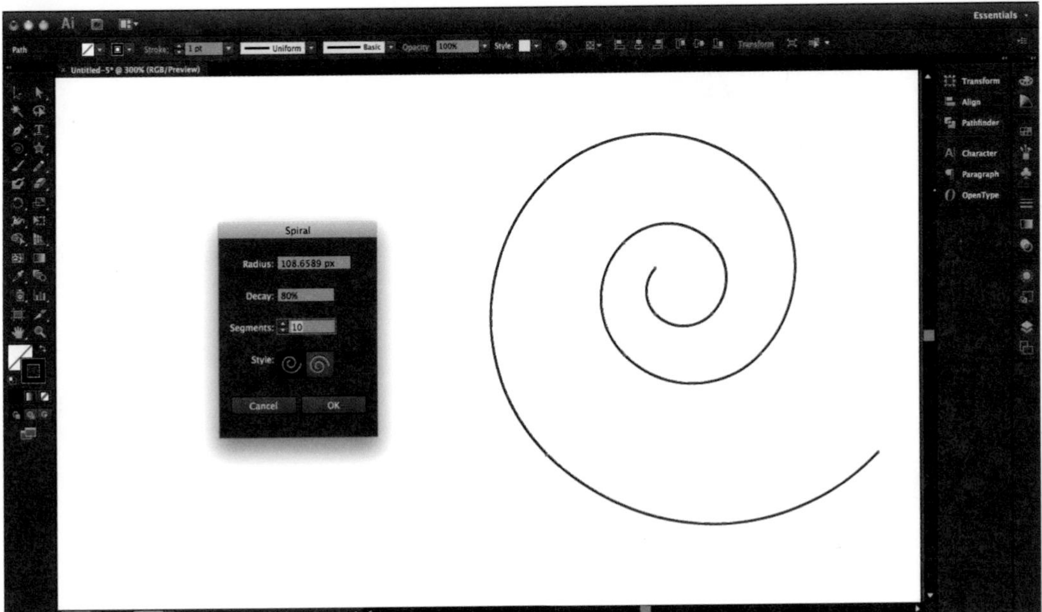

FIG 3-13 The Spiral dialog box

Shortcut

You can increase or decrease the segments using the up and down keys.

Rectangular Grid Tool

This tool creates a grid of rows and columns and can be accessed the same as the other tools. When you click on your document, the dialog box displays the following options:

- Width and Height options, as well as the registration point of the grid.
- Horizontal Divider shows the number of horizontal grids, and the Skew slider sets the space between the grids. For example, if you drag it to the right, the grids will be longer on the top, and vice versa.
- Vertical Divider shows the number of vertical grids, and the Skew slider sets the space between the grids.

- Use Outside Rectangle as a Frame uses a rectangle for the outside frame instead of using individual lines.
- Fill Grid sets the fill of the grid with the current fill color if there is already a fill color.

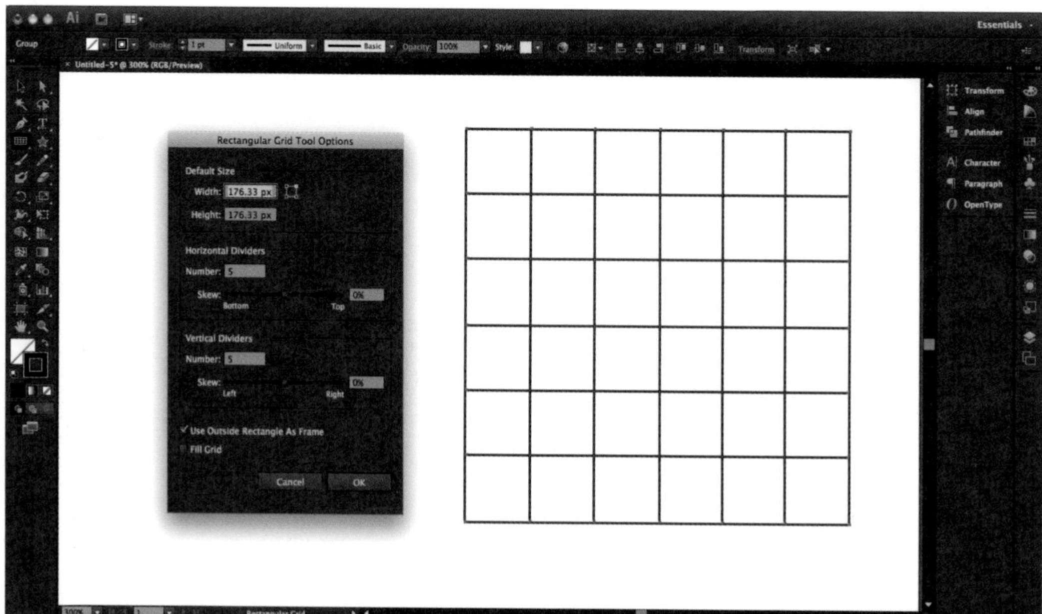

FIG 3-14 The Rectangular Grid Tool Options dialog box

> **Note**
>
> You can click the up and down arrows to increase the columns, and the right and left arrows to change the number of the rows.

Polar Grid Tool

This tool creates a polar chart and follows the same concept as the Rectangular Grid. When you select the Polar Grid tool and click in your document, the Polar dialog box appears with the following options:

- The width and height of the polar grid.
- The number of both concentric and radial dividers and how they arrange in the polar grid. The concentric dividers are the circles that divide the grid, and the radial dividers are the lines that cut these circles.
- Create Compound Path from Ellipse converts the concentric circles to compound paths.

- Fill Grid sets the fill of the grid with the current fill color if there is already a fill color.

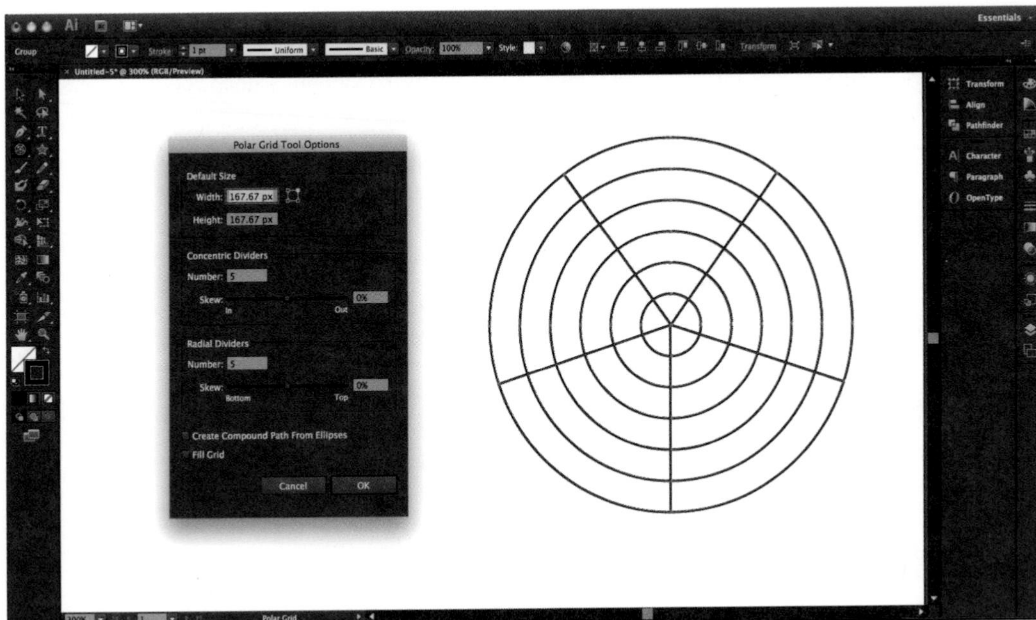

FIG 3-15 The Polar Grid Tool Options dialog box

> **Note**
>
> You can click the up and down arrows to increase the concentric dividers, and the right and left arrows to change the number of the radial dividers.

Modifying Paths

There are other options that you will commonly need when working with paths, such as smoothing, joining, and erasing paths. Let us review each of these features and how it works.

Path Eraser Tool

When you click and hold over the Pencil tool it expands to display the Path Eraser tool. This tool allows you to erase selected paths by drawing over them.

Eraser Tool

The Eraser tool can be used to erase the paths and objects on the stage. Unlike the Path Eraser tool, the Eraser tool erases the whole object.

Join and Average Points

Sometimes you would like to join path anchor points for either open or closed paths, especially when you are working with complex paths. The Join command connects two or more anchor points from different paths or on the same path. In the following example, we have a tree leaf that consists of two paths; let us see how to join the anchor points of the two paths:

1. Open the document Join_average.ai. The first leaf from the left consists of two paths that are not connected with each other.
2. Select the Direct Select tool and select the two anchor points at the top of the leaf.
3. From the Object menu, choose Path > Join or press Cmd+J (Ctrl+J in Windows).

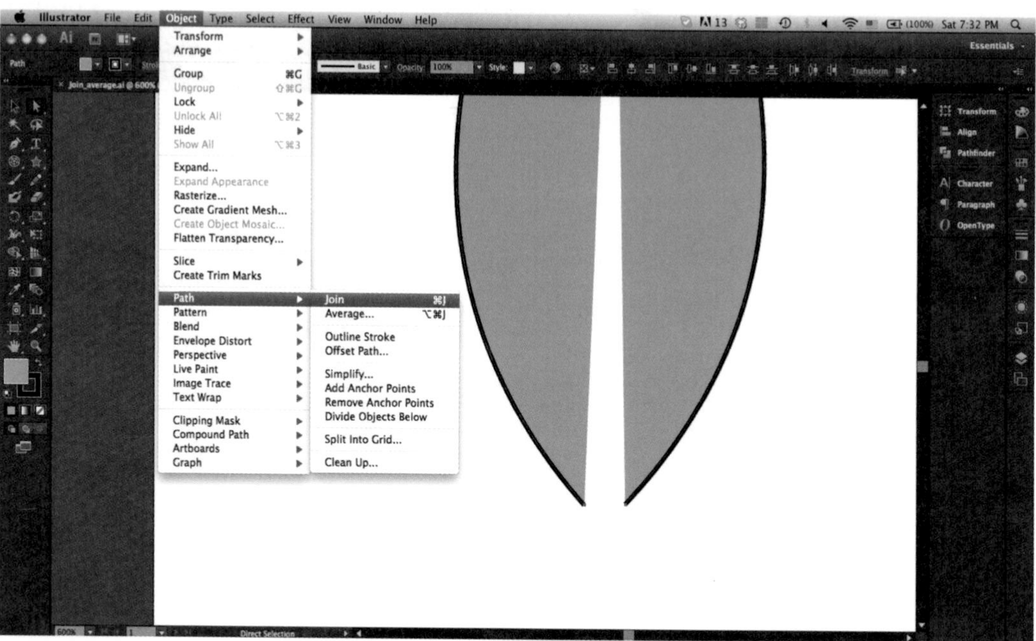

FIG 3-16 The Join command from the Object menu

The two points are joined to be one anchor point. Now, the bottom anchor points are not as far from each other; let us see how they got connected to each other:

4. In the above example, choose the bottom two anchor points.
5. From the Object menu, choose Path > Join or press Cmd+J (Ctrl+J in Windows).

Notice that the two anchor points are still in the same position, and a path is created to join them. In many cases you do not need this path, and you may

FIG 3-17 The Join command and the path that connect the two anchor points

need to have the two points move to a center position and become joined. This done through the Average command, which moves the anchor points to a middle position between them either in the vertical axis, horizontal axis, or both, as follows:

1. Select the Direct Select tool, and select the two anchor points at the bottom of the right leaf.
2. From the Object menu, choose Path > Average or press Alt (Option)+Cmd+J (Alt+Ctrl+J in Windows).
3. A dialog box appears to set how you would like both anchor points to be joined; choose Both and click OK.
4. From the Object menu, choose Path > Join or press Cmd+J (Ctrl+J in Windows).

> **Shortcut**
>
> You can perform both the Join and the Average command together by pressing the Shift+Option+Cmd+J (Shift+Alt+Ctrl+J in Windows).

Simplify Paths

When you get work from outside Illustrator, such as from AutoCAD or another application, you may get paths with a large number of anchor points. The many anchor points increase the file size and make it hard to modify the artwork, because you will need to change many anchor points in order to apply a modification to the artwork, unlike the simple path with few anchor points. The Simplify command helps you to reduce the number of anchor points applied to the object, as we will see in the example below:

1. Open the file Simplify_path.ai; the fish shape in this file includes many anchor points.
2. Select the shape, and from the Object menu, choose Path > Simplify. The Simplify dialog box appears and includes the following options:
   - Curve Precision modifies the precision of the modified path.
   - Angle Threshold controls the number of straight angles created by the corner anchors.
   - The two values show the number of anchor points in the original path and the updated path.
   - Straight Lines converts the lines to straight lines with corner anchor points.
   - Show Original shows the original path as a guide to see how the new one changes from the original.
   - The Preview checkbox lets you see the updated path after changing the values.

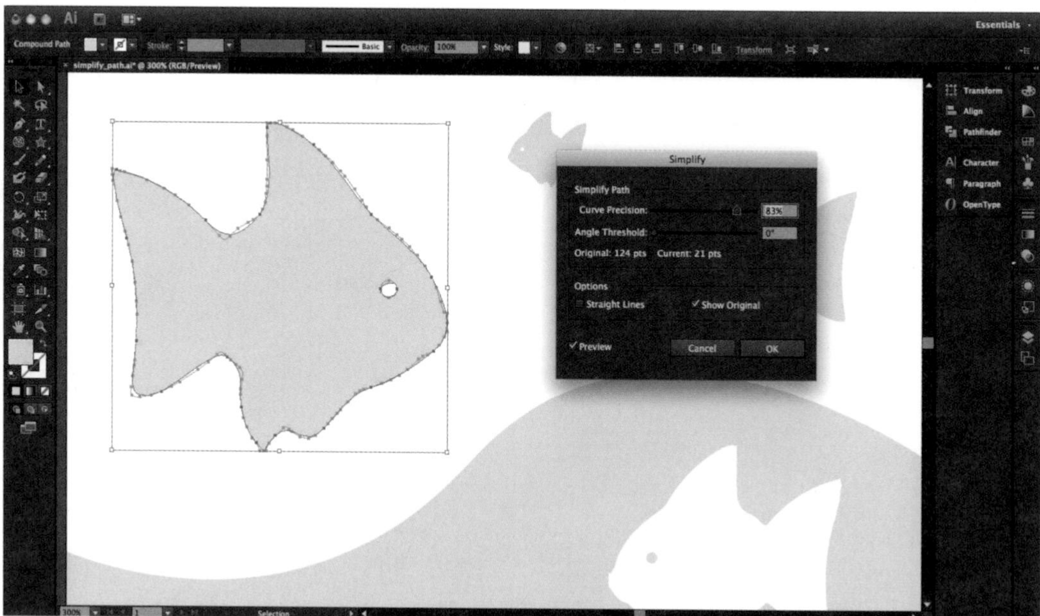

FIG 3-18 The Simplify dialog box

Now, let us apply this to the object we have:

3. Click the Preview checkbox to review the changes in the path.
4. Make sure to check Show Original to display the original look of the path. Notice that the original value shows that the shape had 124 points when the current value shows 12 points.

5. Move the Precision slider to 83% to make the path more similar to the original path. Notice that the current points increase but are still fewer than original points.
6. Click OK.

Clean Up

The last command that we will cover in this chapter is the Clean Up command. This command removes unwanted points, objects, and empty text areas. In complex projects, it is better to keep organized and deliver your project in a professional way with a good file size, but it is normal to have unwanted objects and stray points while creating your artwork.

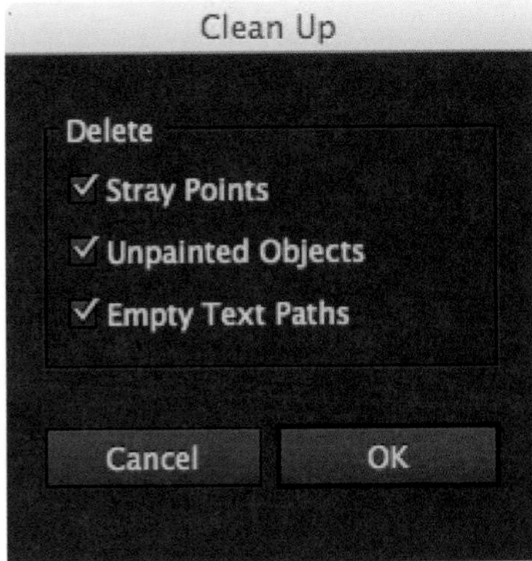

FIG 3-19 The Clean Up dialog box

Thus, this command is very important to make sure that your files do not include unwanted points and objects. You can access the Clean Up command from the Object > Path menu.

At this stage, we should be familiar with paths, including how to use paths to create artwork and how to modify paths by adding, removing, or modifying points. Also, we learned the difference between open and closed paths and how to create both using the Tools panel. The practical side of this chapter includes trying to create your own simple objects, tracing imported objects in your document, and trying to merge both open and closed paths to create complex artwork. In Chapter 15, we will cover more complex techniques to work with paths and shapes and how to arrange them in an Illustrator project.

For examples pertaining to this chapter, visit www.illustratorfoundations.com.

CHAPTER 4

Working with Color

Color is an essential element in your design. It does not matter if your design is for web, printing, desktop, or a cartoon, you will use the color features inside Illustrator frequently to color your artwork. As a vector-based application, Illustrator is used to create artwork, give it the appropriate colors, or modify the colors of existing artwork.

Adobe Illustrator understands the importance of colors and provides many options and features to control your artwork color easily and efficiently. If you are familiar with other applications in Adobe Creative Suite, you many notice that the way that Illustrator handles color is slightly different because it provides more accurate coloring methods than other programs, such as converting the color into different color swatch types, color guides, and recolor artwork features. In this chapter, we will review the different coloring options in Illustrator and how to use the different color panels to work with colors.

Objects in Adobe Illustrator consist of paths, and there are two parts of paths to which you can apply color separately. The first is the fill color, which is defined as the color that fills inside your object path, and the second is the stroke color, which is the color that is applied to the path itself. Coloring your artwork is as simple as selecting your artwork and choosing the color from the fill and stroke color indicator in the Tools panel. Let us review the coloring options in the Tools panel.

FIG 4-1 The file and stroke indicator in the Tools panel

At the bottom of the Tools panel, you find the color icons that represent the fill color and stroke color, which is located behind the fill color. You can activate any of the fill or stroke colors by clicking over it. The active fill or stroke color appears at the top of the fill and stroke color indicator in the Tools panel. At the top right of the color thumbnails is the Swap Fill and Stroke option, which lets you swap the colors between the fill and the stroke colors.

> **Shortcut**
>
> You can switch between the active fill or stroke color by clicking "X" on your keyboard.

At the bottom left of the colors thumbnails, there is an overlapped white and black colors icon (the Default Fill and Stroke icon) that lets you return to the default white for the fill and black for the stroke colors. Under the Default Fill and Stroke icon, there are three icons that let you set the type of color that will be applied to the fill or stroke portion of the path.

The first icon from the left sets the fill or stroke to a solid color, while the second icon applies gradient colors; we will discuss gradient in the next chapter. The third icon, which has a red line across it, shows that the fill or stroke does not have any color applied to it. When you click on either the fill or the stroke color, you bring it to the top of the other thumbnail to show that this is the active part of the object. For example, when you click the stroke thumbnail, it appears on top to let you know that color changes will be applied to the stroke color of the object.

When you double-click the fill color or the stroke color thumbnails, the Color Picker dialog box appears to let you choose the color for your artwork. Color Picker is similar to the one in Photoshop. Generally, it consists of two parts: Color Modes and Color Swatches. When the dialog box appears, it opens Color Modes by default, and you can switch to Color Swatches by clicking on the button on the right side of the dialog box.

Color Mode includes two main sections: the select color area on the left lets you choose the color and its brightness. The section on the right includes the values that represent the specified color. These modes include the following:

- HSB represents the hue, saturation, and brightness of the color.
- RGB is used to identify colors for digital media such as video and digital applications. In the RGB color mode, any color is a combination of red, blue, and green.
- The hexadecimal color system starts with the # sign and is used to define colors for the web. Each color is represented with six values of number, characters, or both.
- CMYK color mode is used in the printing industry and in handling colors with printers; it uses a mix of cyan, magenta, yellow, and black to create the final color.

RGB, hexadecimal, and CMYK are the most-used color modes in different projects. You can choose to handle your colors with any of these modes, based on your project.

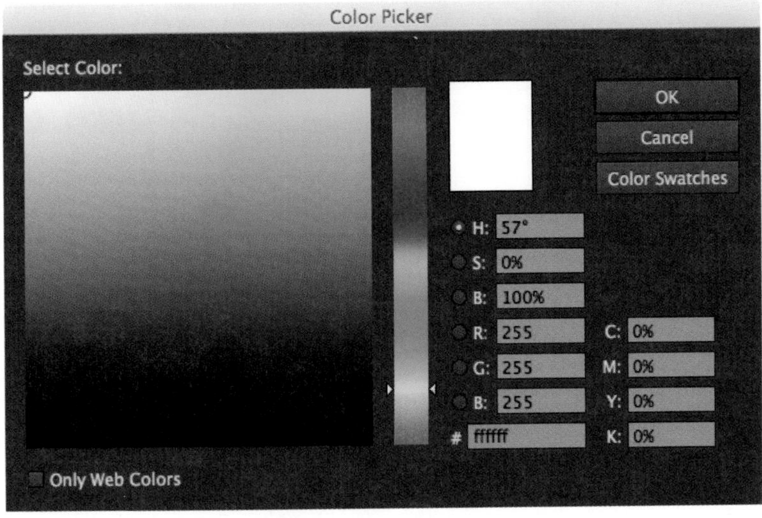

FIG 4-2 The color options in the Color Picker dialog box

The Color Swatches view shows the different colors you can choose by navigating through the Color Swatches list. In the right of the Color Swatches view, there are two color samples, one on top of the other. The top one represents the selected color, and the bottom one represents the currently active color in the fill color thumbnail. Now, let us see a simple example that shows how to easily color your artwork:

1. Open the document Simple_artwork.ai.
2. Click the star shape on the artboard.
3. From the Tools panel, double-click the fill color thumbnail.
4. Use the Color Picker dialog box to change the color of the fill, and click OK.
5. Double-click the stroke color thumbnail, click the Color Swatch button, and change the object stroke color by choosing a color swatch.

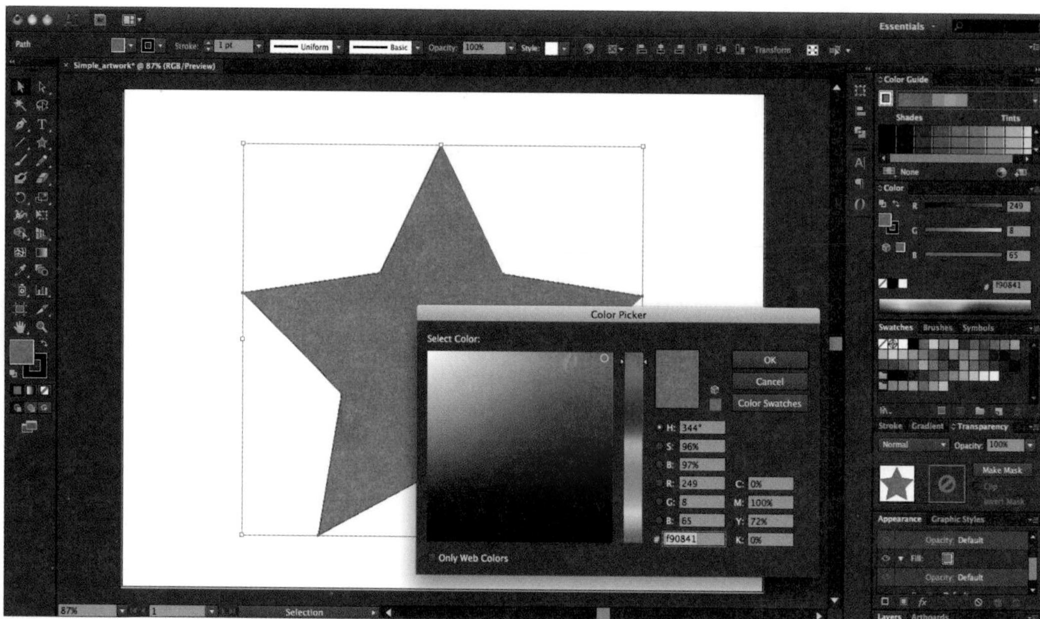

FIG 4-3 Changing the color of the artwork

Changing Artwork Colors

Using the Color Picker is one of many methods you can use to change the color of your object. You can accomplish this from many places in the Illustrator workspace, as outlined next.

Color Panel

The Color panel allows you to change the color of the fill and stroke of the object based on selecting the color from the Spectrum or change its numerical value. The Color panel lets you change the color of the artwork similar to the Color Picker; the only difference is that it has a different structure that may be easier and more reachable than the Color Picker, for which you need to double-click the fill or the strike color indicator to open it. The Color panel allows you to display the colors in different color systems such as grayscale, HSB, RGB, CMYK, and web-safe RGB colors. You can switch between the different color systems from the Panel Context menu.

As you may already know, the grayscale color system indicates the colors are gray levels between black and white. Web-safe RGB colors are used to show only the colors that can be used in old web browsers. Many of the old browsers cannot display all the colors, so web-safe RGB displays only 256 colors from all the colors variations we know. Although most users are already using up-to-date browsers that can display all the colors properly, some projects might require restricting your design to only these 256 colors.

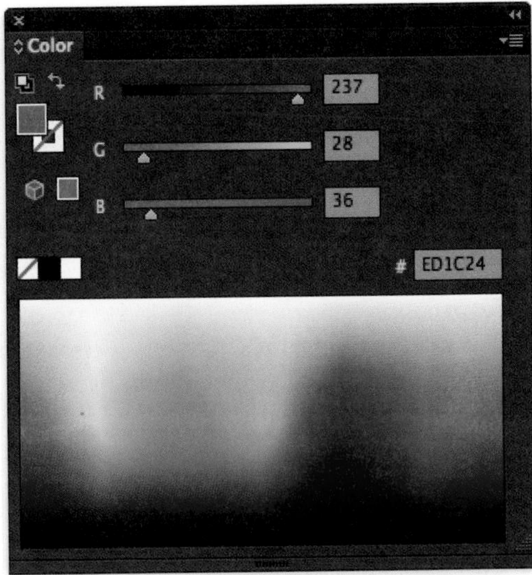

FIG 4-4 The Color panel in Illustrator

The Color panel includes the following main three parts:

1. The top left part includes the fill and stroke colors indicator, which is very similar to the one on the Tools panel.
2. The right side includes the basic colors that mix to create your chosen color. For example, if you selected RGB from the Panel Context menu, the color values will be red, green, and blue. If you choose CMYK, the color values will be cyan, magenta, yellow, and black. Also on the right side, you can find the color values in the hexadecimal option for the use on web.
3. The bottom part includes the color spectrum of the selected color mode where you can move over it with your mouse then click to select specific color.

Control Panel

The top bar includes both the fill and the stroke colors as separated icons next to each other. You can click on each icon to display the Color Swatches panel and choose your color. We will discuss the color swatches in more detail later. When you press the Shift key while clicking over the color thumbnail, the Color panel appears instead of the Color Swatches panel.

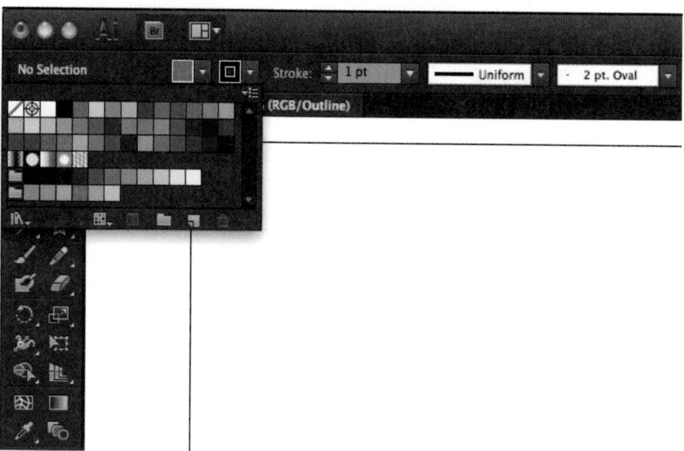

FIG 4-5 The color swatches in the Control panel

Color Swatches

The Color Swatches panel is another method you can use to choose your color in Illustrator based on the color swatches already created in the panel. Many Illustrator projects include different colors and shades that you will want to use often in your designs—you can use this panel to save definitions or swatches of the colors you want to use frequently or even export them to save and use in other documents.

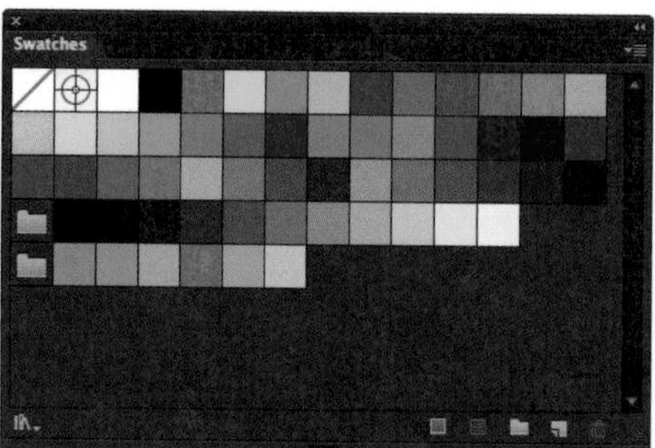

FIG 4-6 The Color Swatches panel

Using the Swatches panel to color your artwork is as easy as three simple steps:

1. Select your object on the artboard.
2. Set the Color/Fill indicator to activate either the fill color or the stroke color.
3. Click on the color that you would like to choose from the Color Swatches panel.

Note

The Color Swatches panel includes the default color swatches in addition to the None icon, which removes any color from the artwork's fill or stroke.

You can click the bottom left icon to reveal other Color Swatch libraries. In many printing projects, the color you see on the screen is different from the actual color you get from the printer, because there are differences between the screen color and the printing ink colors. However, many companies have created color libraries that define each color with a numerical value. Using this value ensures that the color will be exactly as the designer expects it. One of the most famous and commonly used color libraries is the Pantone Matching System.

From the Swatches Library list, you can open any Color library and use it in your design. When you select a Color library, it appears as a separate Swatch panel for this library. Clicking on a color in these libraries will copy it to the Swatch panel for that particular document.

To the right of the Swatches Library icon, there are five icons as follows:

1. The Show Swatches Kinds menu lets you choose which swatches you would like to display, such as solid colors, gradients, and patterns.
2. The Swatches Options icon displays a dialog box that lets you modify the swatch color.
3. The New Color Group option is where you can organize your swatches into groups for easy handling of a large number of swatches.
4. The New Swatch icon lets you create a new swatch using the Swatch Options dialog box. This is one of the methods that allow you to create a color swatch with more control over the color values and the swatch name.
5. Delete Swatch lets you delete a swatch, or you can drag the swatch to the icon to delete it.

FIG 4-7 The Swatch Options dialog box

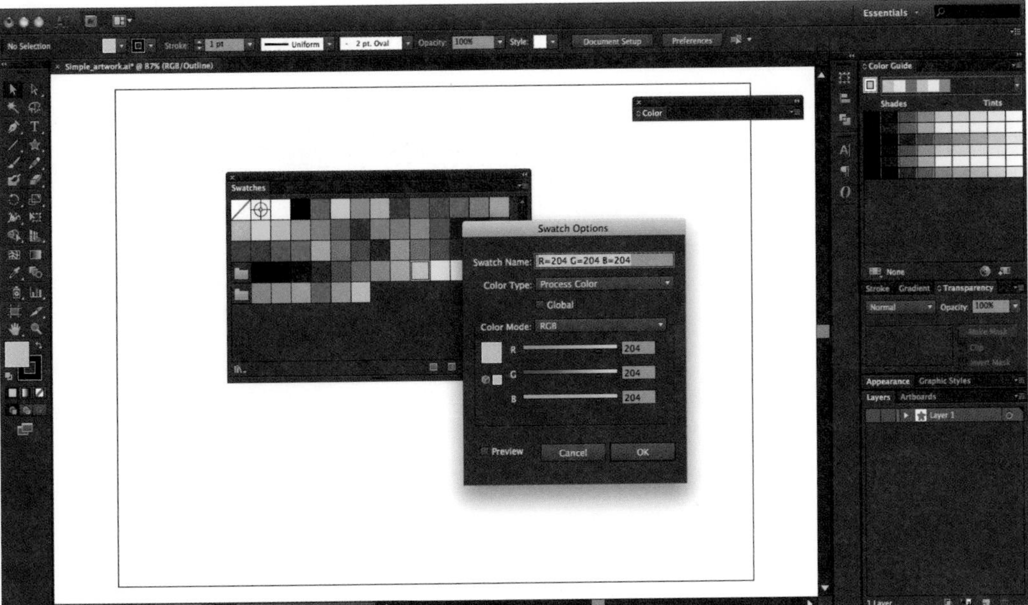

> **Note**
>
> When you create a new swatch, Illustrator names it with its color values. For example, C = 10, M = 50, Y = 30, K = 0. You can use the Color Swatches Options dialog box to give the swatches more customized names, or you can double-click their names if they are in list view.

In the following example, we will see how to use the Swatches panel to arrange the color swatches for one artwork:

1. Open the file Color_donkey.ai. This file includes a colorful artwork—a cartoon donkey character. We need to collect its colors into the Swatches panel.
2. Select each color in the artwork by using the Eye Dropper tool from the Tools panel, and click on the color that you would like to select.
3. Select each of the character's colors. From the Color panel, grab each color and drop it into the Swatches panel. You will see the new colors are added next to each other.
4. Click on the swatches while pressing the Shift key to select all the character swatches.
5. Click the Group icon to create a swatches group for this character.
6. Name the new group Donkey_character. Notice that all the selected swatches are arranged into a new group.

> **Note**
>
> There is another method you can use to select the object color. Select the object using the Selection tool, and you will notice that the object fill and stroke colors appear in the Tools panel and the Color panel.

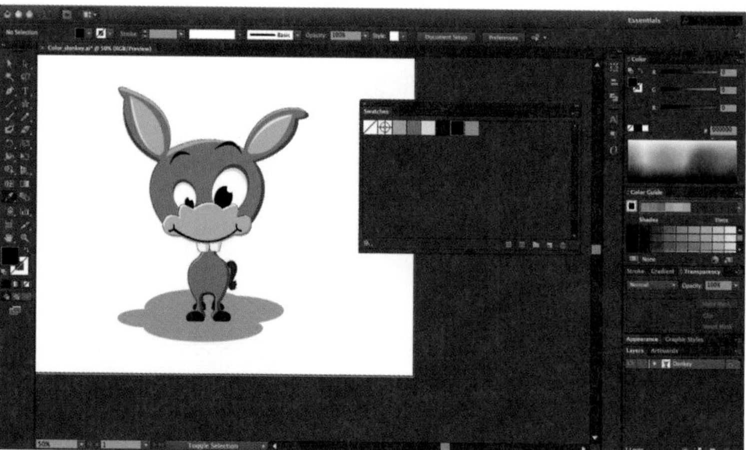

FIG 4-8 Adding the cartoon character colors to the Swatches panel

Note

Sometimes, you click the object but you cannot see its fill or stroke colors—you see only a question mark that appears in the Fill and Stroke indicator. This means that the object is actually a group of multiple objects. In this case, double-click the group to enter the isolation mode of the individual object. Once you select it, you will notice that its color appears in the indicator.

You can save the color swatches as external Adobe Swatches Exchange (ASE) or Adobe Illustrator (AI) swatches to use with multiple documents. To load the swatches document, all you need to do is open the Swatches panel context menu and choose Open Swatch Library > Other Library.

The ASE swatches format integrates better with other Adobe applications such as Adobe Photoshop and InDesign. That's why it is preferred if you are taking the color samples from one application to another. AI swatches libraries are only recognized by Illustrator.

Process colors

Now, let us move to the different color types available and how to use each in Illustrator projects. Select one of the swatches from the Swatches panel and click on the Swatch option from the bottom or by double-clicking on the swatch, you will notice that the color type is set to process color, which is the default type of swatch; the two other types are global or spot. To understand the difference between swatches or color types, let us start with the following simple example:

1. Open the file Color_types.ai. This file includes simple shapes with fill and no stroke color.
2. Select similar star shapes using the selection tool while pressing the Shift key, and make sure that the fill thumbnail is active from the Fill and Stroke Color Indicator at the bottom of the Tools panel or the Color panel.
3. Click on one of the swatches in the Swatches panel to apply the red color to the stars.
4. Click in the artboard to deselect the shapes.
5. Double-click on the swatch and change the color using the color values in the bottom of the Swatch Options dialog box. Make sure to enable the Preview checkbox to check the updates.
6. Notice that the swatch color changes, but the shapes color stays the same and does not update with the new color.

FIG 4-9 Applying the process color swatch on the objects fill

At this stage, this color is a process color. Let us see the difference between this color type and the global process type:

1. Double-click on the same red color swatch, and check the Global box under the Color Type drop-down list.
2. Select the stars object on the artboard and change its color to the global process color swatch we just edited.
3. Now, deselect all the objects.
4. Double-click the swatch again, change its color value, and click OK.
5. Notice that all the objects' colors change even when they are not selected.

FIG 4-10 Change the color type of the swatch to global process from the Swatch Options dialog box

The global process color changes are applied to all the objects that use this color in the document. You can identify the global process color by the small white triangle that is added at the bottom right of the color swatch thumbnail in the Swatches panel. The global process colors are very useful when you would like to change a specific color in your design and would like to have all the changes affect all the objects that use this color.

Whether you use the process color or the global process color depends on your design. For example, some colors are subject to change and applied in many objects in your document. The global process color is a good choice in this situation. On the other hand, if you like to have each object's color change separately or you are afraid of accidental changes in colors, you can choose process color instead.

Spot Colors

In some printing projects, you need to have a special ink or color that is not one of the CMYK colors; for example, a special company color that requires specific ink combinations. When you create these colors in your design, you define them as spot colors. When you apply a spot color to an object in the design, the print house will need a special ink for this color. You can set your color to be a spot color from the Swatch Options panel as follows:

1. Click the New Swatch icon from the Swatches panel.
2. From the Swatch Options dialog box, set the color type to spot color. Click OK.
3. Notice that the spot color icon in the Swatches panel, like the global color, also has a triangle, which also includes a dot inside it.

Note

When you set the color to process or spot colors, you cannot edit it in the Color panel—you can adjust only the tint of the color.

Creating New Swatches

You can also create new swatches directly from the Swatches panel as follows:

1. Click the New Swatch icon on the bottom of the Swatches panel.
2. The New Swatch dialog box appears; set the name of the new swatch.
3. Set the type of the swatch to be process or spot color.
4. Check the global color if you want to apply the global properties that we covered earlier to the swatch.
5. Set the color mode from the list.
6. Change the color values to create the new desired color.

Color Guide

Many designers take a lot of time to choose the best color combination for their artwork or project. Choosing the best colors can be difficult, especially because the colors are a very important part of your design, as we mentioned at the beginning of this chapter. However, Adobe Illustrator provides you with a smart and helpful panel that guides you through the process of using artwork color. This panel is called the Color Guide.

The basic idea behind the Color Guide panel is that each time you select a color from the Swatches panel, the Color Guide panel considers it a primary color and provides you suggestions for color combinations that coordinate with this color. Furthermore, it provides you a clever way to control the color suggestions and limit these suggestions based on your project.

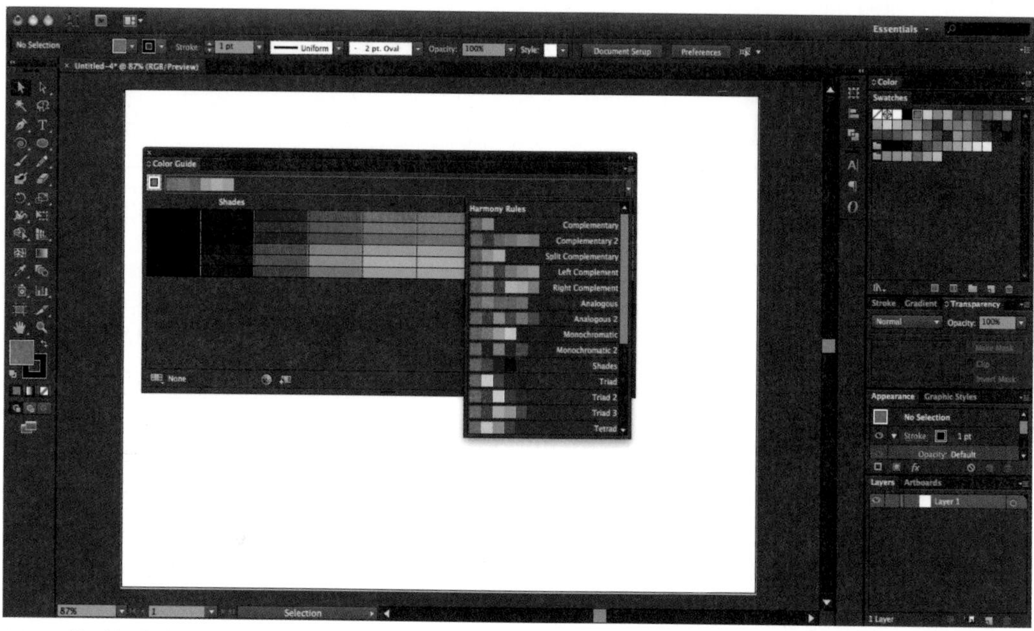

FIG 4-11 The Color Guide panel

When you select a color swatch from the Swatches panel, you will notice it appears in the Guide panel and next to the drop-down Harmony Rule list. You can choose any of these rules to tell Illustrator how you would like it to provide the color suggestions. For example, you can choose Shade to have the suggested colors be shades of the primary color. Or, you can choose Contrast to receive suggestions of colors that contrast with the primary color.

In the preview area below the harmony selector, you can see the suggested colors divided into two parts, with a small arrow in the middle of them. The right part shows suggested colors with different tints, the left side shows suggestions with different shades, and in the middle, under the arrow, you can find the primary color and the main suggested colors.

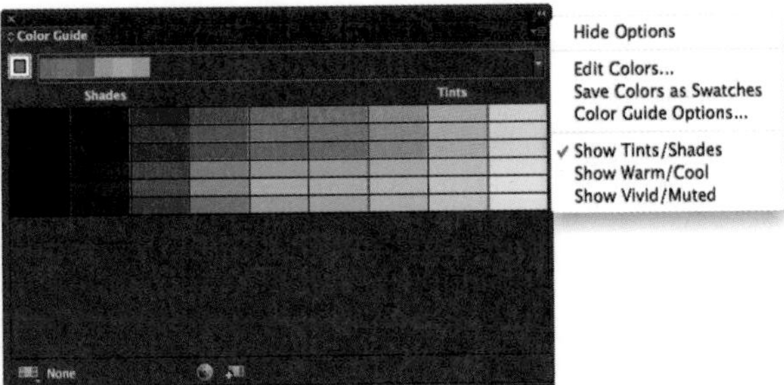

FIG 4-12 The Color Guide panel context menu

From the panel option menu, you can change the two parts to show either Tints/Shades, Warm/Cool, or Vivid/Muted suggestions. Also, you can change the number of the suggested colors from the Color Guide options with a range from 3 to 20 steps.

When you are done with your suggestions, you can click the icon in the bottom right of the panel to add a new color group to the Swatches panel. If you would like to choose only some of these colors, you can click them while pressing Cmd (Ctrl in Windows) to select individual colors. You can also select a single color or more and drag them into the Swatches panel to create swatches.

In some projects, you might want to limit the color suggestions from the Color Guide panel to a specific library. In the bottom right of the Color Guide panel, there is an icon that limits the color group to the colors in a specific swatches library. For example, you can click this icon to expand the available library (note it is the same as the library in the Swatches panel). The colors that appear in the suggestion preview are selected from only the selected color library.

FIG 4-13 The Edit Colors dialog box

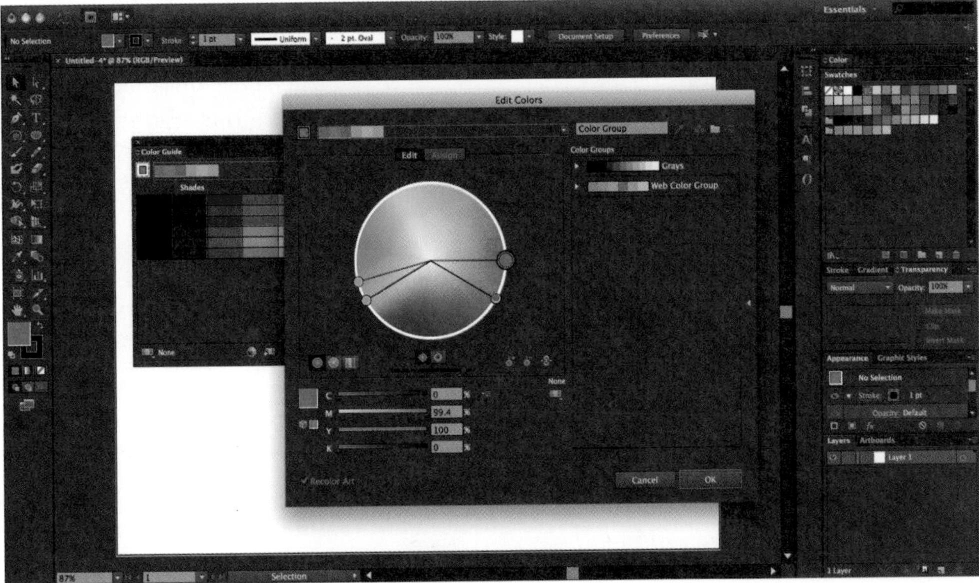

The Edit Colors icon at the bottom of the Color Guide panel gives you more control over the suggested colors based on the color wheel. In the top of the Edit Colors dialog box, you will see the suggested colors, and next to this is the color group name, where you can click and add a custom name for the color group. You can also save the modified color group, create a new one, or delete the group.

On the left side of the Edit Colors dialog box, you will find the color wheel, where you can click and move your mouse to change the color group suggestions. At the bottom of the color wheel, you can change its view, control the brightness of the colors, add more colors to the group, and link or delink the group colors in the color wheel. Thus, you can edit each color separately.

At the bottom of the dialog box, you will find another method to change the color, using the color values based on color modes such as HSB, RGB, CMYK, and Web RGB. When you select a color cycle from the wheel, you can change its value by moving it around the color wheel or through the numerical values in the bottom part of the dialog box. In addition to the above, this dialog box allows you to do the following:

- Create groups of color.
- Assign and reduce color.
- Apply a change to the selected object.
- Invoke it from the control panel or the Edit > Edit Color > Edit Recolor Artwork menu.

We learned in this chapter about one of the very important elements of your artwork—the colors. As we saw, Adobe Illustrator provides a smart and clever method to let you work with the colors in your projects with maximum flexibility and the ability to create, edit, and even have Illustrator suggest color combinations for you using the Color Guide panel. The examples we discussed in this chapter show how to use the color features in Illustrator; you can practice with your own artwork to learn more about the features and how to use them efficiently.

For examples pertaining to this chapter, visit www.illustratorfoundations.com.

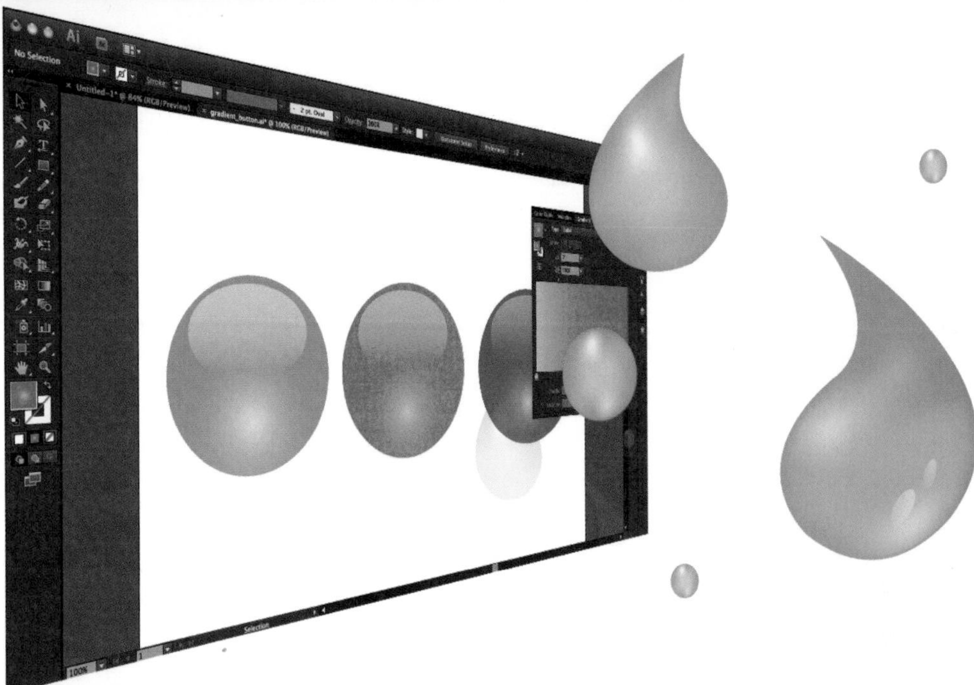

CHAPTER 5

Working with the Gradient Tool

As we discussed in Chapter 4, color is an essential part of your design or artwork. However, the fill or the stroke of your object is not limited to solid colors—it can be filled with other types of fills, such as gradients and patterns. This chapter covers gradient and how to use it to create different effects on your artwork. Gradient is a combination of two or more colors; these colors mix together in different ways to create an artistic effect in your artwork. The effects can be a mixture between colors. Gradient color can also give an object the effect of light and shadow areas, which can give it a more beveled effect or natural appearance.

In the old versions of Adobe Illustrator, it was tedious to work with the Gradient tool to create and apply your gradient. The new versions make it easy for you to create, apply, modify, and save a gradient as a swatch in the Swatches panel, and give you the ability to edit the gradient on the artboard directly using the Gradient Annotator, as we will see later in the Gradient Tool section. Applying a gradient color in Illustrator is achieved in a similar way as solid color, discussed in Chapter 4; there are some minor differences that we will focus on in this chapter.

At first glance, you will notice, in the Fill and Stroke Color indicator in the Tools panel, that there are three small icons under the color thumbnails. The first icon from the left displays the solid color on the active color thumbnail, and the second displays the gradient color. Through this icon, you can easily apply color either in the fill or the stroke. You can create an object and click on the Solid Color icon, which will apply the active solid color, and you can click the Gradient icon to apply the active gradient color on the object. The third icon removes the color to have no fill or stroke color applied to the object.

Let us try the below steps to see how to switch between the solid and gradient fill using the Fill and Stroke Color indicator:

1. Create a new Illustrator document.
2. Use the Rectangle tool to draw a rectangle on the stage.
3. Select the rectangle using the Selection tool.
4. Click on the Fill thumbnail in the Fill and Stroke Color indicator in the Tools panel.
5. Click the Solid icon under the thumbnail to display the active solid color.
6. Click the Gradient icon to display the active gradient color and apply it to the rectangle.

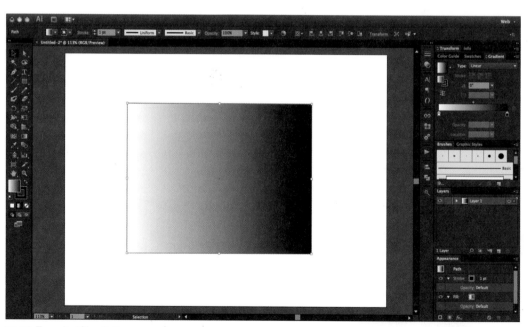

FIG 5-1 The gradient fill applied to an object

Gradient Panel

Before jumping into how to work with the gradient effects, let us discover the Gradient panel options and how to create your gradient effect. The panel includes the following options:

Note

To make sure that all the Gradient panel options are appearing to you, make sure you click the Show Option link in the panel context menu.

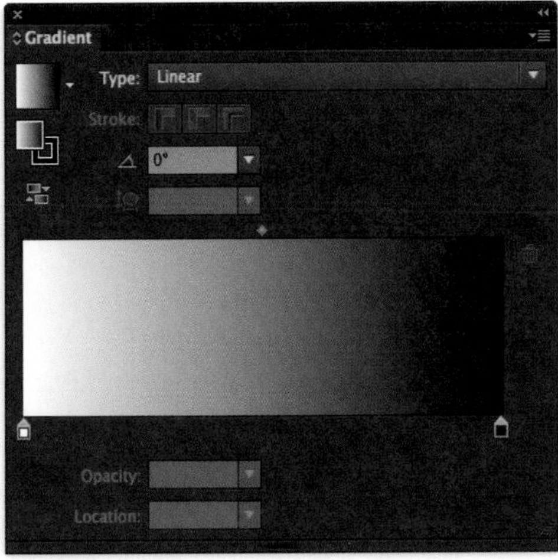

FIG 5-2 The Gradient panel options

- The Gradient Fill list includes the available gradient swatches in the current Swatches panel. At the end of the list is an icon that lets you add your custom gradient to the list. When you click Gradient Fill without opening the list, it activates the gradient fill in the Tools panel.
- The Type list lets you choose between the linear gradient or the radial gradient. The linear gradient arranges the colors parallel to each other, while the radial gradient arranges the color in a circular order and the colors flow from the center of the circle to the outside or vice versa.
- The Reverse Gradient icon reverses the color order in your gradient. For example, if you have a gradient with the white color on the right and black color on the left, clicking this icon reverses the order of the colors, so the white moves to the left and the black moves to the right.
- The Apply Gradient to Stroke icon allows you to choose how a gradient is applied to stroke lines, as we will see later in the Applying Gradient to Stroke section.
- The angle value controls the angle of the gradient or its rotation direction.
- The Aspect Ratio icon lets you modify the size of the gradient applied to the option (available only when using a radial-type gradient).
- The Gradient Slider is the most important option in the panel because it lets you create the custom gradient, as we will see in the next section.
- The opacity value allows you to add transparency to each of the colors individually in the gradient.
- The location value sets where the color is located in the Gradient Slider.

How to Create Gradient

The Gradient Slider is the tool you can use to create a custom gradient in the panel. In the following steps, we will try to create a gradient for a red curtain and add it to the Swatches panel. When you see a curtain, you will see that it has folds that cause bright and dark colors based on their direction from the light. We will create such a gradient with different shades of red colors following the example below:

1. Open the Gradient panel; if you do not see it, you can reveal it by selecting it from the Window menu or Ctrl+F9 (Windows) or Cmd+F9 (Mac).
2. From the Type list, choose a linear gradient.
3. In the Gradient Slider, click on the first color stop arrow from the left.
4. Double-click the arrow to open the Color floating panel. By default, the color floating will be black only, so you need to pick a color mode from the options given in the floating panel or use the Swatches icon. Set the color to light red.
5. While the first color is selected, change the opacity to 65%.
6. Move to the right color stop arrow, double-click on it, and set the color to dark red.
7. While the dark red color is selected, change the opacity to 30%.
8. Create a new color stop arrow by clicking below the gradient, move it to anywhere between the above color stop arrows, and set its color to another degree of the red color and a different opacity.
9. Repeat the above steps to create other color arrows with different red shades, spaces between them, and opacity values. The total number of color spots is 10 colors.

FIG 5-3 The gradient created in the slider

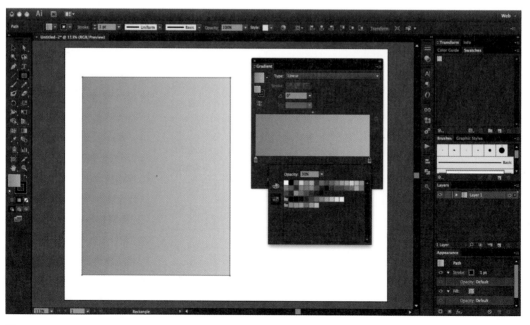

Note

To remove a color from the slider, you can simply drag the color pointer away from the slider.

10. Click the Gradient Fill list and click the icon in the bottom to add it to the Swatches panel.
11. Double-click the gradient swatch in the Swatches panel and name it "curtain red."
12. Select the Rectangle tool and create a rectangle on the stage.
13. While the rectangle is selected, press the gradient swatch we just created to apply it to the rectangle.

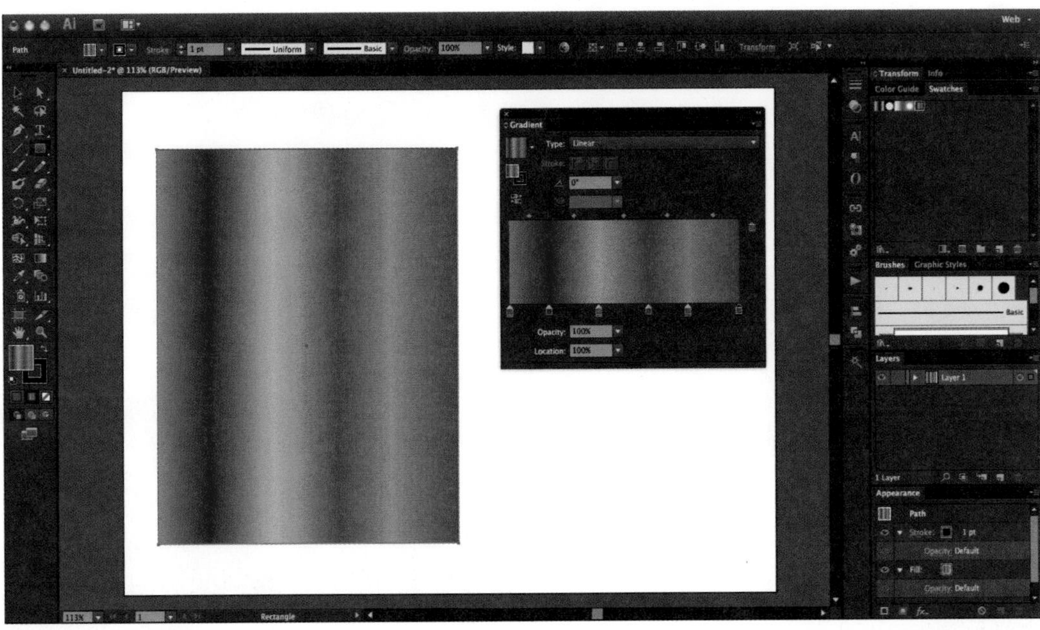

FIG 5-4 The rectangle with the gradient applied to it

Note

When you click on one of the color stops in the Gradient Slider, you can change the color opacity by changing the opacity value, which ranges from zero to 100%.

Applying Gradient to Stroke

In previous versions of Adobe Illustrator, you could not apply gradient to strokes; this was available only for the object fill. We used to have to work around this and use different steps, such as converting the stroke into fill.

Starting with Illustrator CS6, you can apply gradient to stroke as simply as you can apply it to fill, as we saw in the previous example. Although you do not have much control of the gradient that is applied to the stroke, it is now much easier to apply it to stroke than before.

The following steps show how to apply gradient to stroke in a similar way as we did in the previous example:

1. Open the document Gradient_stroke.ai.
2. Select the object on the stage and make sure that the Stroke Color indicator is active from the Tools panel.
3. Apply a gradient from the Swatches panel or create your custom gradient following the same steps we described in the previous example.
4. While the objet is selected, increase the stroke width from the top Control panel to 15 to be able to see the gradient effect applied to the object's stroke.

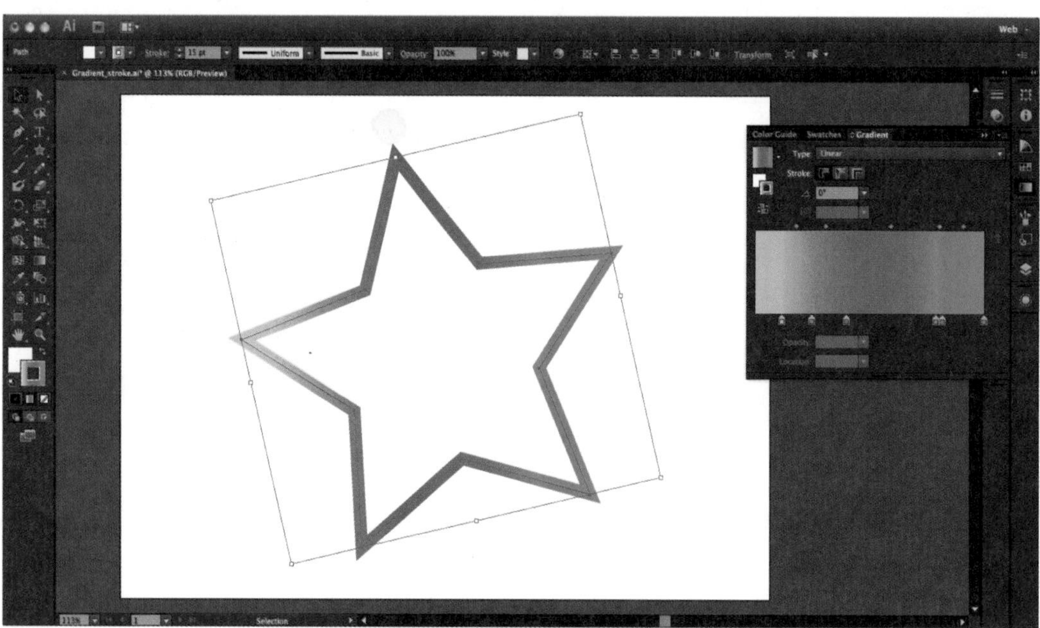

FIG 5-5 The gradient swatch applied to the object's stroke

When you select the object with the gradient applied to the stroke, you can see that there are three stroke icons that have been activated in the Gradient panel. These icons are as follows:

- Apply Gradient Within Stroke: When you click this option, the gradient flows inside the stroke line. You can control the angle of rotation over the path.
- Apply Gradient Along Stroke: This options makes the gradient flow in the same direction of the path.

- Apply Gradient Across Stroke: Applies the stroke inside the width of the stroke. For example, if the stroke is 15 px width, the gradient will be applied across these 15 pixels.

Now, let us try the three different options given above. Select the object on the artboard, and from the Gradient panel, choose the different options to apply gradient to stroke by clicking the three icons.

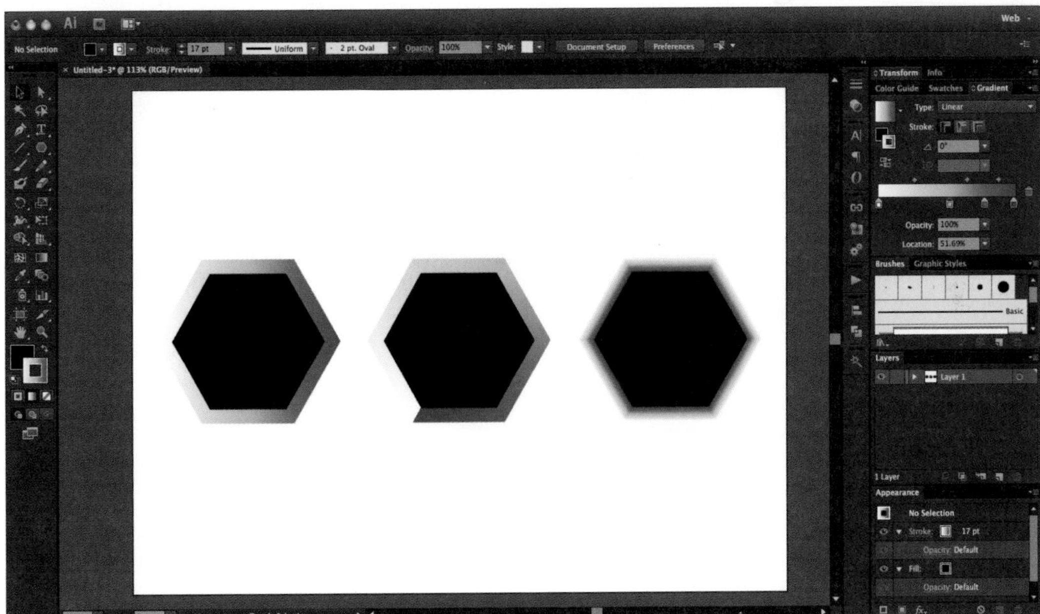

FIG 5-6 The three different options for the gradient applied to stroke

> **Note**
>
> You can also apply gradient to stroke by clicking the Stroke icon in the top Control panel to reveal the Swatches panel and choosing a gradient swatch you would like to apply.

Gradient Tool

In addition to the Gradient panel, you can apply and modify the object gradient using the Gradient tool. When you select this tool and click and drag on the object, the Gradient Annotator appears to give you modification options similar to the Gradient panel. You can create the gradient using the Gradient tool in the Tools panel. When you click on the tool, it gives you the option to modify the gradient in the Gradient panel.

The main difference between applying gradient using the Gradient panel and the Gradient Annotator or Gradient tool is that you only need to select the object and choose the gradient to apply it using the Gradient panel. The tool allows you to have more control over the gradient directly on the object.

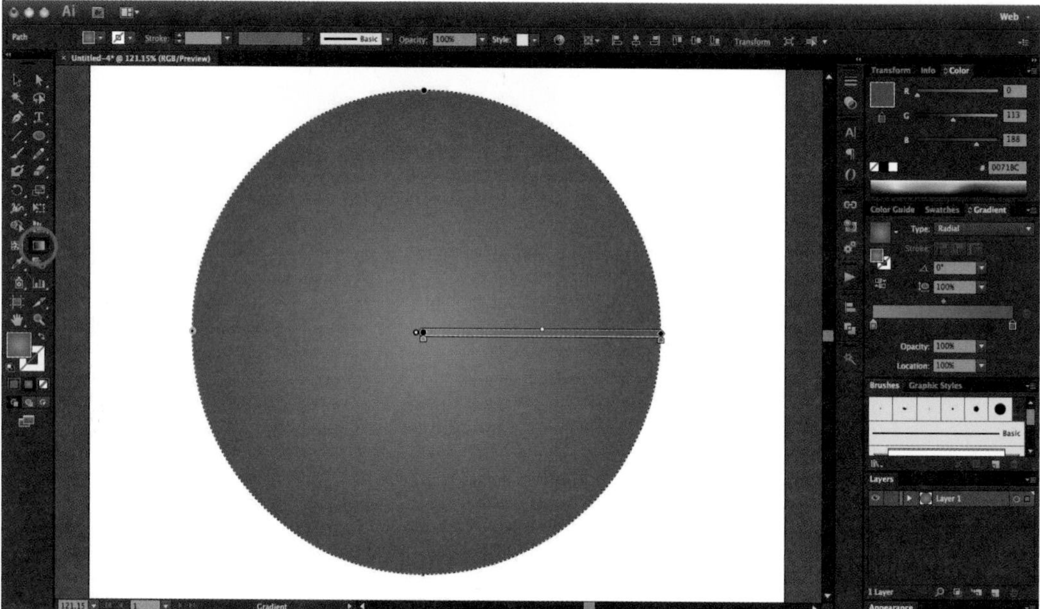

FIG 5-7 The Gradient tool in the Tools panel

Linear Gradient

When you select the Gradient tool while the linear gradient is selected from the Gradient panel, you will notice that the tool gives you a number of settings on the artboard itself. Follow the steps below to create a linear gradient:

1. Create an object on the stage and apply gradient fill to it.
2. Select the Gradient tool from the Tools panel.
3. Click in the object where you would like the gradient to start and drag until the point where you would like the gradient to end.

While you drag, you will notice that the Gradient tool reveals the controls that let you control the gradient options. When you roll the gradient indicator over the object, the following options appear:

- The cycle point at the beginning of the gradient lets you move your gradient's position on the selected object.

- The small square at the end of the gradient indicator lets you change the width of the gradient.
- Along the gradient line, you can see the color indicators. You can click and drag these indicators to modify their position in the gradient. You can also double-click them to change color or opacity.
- On the other side of the color indicator on the gradient line, you will notice small points you can drag to control the center point between each color.
- When you roll over just after the end of the gradient line, the mouse curser turns to a rotation shape, which means that you can rotate the gradient by clicking and dragging.

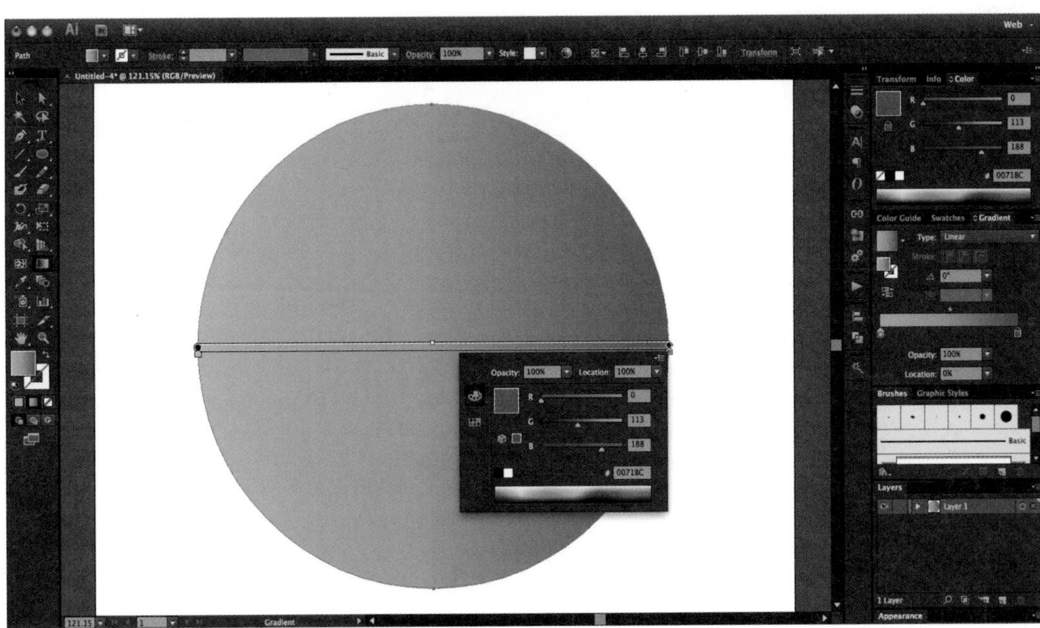

FIG 5-8 The Linear Gradient options

Radial Gradient

The radial gradient has different options that appear when applying the Gradient tool, as follows:

- The black circle on the radial gradient border lets you change the aspect ratio of the ellipse of the gradient circle.
- The other point on the circle lets you change the size of the radial gradient.
- Click on the edge of the circle to rotate it.
- The gradient line includes the same features as the linear gradient.

FIG 5-9 The Radial Gradient options

> **Note**
>
> You can rotate the gradient and scale it from the gradient bar at the same time by clicking the Option key (Alt in Windows) while rotating the gradient.

Similar to other Illustrator guides, you can show or hide the Gradient Annotator from the View menu. Now, after learning about the different gradient options, let us practice a little by using the gradient to create a web 2.0–style glossy button using the gradient options we learned above:

1. Create a new Adobe Illustrator document.
2. Select the Ellipse tool and create a circle on the artboard.
3. From the Color and Fill indicator in the Tools panel, select the Gradient icon.
4. While the circle is selected, open the Gradient panel and create a radial gradient from dark to light blue. Double-click the far right color pointer to create the first dark blue color; double-click the far right color pointer and set the color to light blue.
5. Select the Gradient tool from the Tools panel.
6. Click on the middle bottom of the object to set the radial gradient center in a lower point under the circle center.

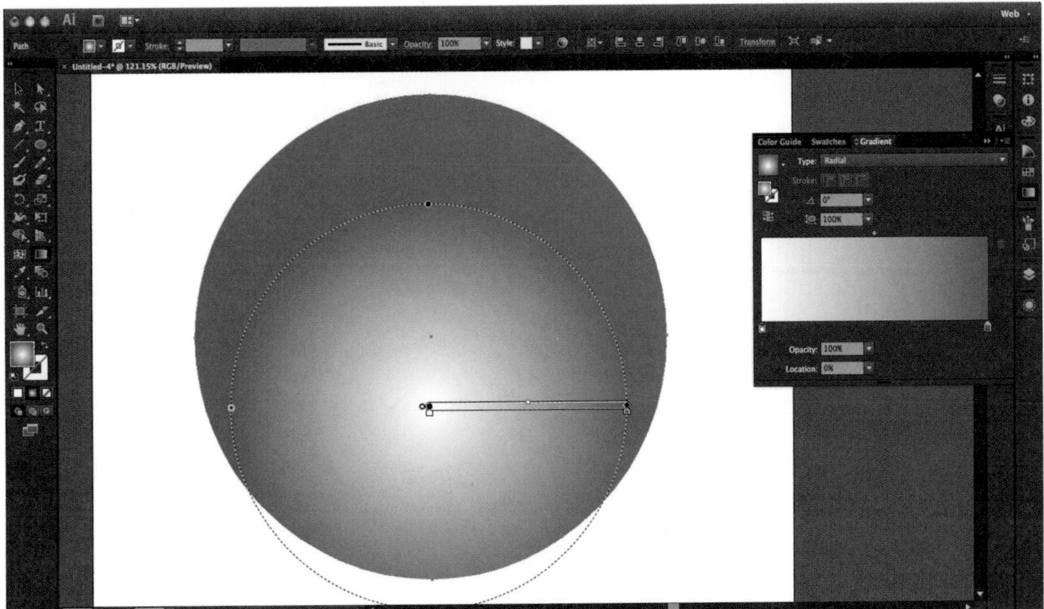

FIG 5-10 The gradient applied to the circle on the stage

7. Create another smaller ellipse over the previously created one. This one is not completely circular; the width is little bit longer than the height.
8. With the second ellipse selected, go to the Gradient panel and create a linear gradient from white to white. Apply it using the Gradient tool as we mentioned in the Gradient Tool section.

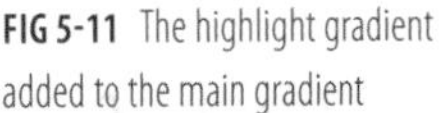

FIG 5-11 The highlight gradient added to the main gradient

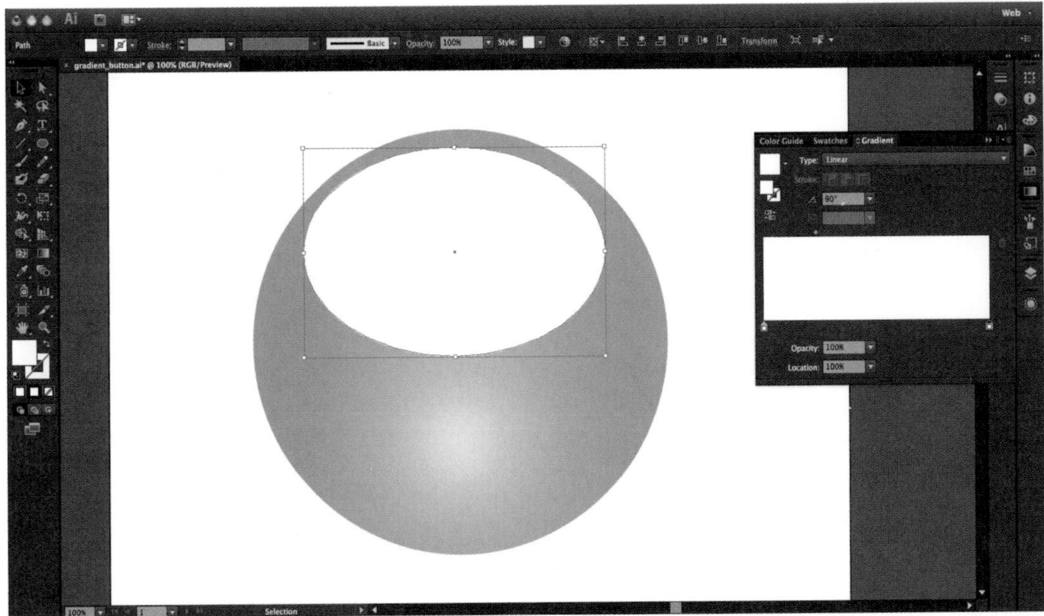

9. With the top ellipse selected, click on the white color from the Gradient Slider that affects the white color at the bottom of the object.
10. From the opacity value, set the value to zero.
11. Select the other white color and set its opacity to 75%.

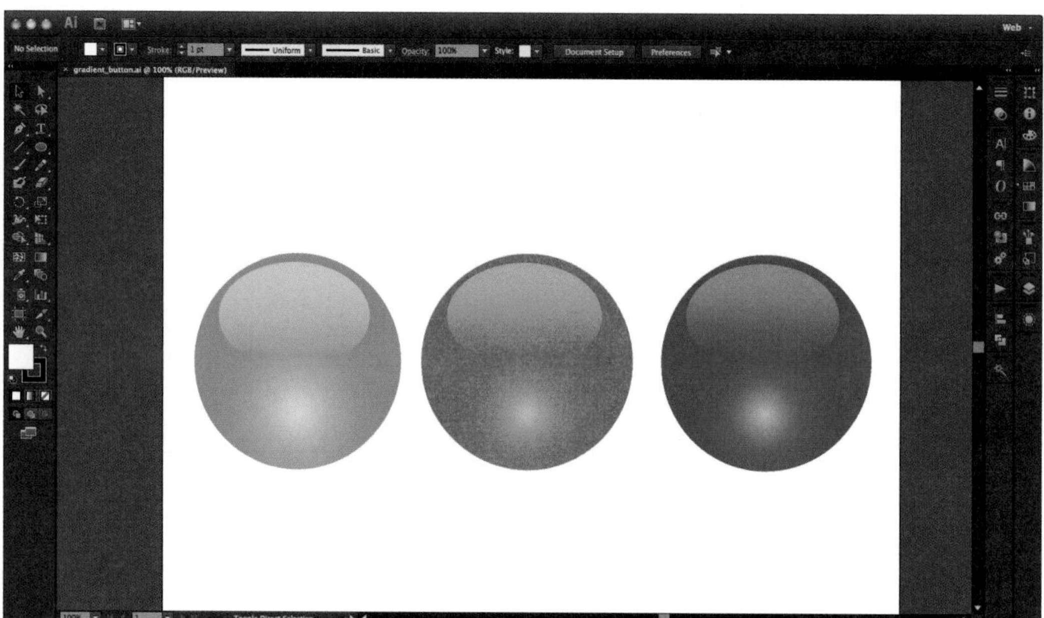

FIG 5-12 The final button appearance

Note

The Gradient tool and Annotator do not work when applying gradient to strokes.

Working with Meshes

The mesh feature converts the object fill into a mesh of paths and points; each point in this path can have a specific color and opacity applied to it, and each color blends with the colors of the other points. In old versions of Illustrator, gradient was either linear or radial, which did not allow much control of the object shades, light, and the color distribution on the object fill, because we had to add colors in either linear or radial order, which generates an unrealistic effect. This was one of the common problems in creating artwork or cartoon characters in Illustrator. We used to work around this issue using complex objects above each other with different shades to create the final effect.

The mesh feature solves this problem by converting your object into a mesh of anchor points that is called a mesh point. Changing the color of each mesh point affects the fill under it. This creates different color spots on your object fill that you can control separately and allows artwork to have more complex color mixtures or light and shadow effects, and above all, smooth transitions in directions you can control.

In the following example, let us see how to use the Mesh tool to create a realistic water drop by adding a mesh point and using it to create light reflection over the water drop surface:

1. Open the file Water_drop.ai. This file includes a water drop flat shape.
2. Choose the Mesh tool from the Tools panel.
3. Click on the shape to add a mesh point as shown in the figure below. By clicking on the object using the Mesh tool, you convert the object fill to gradient mesh.

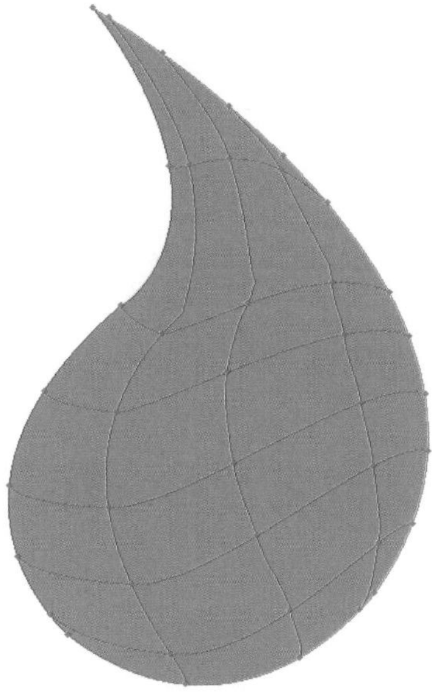

FIG 5-13 The mesh points arrangement on the water drop

4. Select the Direct Selection tool or press "A" on your keyboard.
5. Select the points on the left and the right of the water drop as shown in the figure below. You can select multiple points by pressing the Shift key while choosing the mesh points, or even use the Lasso tool.
6. Double-click the fill color thumbnail in the Tools panel.
7. Choose the lighter blue color and click OK to apply it to the mesh anchor points.
8. You can repeat the above step with other points to create different spot light areas.
9. Select the Mesh tool or Direct Selection tool, and click any of the mesh points to modify its position, similar to working with the path anchor points.

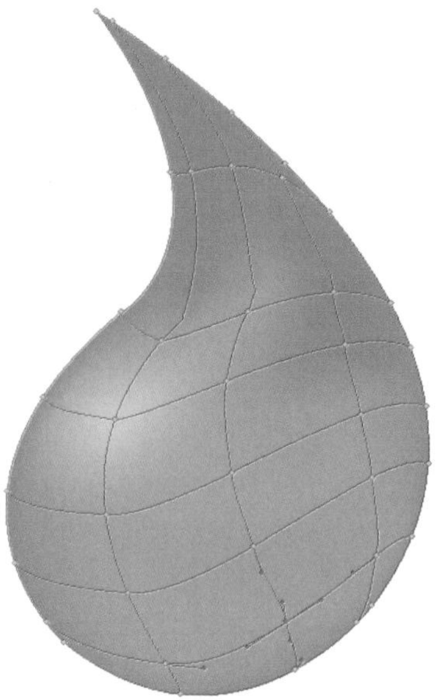

FIG 5-14 The water drop with the lighter color applied to it

10. Use the Direct Selection tool to select the point in the figure, and from the Fill Color option choose the white color and click OK. This will apply light spots over the water drop.
11. Choose the top right mesh point and change its color to a darker blue.

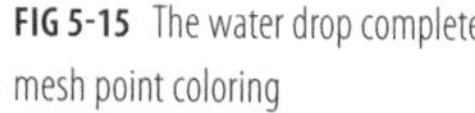

FIG 5-15 The water drop complete mesh point coloring

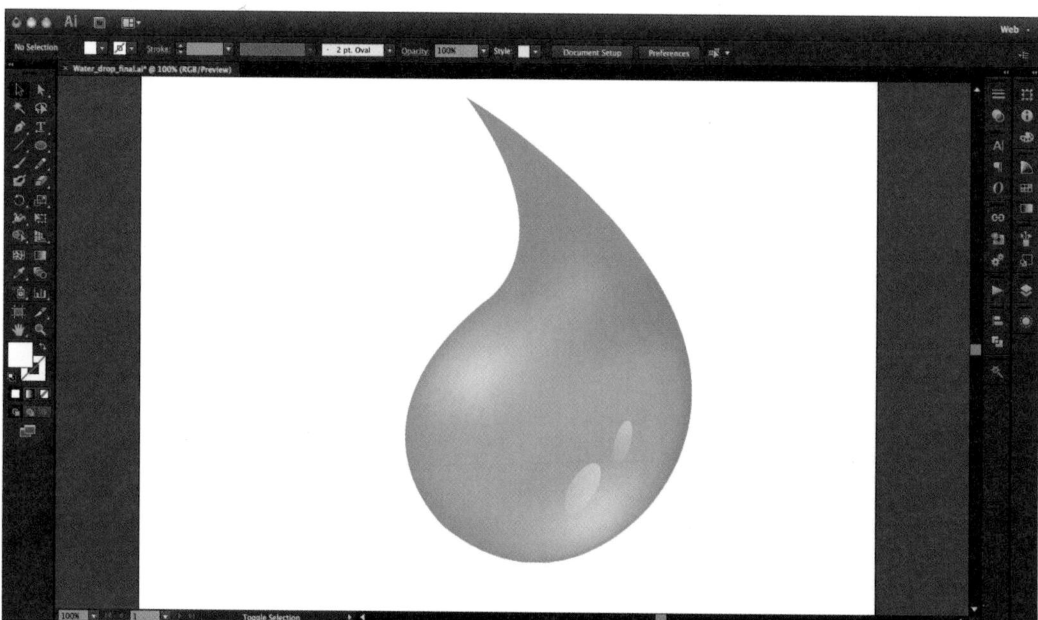

You can repeat the above steps with different shapes of water drops. Also, I added some gradient circles to serve as spots of light. The final result should look like the figure below.

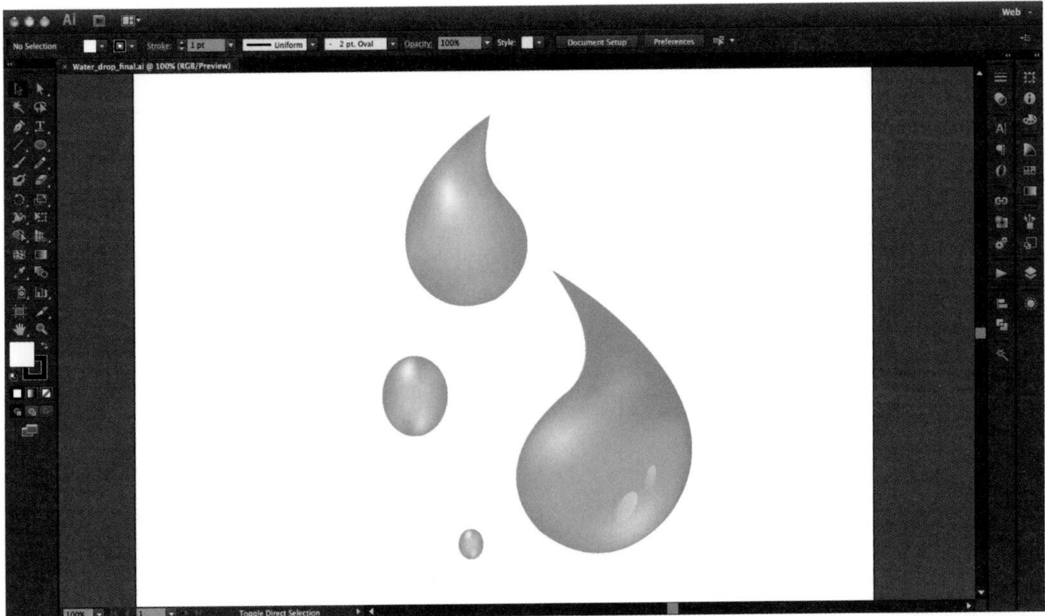

FIG 5-16 The final water drop effect

The Mesh tool is not the only way to create gradient mesh. The Mesh tool lets you create a customized mesh arrangement for the mesh points based on your own desires for the color arrangement. You can also choose the Create Gradient Mesh option from the Object menu to create the mesh through the dialog box.

> **Note**
>
> You can convert a regular gradient to a mesh gradient by selecting the object, and from the Object menu, choose Expand and select Gradient Mesh from the dialog box.

The Create Gradient Mesh dialog box lets you create mesh over the object by deciding the number of mesh rows and columns. You can choose the appearance of the highlight from the Appearance drop-down list as below:

- The Flat option does not add any highlights to the object and adds only the mesh. This option can be used when you would like to choose your own mesh color combination.
- To Center displays the highlight at the center of the object to give it more depth.

- To Edge reverses the To Center effect as it displays the highlight on the edges of the object and the main color in the center.

You can also modify the highlight level applied on the object by editing the highlight percentage.

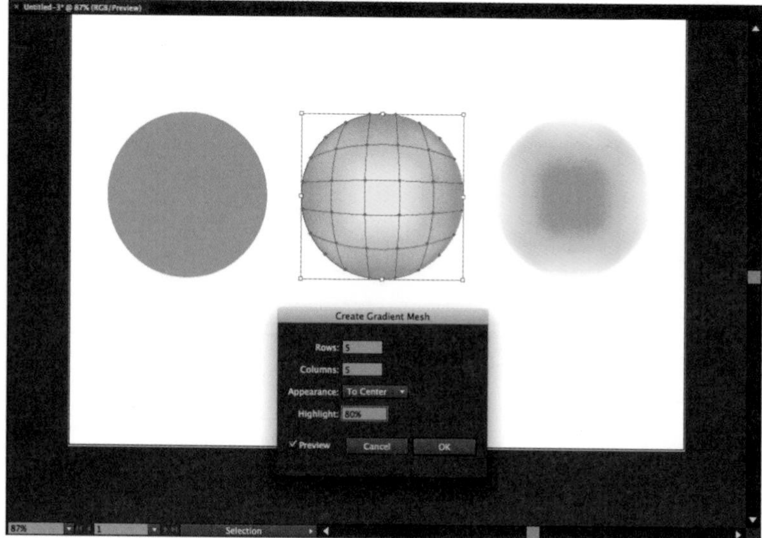

FIG 5-17 Different gradient mesh highlight options: the first one from the left represents the Flat option, the second is To Center, and the last is To Edge.

At this point, we should be able to work with the different gradient features in Adobe Illustrator and understand the different types we can use to create and modify gradient fill and stroke applied to the object. Also, we covered one of the most important features in Adobe Illustrator—the mesh gradient, which can maximize your ability to work with custom gradient effects. Practicing the gradient features a lot can help you create more realistic effects on your artwork or illustrations, because it allows you to simulate the real effects of shadow and light applied to the object and add depth and shadows to flat artwork to simulate real-life objects.

For examples pertaining to this chapter, visit www.illustratorfoundations.com.

CHAPTER 6

Working with Patterns

In Chapters 4 and 5, we learned that we can fill the vector object with either a solid color or a gradient, and this can be applied either as an object's fill or applied to the object stroke. In addition to these two methods to fill our object, there is another method—filling the object with a pattern. As the name implies, patterns are graphic elements that repeat next to each other to create seamless fill for Illustrator artwork. Working with patterns is similar to working with solid color. When you create a pattern, it is added to the Swatches panel.

In this chapter, we will learn more about patterns in Adobe Illustrator and how to understand and create patterns. Also, we will cover the new Pattern Options panel, which was added to Illustrator CS6 to make creating patterns and modifying them easier.

Understanding Pattern Design

Patterns are small artwork that is repeated next to each other in a seamless way that appears to be one single artwork. In order to achieve this, you have to analyze the artwork that will be used in the pattern design. For example, the artwork on right side of your pattern should complete the left side of the pattern next to it; the same goes for top and bottom positioning. Let us see how to create a background with repeated circles on it using square defined patterns. The pattern unit can contain two options. The first option is to have a full circle drawing in the pattern as shown in the figure below.

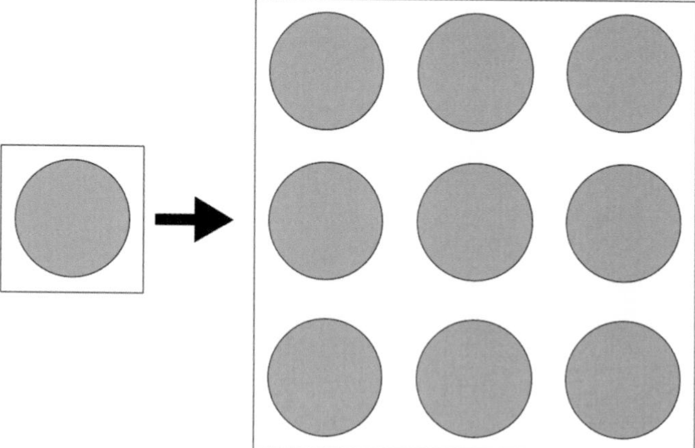

FIG 6-1 The pattern with a full circle drawing in it

This is the easiest method, but the pattern can include more complex artwork. In many cases you need to divide the artwork into parts that are arranged in the pattern area. In the figure below you can see that instead of adding the whole circle in the pattern area, we divided the circle into four parts and added each part at the edge of the pattern. When the patterns are repeated, the circle shape is formed.

The benefit of the second method is that it allows you to add artwork inside your pattern in a random way. In this case you would divide the artwork as we described above. The figure below shows sample artwork that is converted to a seamless pattern.

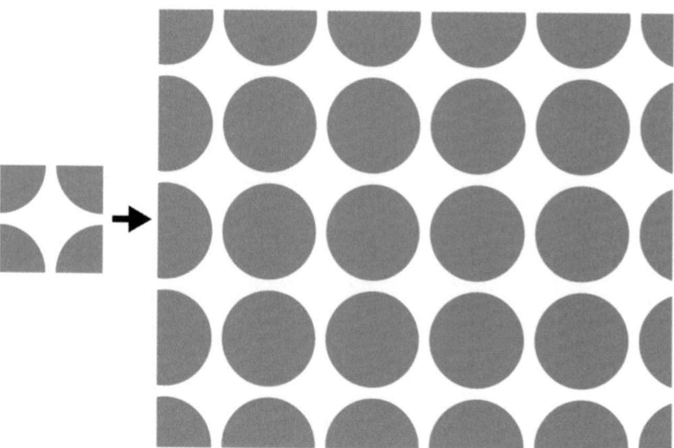

FIG 6-2 The pattern with circle divided into four parts

Converting Artwork into a Pattern

At this stage the artwork we created above is not actually a pattern; we have to define it as a pattern, so it can be added as a pattern swatch that you can use and apply to your objects. In order to convert the artwork to a pattern, follow the steps below:

1. Open the file Pattern_making.ai. This file includes artwork on the stage. One good practice when creating patterns is to have a background square with no fill and stroke to define the pattern edges. As you can see in the shape on the artboard, there is a transparent square behind the shape in order to define the white space around it.
2. Select the artwork. From the Object menu, choose Pattern > Make. An alert message appears to mention that the pattern is added to the pattern swatch and any modifications will affect the pattern swatch.

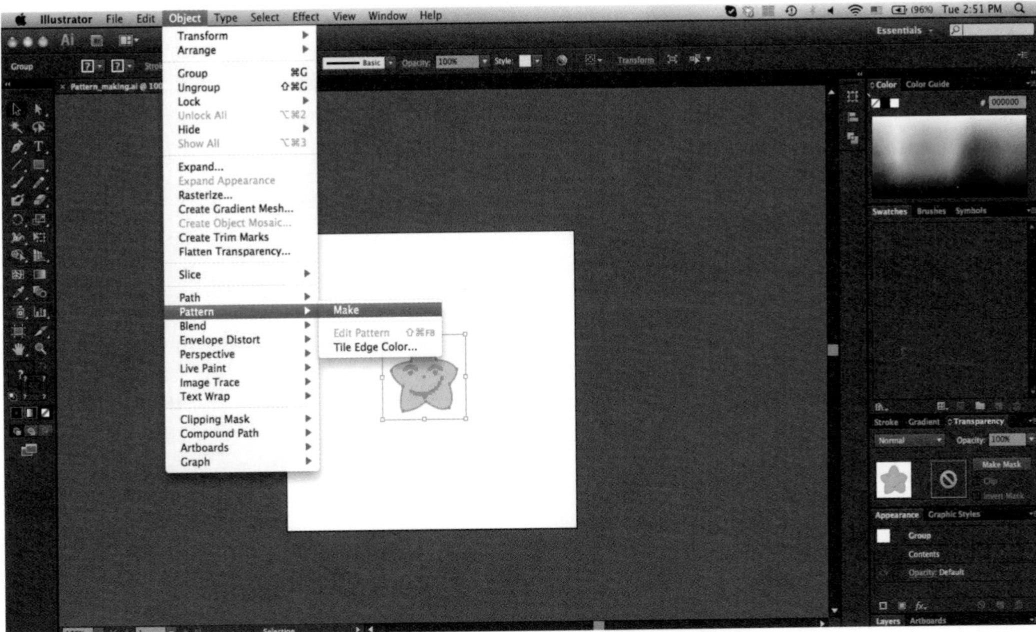

FIG 6-3 Converting an object to a pattern through Pattern > Make from the Object menu

The file Pattern_making-final.ai shows how the pattern we just created is applied to a rectangle shape. When you convert the artwork into a pattern, you can find it listed in the Swatches panel. Now, let us see how to create a cartoon pattern from different shapes and arrange it in the pattern area, so the objects look complete and not cut off when the pattern is repeated in the object fill.

1. Open the Illustrator document Cartoon_pattern.ai. This document includes the elements that we will use in our pattern.
2. Arrange the artwork as shown in the figure below.

FIG 6-4 The artwork arranged on the artboard

3. Group all of the objects by first selecting all (Cmd/Ctrl+A), and choose Group Cmd+G (Ctrl+G in Windows) from the Object menu.
4. Double-click the group to edit it.
5. Draw a rectangle over the objects. Select the Rectangle tool and click on the artboard; set the width and the height of the rectangle to 400 × 400 px.
6. Set the fill color to None, the stroke to black, and its stroke to 1 px.
7. Select the rectangle, and from the top Control panel, make sure to set the alignment to Artboard.
8. Set the alignment of the rectangle to both horizontal and vertical center.
9. Exit the group editing mode; make sure that the Preview checkbox is selected to see live updates for your changes.
10. Set the horizontal value to 400 to move the group to the right of the artboard. Click Copy to create a copy of the group on the right side of the document.
11. Select the original group again, and from the Move dialog box, set the horizontal value to –400 to move it to the left side of the document.
12. Repeat the same steps with the vertical values to create two groups on the top and the bottom of the document.

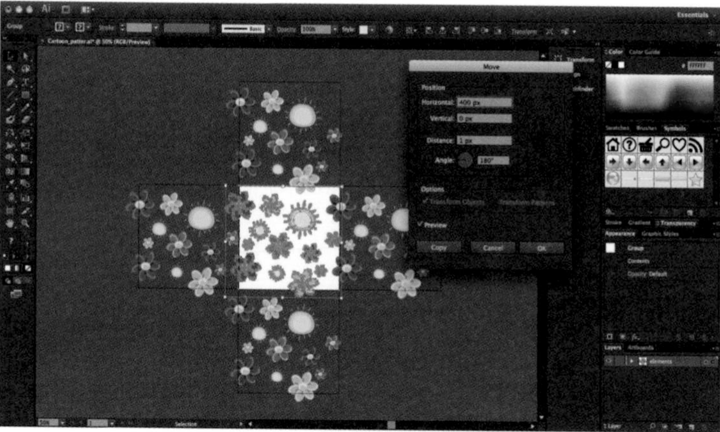

FIG 6-5 The repeated pattern group in four sides

13. Now, select all the groups on the stage, ungroup those that are around the pattern area, and delete the artworks that do not intersect with the pattern edges.

FIG 6-6 The pattern with the artwork completely arranged inside it

14. Go back to your main group. Double-click the group to enter its editing mode.
15. At this stage, your artwork is not yet a pattern. To convert it into a pattern, select the artwork and from the Object menu, choose Pattern > Make. Or you can simply drag the artwork to the Swatches panel to covert it into a pattern.
16. Now, create a new big circle on the artboard. Make sure that the fill color is selected in the Tools panel. Click on the pattern to apply it to the circle.

FIG 6-7 The created pattern applied to a circle on the artboard

The final results of this method can be found in the file Cartoon_pattern_ordinary_way.ai in the chapter folder on the companion website, http://www.illustratorfoundations.com.

Working with the Pattern Options Panel

While the previous steps show the manual way to create a squared tile pattern, the new Adobe Illustrator CS6 makes it much easier through the new Pattern Options panel. It also offers a way to create more complex patterns using other types of tiles. In this pattern you can easily modify and edit your artwork to be a perfect pattern for future use.

The Pattern option lets you enter a pattern editing mode, where you can create or edit artwork in an interactive way and preview how the pattern will look when applied to an object. You can work from scratch or use existing artwork in your pattern. You can also use the Pattern option to edit a pattern already created and already available in the Swatches panel by simply double-clicking on its thumbnail. Before learning how to use the Pattern Options panel in creating patterns, let us overview the different options in the panel.

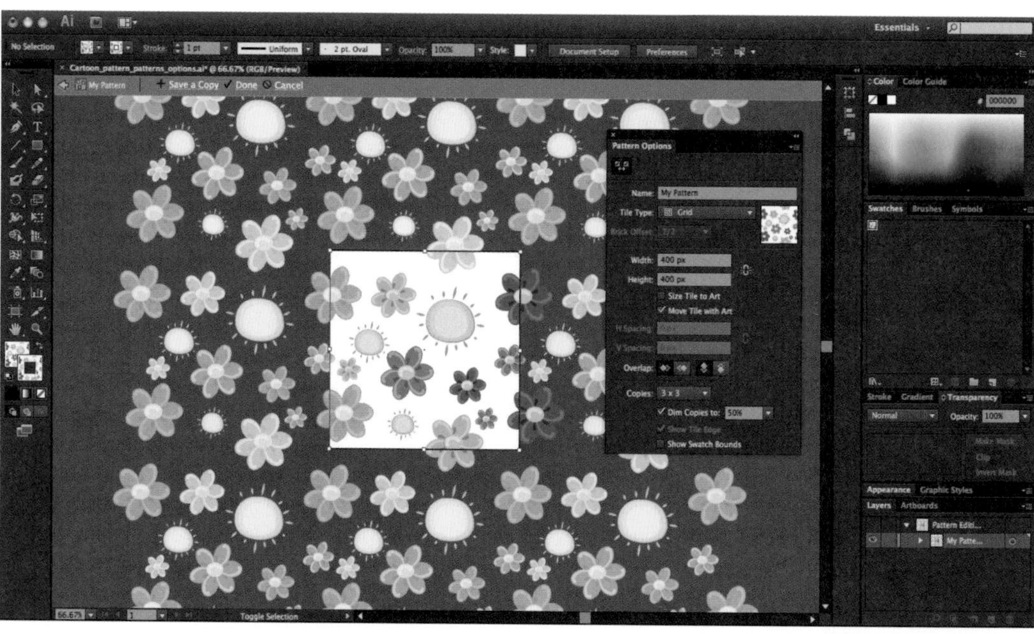

FIG 6-8 The pattern editing mode

When you double-click on a pattern swatch in the Swatches panel, the pattern is opened in editing mode and opens the Pattern Options panel. In the top left of the editing mode workspace, you can do the following:

- Return to the Illustrator main stage by clicking the back arrow.
- Save changes as a new pattern by clicking the Save As link.

- Save changes on the current pattern by clicking the Done link.
- Discard the changes by clicking the Cancel link.

Now, let us see the different options in the Pattern Options panels. At the top left of the panel, you can find the Patterns Tile tool, which allows you to set the size of the pattern and modify its position over objects.

- The name field lets you name or rename the pattern.
- Tile Type is a very useful option because it easily allows you to set the repeating behavior of the object in your pattern without having to figure out the math that is needed to do it manually. The pattern preview thumbnail square gives you a small idea what the final look of the applied pattern will be. The Tile Type option includes:
    - Grid
    - Brick by Row
    - Brick by Column
    - Hex by Column
    - Hex by Row
- You can set the Brick Offset from the offset value that is activated when you select any of the Brick Tile options.
- The Width and Height options set the size of the pattern tile. You can click the Chain icon next to it to change the size with the original artwork proportion.
- Check the Size Tile to Art checkbox to set the tile size to be as the same as the artwork.
- Check the Move Tile with Art to link the tile area with the artwork. When you change the position of the artwork, the tile will also change based on the new position.
- The H and V spacing value sets the space between tiled patterns (available only when Size Tile to Art is enabled).
- The Overlap icon controls how the tiles overlap each other and includes the following options:
    - Left on Front
    - Right on Front
    - Top in Front
    - Bottom in Front
- The Copies option sets how many tiles will appear for a preview of the tile arrangement.
- Dim Copies changes the opacity of the tile copies to differentiate them from the original tile.
- Show Tile Edge sets how the tile edge appears.
- Show Swatch Bounds sets whether or not the objects outside the tile bounds are repeated.

After this overview for the Pattern Options panel, let us repeat the above example using the Pattern options:

1. Open the Illustrator document Cartoon_pattern.ai. This document includes the elements that we will use in our pattern.

2. Arrange the artwork as we did in the previous example.
3. Select all artwork on the artboard. From the Object menu, choose Pattern > Make.

Shortcut

You can enter the pattern editing mode from the Object menu by choosing Pattern > Edit or by pressing Cmd+Shift+F8 (Ctrl+Shift+F8 in Windows).

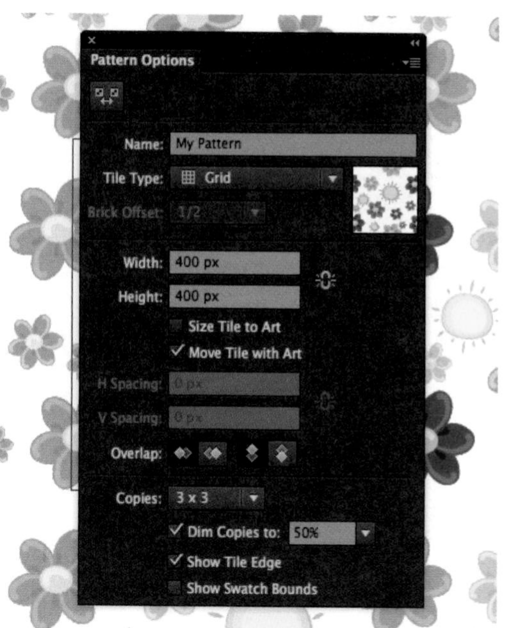

FIG 6-9 The Pattern Options panel

Note

You can change the tile edge color from the Object menu by choosing Pattern > Tile Edge Color.

4. In the pattern name field, add the name "my pattern."
5. Set the width and height of the pattern to 400 px.
6. Select the Pattern Tile tool to move the pattern bouncing box to fit with the document.
7. Make sure that Grid is selected from the Tile Type option and set the copies to 3 × 3 in the Copies drop-down list.
8. Check Size Tile to Art.
9. From the Pattern Options panel, select the Pattern Tile tool.

10. Drag the tile bounds to fit with the pattern design as shown in the figure below.

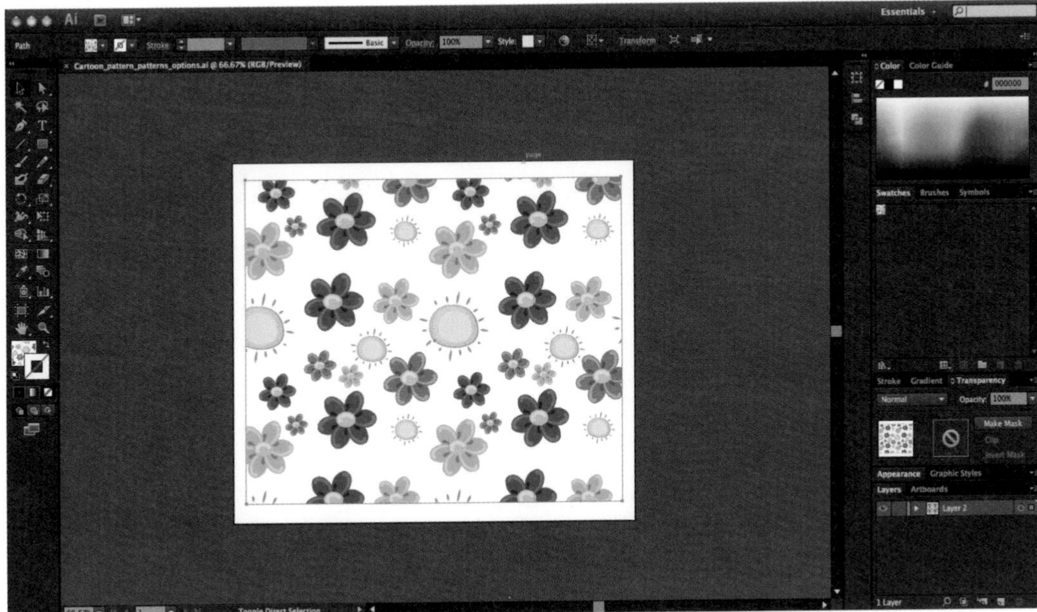

FIG 6-10 The modified pattern artwork applied to a rectangle shape

11. Click Done from the top of the workspace to save and exit the editing mode.
12. Delete the objects from the stage.
13. Select the Rectangle tool and create a rectangle in the stage.
14. Make sure that the fill color is active from the Tools panel.
15. While the rectangle is selected, click the pattern we created from the Swatches panel. If the patterns are not visible, you can choose Show Pattern Swatches from the Show Swatches Kind icon in the Swatches panel.

Note

If you want to change the pattern size or modify the artwork, you can double-click the pattern swatch to open it in the pattern editing mode. Then, you can click Done or Save As to save the pattern modifications.

You can preview the results of this method in the file Cartoon_pattern_patterns_options.ai in the chapter folder on the companion website.

As we saw in this chapter, you object's fill or stroke may not be only solid color or gradient; it can also be filled with artwork as a pattern. In previous versions of Adobe Illustrator, creating patterns was not as simple as it is in Illustrator CS6. The new Pattern Options panel allows you to create and edit patterns easier and faster than the old method. In this chapter, we have gained understanding of the structure of patterns, described both the ordinary and the new method to create patterns, and learned how to apply these patterns to artwork and objects.

For examples pertaining to this chapter, visit www.illustratorfoundations.com.

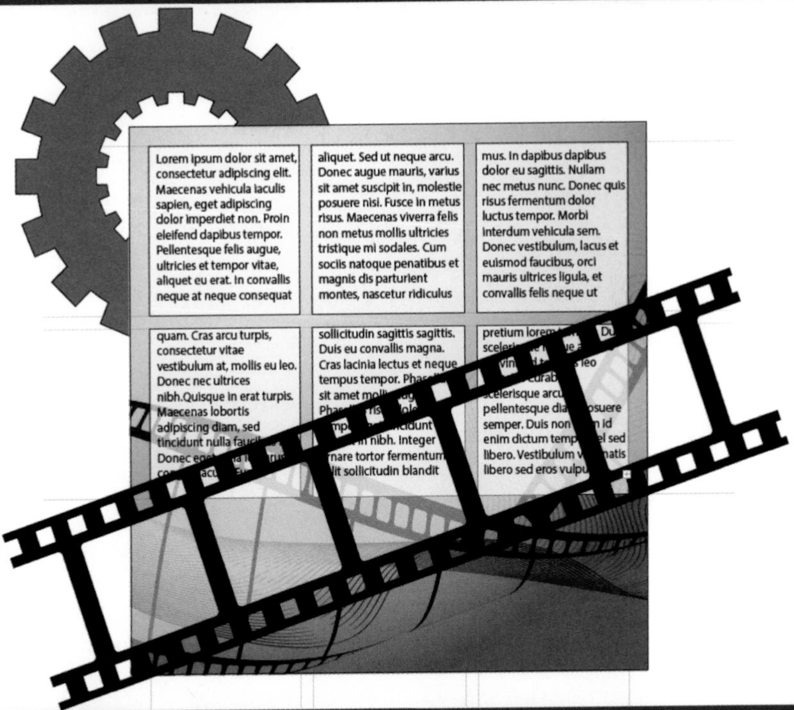

CHAPTER 7

Editing Artwork

Building artwork in Adobe Illustrator requires not only a good understanding of the tools and how to use them in combination to create your artwork, but also of how to edit and modify artwork to reach the results you visualize. Actually, editing artwork plays an essential role in creating artwork, because you usually need to compile, edit, and modify shapes and lines in order to create more complex artwork.

In Chapter 3, we learned how to use Illustrator drawing tools to create basic shapes and how to edit these shapes using the available tool options. However, this chapter will take your drawing skills to another level by teaching you how to edit shapes and use the different editing features to create more complicated artwork based on a combination of simple shapes and objects. In many cases, developing complex artwork based on editing and compiling simple shapes is better than drawing it from scratch because building it from shapes maintains more precise lines and symmetric results.

Working with Compound Paths

Unlike simple paths that we covered in Chapter 3, compound paths consist of multiple paths that are joined together. Adobe Illustrator treats compound paths as one object. To gain a better understanding of how compound paths work, follow the steps below:

1. Open a new Illustrator document.
2. Select the Rectangle tool and create a rectangle. Make sure that the fill color is white and the stroke is black.
3. Select the Ellipse tool and create a circle next to the rectangle shape.
4. Select the rectangle and the circle.
5. From the Object drop-down list, choose Compound Path > Make.

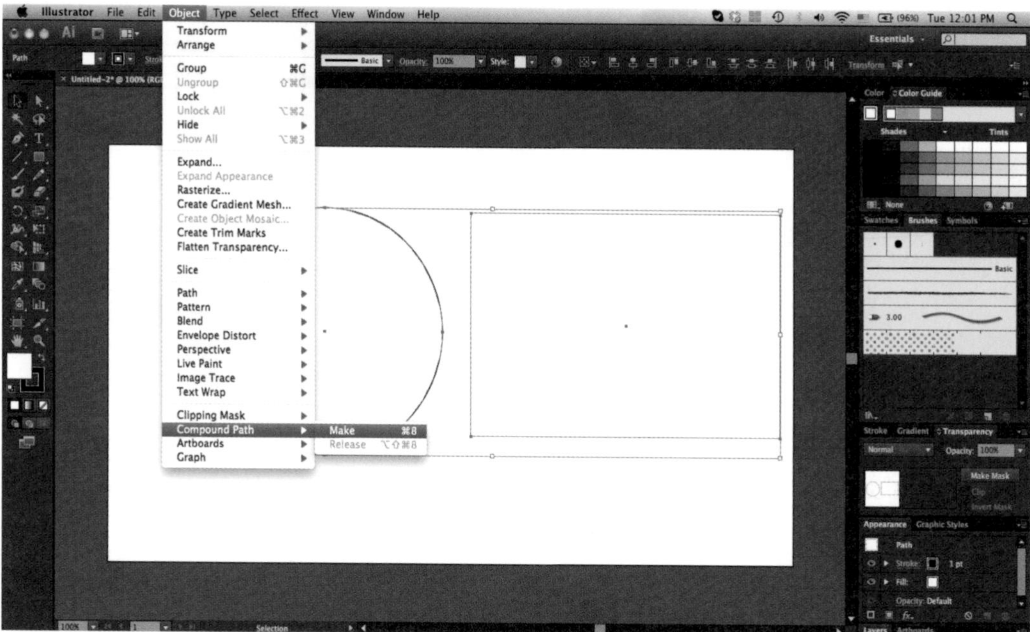

FIG 7-1 A simple compound path in Illustrator

Notice that the two paths are merged in one compound path object. When you try to select any of them, both paths are selected. To edit the path, you need either to double-click the path to enter the compound path isolated mode or right-click the object and choose Isolated Selected Compound Path. You can also release the linkage between paths and convert it into the initial two paths by choosing Compound Path > Release from the Object menu or right-clicking the compound path and choosing Release Compound Path.

This example shows how the paths are compiled together in the compound path, but what if the paths are inside each other? Imagine a letter "O"; this letter includes two paths, the outer one that is represented by a large circle and the inner one that is represented by a smaller circle that contains the empty part of the letter, or the hole. As this shape cannot be created with one path, we will see how to create it using two eclipse paths in the steps below:

1. Open a new Illustrator document.
2. Select the Ellipse tool.
3. Create a circle as shown in the figure below.
4. Create another smaller circle inside the first one.
5. Select both circles, and, from the Object menu, choose Compound Path > Make.

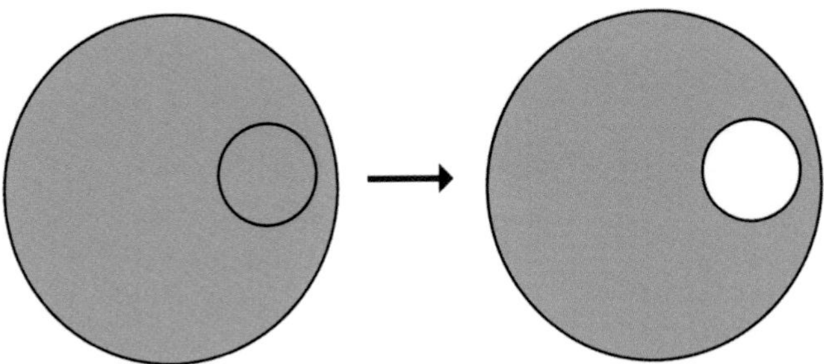

FIG 7-2 The circle compound path in Illustrator

Notice that the inner path turned to a hole. This is because of how Illustrator reads the several paths in the compound path. Usually, Illustrator reads the compound path from outside to inside in a clockwise order. So, all the paths that flow with the outside path are considered a fill area, while Illustrator reads the inner paths in a counterclockwise order. Thus, the inner paths turn to a hole in the shape.

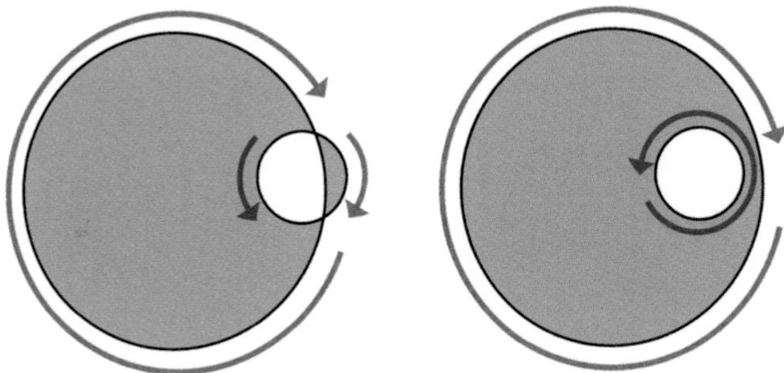

FIG 7-3 How Illustrator reads the compound paths

Working with Pathfinder

Creating artwork using the pencil is not always the best way to build artwork in Illustrator. In many cases you need to build artwork by merging simple objects, which is not only much easier but also more accurate and symmetric. The Pathfinder panel is one of the most commonly used panels in Illustrator, and you can use it to build complex artwork from basic shapes. The Pathfinder panel consists of the Shape Modes icons and the Pathfinder icons.

Let us start with the Shape Modes icons and see how icons affect the object:

1. Create a new Illustrator document.
2. Select the Ellipse tool.
3. Create two circles intersected with each other, similar to the figure below.
4. Open the Pathfinder panel. If it is hidden, you can show it by selecting it from the Windows menu.
5. Select both circles.
6. Click on the Unit icon in the Pathfinder panel.

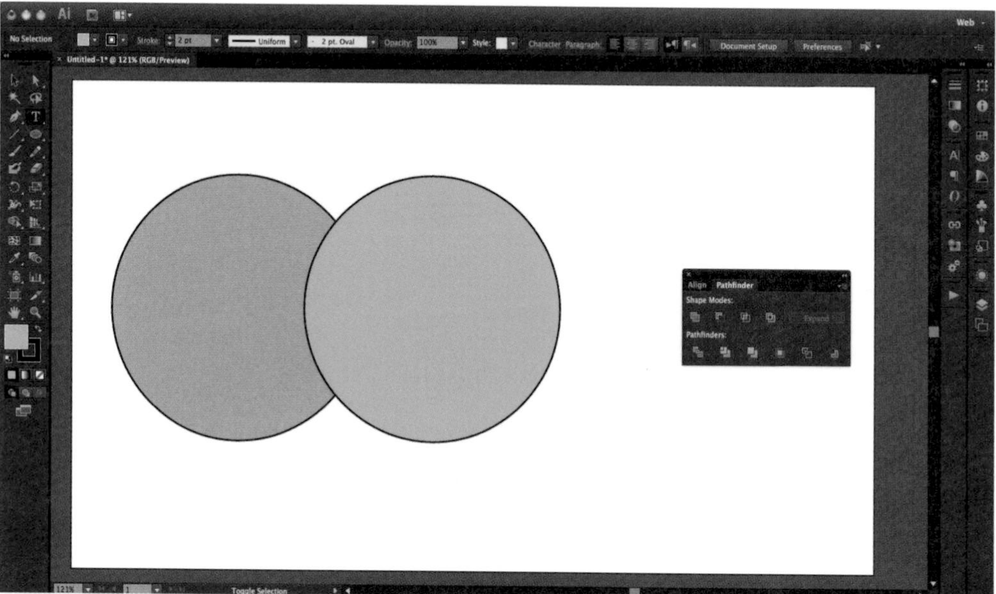

FIG 7-4 The two circles and the Pathfinder panel

The Pathfinder includes the following icons from the left to right. The Unite icon unites the selected object and converts it to one path. It removes the inner paths and keeps the outer paths of objects, as we can see in the below figure.

FIG 7-5 Apply Unite option from the Pathfinder panel

The second icon is the Minus Front icon, which removes the front shape and the intersected part from the bottom shape. Let us apply this to the above circle example and see the results:

1. Repeat the steps we did on the previous page to create two intersected circles.
2. Change the color of the circles so you can identify how they are arranged.
3. Select both circles.
4. From the Pathfinder panel, click the Minus Front icon.
5. Notice that the top circle and the intersected part between both is removed.

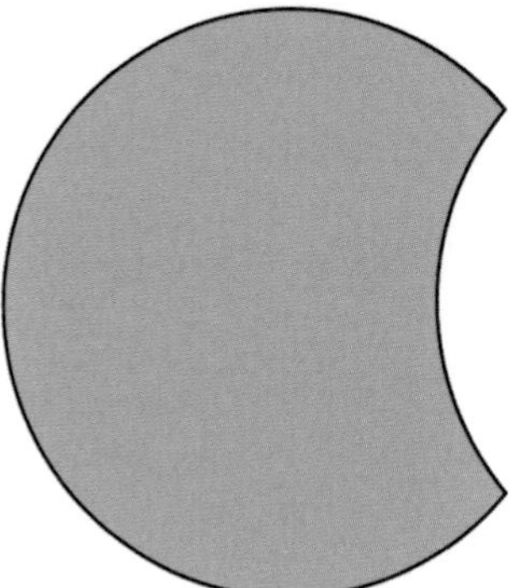

FIG 7-6 Apply the Minus Front option from the Pathfinder panel

The Intersection icon removes both objects and keeps only the intersected area between them. If there are more than two objects, the icon keeps only the intersected area between all the objects. The figure below shows the intersected option results.

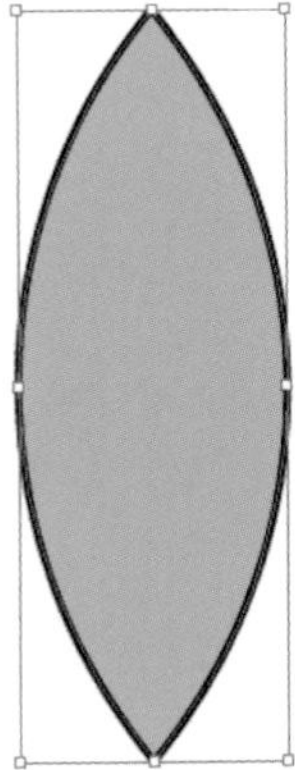

FIG 7-7 Apply the Intersect option from the Pathfinder panel

The Exclude icon acts in the opposite way from the Intersection icon. The Exclude icon removes the intersected areas between objects. If there are many intersected objects, the Exclude icon removes any intersected areas between any of the objects.

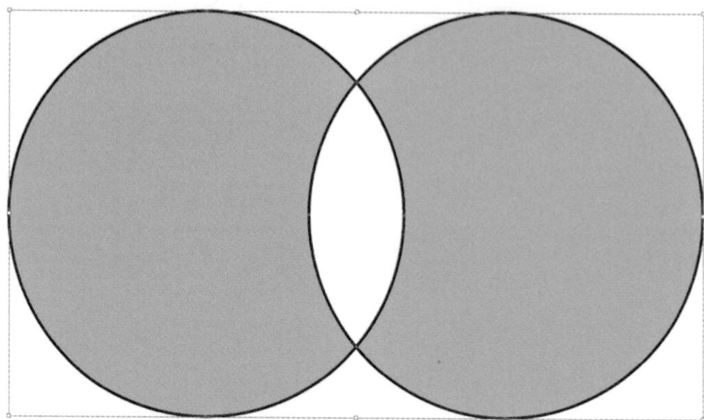

FIG 7-8 Apply the Exclude option from the Pathfinder panel

In the following example, we will learn how to create a gear in Illustrator using the above icons from the Pathfinder panel:

1. Open the document Gear.ai from the Chapter 7 folder on the companion website associated with the book, http://www.illustratorfoundations.com. This document includes a circle and rectangles that we will use to create a gear shape.

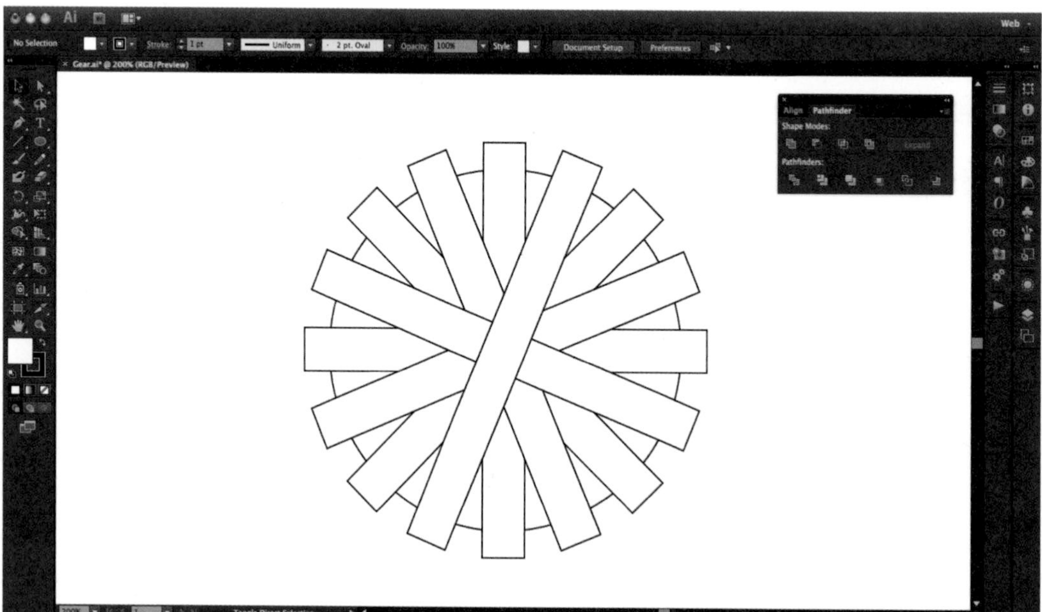

FIG 7-9 The circle with the rectangles on it

2. Select all the rectangles and the circle in the middle.
3. From the Pathfinder panel, click the Unit icon. This command will merge the paths and create the outer part of the gear.
4. Select the gear shape.

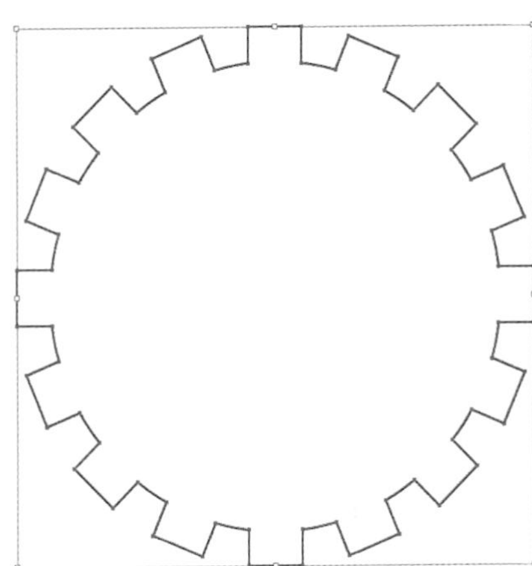

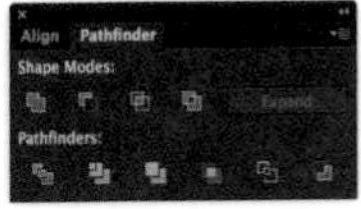

FIG 7-10 The gear shape outline

5. From the Object menu, choose Transform > Scale.
6. Set the scaling ratio to 50%. Click Copy. A new, smaller gear appears in the middle of the first one. Make sure to keep the new gear on top of the first one. If it does not appear on top, right-click on the large gear and select Arrange > Move to Back.

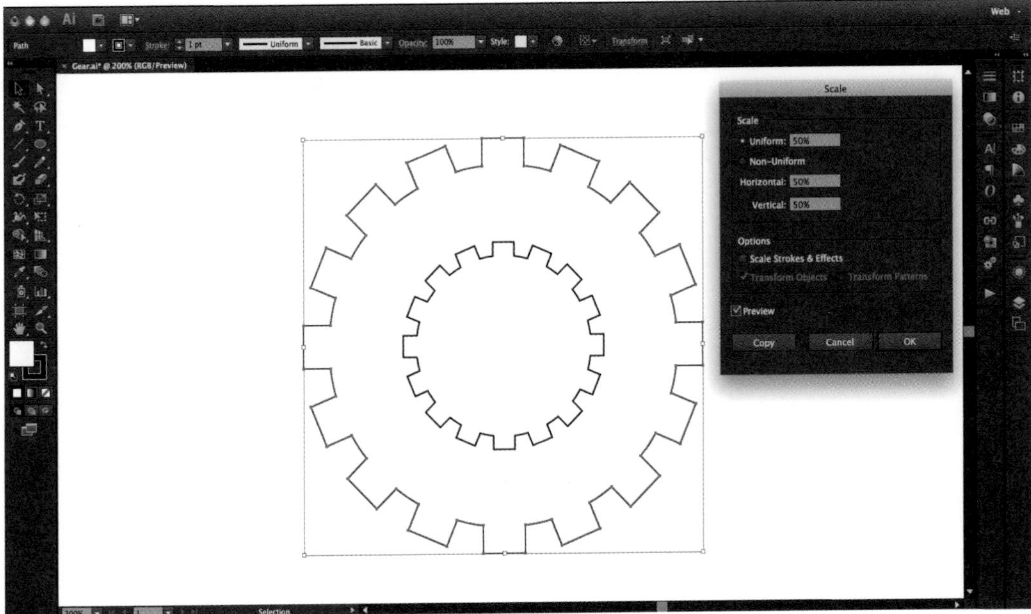

FIG 7-11 The inner gear outline scaled to 50%

7. Select both shapes, and, from the Pathfinder panel, choose the Minus Front icon to create a hole in the big gear based on the size of the smaller one we created.

FIG 7-12 The final look for the gear artwork

Note

We will cover Transform options and how to edit objects using the Transform tools in more detail later in the Transform Artwork section.

Under the Shape Modes icons are the Pathfinder icons. These icons include more options and handle differently from those given in the shape modes.

Shortcut

When you click the Option (Alt in Windows) key while pressing the Shape Mode icons, you can create a compound shape while preserving the original paths.

The Divide icon, as the name implies, divides the objects and creates a new part for the intersected part. Follow the steps below to see how the Divide icon affects the shapes on the stage:

1. Create a new document and use the Rectangle tool to create two intersected rectangles.
2. Select both rectangles.
3. From the Pathfinder panel, press the Divide icon in the Pathfinders part. Notice that the two rectangles become one group.
4. Double-click on the group object to access isolated mode. Notice that the divide results in three paths: two for the rectangles and one for the intersected area of the rectangles.

Note

The best way to understand the difference between the Pathfinders icon's results is to enter the created group objects in isolated mode to see how each path has been affected by each icon's behavior.

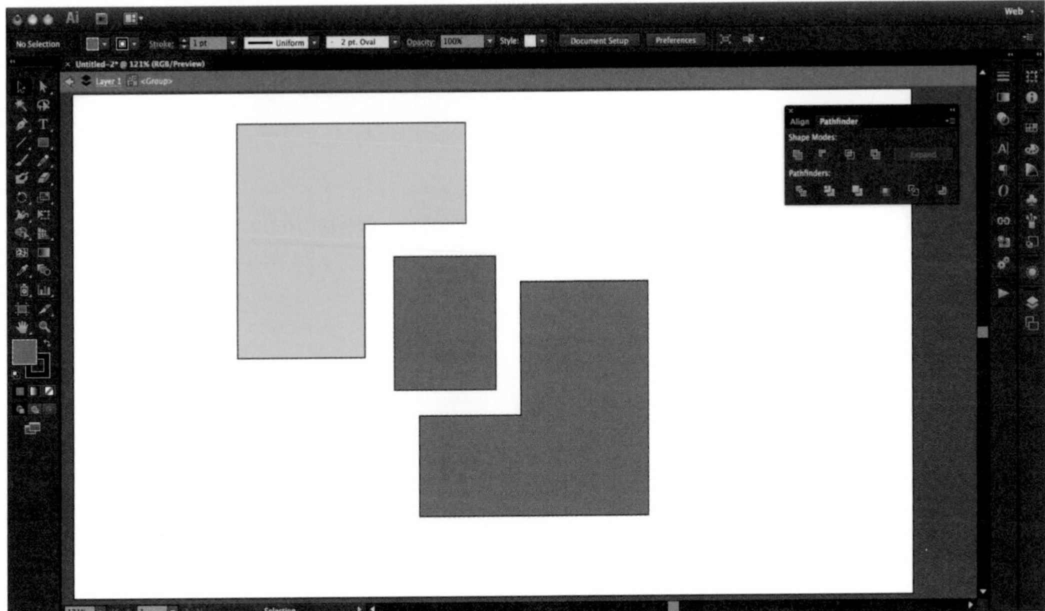

FIG 7-13 Clicking the Divide icon converts the two rectangles into one group with three paths inside it

Next to the Divide icon is the Trim icon. This icon creates a group out of the selected paths, but when you access the created group in isolation mode, you can see from the figure below that the front path trims the other path in the compound object. I tried to move the two paths apart so you could see how the paths are trimmed.

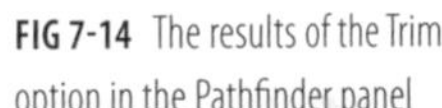

FIG 7-14 The results of the Trim option in the Pathfinder panel

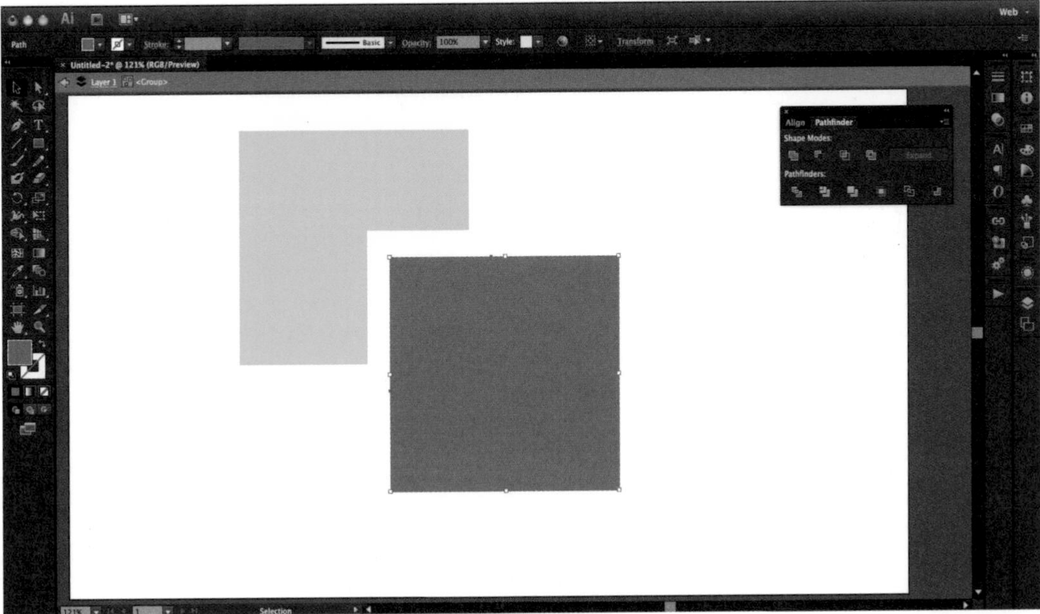

The third icon under the Pathfinders in the Pathfinder panel is the Merge icon, which acts very similar to the Unite icon in shape mode. The only difference is that the Merge icon removes the outline applied to the merged objects and merges the shapes based on the similarity of the colors in the shapes.

The next icon is the Crop icon, which makes the top shape crop the bottom shape and display only the intersected area between them as a separate path; the rest of the top shape path appears as another transparent separate path, as shown in the figure below.

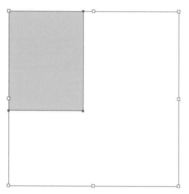

FIG 7-15 The results paths of the Crop option in the Pathfinder panel

The Outline icon removes the fill from the selected shapes and separates the intersected path from the other paths into one single object. The Minus Back icon acts very similar to the Minus Front icon in shape mode. The only difference is that the Minus Back icon removes the back path and the intersected area between it and the front path. Thus, it keeps only the nonintersected part of the front object path.

While the icons in the Pathfinder panel give you easy access to the commonly used options, you can also reach the Pathfinder options from the Effects menu under the Pathfinder. The Effects menu includes the same options in addition to an extra three options that affect the colors of the intersected objects. These three options are Hard Mix, Soft Mix, and Trap. Pathfinder effects should be applied to groups, layers, or type objects.

The Pathfinder panel allows you to create compound paths from the Panel Context menu, where you can choose Make Compound Shape, Release Compound Shape, and Expand Compound Shape. To create a compound shape, select Make Compound Shape from the Pathfinder panel context menu. Then, you can either release it by choosing Release Compound Shape or expand it by choosing Expand Compound Shape.

FIG 7-16 The Pathfinder panel context menu commands

The essential different between releasing a shape and expanding a shape is that the Release Shape option reverts it to its original state and paths, while the Expand Shape option converts the compound shape to a normal one-path shape and causes it to lose the ability to access its paths.

> **Note**
>
> You can expand the path by clicking the Expand button in the Pathfinder panel.

You can set the Pathfinder options from the context menu using the command Pathfinder Options, which includes the following:

- Precision controls how precisely Pathfinder calculates and detects the object path.
- Remove Redundant Points removes the unnecessary points when you apply the Pathfinder command.
- Remove Unpainted Artwork removes the unfilled objects when you choose the Divide or Outline options.

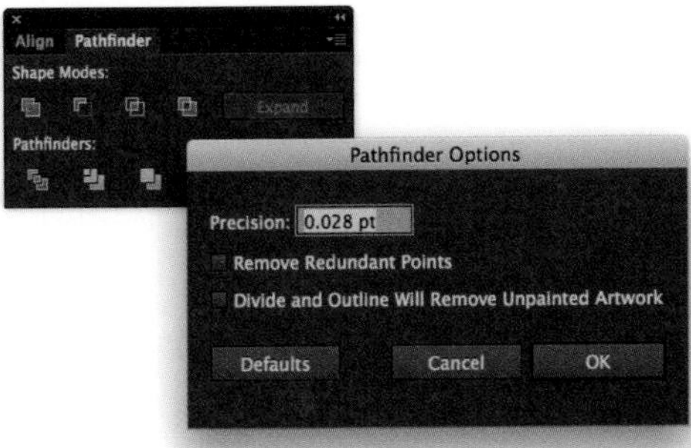

FIG 7-17 The Pathfinder panel options dialog box

> **Note**
>
> When you apply any Pathfinder option, it appears in the Context menu in the Repeat command.

As we saw from the above preview of the Pathfinder panel, the panel includes various options that let you create complex artwork based on simple paths.

Shape Builder Tool

While the Pathfinder gives you an easy way to build shapes, the Shape Builder tool is even easier. You do not have to use different icons to build your object—just choose the Shape Builder tool from the Tools panel or press Shift+M. The Shape Builder tool lets you drag over a selected shape to merge or delete the shape with the help of the modifier keyboard keys, as we will see in the simple example below:

1. Create a new Illustrator document.
2. Select the Ellipse tool and create two circles.
3. Using the Arrow tool, drag over the circles to select them both.
4. Select the Shape Builder tool from the Tools panel.

To unite the shapes, click on one of the shapes and drag over the intersected area to reach the other shape. To divide the intersected shapes, click on the intersected area to convert it into a separate shape. To exclude (delete) part of the shape, click on it with the Shape Builder tool while pressing the Alt key on the keyboard.

Now, let us follow the example below to create an old camera-film shape using the Shape Builder tool:

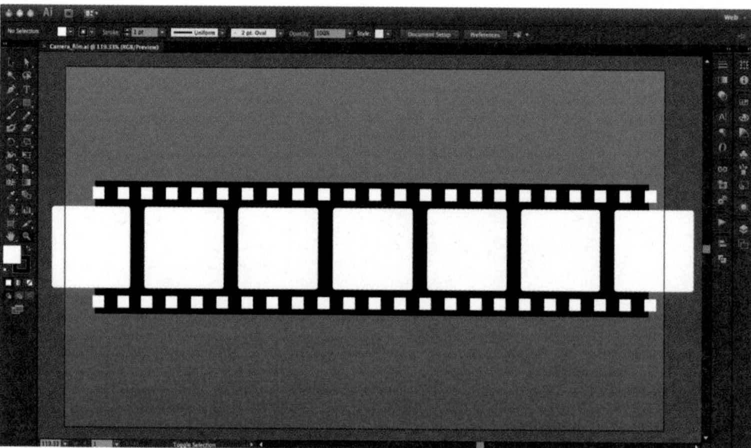

FIG 7-18 The Camera_film.ai file in Illustrator

1. Open the document Camera_film.ai from the Chapter 7 folder on the companion website associated with the book. This document includes the shapes that we will use to create the film shape.
2. Select the Arrow tool.
3. Select the black background and the small white rectangles. You can drag over the rectangles while holding the Shift key to select them.

4. Select the Shape Builder tool.
5. Click on the small white rectangles while holding the Alt key to subtract them from the black background.

FIG 7-19 The small rectangles excluded from the black background

6. Deselect the shapes and select the Arrow tool.
7. Drag to select the black background and the large white rectangles.
8. Select the Shape Builder tool.
9. Click on each large rectangle; this will keep the rectangle but cut a similar space under it in the black background.
10. Using the Arrow tool, select all the white large rectangles.
11. From the Appearance panel, expand the fill section.
12. Click on the opacity, and, from the panel, set the opacity to 50%.

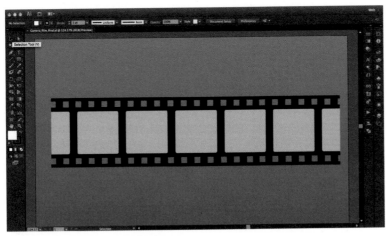

FIG 7-20 The final look of the camera film shape

When you double-click the Shape Builder tool, you bring up the options dialog box. It includes the following options:

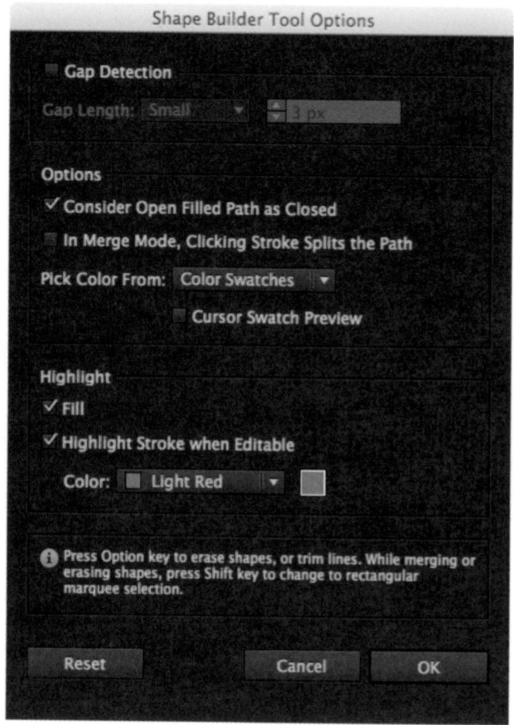

FIG 7-21 The Shape Builder Tool Options dialog box

- Gap Detection sets the gap length and can be set to different values or your customized value. It is used to detect the gap length between shapes, and you can set it to small, medium, large, and custom length.
- Consider Open Filled Path as Closed means that the open-path shapes with fill will be handled as if they were closed paths.
- In Merge Mode, Clicking Stroke Splits the Path allows you to split the output paths into two paths while you are doing a merge using the Shape Builder tool. Note that the tool pointer changes when you try to click on the path with this option active.
- Pick Color From lets the Shape Builder tool take color from either the artwork or the color swatches. When you select the Color Swatches option from the drop-down list, you can activate the Curser Swatch Preview to display the current swatch in a small swatch box next to the Shape Builder tool cursor.
- Highlight Fill lets you highlight the fill when you roll over it with the Shape Builder tool.
- Highlight Stroke When Editable lets you highlight the stroke when it is editable. Also, you can choose the highlight color from the list.

Splitting Objects into Grids

In many designs, you need to split a single object into grids or lines crossing the object, such as the chessboard, or divide your layout into a grid of content areas, such as in web layout design. The Slip into Grids option from the Object > Path menu can help you to carry out this grid effect in a single step without the need to do many workaround steps to reach your desired grid. Also, it helps you to do it with accuracy and a symmetric grid shape.

In the web layout below, we need to convert the one large content area into multiple areas by splitting the large area into several grids as follows:

1. Open the document Grid_ layout.ai from the Chapter 7 folder on the companion website associated with the book.
2. Select the large white square in the layout.
3. From the Object menu, choose Path > Split into Grids.

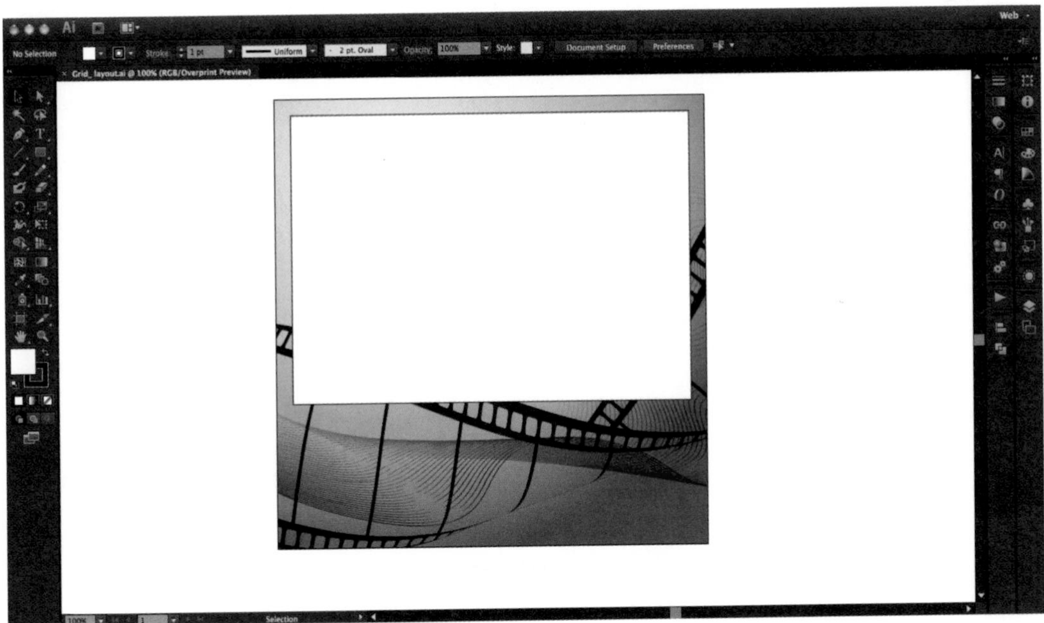

FIG 7-22 The layout without the grid applied to it

The Split into Grids dialog box appears and lets you add rows and columns into the grid. Each row and column value includes:

- The number of the rows or columns you would like to create.
- The height or the width of the rows or the columns.
- The gutter or the space between cells in the row or column.
- The total size of the row or the column, including the gutters.
- Under the rows and columns sections, you can check the Add Guide option to display guides on the grid.

4. With the Split Into Grids dialog box open, set the number of rows to two and the number of columns to three.
5. Change the gutter value to 5 px in both rows and columns.
6. Click OK.

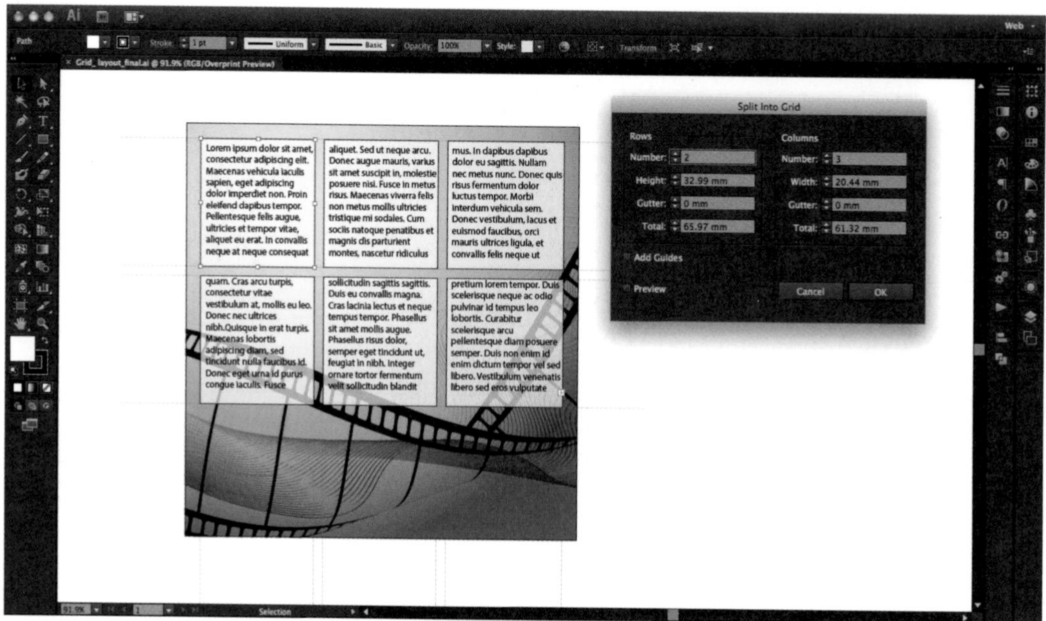

FIG 7-23 The layout with the grid applied to it

Transform Artwork

Similar to most design applications, Adobe Illustrator provides tools to allow you to scale, rotate, skew, shear, and reflect. You can use these tools directly from the Tools panel, or you can choose them from the Objects > Transform top menu. When you work with these tools, you can apply the transform effects directly to the object. The Tool Properties dialog box gives you more accurate results because you add specific values and apply them to the object with a live preview of your changes through the Live Preview checkbox that is available in each Tool Properties dialog box. In this section we will go through these Transform tools and how to use them to edit artwork.

Move Objects

While you can use the Arrow tool to click and drag your object to move it around the stage, this method does not provide accuracy, especially when you need to move objects for specific values. You can choose Transform > Move from the Object menu to open the Move dialog box that lets you specify exactly how you want to move your object on the stage.

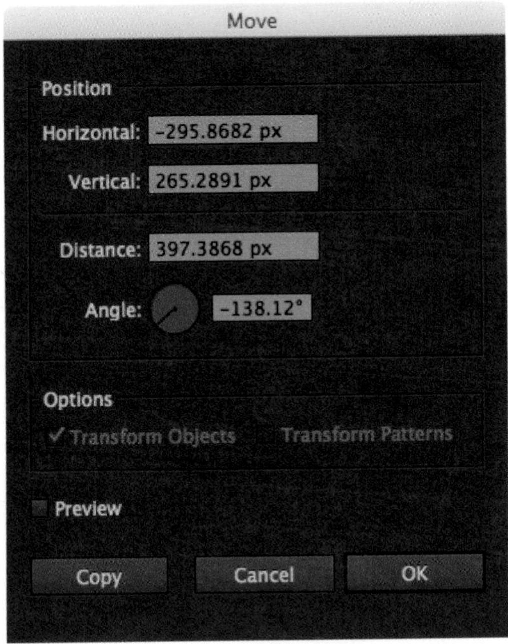

FIG 7-24 The Move dialog box options

The Move dialog box lets you move the object by entering the horizontal or vertical distance you would like to move the object. Also, you can change the angle if you want the object to move in a specific angle direction. Note that adding a positive value in the height and width moves the object to the right, while adding a negative value moves the object to the left. You can also click the Copy button to create a copy of the object and keep the original in its position without moving it.

Note

You can access the Move dialog box by double-clicking the Selection tool or hitting the Enter key when the Selection tool is selected.

Rotate Objects

You can rotate objects in your artboard using either the Rotate dialog box from Transform > Rotate from the Object menu or from the Rotate tool in the Tools panel. To rotate an object using the Rotate dialog box, do the following:

1. Open a new Illustrator document.
2. Create an object and select it.
3. From the Object top menu, choose Transform > Rotate.
4. In the dialog box, add the angle you would like the object to rotate and click OK.

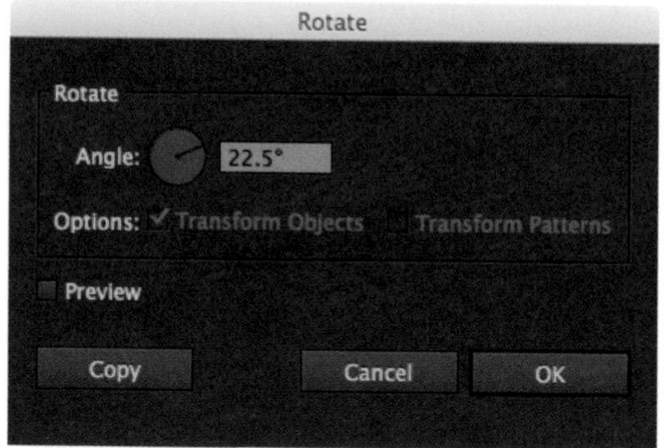

FIG 7-25 The Rotate options in the dialog box

> **Shortcut**
>
> You can display the Rotate tool by pressing the R key on the keyboard.

The Rotate tool is less accurate but allows you an easy and fast way to rotate objects on the stage:

1. Create an object on the stage and select it.
2. From the Tools panel, choose the Rotate tool.
3. Click on the stage to create the rotation point around which the object will rotate.
4. Click again and drag to start rotating the object.

> **Shortcut**
>
> While dragging the object using the Rotate tool, you can press the Alt key to create a copy of your object and keep the original object in its same position.

> **Note**
>
> You can double-click the Rotate tool to open the Rotate dialog box. Actually, this is a fast method to reach the Tool options that you can apply to any of the tools in the Tools panel.

Reflect Objects

The Reflect option works in a similar way to the Rotate option in Illustrator. The only difference is that the Reflect option reflects the object based on either horizontal or vertical axes, as you can see in the Reflect Options dialog box below.

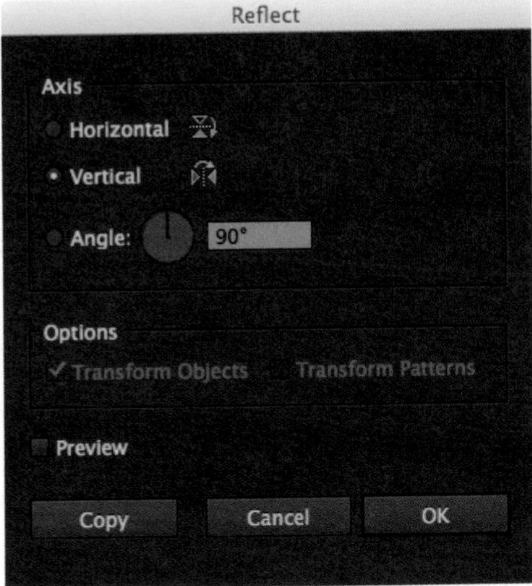

FIG 7-26 The Reflect options in the dialog box

Note

You can double-click any one of the tools to access its Properties dialog box without the need to access it from the Object top menu.

When you select the Reflect tool, you can use it as follows to reflect an object:

1. Select an object.
2. From the Tools panel, choose Reflect tool.
3. Click to create the reflection axe point.
4. Click again and drag to reflect the object. You can click the Alt key to create a reflected copy of the object.

Shortcut

You can activate the Reflect tool by pressing the O key on the keyboard.

Scale Objects

This option lets you either increase an object's scale or decrease it. You can access the Scale Properties dialog box from the Object > Transform menu. The Scale dialog box allows you to scale the objects on the stage with the following options:

- Uniform lets you scale the object while saving the size proportions.
- Non-Uniform lets you scale both height and width with different values, which may cause the shape to be distorted.

- Scale Strokes & Effects allows the scale to affect the strokes and effects applied to the object.

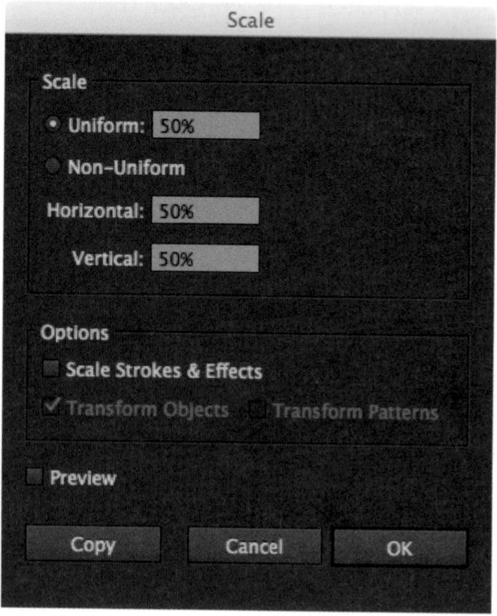

FIG 7-27 The Scale options in the dialog box

From the Tools panel, you can select the Scale tool to start scaling your object on the stage.

> **Shortcut**
>
> You can activate the Scale tool by pressing the S key on the keyboard.

Shear Objects

Shear or skew objects is one of the options that can give your shape on the stage virtual depth by skewing it and giving it perspective. You can apply the shear using the Shear Options dialog box from the Object > Transform top menu. It allows you to skew your object based on the below options:

- Shear Angle is the angle to which you would like the object to shear or skew.
- Axis lets you select the shear axis to be horizontal or vertical or select the angle of the axis if you would like to have a custom-angle axis.

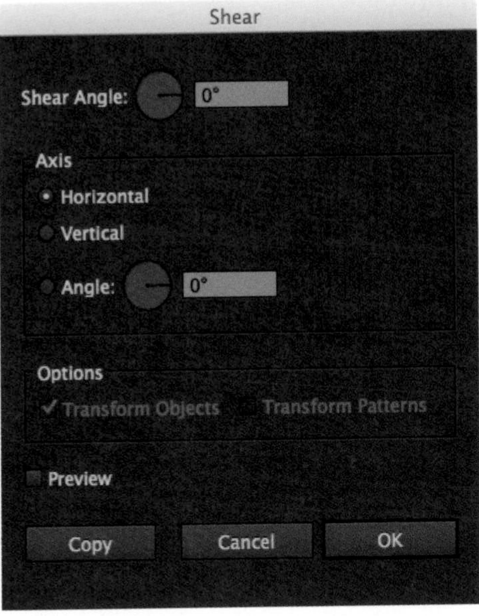

FIG 7-28 The Shear options in the dialog box

Using the Shear tool from the Tools panel is similar to the Reflect and Rotate tools, as shown in the below steps:

1. Select an object.
2. From the Tools panel, choose the Shear tool.
3. Click to create and drag to shear the object.
4. You can click once to create a shear axis and then click and drag to shear the object around this axis.

Free Transform

While the above Transform tools allow you to edit and modify your object, the Free Transform tool is the most commonly used tool to edit artwork. This is because it lets you perform common transformation tasks while selecting your object, as we will see from the following steps:

1. Create a new Illustrator document.
2. Create a new object—a rectangle, for example.
3. Select the Free Transform tool from the Tools panel and select the object.

There are eight small squares around the object on the Free Transform sides: four on each side and one in the middle distance between each of the two corners. You can interact with them as follows:

> **Shortcut**
>
> You can activate the Free Transform tool by pressing the E key on the keyboard.

Click and drag on each side point to scale the object. If you click on any of the corner points while pressing the Shift key, you can scale the object while maintaining its original size aspect ratio.

Note

When you scale the object with the Alt key pressed, the object is scaled based on its center point as the center of the registration.

Roll over any of the corners and notice that the curser changes to an arc—this means that you can drag to rotate the object. If you click the Shift key while rotating the object, you can rotate the object at specific angles: 45 degree, 90 degree, 180 degree, and 270 degree.

Shortcut

You can click the middle square of the Free Transform boundary box while holding Cmd (Ctrl in Windows) to shear the shape. Also, you can click the corner while holding Cmd (Ctrl in Windows) to transform the perspective for the shape.

When you have pattern fill applied to the object, you can choose the following options from the Transform panel: Transform Object Only, Transform Pattern Only, or Transform Both. This feature is very important when you are working with pattern fill and would like to control the pattern fill while applying the object transform.

Creating artwork in Illustrator depends on using basic shapes and integrating them together. The Transform tools and options are your main tool to build your artwork, and you will notice that you will use them more frequently than you can imagine. However, it is good idea to try to use it in your work and practice its different options.

At this point, we understand the basic tools that allow us to modify and edit artwork in Illustrator. We have learned how to work with two more very important features in Illustrator: the Pathfinder and the Transform tools. These are the initial tools that you will depend on in your work. In the advanced chapters of this book, you will notice that we will use some of these tools frequently in our examples. Thus, it is good idea to start practicing them and begin to understand how these tools work to help you easily create more complex artwork.

For examples pertaining to this chapter, visit www.illustratorfoundations.com.

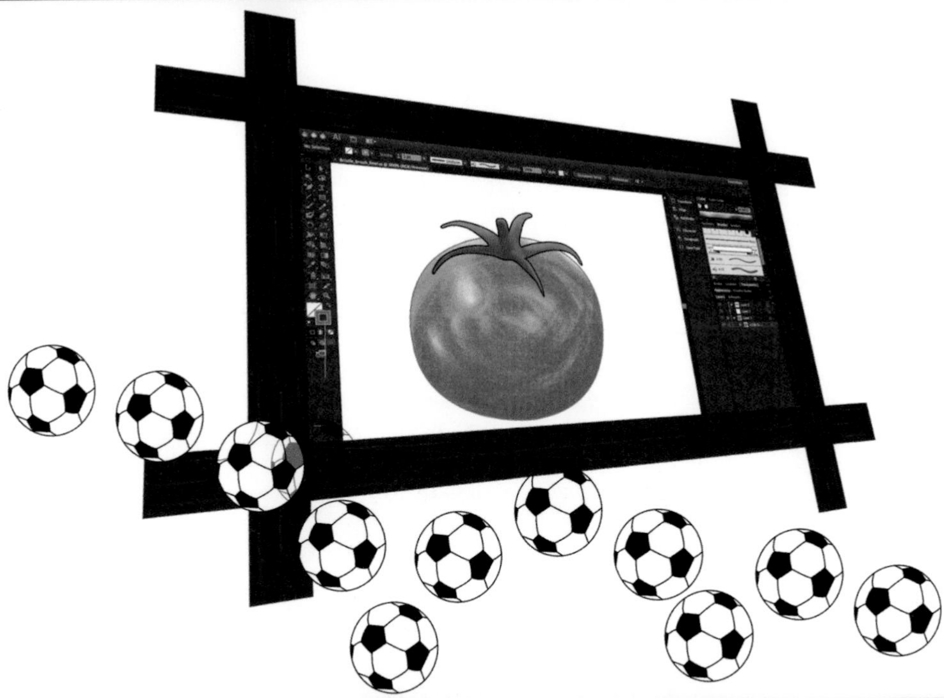

CHAPTER 8

Brushes

While the paths in Illustrator are the main way to create objects, the Pen and Pencil tools are not the only tools that let you create artwork. Brushes extend your drawing capabilities by giving you the option to stylize your artwork paths. Brushes can be applied using the Paintbrush tool or by applying the brush styles to an existing path. There are many brush styles in Illustrator. In this chapter we will continue to learn more about brushes and painting and how to use them in creating artwork. We will learn how to apply brushes to paths, different brushes and their options, and managing brushes through the Brushes panel.

The amazing thing in Illustrator brushes is that you can customize and add various styles to them, such as drawing with a special pattern that you would like to repeat and apply in your design. This way, brushes can save you time and effort in creating the same object in your document multiple times.

The Paintbrush tool acts very similar to the Pencil tool. To see how it works, select the Paintbrush tool (the keyboard shortcut is the B key on the keyboard) from the Tools panel and start trying to draw some lines. When you double-click the Paintbrush tool, a dialog box appears to let you set the brush settings; it is similar to the Pencil Options dialog box that we covered in Chapter 3.

Brushes Panel

You may not notice the real difference between the Paintbrush and the Pencil tool. Let us see the Brushes panel and how to use it to stylize your brush. The Brushes panel lets you manage, create, and delete brush styles. Each brush style appears as a thumbnail in the panel. You can reveal more Brush libraries from the Brushes Library Menu icon at the bottom left of the panel. When you click on this icon, it reveals more libraries, and you can select any of these libraries to open them in a separate panel. Each library includes special brush sets that allow you to create different effects. For example, the Arrows libraries include different arrow shapes. The Artistic libraries include artistic-style brushes such as calligraphy brushes and paintbrush brushes.

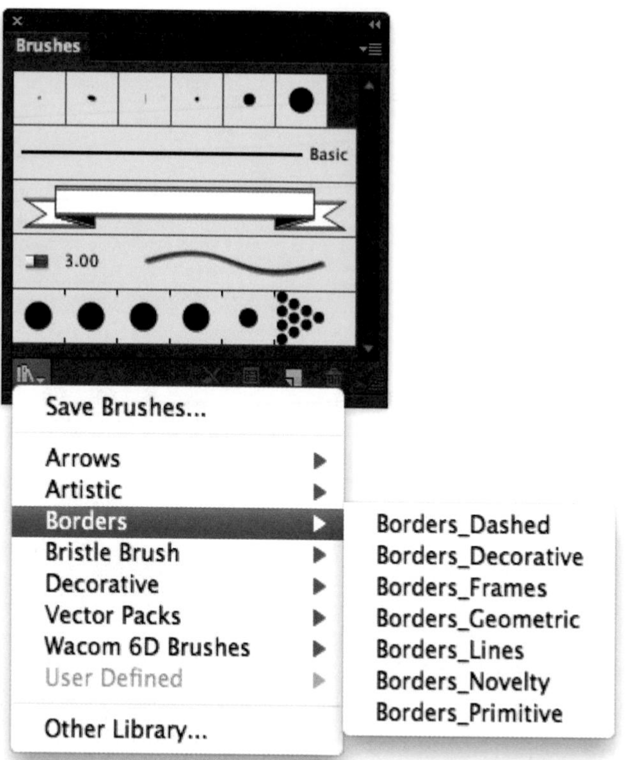

FIG 8-1 The Brushes libraries in the Brushes panel

You can also import other libraries by clicking on the Other Library command to load external brushes from other documents into the Brushes panel.

To the right of the Library icon, you will find the following icons:

- Remove Brush Stroke removes the style that was applied to the brush shape to return the path to the initial regular path shape.
- Options of the Selected Object lets you edit the properties of the currently selected brush strokes.

- New Brush lets you create a new brush from the different types of brushes that are included in Illustrator, as we will see later in page 126.
- Delete Brush lets you select any of the brushes and click the Delete Brush icon to remove it from the Brushes list. You can also simply drag it to the Delete icon to remove it.

In the Option menu of the Brushes panel, you will see the same commands as in the icon, and you can set the brush options. You can see two commands that are concerned with the brush options, which may be confusing. The first command is Options of the Selected Object. This option lets you edit the brush setting for only the selected object. Thus, it does not affect the other objects with the same brush applied to them or affect the general brush setting in the Brushes panel.

Note

In the Brushes panel, you can also find the Show command, which lets you specify the type of brushes that you would like to display in the panel. The Brushes panel also includes the View command, which lets you choose to view the brushes as thumbnails or lists.

The other command is the Brush option, which affects the brush setting in the Brushes panel and all the objects in the stage that have the brush applied to them. To understand the differences in each command, let us follow this example for the results of each command:

1. Open the document Brushsetting.ai. This document includes a number of strokes with brushes applied to them.
2. Select one of the arrow brushes.
3. Click Options for Selected Object; the Brush Options dialog box appears.
4. Make sure that the Preview checkbox is selected.

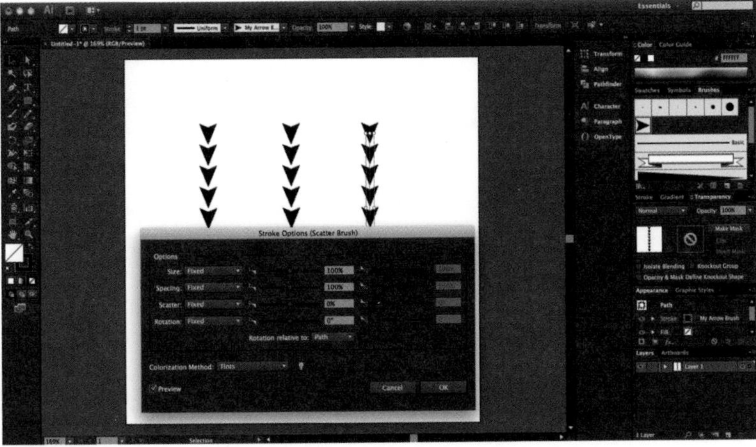

FIG 8-2 The brush setting when clicking on the Options for Selected Object icon

5. Change any of the values. We will cover these settings later in the Calligraphic Brush section, so do not worry much about it at this stage.
6. Notice that this affects only the current selected brush and does not affect other similar brushes.
7. Click the Cancel button.

Now, let us see how the global Brush Options affect the brushes on the stage:

1. Deselect any of the brushes on the stage.
2. Select the arrow brush thumbnail you would like to change from the Brushes panel.
3. From the Brushes panel, open the panel's Option menu.
4. Select the Brush option. This opens the Brush Option dialog box.
5. Make sure that the Preview checkbox is selected.
6. Change any of the brush setting values.
7. Notice that the changes affect all the brushes on the stage, even when they are not selected.

Note

You can click the thumbnail brush to open the Brush Options dialog box.

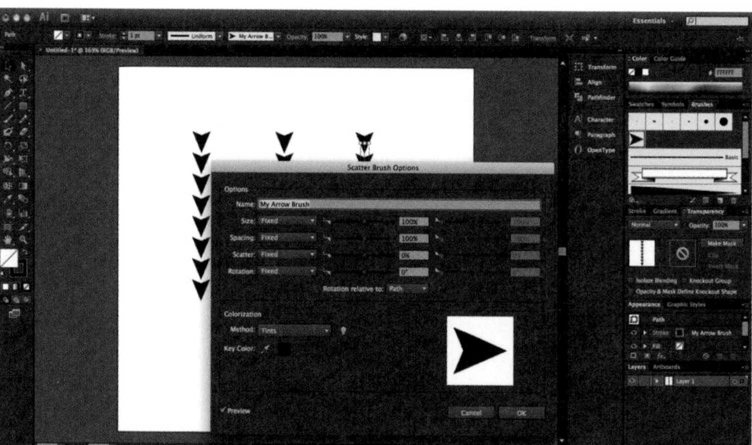

FIG 8-3 The global Brush Options dialog box

Brush Types

After understanding the anatomy of the Brushes panel, let us move to the different types of brushes in Illustrator. One of the powerful features is that you can create different types of brushes, and each type has its own style and results. When you click the New Brush icon in the Brushes panel, the New Brush dialog box appears to let you choose the type of brush. The Brush options are as follows:

FIG 8-4 The New Brush dialog box

- Calligraphic Brush creates a brush that is similar to drawing with a calligraphy pen. The brush outline appears on both sides of the path.
- Scatter Brush has an object defined as the brush shape. When you draw with this brush, it spreads the object around the drawing path.
- Art Brush stretches an object and applies it to the path as a brush.
- Bristle Brush mimics the look of bristles, creating a real brush effect in Illustrator.
- Pattern Brush uses objects or patterns to fill the path stroke. The difference between this brush and the scatter brush is that the pattern brush tiles the patterns to each other with different options, as we will see later in the Pattern Brushes section.

These are the available brushes in the Brushes panel; let us dig deeper and understand each Brush option and how it works.

Note

The scatter and art brushes require you to select an object in your document before defining it.

Calligraphic Brush

This option creates a calligraphy pen–like brush and applies it to the drawing path. When you use this brush, you can control the thickness of the outline while you move or rotate the brush, creating a varied thickness along the line. Therefore, this brush is useful when you are creating artwork with different thickness outlines, such as cartoon characters. It gives a more artistic effect in the lines compared with the normal Pencil tool.

While you can access various calligraphy brushes from the Artistic library in the Brushes libraries, you can create new calligraphy brushes at any time from the New Brush icon at the bottom of the Brushes panel. When you click this icon, the New Brushes dialog box appears to let you choose the type of brush you would like to create. Choose the calligraphy brush and see its different settings. You can use these settings to create your own calligraphy brush that you can use to create different line sizes and angle effects.

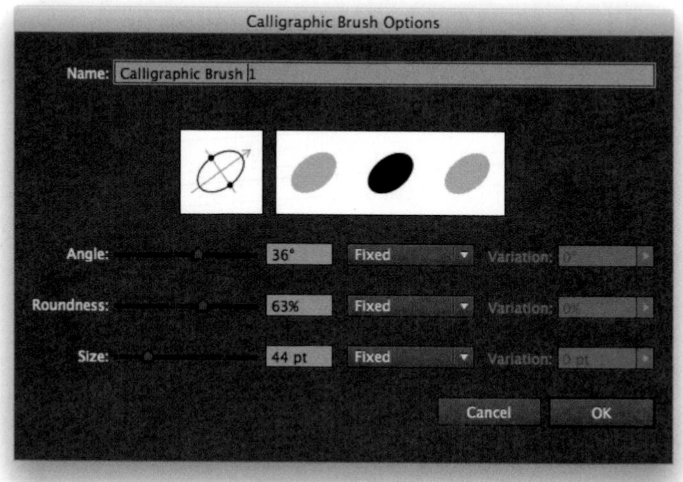

FIG 8-5 The Calligraphic Brush Options dialog box

The Calligraphic Brush Options dialog box includes the following. The calligraphic brush name field lets you name your new brush. It is always good to name your brush to organize your work, especially when you need to create many custom brushes. Under the name is the preview area where you can preview the changes made in the brush parameters, which include the following:

- Angle sets the angle of the brush tip. It is marked with an arrow in the brush preview area.
- Roundness changes the ellipse of the brush and its round edges.
- Size increases or decreases the size of the brush.

On the right side of each value, there is a drop-down menu that includes a variety of options that control the behavior of each value and how it will interact with your lines while drawing manually or with the help of a graphic tablet. Next to these options, you can control the variation of each setting using the variation option slider. This variation value affects how the brush will change. To activate this option, you need to change the Fixed option from the left list. For example, if you set the brush size to 20 degrees and the variation is 5 degrees, this means that the change value in the brush angle range is between 15 and 25 degrees. Thus, when you draw with this brush, its size will vary from 15 to 25 in a random way throughout the line.

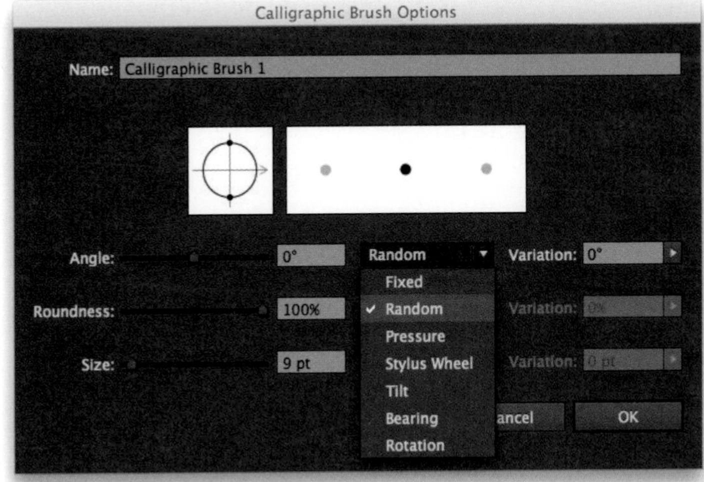

FIG 8-6 The calligraphy brushes variation setting

Let us see how these different options affect your drawing style and stylus:

- Fixed is the default value and does not affect the options in the Calligraphic Brush Options dialog box. You will notice that the variation slider is not active in this option.
- Random creates random angles, roundness, and size while drawing with the brush. This option does not interact with your tablet's stylus pressure.
- Pressure changes the brush values based on the pressure of the stylus pen, as you can tell from the name. For example, if you set the brush size variation to Pressure, increasing the pressure on the stylus pen increases the size of the brush.
- Stylus Wheel lets your newly created brush be affected by the stylus wheel.
- Tilt works when you have a stylus pen that can detect the pen tilt, and works more properly with the roundness option.
- Bearing works with the paintbrush styles that can detect the pen's vertical position.
- Rotation is affected by the stylus pen tip rotation, while the Pressure option is affected by the stylus pen pressure.

As we can see, most of the above options are used to extend your work with the calligraphy brush while using the stylus pen. This can help you to create different artistic effect lines for your artwork. The best practice for these options is to use and try them to see their different impacts on your Illustrator artwork, as we can see from the example below:

> **Note**
>
> It is preferred to use stylus pen in this example to be able to experience the pressure of the pen and the rotation of the pen tip.

1. Open a new Illustrator document.
2. Select the Paintbrush tool.
3. From the Brushes panel, click the New Brush icon at the bottom of the panel.
4. The New Brush dialog box appears, choose calligraphy brush.
5. From the Calligraphic Brush Options dialog box, set a new name for the brush.
6. Set the angle to 40 degrees, and set the roundness to 10%.
7. Set the size to 20 pt, and set the variation to pressure and the value to 10 pt. Thus, when you draw with the stylus pen, the size of the brush will vary between 10 and 30, based on your pressure on the pen.

FIG 8-7 The Calligraphic Brush Options set to pressure

8. Click OK and start drawing with the stylus pen; change the pen pressure to see a change in the size of the brush.
9. Double-click the brush from the Brushes panel to edit its properties.
10. Change the variation setting to a different option, and click OK to try it.

> **Note**
>
> You can change the brush setting by double-clicking the brush thumbnail in the Brushes panel.

Scatter Brush

The scatter brush uses an object as a brush and spreads it along the brush line. Unlike the calligraphy brush, you cannot create the scatter brush from scratch. You need to define the basic shape for the brush by selecting an object in your document.

> **Note**
>
> The shape selected to be a scatter brush should be very simple; otherwise, an alert message appears to say that the object cannot be used for the brush.

To learn more about this brush, follow the example below and see the different options for this brush:

1. Open the document Scatter.ai. This document includes a shape of a soccer ball, which will be used in the scatter brush.
2. Select the shape.
3. From the Brushes panel, click the New Brush icon and choose scatter brush from the New Brush dialog box.

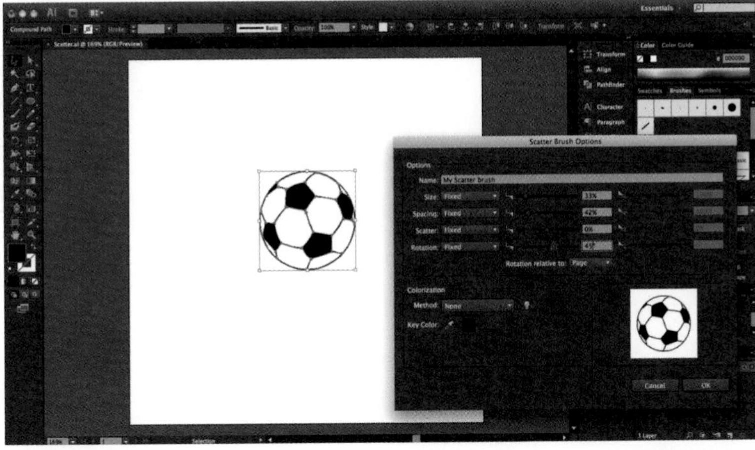

FIG 8-8 The new scatter brush

Before we create the new brush, we will need to learn more about the scatter brush options in the Scatter Brush Options dialog box. The dialog box includes the following features:

- Size, similar to the calligraphy brush, sets the size of the brush.
- Spacing sets the space between the objects on the path.
- Scatter controls how close the object is from the path sides.
- Rotation sets the rotation of the objects.
- "Rotation relative to" directs the rotation of the objects to be relative to either the path or the page. For example, when you set it to the page, the object rotation will be relative to the page. The same applies to rotation relative to the path.

At the right side of this section, you will find the Variation options. These options are very similar to the calligraphy brush and react the same way. The Colorization section sets the color method for the object used in the scatter brush. You can set the colorization options to None, Tints, Tints and Shades, and Hue Shift.

Now, let's continue our example and see how the scatter brush interacts with the object:

4. In the Scatter Brush Options dialog box, name it "my scatter brush."
5. Set the size to 33%, spacing to 42%, and rotation to 45 degrees. Click OK.
6. Choose the Pen tool from the Tools panel. Draw a path as in the figure below.

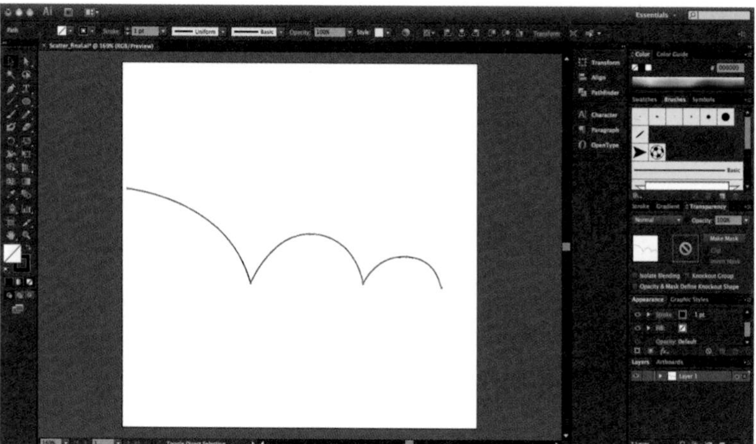

FIG 8-9 The created path using the pen tool

7. With the path selected, choose the scatter brush we just created from the Brushes panel. Notice the results of the scatter brush and how it differs from the calligraphy brush.

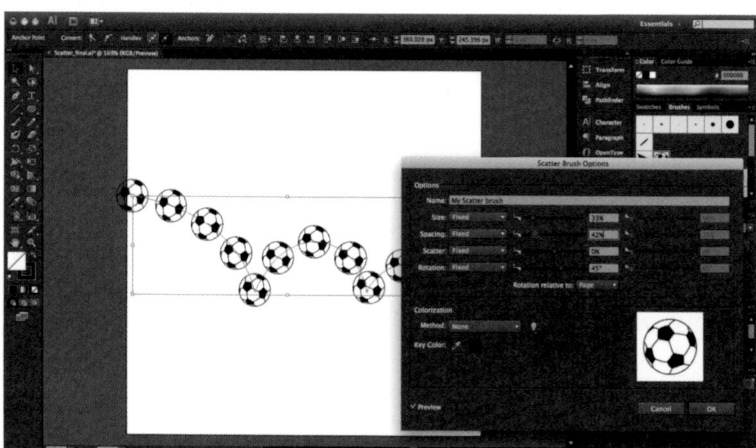

FIG 8-10 The path with the scatter brush applied

Art Brush

As we mentioned previously when we defined how each brush works, the art brush uses a specific selected object and applies it to the entire length of the path. Similar to what we did with the previous brushes, follow the example below to have a better idea about the art brush and how it is different from the other brushes:

1. Open the document Artbrush.ai. This document has a simple circle shape on the artboard; we will create an art brush out of this object.
2. While the object is selected, click New Brush from the Brushes panel. Select Art Brush from the New Brush dialog box.

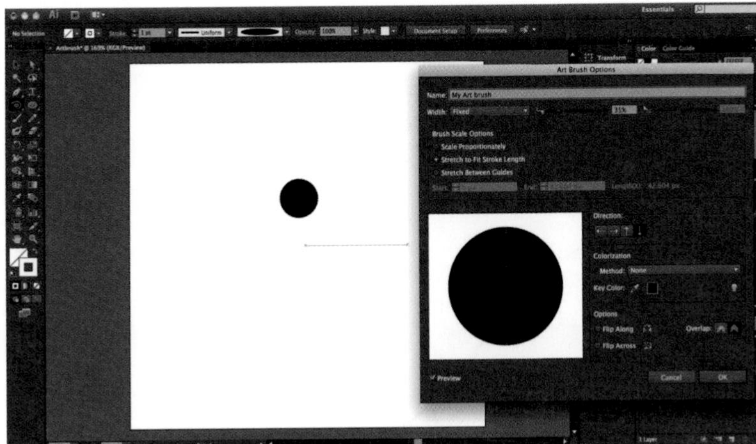

FIG 8-11 The Art Brush Options dialog box

The Art Brush Options dialog box appears and includes the following options:

- Width sets the size of the object applied to the brush in relation to its original size.
- Brush Scale Options controls how the brush is scaled. For example, the brush can be scaled proportionally, stretched to fit with the brush length, or scaled between two guides.
- Direction sets how the art brush shape is directed to the path. You can do this by clicking any of the arrow icons; each arrow sets the shape direction to the end of the path. For example, the right arrow sets the right side of the object toward the end of the path.
- Flip Along or Flip Across sets the orientation of objects toward the path.
- Colorization lets you colorize the brush artwork with one of the color methods: None, Tint, Tint and Shades, and Hue Shift.
- Overlap lets you set the overlap options for the object applied to the brush.

Now, let us continue our example by setting the Art Brush options:

3. Name the new brush "my art brush."
4. Set the width to 35%, and set the brush scale to Stretch to Fit the Stroke Length.
5. Use the Pen tool to create different paths on the stage.
6. Select these paths, and apply to them the art brush we created.

> **Note**
>
> If you would like to modify the brush type assigned to each path separately, you can select the path and click the Options of the Selected Object icon from the bottom of the Brushes panel.

FIG 8-12 Paths with the art brush applied to it

Bristle Brush

This brush is one of the newly added brushes to Adobe Illustrator, it simulates the look and the feel of the real painting brushes. It extends your artistic painting for artwork by giving your object a similar effect as digital painting. The bristle brush does not require you to have an object selected on the stage, unlike the scatter and art brushes, because it is not created based on an object. You can create a new bristle brush by clicking the New Brush icon and choose Bristle Brush from the New Brush dialog box.

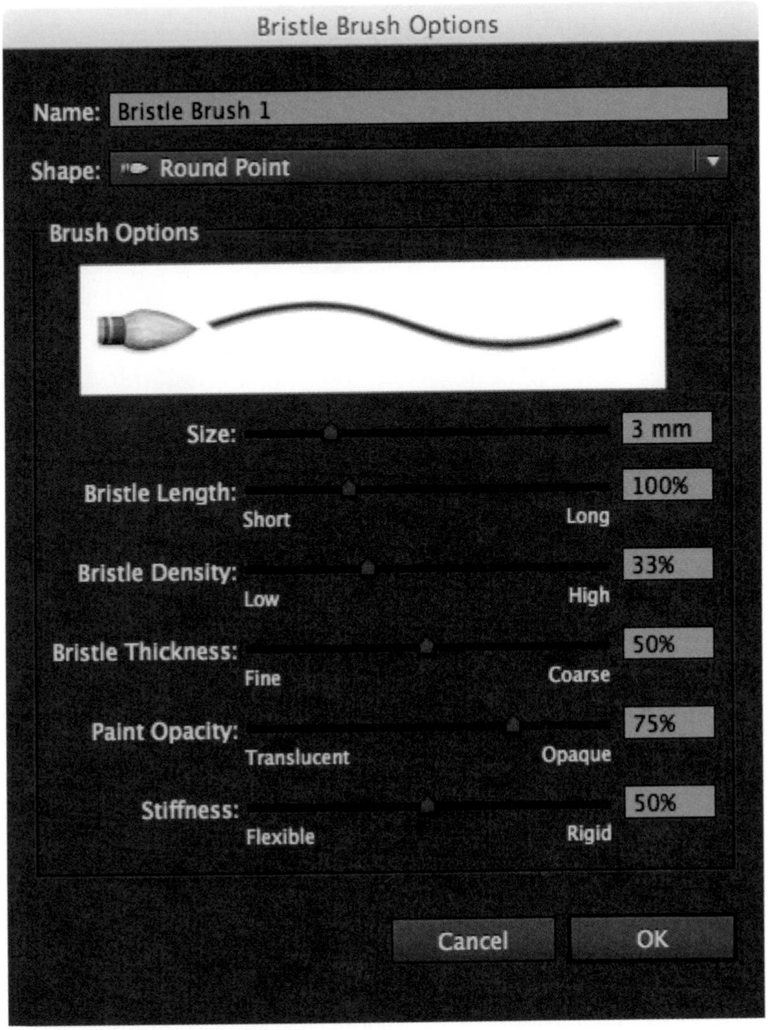

Bristle Brush Options

Name: Bristle Brush 1

Shape: Round Point

Brush Options

Size: 3 mm

Bristle Length: 100% Short Long

Bristle Density: 33% Low High

Bristle Thickness: 50% Fine Coarse

Paint Opacity: 75% Translucent Opaque

Stiffness: 50% Flexible Rigid

Cancel OK

FIG 8-13 Bristle Brush Options dialog box

The options for the bristle brush are different from the other brushes, as we will see below:

- Name: It is good to have unique name for each brush you create to organize your work and distinguish it from other brushes.
- Shape: There are a variety of shapes that you can choose for the bristle brush; each shape mimics real brushes and their effects.
- Size: Similar to the other brushes, this option lets you choose the brush size.
- Bristle Length: This option affects the bristle effect that is applied to the brush. Decreasing this value reduces the bristle effect of the brush.

FIG 8-14 The left brush has the bristle length value set to 25% and the right brush has the value set to 300%

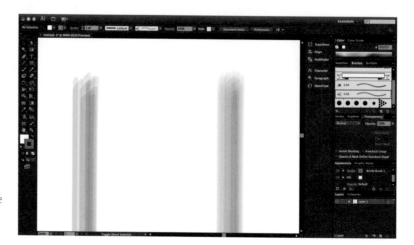

- Bristle Density: This value sets the density of the brush; the high value means that the brush looks more realistic, but at the same time it becomes more complicated, which affects the computer CPU performance.
- Bristle Thickness: This value sets the thickness of the bristle effect applied to the object.
- Paint Opacity: Similar to the rest of the brushes, this value sets the opacity of the brush.
- Stiffness: This value sets the smoothness of the bristle brush; a more smooth brush makes it more realistic and is similar to the real brush.

The bristle brush is a very artistic tool; you can try it to create different effects and results. The example below shows how to set the bristle brush to do a digital painting for artwork in Illustrator:

1. Open the document Bristle_brush.ai; this file includes a tomato outline shape to which we would like to apply the bristle brush.
2. Click the New Brush icon from the Brushes panel. Choose Bristle Brush from the dialog box.
3. In the Bristle Brush dialog box, name the new brush "Tomato body."
4. From the Shape drop-down menu, choose Round Fan. Set the brush values as follows:
    a. Size: 4 mm × 4 mm
    b. Bristle length: 240%
    c. Bristle density: 80%
    d. Bristle thickness: 90%
    e. Paint opacity: 75%
    f. Stiffness: 50%
5. Click OK. In the artboard, select the tomato and set the stroke color to red.
6. Select the tomato body, and from the Tools panel, choose Draw Inside from the bottom of the panel. This will give you the option to draw inside the tomato without the brush color going outside the outline.

7. Start painting with the bristle brush as shown in the figure below.

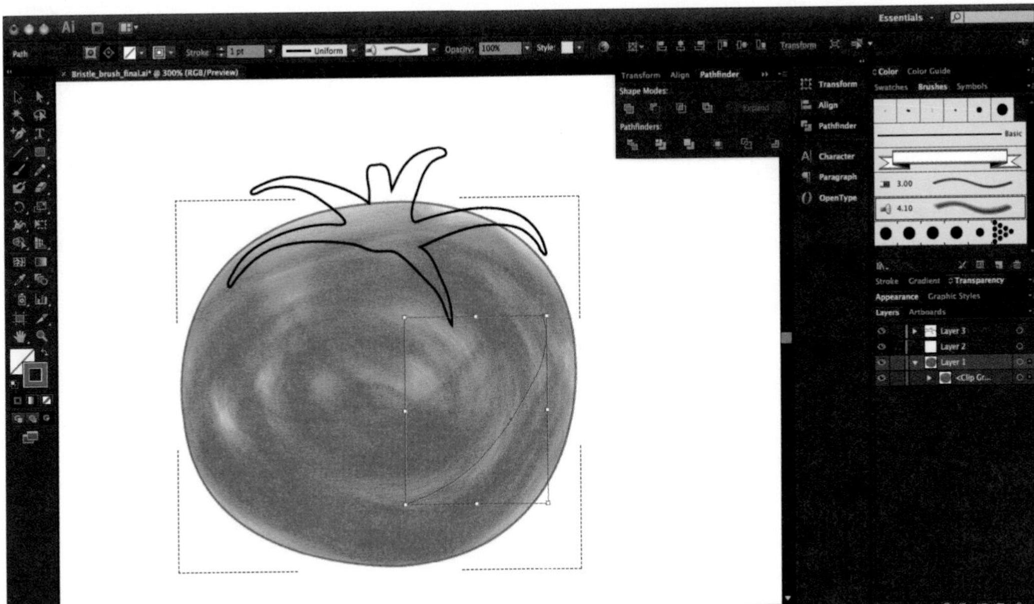

FIG 8-15 The tomato body with the bristle brush painting

8. Change the brush outline color to dark red to paint the shaded areas of the tomato.
9. Change the brush color to light red to paint the bright areas of the tomato.

Note

You can press the open bracket or close bracket ([or]) on your keyboard to increase or decrease the brush size when desired.

10. Select the top part of the tomato. Choose Draw Inside from the bottom of the panel. This will give you the option to draw inside the tomato without the brush color going outside the outline.
11. Set the stroke color to green.
12. Start to paint the top part of the tomato.

Note

You can always change the bristle brush setting for the whole shape by double-clicking the brush on the Brushes panel or change only the selected path by clicking Options of the Selected Objects.

FIG 8-16 Apply the bristle brush to the tomato artwork

Shortcut

You can change the paint opacity of each brush stroke by selecting it and pressing any of the numbers in the keyboard from 1 to 0. For example, number 1 means 10% opacity, number 5 means 50%, and number 9 means 90%.

Pattern Brushes

Unlike the scatter brush, the pattern brush applies an object as a brush in a more organized order and gives you control over the different parts of the brush. You can choose different shapes for the beginning, corner, and the end of the brush, which makes it useful to create borders, as will see in the next example.

Mainly you can define an object as a pattern brush or choose one of the patterns in the Swatches panel. Let us see how to use the second method to create a pattern brush:

1. Open the document Pattern_brush.ai. This document contains the elements that we will use in the patter brush.
2. Select each element individually and drag it to the Swatches panel to convert it into a pattern.

3. From the Brushes panel, click the New Brush icon. Select Pattern Brush from the New Brush dialog box.

The Patterns dialog box is a little different from the other brush dialog boxes because it lets you set up each part of the brush line. The pattern brush options are as follows:

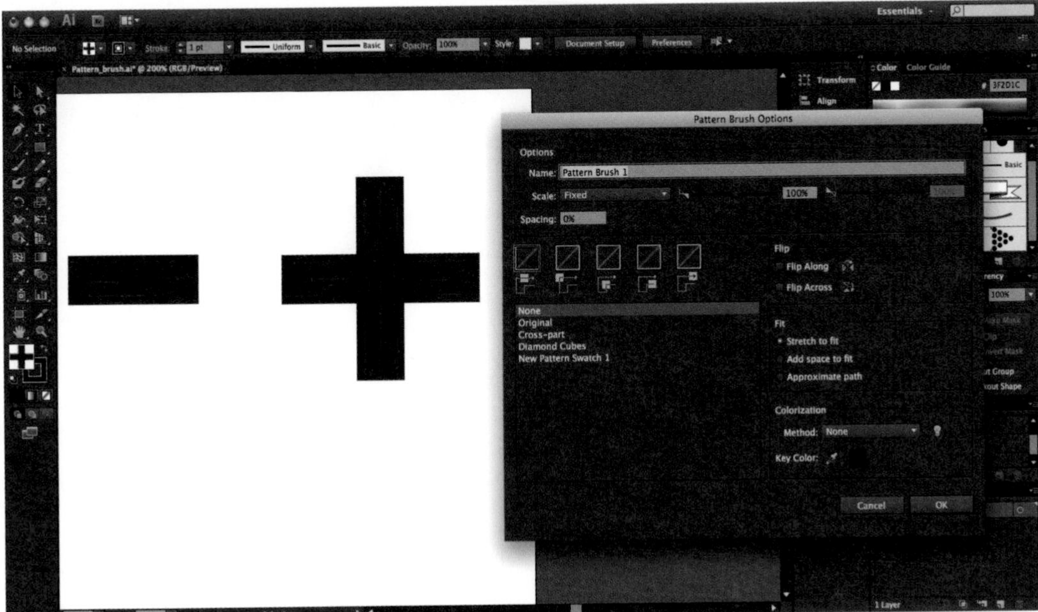

FIG 8-17 The Pattern Brush Options dialog box

- The Name area lets you unify your brush by giving it a unique name.
- The Size Slider lets you change the size of the brush. The drop-down list next to it controls how the size will affect the mouse or the tablet pen, as we learned earlier in this chapter.
- Spacing lets you change the space between the patterns in the brush.
- The Tile five boxes let you customize different parts of the pattern brush. You can choose different patterns from the list below each part. The patterns that appear in the list are the patterns that are available in the Swatches panel.
- Flip changes the orientation of the patterns that are included in the brush.
- Fit changes how the brush parts fit with each other; the brush can be stretched, filled with space, or set based on the path.

Now, let us continue our example:

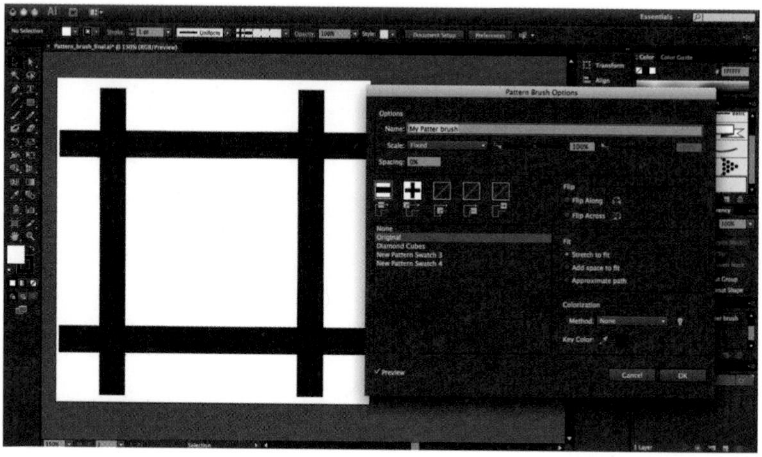

FIG 8-18 The pattern brush applied to document frame path

4. In the Pattern Brush Options dialog box, name the new brush "my pattern brush."
5. In the Tile five boxes, select the first box from the left and choose the first-created part of the pattern from the Swatches list under it.
6. Select the second tile, and from the list, choose the second-created corner part. Click OK to apply the changes. You will notice that the new brush appears in the Brushes panel.
7. Select the Rectangle tool and create a frame around the stage.
8. While the rectangle is selected, choose the brush we just created from the Brushes panel. Notice how the brush is applied to the path and the corners are different from the horizontal or vertical parts of the path.

At this stage we have covered the different types of the brushes in Illustrator, and we have learned how each brush is unique in its properties and can extend your creative experience when creating artwork.

Note

You can choose the colors of the brushes through the Stroke Color option. Also, you can choose to save your custom brushes as a Brush library from the Brushes panel context menu using the Save Brush Library command.

Blob Brush

The blob brush is one of the newly added features in Illustrator CS5 and gives the artist more control over the artwork and artwork outline. Unlike the previous brushes, the blob brush is not applied as a stroke to the path; it is applied as a fill. Because it actually does not create a path line, it creates a filled area.

While the other brushes' thicknesses are hard to control because they consist of one path, you can change the thickness of the blob brush by modifying its fill path. To give you a better idea of how the blob brush is different from the other brushes, the figure below shows the difference between the path that the calligraphy brush created and the one created by the blob brush.

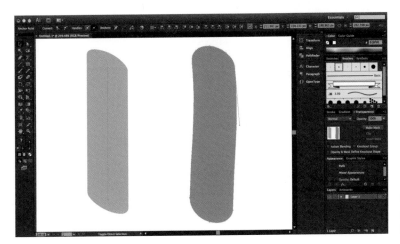

FIG 8-19 The difference between the calligraphy brush on the left and the blob brush on the right

You can start experiencing the blob brush by selecting the Blob Brush tool from the Tools panel. When you double-click the Blob Brush tool, the Options dialog box appears to give you more control over the brush through a number of options from which you can choose.

Blob Brush Tool Options
✓ Keep Selected
✓ Merge Only with Selection
Tolerances
Fidelity: 20 px
Smoothness: 32%
Default Brush Options
Size: 9 pt Fixed Variation: 0 pt
Angle: 56° Fixed Variation: 0°
Roundness: 23% Fixed Variation: 0%
Cancel
OK

FIG 8-20 The Blob Brush Tool Options dialog box

The blob brush includes the following options. The first two options are Keep Selected and Merge Only with Selection. To understand the behavior of those two options, we should see the blob brush in action. So, let us follow the steps below:

1. Open a new Illustrator document.
2. Select the blob brush from the Tools panel.
3. Start to draw a line with the blob brush.
4. Draw another cross line above the first one.

Notice that both the first and the second brush lines are merged together into one path filled with the active fill color. Now, double-click the blob brush and check the Keep Selected option. Then try to follow the above steps; you will notice that the drawn line is selected even after you are finished drawing the first line and move to create the second one.

This second option is Merge Only with Selection. True to its name, this option only allows merging the paths of the intersected selected blob brushes. This option works along with the first to give you more control over which brushes merge with each other while creating artwork. With two of these options checked, only the selected overlapped paths merge together.

In the Tolerances section, you can set the fidelity, which controls how far you need to move with your mouse or tablet before a new anchor point is added to the blob brush path. The higher value means a smoother and simpler path. The other option in the Tolerances section is the smoothness value, which sets how smooth the brush is. In the Default Brush Options section, you can find the regular brush settings, such as the size, angle, and roundness.

At this stage, we should be aware of the different brushes in Illustrator and be able to use them and their different options to create artwork or outlines for your artwork. The choice of proper brush and properties for the brush depends on your artwork and the style you would like to create. The examples in this chapter are meant to give you an idea about the brushes and how to use them. Start practicing the different options, and try to use them in your Illustrator artwork; this will give you more experience with the brush options and how to implement them in your work.

For examples pertaining to this chapter, visit www.illustratorfoundations.com.

Working with Type

As you may know, Adobe is one of the pioneer companies in the typeface and fonts industry. Many of you may get the chance to play with one of those amazing Adobe fonts. Actually, Adobe has one of the largest font stores, where you can find a large variety of fonts. Because of this, Adobe Illustrator is one of the applications that handles type and fonts efficiently and provides amazing options and features to handle your text writing, as we will see in this chapter.

Typeface and fonts are an essential part of your design, regardless of whether it is for printing, web, or video. It is considered the most important visual element in your design, because it handles the content or design message that you would like to address to the design viewer. Therefore, understanding the type setting and how it works can affect your workflow and help you create a better type experience in your design, professionally and in less time. Type in Illustrator is not just for writing text. Some fonts are decorative fonts that allow you to add decorative motifs and shapes into your document as you type the font on your keyboard.

In this chapter we will cover how to work with type and paragraphs in Adobe Illustrator and how to use the different features to create the type in your design. Generally, there are two main ways to add text to your Illustrator document. The first way is to import text from an external text file such as Notepad, Typepad, or Microsoft Word through the Place command. The second method is to write or copy the text directly into the Illustrator workspace using the Text icon in the Tools panel. Let us first see how to use the Place command to bring text into an Illustrator document.

Placing Text into an Illustrator File

The advantage of using this method is that you can import a large text document directly into Illustrator without the need to copy or even open the text document. Also, Adobe Illustrator supports a wide variety of text files, such as Microsoft Word, TXT, and RTF. Sometimes the original text had styles or formats applied to it in applications such as Microsoft Word; Adobe Illustrator then gives you the option to import the text with the applied format or just ignore the original text formats.

Let us see in the example below how to place external text into Illustrator document:

1. Create a new document from File > New Document.
2. From the Document Profile, choose Web.
3. In the Size drop-down list, choose 1024 x768 px and click OK.
4. From the File menu, choose Place.
5. Navigate to Chapter 9 in the companion website that accompanies this book (http://www.illustratorfoundations.com), select Simple_text.txt, and click the Place button.
6. A dialog box appears to let you modify the imported text options. Press OK.

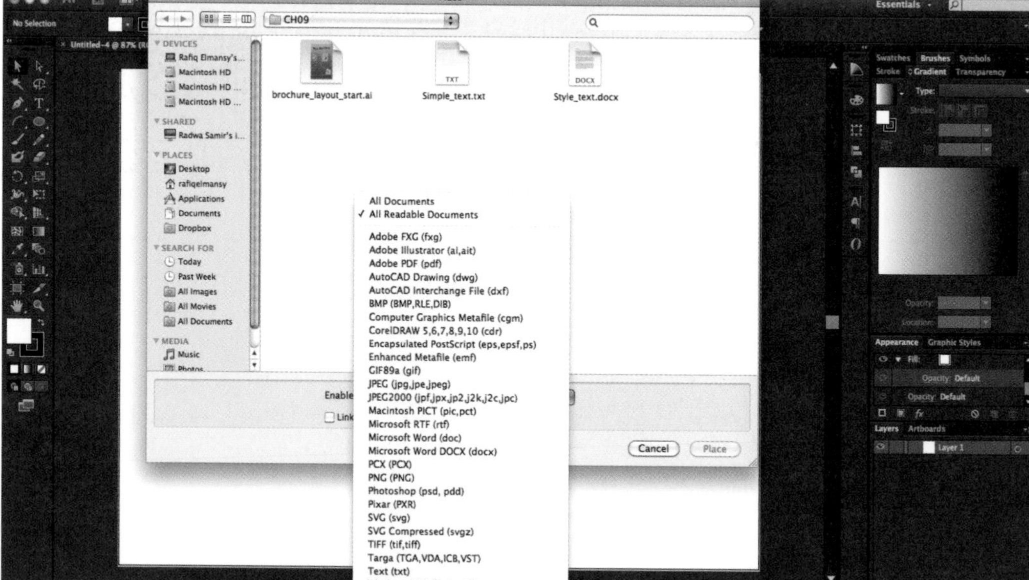

FIG 9-1 The Place command dialog box

Notice that the text is placed in the document. Do not worry about the formatting at this stage. We will see later in the Text Properties section how to work with the text and how to improve the text formatting in Illustrator.

Note

If you use the Text tool to click on an existing text frame, this will let you edit the current text. If you click on an empty area in the artboard, this will let you create a new text.

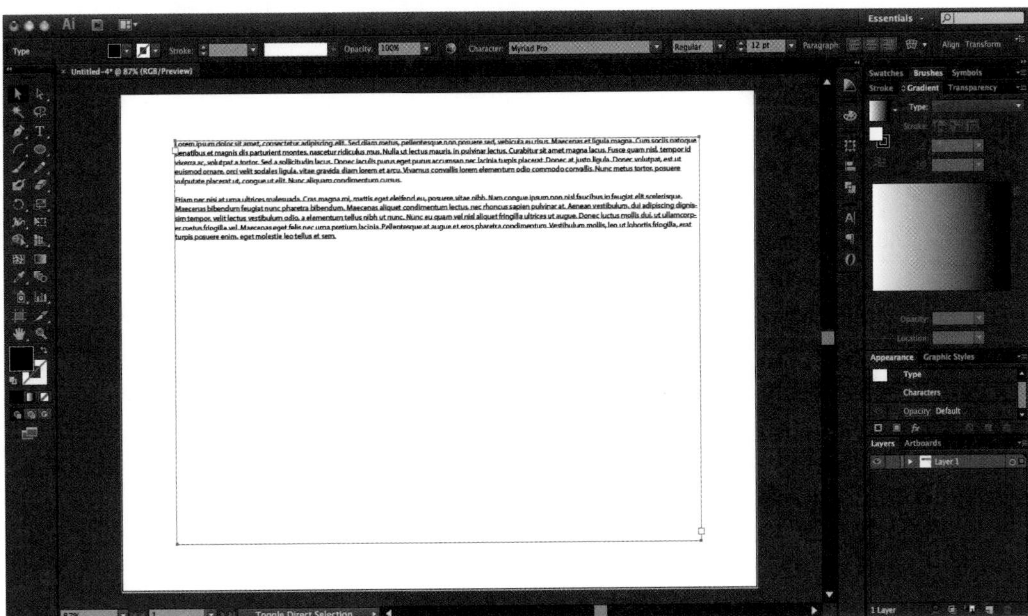

FIG 9-2 The text places in the illustrator document

Now, let us try to import a Microsoft Word document with styles applied to it:

1. Repeat the above steps, navigate the companion website to Style_text.doc in Chapter 9, and click Place.
2. A dialog box appears to let you choose the type of the content you would like to place and if you would like to ignore the original text format. Keep Remove Text Formatting unchecked and press OK.

Notice that the text is inserted into your document with the format applied to it, and the colors * paragraph/character is also imported.

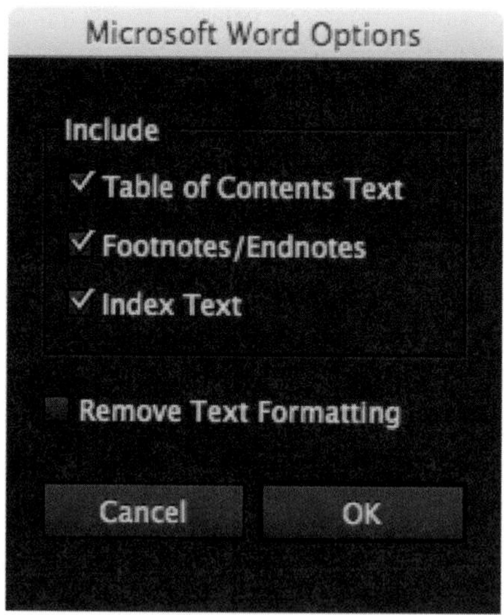

FIG 9-3 The Place command dialog box for the Microsoft Word document

After briefly previewing the above method to insert text into Illustrator, let us move to the most commonly used method to add text in Illustrator—through the Text tool. Adding text in Illustrator is as simple as choosing the Type tool from the Tools panel, clicking in the document artboard to show the text cursor, and typing your text. There are two ways to write text in Illustrator.

The first way is called point text, where you just click once in your Illustrator document using the Type tool (you can access it using the letter T on your keyboard). The second method is called text area, where you click and drag to create a text area in which you can write text. Let us try both ways and see the difference between them.

Note

You can choose the Vertical Type tool to create vertical text instead of horizontal. You can toggle to the Vertical Text tool using the Shift key when you are using the Type tool.

As we mentioned, you can start using the point text method by selecting the Type tool from the Tools panel and clicking on the stage. The text indicator appears to let you use your keyboard to write your text. Notice that there is no rectangle around the text, and it appears only when you finish your text and click any other tool to exit the text-writing mode. Also, notice that your text line does not wrap; it just keeps getting longer as long as you keep writing. The only option to get a new line is to click the Return or Enter keys on the keyboard and continue writing.

This method is not suitable for typing paragraphs and large amounts of text, because you will have no restriction on the text line width. It is more suitable for free text such as writing titles and small text or words. Also, when you use the Selection tool to select the text after writing it, you will notice that changing the boundary box that is around the text changes the text size of the text itself and may distort it.

The second method to create text in Illustrator is to create a text area. You can do so using the following steps:

1. Select the Type tool from the Tools panel.
2. Click in the artboard where you would like your paragraph area to start. Drag to create a rectangle.
3. The text cursor appears to let you type or copy text inside the text area.

Notice that when you write inside the text area, the text line wraps once it reaches the end of the rectangle width, which makes it more efficient for writing paragraphs and text areas than the point text described previously. When you try to scale the text area, this does not affect the text size because you just change the size of the area that includes the text, not the text itself.

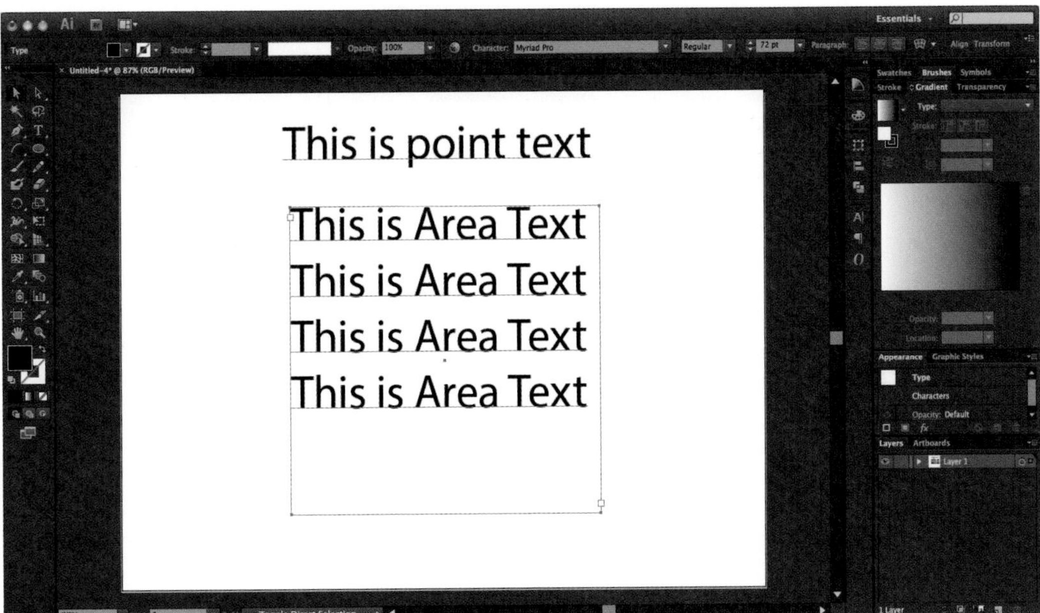

FIG 9-4 The point text and the area text

Notice that both text types have their own usages. We will use both while we move forward in this chapter.

Text Properties

Similar to any other graphic application, when you select the Type tool, it provides you with properties that allow you to format your text based on your desired design. You can display the text properties by either selecting the text area or the text line created by double-clicking the text to activate it, then clicking on the first line in the text and dragging to select part of the whole text, if you prefer.

> **Note**
>
> When you are in text editing, you can use Cmd+A (Ctrl+A in Windows) to select all the text at once. Also, you can double-click on a specific word to select it or triple-click to select an entire paragraph.

When you select the text, the type properties appear in the Control panel in the top of your document. These features should provide the essential options that are used commonly to format the text in Adobe Illustrator. Let us first overview the type properties from the left side to the right:

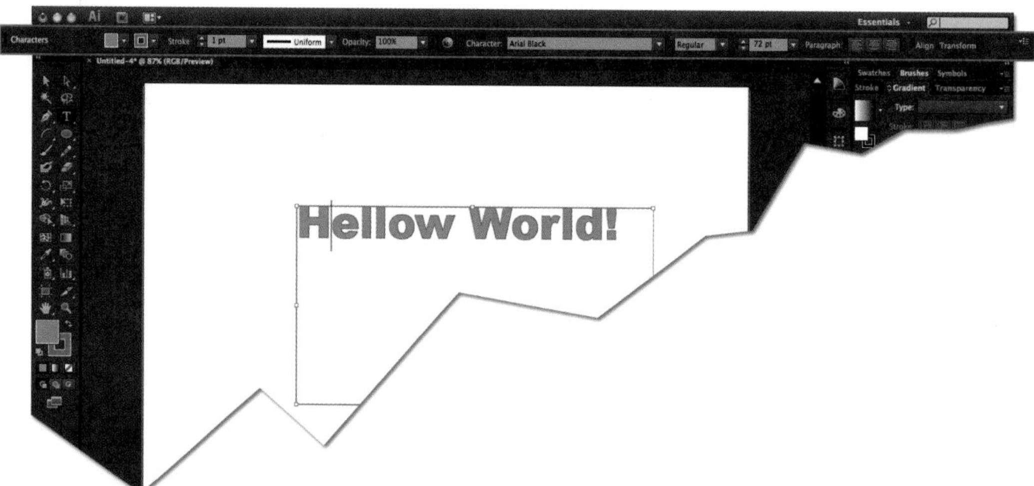

FIG 9-5 The type properties in the Properties bar

- The first color icon lets you choose the text fill color. You can click on the arrow next to it to display the color swatches, and you can pick a color or click on the New icon at the bottom of that floating panel to create a new color.
- The second color indicates the color of the stroke that surrounds the type letters.

- The Stroke Size drop-down list lets you choose the weight of the stroke from a predefined list, or you can write your number directly.
- Stroke Shape lets you choose the shape of the stroke applied to the text, but it does not affect the editable text.
- Opacity lets you set the opacity of the text. Zero percent means that the text is fully transparent and 100% means that the text is fully in color. Clicking the blue opacity word will bring up the full transparency option in a floating panel.
- The Recolor Artwork icon displays the Recolor dialog box that allows you to change the text fill and stroke colors from different color combinations.
- The Character menu lets you choose the font that you would like to use in your type. Clicking the blue character word will display the paragraph panel.
- The Font Size list lets you change the font size to any of the sizes in the list, or you can type the value of your font size directly in the numerical field.
- The Paragraph Direction is three icons that let you align the text to right, center, or left. Clicking the blue paragraph word will display the paragraph panel.
- Next to the Paragraph Direction icons, there are two icons, between which you can switch using the arrow next to them. These icons are Make with Warp and Make with Mesh. You can use these icons to apply a distortion to your text, as we will see later in the Make with Warp and Make with Mesh sections.
- When you select the text area or the text frame, you will notice that the Make Envelope icon appears to let you apply warp effects. You can switch between Make with Warp and Make with Mesh options.
- The Align panel lets you align the text to the document or to the other object in the document.
- The Transform panel lets you change the position, scale, rotation, and skew options of the text.

Make with Warp

This option lets you apply a distortion to the text using a variety of options. The amazing thing in this feature is that the text is still editable even after you modify it, as we will see in the below example:

1. Create a new Illustrator document. Set the Document Profile to Web and the size to 1024 x 768 px.
2. Select the Type tool from the Tools panel.
3. Click on the artboard and write the text "Hello World."
4. Set the text color to black from the Swatches floating panel.
5. Set the stroke color to None.
6. From the Character menu, change the font to Arial Black and the size to 130 pt. It is not listed in the current sizes, so you need to write it in the size numerical value.
7. Click Align to reveal the Align panel. Set the align value to Artboard.
8. Click Align Horizontal and Align vertical icons. At this stage the text should be aligned to the center of the document artboard.

FIG 9-6 The text was centered in the artboard using the align buttons

9. Click the Make with Warp icon to open the Warp Options dialog box. It includes different styles of warping, and each warp can be applied either horizontally or vertically and has settings associated with it.
10. Make sure to select the Preview checkbox to be able to preview the changes you create applied to the text.
11. Set the style to arc, check Horizontal, and set the bend to 50%.
12. Move the horizontal value to −100% and click OK.

FIG 9-7 The type with the warp applied to it

This is one of the distortions that we can do with the text warp. You can practice different styles and effects to choose the best fit for your design.

Make with Mesh

Before Illustrator added this feature, it was hard to modify text, especially when you wanted to keep it editable; this is the most useful part about this feature. Editing the text after applying either Make with Warp or Make with

Mesh is very easy. You can edit it by double-clicking on the text or by using the Control panel buttons. When you select the text and click the Make with Mesh icon, the Envelope Mesh dialog box appears to set up the mesh that will be applied to the text, as below:

1. Click the Make with Mesh icon; the Envelope Mesh dialog box appears. Set the rows and columns value to 5 and click OK. Notice that the text has mesh applied to it.

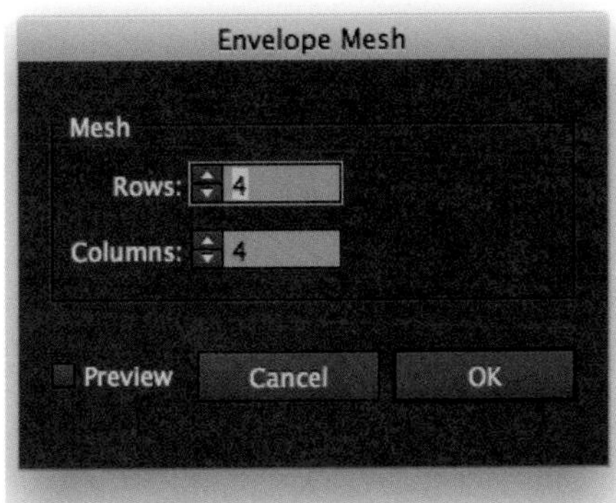

FIG 9-8 The Envelope Mesh dialog box

2. Choose the Direct Selection tool, select each of the mesh points, and drag them to reach the below shape (you can also use the Mesh tool).
3. You can double-click the text to enter isolated mode and edit the text or use the Control panel. Notice that your edited text will have the mesh applied to it also.

FIG 9-9 The text with the envelope mesh applied to it

Working with Paragraph

Paragraph is actually a set of multiple text lines added in a text area. Thus, the paragraph text includes the same properties of the line text, in addition to other options that control the paragraph in order to make it useful in your layout design, such as web pages, printing brochures, and so on.

In addition to the type alignment options such as the right, left, and center alignment, the Paragraph panel provides extra options to control your text. You can create a paragraph by choosing the Type tool and dragging over the artboard to create an area of text. Then you can write your own text or copy text from an external source. If the Paragraph panel is not available, you can view it from Window > Type menu. Now, let us create a paragraph of text, select it, and then open the Paragraph panel and see the available options in it:

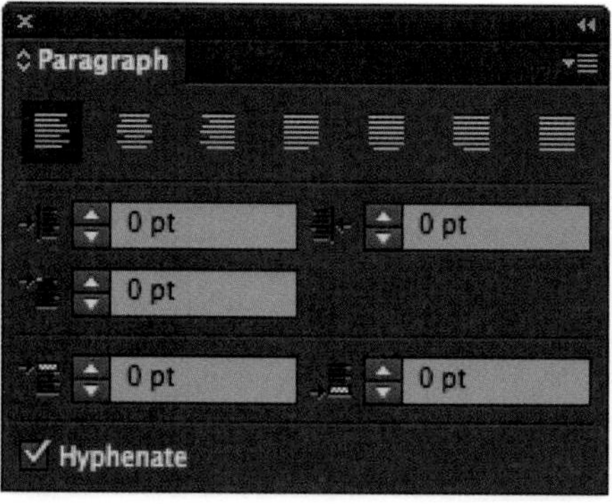

FIG 9-10 The Paragraph panel options

At the top of the Paragraph panel are the alignment icons that allow you to align the text to the left, center, and right. Next to these icons, the justification icons let you justify the text in the text area; the way last line will be treated will differ. For example, you can justify the text and leave the last line in the paragraph without justification, justify right, justify left, or justify from both right and left sides.

The Left Indent and Right Indent icons allow you to add margins on the left and the right side of your paragraph. The First Line Left Indent icon lets you add a left margin before the first line only; it is useful in some paragraph formats, such as magazines and articles. The Space Before Paragraph and Space After Paragraph icons allow you to increase or decrease the area above or below your paragraph and between the paragraphs. The Hyphenation checkbox lets you enable hyphenation on words that are not completed by the end of the line. If it is not enabled, the word will move to a new line.

Area Text Options

These options are very important when you handle paragraph layouts. The settings in the Area Text options let you arrange and organize the text inside the text area and text flows. You can also use the Area Text options to create columns and rows from the current text and set the spaces between them, as we will see below. You can reach the Area Text options from the top Type menu. In order to understand the Area Text options, we need to create a paragraph on the Illustrator stage, as follows:

1. Create a new document in Illustrator. Set the Document Profile to Print, and choose a format.
2. Select the Type tool and click and drag on the artboard to create an area of text.
3. Write any text inside the text area. You can add the famous Lorem Ipsum text from the website www.lipsum.com. This is a dummy text, and you can use it in your practice and draft designs.
4. Select the Selection tool and select the text area. From the Type menu, choose the Area Text Options dialog box.
5. Make sure to have the Preview checkbox enabled to preview the results as you make changes in the dialog.

Now, let us see the different options and how they affect the paragraph:

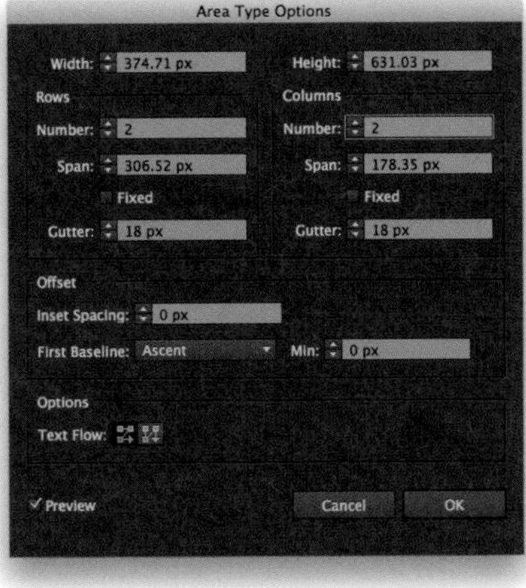

FIG 9-11 The Area Type Options dialog box

- The width and height values let you set the text area dimensions.
- The rows and columns sections divide your paragraph into either rows or columns or both. And you can set the number of rows or columns.
- The span value sets how the text flows outside the text area, and the fixed value provides a fixed change in the span.
- The gutter value determines the space between the columns and the rows.
- The offset section lets you set how and where your text will appear inside the text area. It includes the following options:
  - Inset Spacing lets you set the space of the offset between the text and the text area borders.

- First Baseline sets how you would like your first line of text to start inside the text area. The baseline of the first line can be determined based on the ascent, cap heading and leading, and so on, and a minimum value can be used in the min field to fine-tune your choice.

At the end of the Area Text Options dialog box, you can set the flow direction of the text by columns or by rows.

Text Area Threading

When you add a lot of text in the text area, you can easily notice that the bottom right rectangle turns to red with a plus sign in it, which indicates that there is some overset text in this text area. Threading the text area allows you to create multiple text areas that are linked to each other. This is one of the commonly used features in printing and magazine layout.

Let us see in the following example how to create a link between text areas:

1. Create a paragraph of text as we did before. Add a lot of text until the extra text is longer than the text area and the bottom right rectangle appears in red.
2. Click the red rectangle and click in another place in the artboard.
3. A new text area is created and the text flows from the first text area to the second.
4. Notice that there is a blue line running between the two text areas to show that they are linked.

FIG 9-12 The threaded text areas in Illustrator document

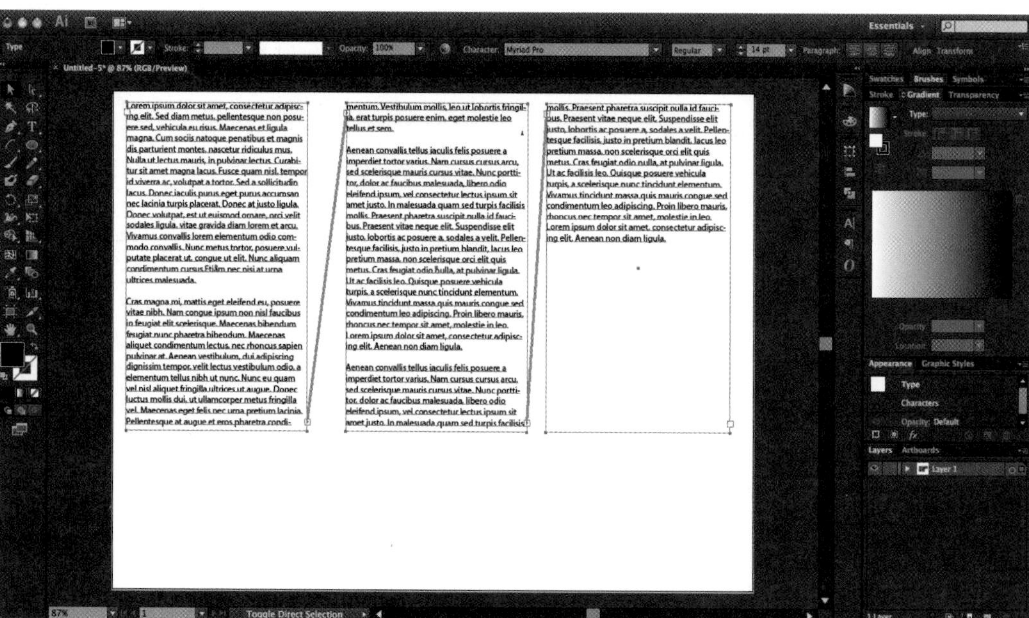

Before we move to other text options in Adobe Illustrator, let us see how to use the above options and features to create a draft brochure layout:

1. Open the document Brochure_layout_start.ai. This document includes the basic elements for our brochure layout. It is in A4 printing size and has two artboards.
2. Select the first artboard and choose the Type tool from the Tools bar.
3. Click on the top of the artboard once to create a point text and write "New Brochure."
4. Set the font size to 60 pt and the font type to Arial Black. Also, set the color to "CMYK Blue."
5. Select the text using the Selection tool, and from the Control panel, select the Warp Text icon to open the Warp Text dialog box.
6. Make sure that the Preview checkbox is selected and set the style to flag. Check the Horizontal checkbox and set the bind to 50%.
7. Open the Align panel. Make sure that the Align To option is set to artboard.
8. Click the Horizontal Align Center icon to align the text center of the active artboard.

FIG 9-13 The warp text in the brochure example

9. Select the Type tool and drag on the artboard to create the first column on the left side of the first artboard under the title. Add any text, such as the Lorem Ipsum text, and set the color to black, the size to 18, and the font to Arial Regular. Also, align the paragraph to the left. Make the text exceed the size of the area in order to see the red rectangle.

> **Note**
>
> You can change the case of the text from Type > Change Case. In this option you can set the text to uppercase, lowercase, title case, or sentence case.

10. Click the red rectangle icon and click where you would like to create the second column. Make sure that columns fit together in the artboard; if not, you can change the width of the text area to make the text fit inside the artboard.
11. Repeat the above step to create another threaded text area at the bottom of the two columns as shown in the figure below.

> **Note**
>
> There is another method to create linked text. You can create three text areas, and, while selecting them, choose Threaded Text > Create from the Type menu. When you add the text, you will notice that it flows from one text area to another.

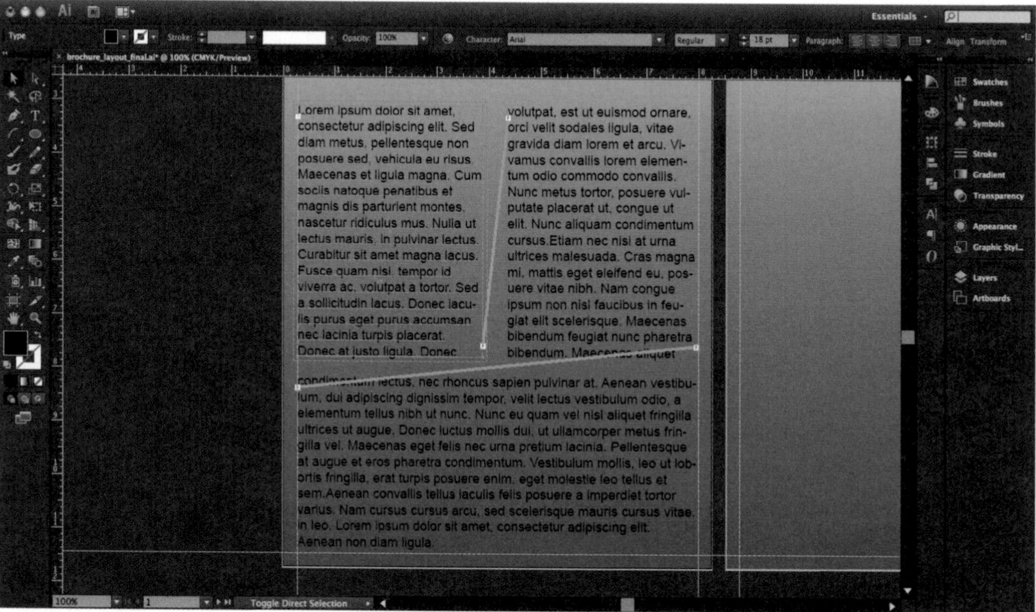

FIG 9-14 The brochure with the linked text paragraph applied to the first artboard

12. Reveal and unlock the Thumbnail layer from the Layer panel. This layer includes a thumbnail that we will use to wrap the paragraph text around it.

13. Move the content of the Thumbnail layer to the Text layer so both are in the same layer. Make sure the thumbnail is above the text area.
14. Select both the first thumbnail and the paragraph under it.
15. From the Object menu, choose Warp Text > Make.
16. Click OK for the alert message.
17. Repeat the same action with the rest of thumbnails. The final layout should look like the figure below.
18. Save your document.

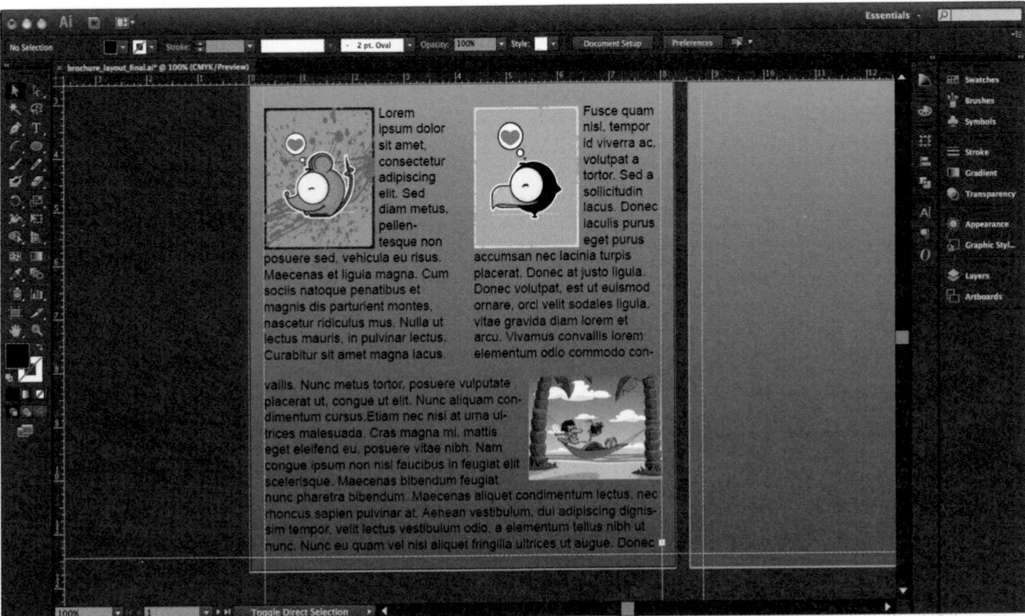

FIG 9-15 The text paragraph wraps around the thumbnails

You can apply these options and effects on different designs with different styles. Try to follow the above steps in creating your layout.

Working with Text and Paths

In addition to above great type features, Adobe Illustrator allows you to add text inside any path, such as a rectangle, circle, or any shape. This is called adding text inside a path. It also allows you to add text on the path, as we will see later in this part.

Let us start by adding text inside a path in the following steps, which completes the second page of the brochure in the previous example:

19. Open the file Brochure_layout_start.ai that we already started. Select the second artboard.
20. Choose the Ellipse tool and drag to create a large cycle. Do not forget to press Shift while dragging to create a precise rounded circle.

21. Choose the Type tool and move over the inside of the circle. You will notice that the Type icon has changed to identify that you can write inside this shape.
22. Click on the shape and start adding your text.
23. Open the Align panel and make sure it is set to Align to Artboard. Align the text to the horizontal and vertical center of the artboard.
24. Select the text, and from the Pargaraph panel, choose Justify All to have all the text lines to fully fill the circle shape.

Note

You can choose the Area Type tool directly from the Tools panel to write inside the shape or choose the Vertical Area Type tool to create vertical text.

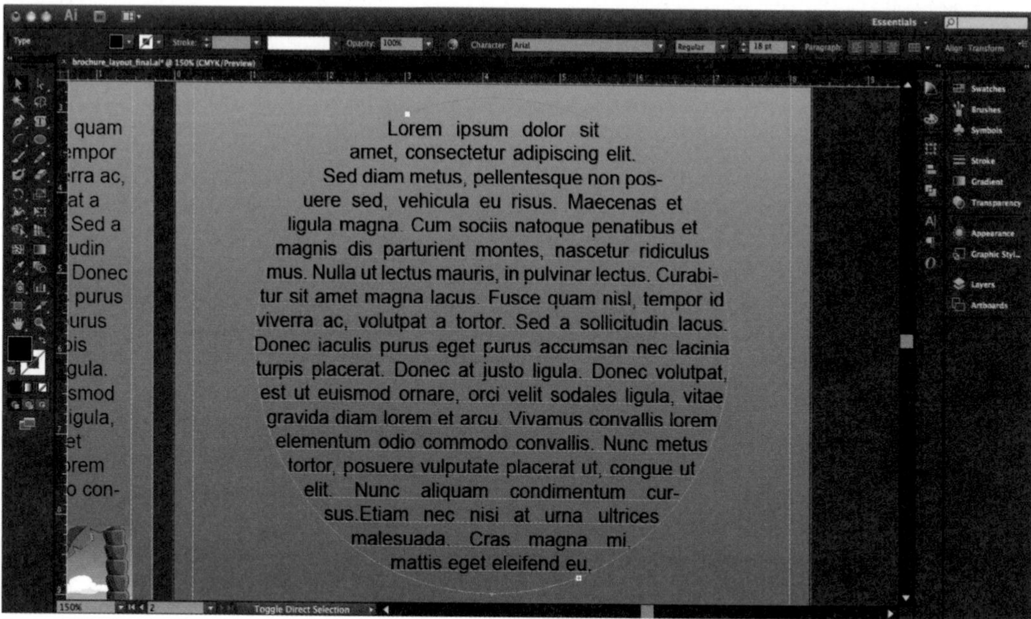

FIG 9-16 The text applied to the circle shape

While you work in the above example, you may notice that the Type tool changes its shape when you roll over different parts of the path. For example, it turns to the Area Type tool when you roll over inside the path and turns to the Type on a Path tool when you move over the path line itself.

Let us add text on a path in our example and see the different options for it:

25. Open the file Brochure_layout_start.ai that we already started before. Select the second Artboard.
26. Create a path under the text circle as shown in the figure below.
27. Select the Type tool or the Type on a Path tool.

28. Place your cursor on the edge of the path until the tool shape changes to the Type on a Path tool. Then click to start adding your text.
29. Notice that the text appears on the path. Sometimes, the text appears flipped due to the direction of the path, but this is not a problem because we can control this from the Type on a Path Options dialog box.

FIG 9-17 The text on a path applied to the brochure design

If you select the text that is applied to the path, you can change its appearance from the menu Type > Type on a Path. You can choose from different effects such as rainbow, skew, 3D ribbon, and gravity.

> **Note**
>
> You can choose the Type on a Path tool directly from the Tools panel to write over the path or choose the vertical Type on a Path tool to create vertical text.

Under these effects, you can choose the Type on a Path Option dialog box that includes the following options. You can choose any of the above effects from the Effects drop-down list, and you can flip the text and the effect by checking the Flip checkbox. You can choose the alignment base of the text, as it can be aligned on the path based on baseline, ascender, descender, or center. Also, you can change the spacing between characters using the spacing value.

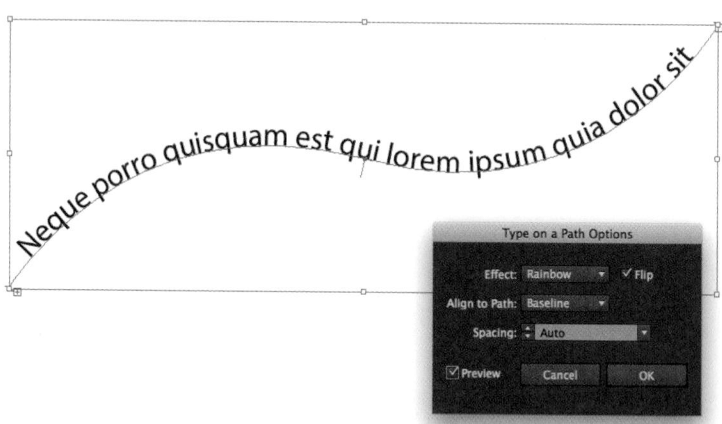

FIG 9-18 The Type on a Path Options dialog box

Convert Text into Path

The nature of text is different from any vector object in Illustrator. You can edit and resize it using the text features in Illustrator. In some cases, you will want to convert the text into a normal vector shape in order to be able to create more complex effects. You can convert any text into a path by simply selecting the text and choosing the menu Type > Create Outline.

At this point, we have reviewed the most important text and paragraph features in Illustrator, such as how to work with point and area text and how to use area text to create paragraphs. Also, we learned how to work with the different paragraph options that can help you create text layout easily and efficiently. The example we described showed how to compile different features and options to create one simple project, a brochure layout. You can practice with your own ideas and try to apply the different options we covered in this chapter.

For examples pertaining to this chapter, visit www.illustratorfoundations.com.

CHAPTER 10

Masks, Blends, and Blending Modes

Designing a complex piece of artwork involves adding objects and artwork to construct the final design. In many cases, you would like to display part of the image or artwork in the Adobe Illustrator document and hide the rest of it. However, cropping and cutting artwork or images is not available in Illustrator in a direct way; instead, Illustrator provides the mask feature, which allows you to reveal parts of the artwork and hide the rest of it using a comprehensive feature.

In this chapter we will cover two of the important Illustrator features that many designers commonly use in their work—the mask feature and the blending modes found in the transparency panel—and how to use them to create artwork effects. Similar to many Adobe Illustrator effects, these are more practical features that you need to learn how to implement in your design projects. Thus, let us move to learn more about these two features.

Working with Masks

The mask concept is very common in many design applications, such as Adobe Photoshop, Flash, and After Effects. The idea of the mask is to hide parts of the objects and display specific parts using another object, which is called the clipping path. One of the benefits of using masks is that you do not need to cut, modify, or distort the masked object in order to remove parts of the artwork. All you need to do is hide the parts that you do not want to appear in the document, as we will learn next.

The Mask Concept

If you are already familiar with any of the design applications, you can skip this part. We will try to describe the idea behind the mask function in Illustrator, using the following example. This will provide a better understanding of how the mask concept works. The figure below includes two shapes: a large rectangle shape and a circle shape above it. If we consider the circle to be a mask applied for the rectangle, then we will be able to see only the circular area of the rectangle under the mask circle, as we can see on the right side of the figure below.

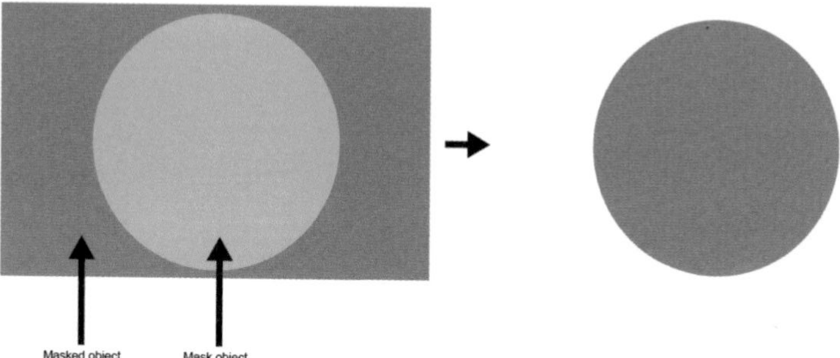

FIG 10-1 The mask concept

In a more in-depth review of the mask concept, the masked object could be one shape, complex artwork or an imported bitmap image, or even an entire document.

Applying Mask to Artwork

As we mentioned in the previous section, you can apply the mask to various types of objects in Illustrator. In this section we will see how to create a mask and apply it to an artwork that was created previously. You can begin with the following example:

1. Open the Document Artwork_mask.ai, which includes an artwork to which we will apply the mask to hide the extra areas outside the document stage.
2. Select the Rectangle tool and create a rectangle over the artboard area.

FIG 10-2 The artwork without the mask applied to it

3. With the Selection tool, select the artwork and the mask rectangle. You can click Cmd+A (Ctrl+A in Windows) to select all the objects.
4. From the Object menu, choose Clipping Mask > Make.

FIG 10-3 The artwork after applying the clipping mask

> **Shortcut**
>
> You can apply the mask directly by pressing Cmd+7 (Ctrl+7 in Windows).

When we check how the layers are affected by applying the mask, we see that the layer that includes the rectangle that we used as a mask has become a mask clipping path, and the rest of the artwork layers have become a masked layer relative to the main one. In the figure below, you can see the original layer arrangement before and after applying the mask. Also, you can see that the mask's layer in the Layer panel appears underlined to identify it as the sublayer that includes the mask.

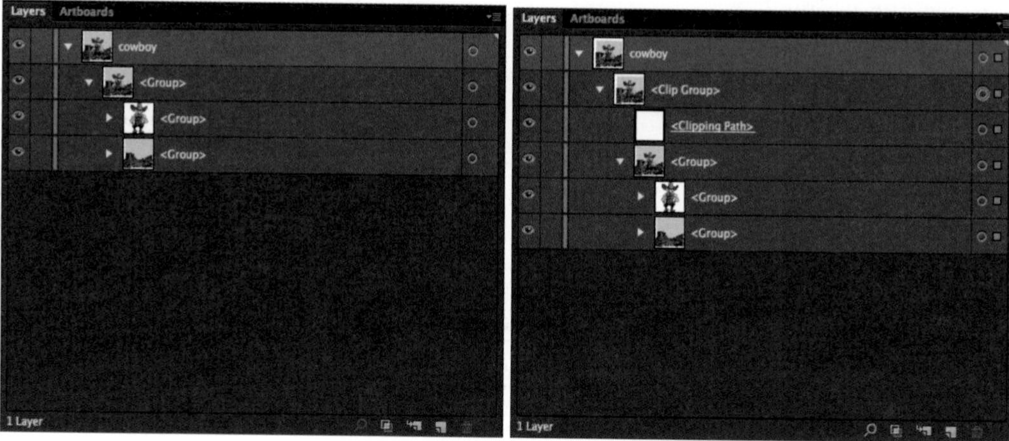

FIG 10-4 The original layer arrangement vs the masked layer arrangement in the Layer panel

While both the mask and the masked artwork become a group in the artboard, you can still edit the masked artwork by choosing Edit Content from the Object > Clipping Mask menu. This command allows you to edit the artwork under the mask, but what if we wanted to edit the mask itself? This is easy—all you need to do is double-click the clipping group that includes both the mask and the masked artwork. This action lets you access the clipping group isolated mode, similar to editing artwork. You can also right-click the clipping group and choose Isolated Selected Clipping Mask.

Based on steps 1–4 above, let us learn how to edit the mask and subsequently affect the viewable area of the artwork:

5. Double-click the clipping mask group that we created in the first steps.
6. Select the mask rectangle; it will appear as transparent without fill or strokes. Thus, you will need to select the rectangle path.
7. Change the size of the rectangle. For example, make it smaller.

8. Double-click outside the artwork to exit isolated mode.
9. Notice that the viewable area of the artwork becomes smaller due to the decrease in the mask dimensions.

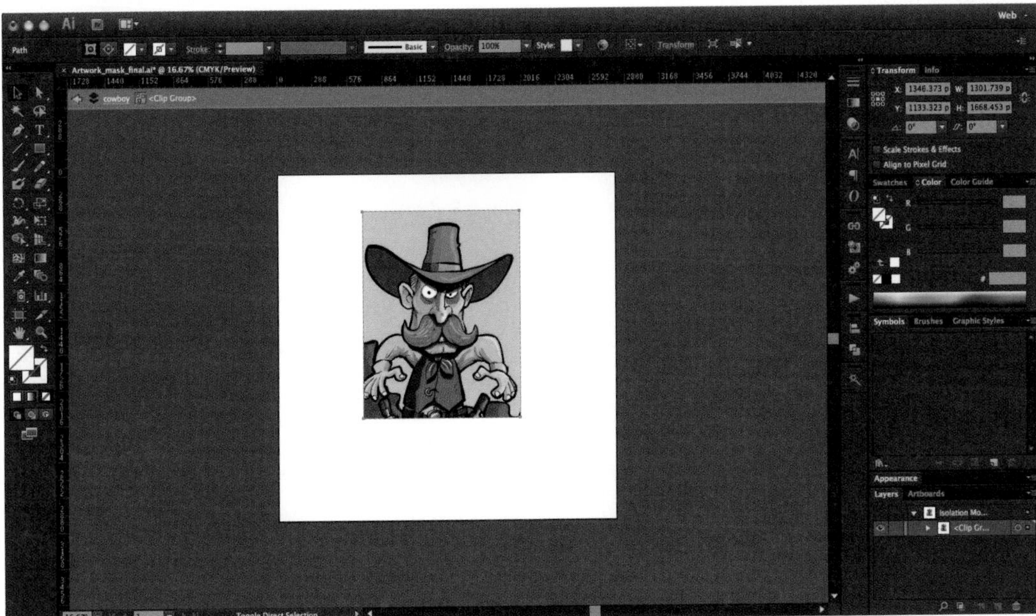

FIG 10-5 Decreasing the dimensions of the mask

> **Note**
>
> If you would like to release the mask and revert the artwork to its original status, you can remove the mask using the Release command from the Object > Clipping Mask menu when the mask is selected.

Applying Mask to Images

You can apply the mask to any imported image in an Adobe Illustrator document, similar to what we did in the artwork above. Working with masks with images is very helpful in Illustrator, as Illustrator does not provide tools to modify the image by removing parts of it. In the following example, we will see how to use the mask to separate an image from its background in Illustrator:

1. Open the document Image_mask_start.ai. This document includes an image to which we would like to apply the mask.
2. Select the Pen tool, or simply press the letter P on your keyboard.
3. Draw a path around the object that we would like to separate from the background.

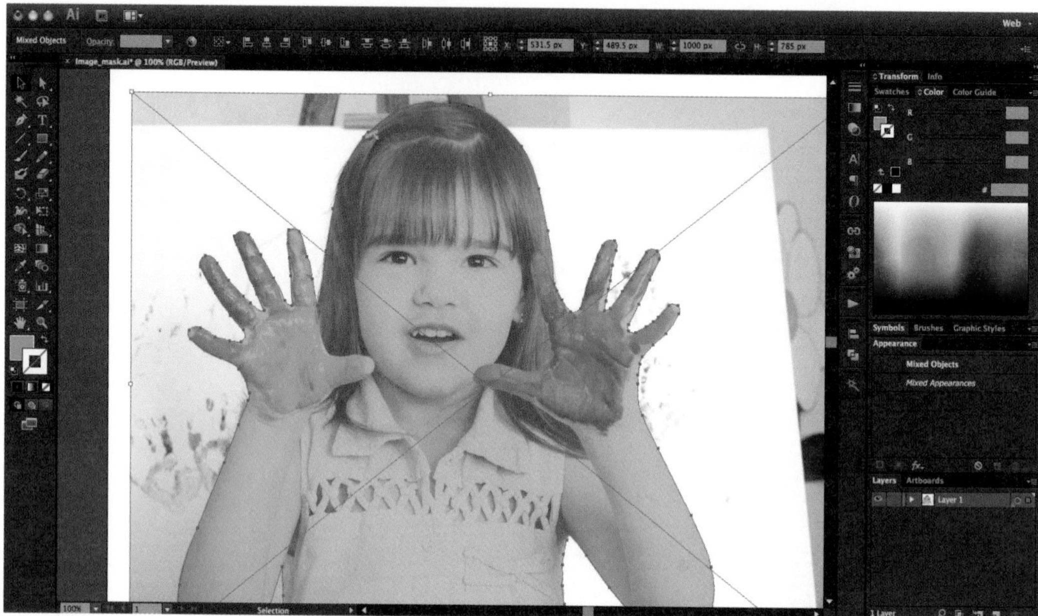

FIG 10-6 Drawing a path around the object in the image

4. Set the fill color for the path to white and the stroke to none, as we do not need a stroke for the mask.
5. With the Selection tool, select both the path and the image.
6. From the Object menu, choose Clipping Mask > Make.

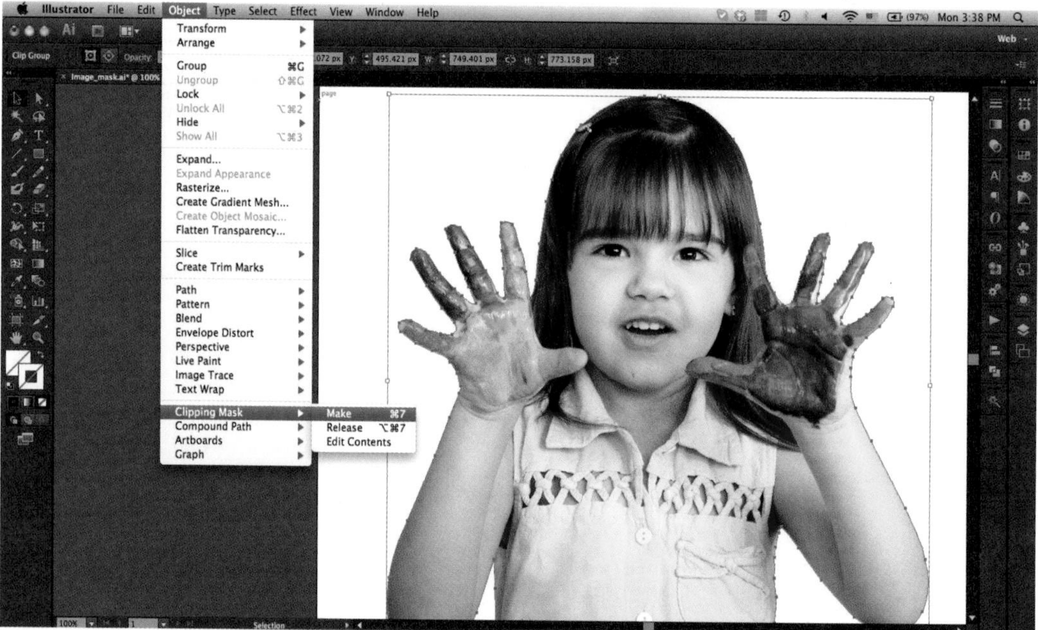

FIG 10-7 The final image after applying the mask

You can also create the mask from the Layer panel. When you have a number of objects in an Illustrator layer, you can select one object and click the Make/Release Clipping Mask icon from the Layer panel to convert it to a mask; the rest of the objects under it will become masked objects. We can apply this to the above example:

1. After creating the path that we will use as a mask in the above example, select it using the Selection tool.
2. From the Layer panel, click the Make/Release Clipping Mask icon. It is the second icon from the left in the panel bottom icons.

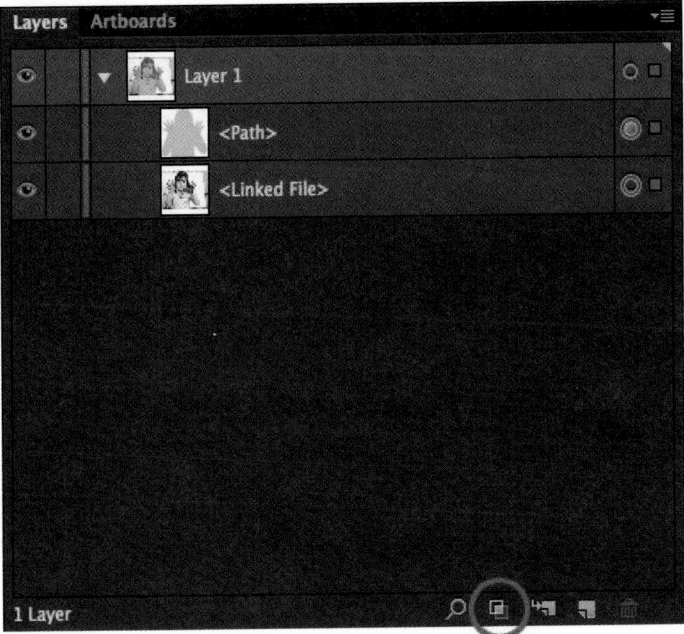

FIG 10-8 The Clipping Mask icon in the Layer panel

> **Note**
>
> It is also possible to draw inside a selected object using the Draw Inside command.

Working with Opacity Mask

In the above examples, we learned how to create a mask and apply it to artwork in Illustrator. But it is obvious that the masks we created are solid masks and their edges are sharp. How can we create a mask that includes soft edges or transparency? We can do this in a different place than the Object menu, as we will see in the example below:

1. Open the document Gradient_mask.ai; this document includes the image to which we will apply the mask.

2. Select the image and drag it to the New icon in the Layer panel.
3. Select the image on the layer that we just duplicated.
4. From the Object menu, choose Transform > Reflect.
5. In the dialog box, set the axis to horizontal and press OK.
6. Move the reflected image and place it at the bottom of the original image as shown in the figure below.
7. Decrease the height of the flipped image using the bounding box.

FIG 10-9 The reflected image placed under the original image

8. Select the rectangle tool and create a rectangle that covers the entire image duplicate.
9. Open the Gradient panel and apply a black to white gradient. Set the bottom color to black and the top to white.

FIG 10-10 The gradient rectangle above the reflected image

10. Select the gradient rectangle and the flipped image.
11. Open the Transparency panel. If it is not open, you can display it by choosing it from the Window panel.
12. Click the Make Mask button on the panel. This action will apply the gradient as an opacity mask on the image.

FIG 10-11 The opacity mask applied to the image

> **Note**
>
> You can release the mask by pressing the Release button in the Transparency panel.

When you apply the opacity mask using the Transparency panel, you can see that there are two thumbnails that appear on the panel: the left one is for the image or artwork, and the right one is for the mask applied to it. The Chain icon between both thumbnails causes any transformation to affect both the artwork and the mask.

In the following steps, we will try to modify the size of the mask using the mask thumbnail in the Transparency panel:

1. After creating the mask in the previous example, open the Transparency panel.
2. Click the mask thumbnail on the left.
3. Drag the mask boundary box to make it smaller. Notice that the revealed area of the image decreases with the mask size change.

In the next example, we will see another tip for creating a web banner with faded edges in Illustrator using the mask feature with the gaussion blur effect:

1. Open the document Blur_mask.ai. This document includes an image that we will use in our banner.

2. Select the Rectangle tool and create a rectangle as shown in the figure below; set the rectangle color to white.
3. From the Effects menu, choose Blur > Gaussion Blur.
4. In the Gaussion Blur dialog box, set the radius value to 10 pixels.

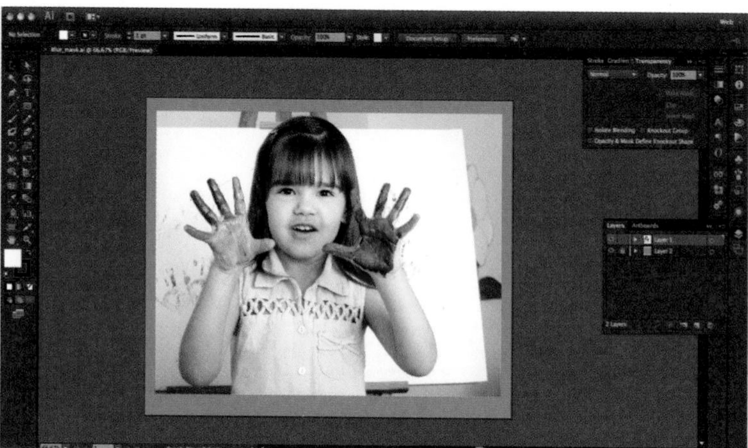

FIG 10-12 The rectangle with the blur effect applied to it

5. Select both the image and the blurred rectangle.
6. From the Transparency panel, click the Make Mask button.

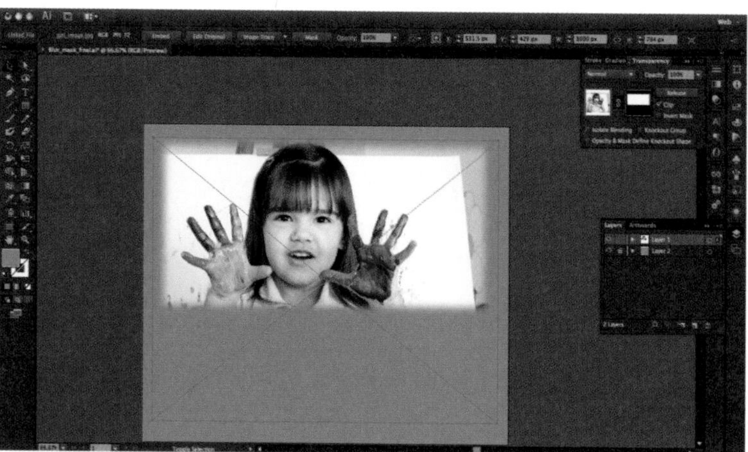

FIG 10-13 The final look for the banner with the blur mask applied to it

The transparency mask is one of the important features that many designers use frequently to build nondestructive blurred masks and gradient shadows on objects without the need to use other applications such as Photoshop.

Note

When you apply an opacity mask, the mask colors are interpreted to gray colors even if it is colored. These grays determine the level of opacity applied to the object.

The above examples show how we can use the mask feature to create practical artwork effects. You can start from there when you are trying your own ideas and learning how to use the mask feature.

Blends

The other topic that we will cover in this chapter is blends, which refers to the ability to blend the color between two shapes on the Illustrator stage. There are two methods to apply the blend effect. You can apply it using the Blend tool or you can apply it through the Blend commands in the Objects menu.

Blend can be applied to objects with different shapes and colors. Thus, it is more flexible than the gradient, which you can apply only to one object and with specific gradient flow styles. In the blend structure, you can edit the look and the feel of the blended objects, as we will see in the examples in this section. Let us learn more about blends and start using the Blend tool to learn how to apply the blend effect.

1. Open the document Gear_blend.ai. We created this gear object in Chapter 7.
2. Now, we will duplicate the gear shape. From the Object menu, choose Transform > Move.
3. In the Move dialog box, set the horizontal and vertical move to 30 pixels each, and click the Copy button.
4. Select the back gear and from the Color panel, set the color to R = 100, G = 0, and B = 140.

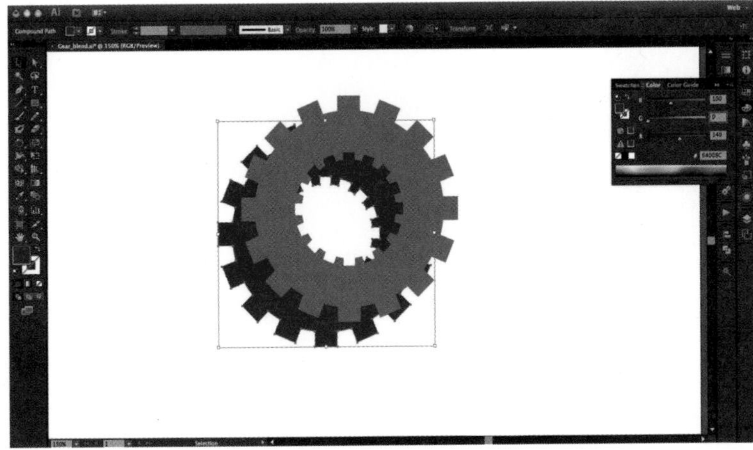

FIG 10-14 The front and back gear shapes

5. Select both gear shapes.
6. From the Tools panel, choose the Blend tool.
7. Click on the top gear shape, and click on the back gear shape.

FIG 10-15 The final look for gear with blend effect

As we mentioned, the blend effect gives you flexibility to edit the blend's structure. In the next steps, we will increase the depth of the gear extraction:

8. Select the Direct Select tool from the Tools panel.
9. Click to select the back gear shape. Make sure to click inside the gear path to select the whole path.
10. Drag the back gear a few pixels away from the front gear to see how the shape of the gear changes and how the blend changes with the distance

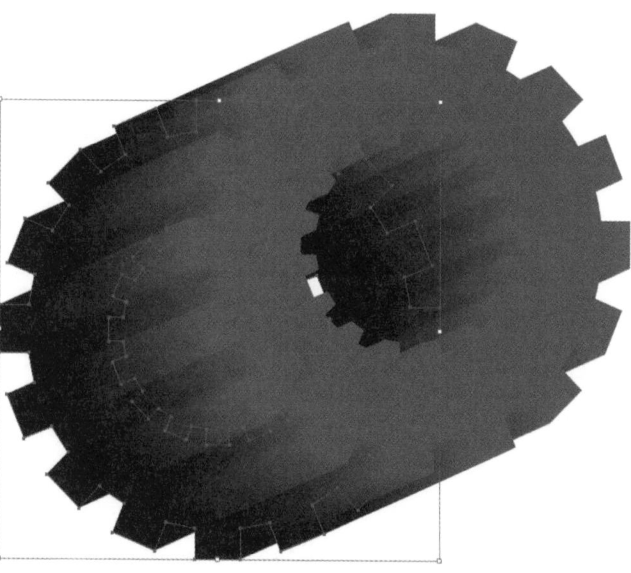

FIG 10-16 The gear shape after extending it

of the two gear shapes. You can also change the colors of the back gear to white or any color to see how the blend appearance changes.

The second method to create blends effect is through the Object > Blend menu. In some cases, such as applying a blend to thin paths, it is hard to apply the blend using the Blend tool. There is another way to apply the blend effect through the top menu. In the example below, we will use the blend from the top menu to apply a customizable blend effect that creates a green plant stem that can be edited later.

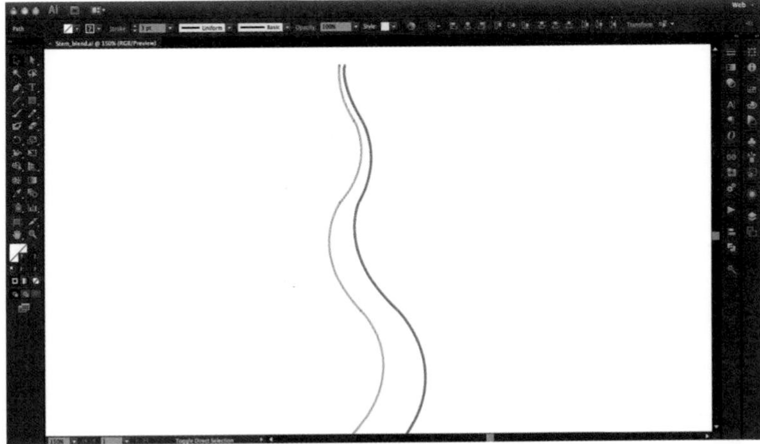

FIG 10-17 The stem paths on the document

1. Open the document Stem_blend.ai. This document includes two paths that represent the stem sides.
2. Using the Selection tool, select both paths.
3. From the Object menu, select Blend > Make.

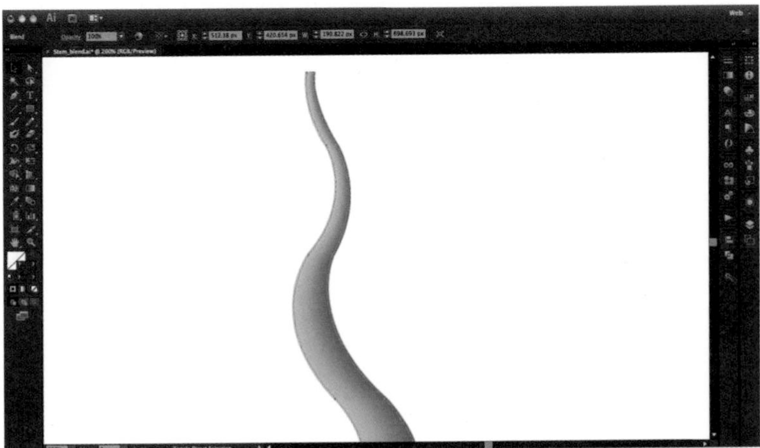

FIG 10-18 The stem shape after applying the blend effect

Note

You can edit the stem shape using the Direct Select tool and modify its anchor points and color. This will affect the blend as well.

Now, let us see another example for using blend in place of the regular blending. In this example, we will create a rainbow blending effect without the use of the gradient.

1. Open the document Rainbow_blending.ai.
2. Select the rainbow lines.
3. From the Object menu, select Blend > Make.

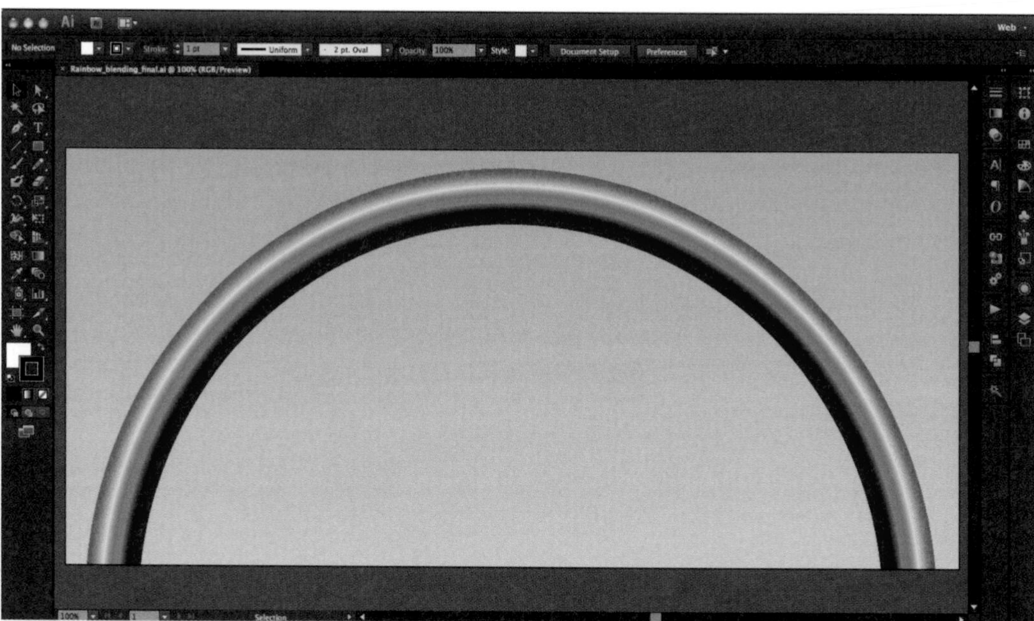

FIG 10-19 The rainbow with the blend effect applied to it

When you double-click the Blend tool in the Tools panel, you can set up more options for applying blending to the selected object through the Blend options. Spacing determines how the blend handles the intermediate transition between the first and last shapes, and it has the following options:

- Smooth Color creates a smooth blending effect between the start and the end shapes.
- Specific Steps lets you specify the number of the blending steps. A smaller number means a less smooth effect, while increasing the number of steps creates a more smooth effect.
- Specific Distance lets you determine the space between transition steps.

Orientation lets you set how the shapes are oriented to the blending path. From the Blend menu in the Object top menu, you can find more blending commands that can extend your experience with this effect, such as:

- Release removes the blending effect and reverts the shape to its initial state.
- Expand applies the blend to be part of the object. After expanding objects, you cannot revert to the original shapes status.
- Replace Spine changes the blending line direction to the blending effect. Select the blended objects and the new line and apply this command to have the blending follow the new object shape.
- Reverse Spine reverses the blending effect applied to the shape.
- Reverse Front to Back sends the front object to the back, which affects how the blending appears.

This chapter covered the blends features and how to use them to blend colors and objects in a comprehensive way that allows you to build more customized color blends and gradients. At the end we covered the blending modes and how they affect the overlapped shapes. The examples we provided in this chapter taught you how these features are used. You can start applying these features, along with other features, to build more complex artwork.

For examples pertaining to this chapter, visit www.illustratorfoundations.com.

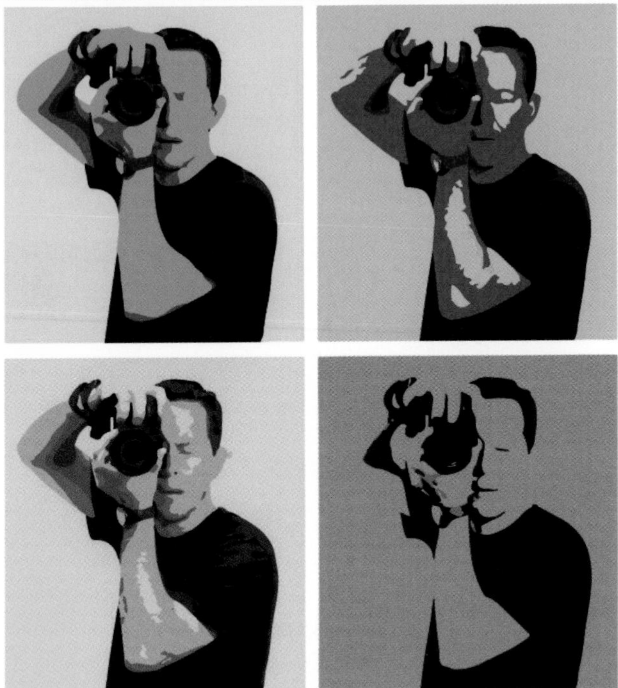

CHAPTER 11

Working with Images and Image Trace

As we mentioned in Chapter 1, distinguishing the graphic tools as vector-based or bitmap-based does not mean that each tool cannot handle the other type. Each type of tool can interact with both vector and bitmap images on different levels. For example, vector applications can import and use bitmap images, but they will not give you the full editing features that the bitmap applications do.

Both vector and bitmap images are important in the design process. While you are designing a web layout, you need bitmap images to add to the design and vector elements to draw the lines, curves, and layout. The same applies to other design projects, such as printing and video projects. While Adobe Illustrator is a comprehensive vector-based application, it gives you the ability to add bitmap images to your file, and edit and convert them through the amazing Image Trace feature. Adobe Illustrator supports most of the common bitmap formats, such as JPG, BMP, PNG, TIFF, PSDs, and so on.

When you would like to add bitmap images to Adobe Illustrator, there are two methods. The first is to open the image using the Open command from the File menu. This command will open the image in a new Illustrator document that holds the same image name. You can also drag the image to the Illustrator icon to open it.

FIG 11-1 Add image to illustrator using Open command; the image is imported in a document with the same image name

The second method is through the Place command, through which you can add an image to your Illustrator document without the need to open it in a new file. To place an image into the document, follow these steps:

1. From the File menu, choose New to open a new Illustrator document.
2. From the File menu, choose the Place command to add a new image.
3. Navigate to Chapter 11 on the companion website that accompanies the book (http://www.illustratorfoundations.com) and select the image Apple.jpg. Click OK to insert the image to the document.

FIG 11-2 Using the Place command to insert image to the document

Links Panel

Inserting images into an Adobe Illustrator document does not mean that the image is included with the document. Actually, the image is linked to the external source for the image, and what you see is a reference for the image.

> **Note**
>
> When you are working with bitmap images in Illustrator, make sure to save the images in the same location as the Illustrator file to keep them linked to the file; this way they will not get lost when transferring files between computers and clients.

Unlike saving the bitmap images inside the Illustrator document, referencing an image from an external source can help reduce the document size and therefore the resources required to open and work with the document. Linking to an external reference for the image is very important, especially when you are working with a large Illustrator document that has a lot of bitmap images in it.

One of the other benefits of using linkage images is that you can edit and replace the images without the need to do it manually in the Illustrator file, which is especially useful when you have a large document with images. Through the Links panel, you can handle images that are externally linked and replace them without the need to touch the image itself. The Links panel includes most of the required feature that allow you to work with image links, as we will see below.

FIG 11-3 The Links panel in Illustrator

In the Links panel, you can find a list of the images that are used in the Illustrator document. You can double-click each image to find more information about it, such as the image name, location, size, format, the changes applied to it in Illustrator, and so on.

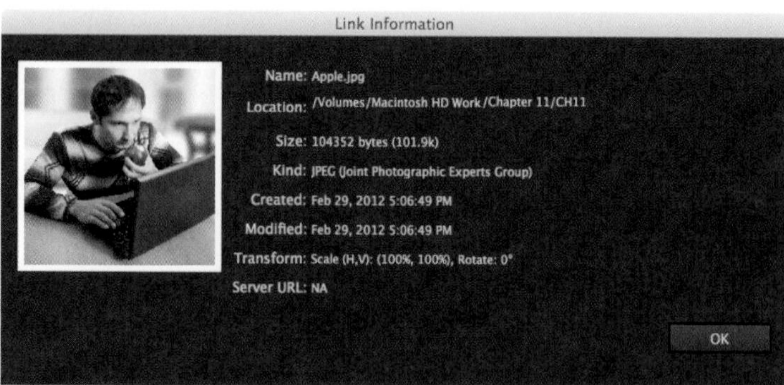

FIG 11-4 The image information in the Links panel

When you select one of the image's links, you will find the bottom icons become active. These are discussed next, from left to right. The Relink icon allows you to change the image linkage. When you click on this icon, it lets you navigate the image URL, so you can change the link for the image by browsing the new image path, and Illustrator will update the image in the document with the new one. This can save you time and prevent messing up with the document design, especially when the new image has the same properties as the previous one.

The Go To Link icon lets you navigate to the selected image in the document—for example, if you would like to select or find a specific image. When you select the image from the Links panel and click Go To Link from the bottom of the menu, Illustrator finds and selects the image in the document. The Update Link icon checks if there is a change in the linked images. You can click on this icon to make sure that the image is synchronized with the original source.

The Edit Original icon opens the original image in your system's default image viewer in order to edit it. When you finish editing the image and save it, a message appears in Illustrator to lets you know that there have been changes to the image and asks if you would like to apply the changes. When you accept the changes, they are applied directly to the image, but if you do not accept them, a yellow alert rectangle appears next to the image to let you know that this image has unapplied changes. Then, you can click the Update Link icon to apply the changes to the image in Illustrator.

Note

When the original image is deleted or renamed, a red alert appears next to the image in the Links panel.

In the following example, we will use the above features to add and modify an image in a poster design:

1. Open the file Poster.ai from the Chapter 11 folder on the companion website associated with the book; this is a poster that includes a design with a place to add our image.

2. From the File menu, choose Place and navigate to Poster_image01.jpg from the same folder with the poster design.
3. Click OK and place the image to the left of the text and aligned to the top of the poster.
   We can replace the image through the Links panel as follows:
4. Open the Links panel. If it does not appear in the Illustrator workspace, you can open it from the Window panel.
5. Select the image Poster_image01.jpg from the panel.
6. Click the Relink icon from the bottom right of the Links panel. Navigate in the Chapter 11 folder to Poster_image02.jpg and click OK.
7. Notice that the old image is replaced with the new one in both the Links panel and the poster design folder.

FIG 11-5 The poster with the image placed in it

Along with the above features, the Links panel includes more features in the panel context menu that you can access by clicking on the top right of the panel. The menu includes the following:

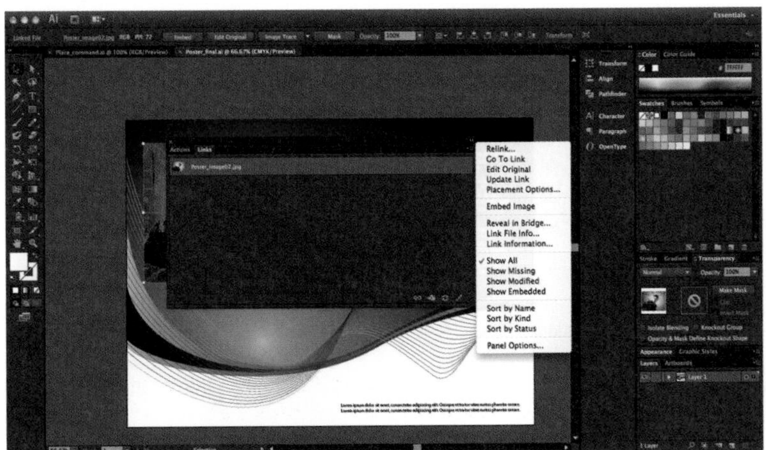

FIG 11-6 The Links panel context menu

Placement Options lets you set how the image is updated or replaced in the bounding box. When you click the Placement Options command from the context menu, a dialog box appears to let you choose from different options.

Note

You need to have the placed image selected in order to have the commands in the context menu activated.

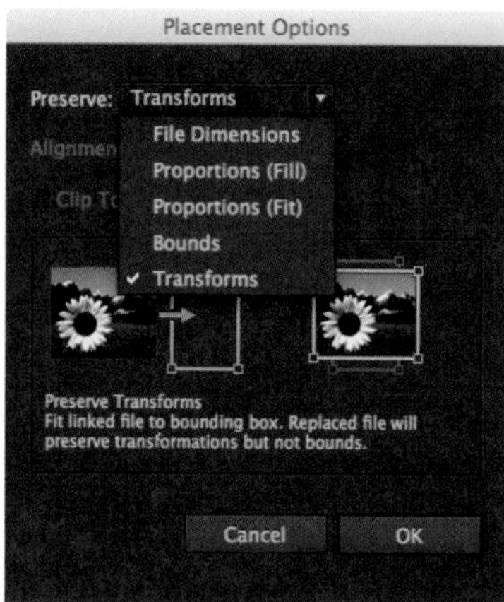

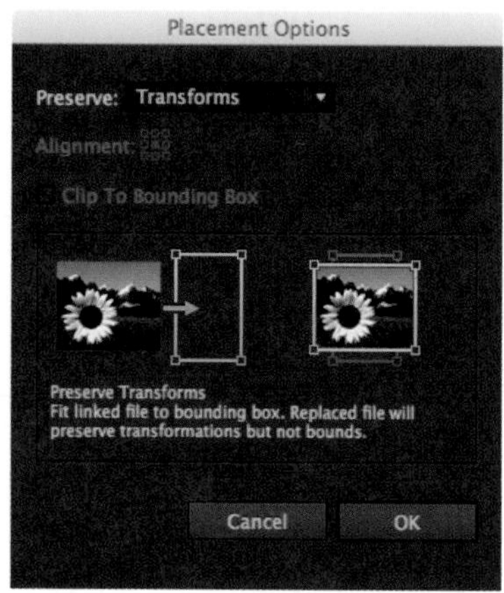

FIG 11-7 The Placement Options dialog box

The Reserve drop-down list lets you set how the image is placed inside the bounding box and includes the following options:

- File Dimensions preserves the original image dimensions. Thus, the image appears in its original size even when you change the bounding box dimensions.
- Proportions (Fill) sets the image to fill the bounding box and preserves its original proportions as well.
- Proportions (Fit) resizes the image to be inside the bounding box while preserving its proportions.
- Bounds resizes the image to make it fit within the bounding box.
- Using Transforms, the image fits within the bounding box; the file replacement will preserve only the transformation of the image.

FIG 11-8 The different Placement options from left to right (File Dimensions, Proportions FIll, Proportions Fit, Bounds, and Transforms)

Under the Preserve drop-down list is the Alignment option, which allows you to set the alignment of the placed image in the bounding box. Just click on either of the points to set the image alignment to this point. Clip To Bounding Box is a useful option because it clips the image parts that flow outside the bounding box and shows only what is included in the box. This makes the bounding box act like a mask for the placed image.

After the Placement Options command, you will find the Embed Image command. As we mentioned earlier, images placed in Illustrator are linked to their external original sources. This command gives you the option to break this linkage and embed the image in your Illustrator document. This command is helpful when you are sending final Illustrator files to end production, such as the printing house, and you would like to make sure that the linked images can be found in their links paths and are not lost. When you click on this command, an icon appears next to the image in the Links panel to indicate that the image is embedded in the document.

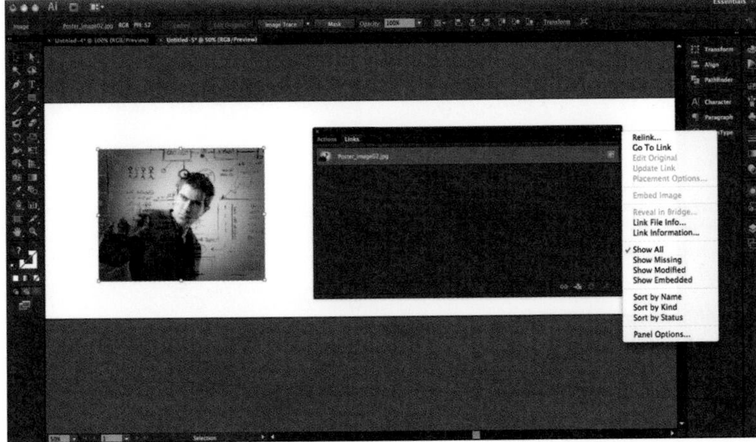

FIG 11-9 The embedded image in the Links panel

The Show section in the context menu lets you filter the images in the Links panel as follows:

- Show All displays all the images regardless of status.
- Show Missing displays only the images with missing links.
- Show Modified displays only the images that have been modified.
- Show Embedded displays only the images that have been embedded into the document.

The Sort section lets you arrange the images by name, kind, or status. In the bottom of the Links panel context menu, you can find the panel options.

> **Note**
>
> When you select an image on the stage, you can find the Embed and Edit Original buttons in the top Control panel.

Image Trace

We mentioned in Chapter 1 that, compared with bitmap images, vector graphics are easier to scale and modify without losing quality. Also, vector graphics give a more artistic look than bitmap images do. Therefore, many designers may like to convert bitmap images to vector graphics or vector lines. This can be done in two ways; the first is through manual trace. In this method, you use the Adobe Illustrator drawing tools to draw over the bitmap and recreate it from scratch. Of course, this method is effort- and time-consuming, and may not produce the best results.

The second method is through the Image Trace feature. This feature has been added to Illustrator since version CS2 (version 12) and has been revamped in CS6. It allows you to convert any bitmap image to become vector based by using automatic tracing for the image based on various types of trace presets and settings, as we will see next. You can change the image trace settings from the presets in the drop-down list, or you can choose the Custom option to set customized options.

FIG 11-10 The Image Trace Presets options

When you select an image, you will notice that the Image Trace button becomes active on the top Control bar. When you click on this button, it applies the default tracing option. Next to the Image Trace button is a small arrow that allows you to open the Presets drop-down list. The list includes a variety of commonly used Image Trace options that you can apply just by clicking them. You can also click on the Image Trace button to apply the default trace settings. The presets include the following options:

- Default traces the image based on the default tracing option.
- High Fidelity Photo creates a traced photo with high details to simulate the original bitmap photo.
- Low Fidelity Photo creates a traced photo with low details and curves.
- 3 Color traces the image and produces a 3-color-traced vector image.
- 6 Color traces the image and produces a 6-color-traced vector image.
- 16 Color traces the image, and the final result includes a maximum of 16 colors. This is one of the options that you can use to convert the image to an artistic-style image.
- Shades of Gray converts the image to a grayscale image with different varieties of black, white, and gray colors.
- Black and White Logo converts the image to only black and white colors.
- Sketched Art creates sketch-style images with a black-and-white color drawing style.
- Silhouette converts the image to a silhouette like a vector image.
- Line Art converts the image to lines.
- Technical drawing creates a technical-style image with black and white colors and zero blur effects.

Note

Large bitmap images may take a long time to trace, especially when you try to produce a very detailed trace of the image.

FIG 11-11 From left to right, Image Trace results using the High Fidelity Photo, 3 Color trace, and Silhouette options

When you apply any of the above Image Tracing options, the image is converted to a vector-based image, and the Control panel in the top displays the different tracing options and settings. The available options are as follows, from left to right. The Presets drop-down list gives you easy access to the available Image Trace presets, similar to those we discussed earlier. You can use the Image Trace panel to create your own custom image tracing settings; we will discuss its different options in the next section.

The View list lets you choose how you would like to view the image on the stage. When you trace the image, you have the option to view it as any of the following:

- Tracing Results lets you view only the traced results of the image.
- Tracing Results with Outline displays an outline for the different color areas in the image.
- Outline shows the results as only outlines for the different color areas.
- Outline with the Source Image shows the original image and the outline for the different color areas.
- Source Image displays only the original image without the traced result or the outline.

Image Trace Panel

You can reach the Image Trace panel from the Control panel for the traced image or from the Window menu. The Image Trace panel includes all the settings and values that you can play around with to change how the image is traced. With the Preview checkbox selected, you can view your changes immediately and see how close your image is to your desired tracing effect.

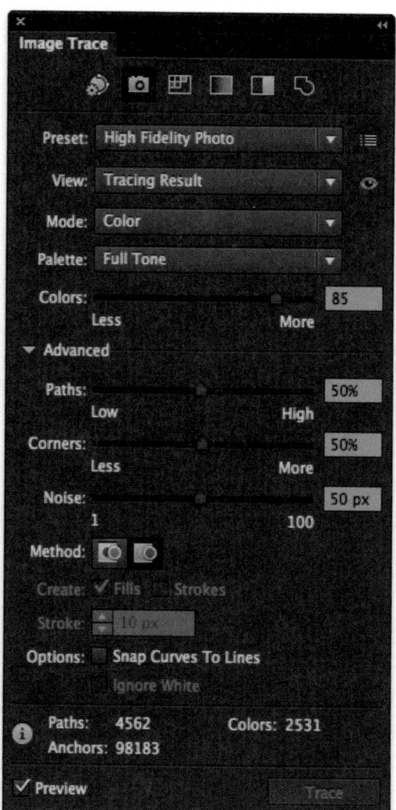

FIG 11-12 The Image Trace panel

At the top of the panel, there are icons that represent six different main settings: Autocolor, High Color, Low Color, Grayscale, and Outline. In the Presets drop-down list, you can find more presets from Image Trace. When you create your own settings, they appear as Custom presets in the Presets list. Then you can give your presets a name and save them from the context menu that appears when you click the icon next to the Presets list. You can also delete or rename current presets.

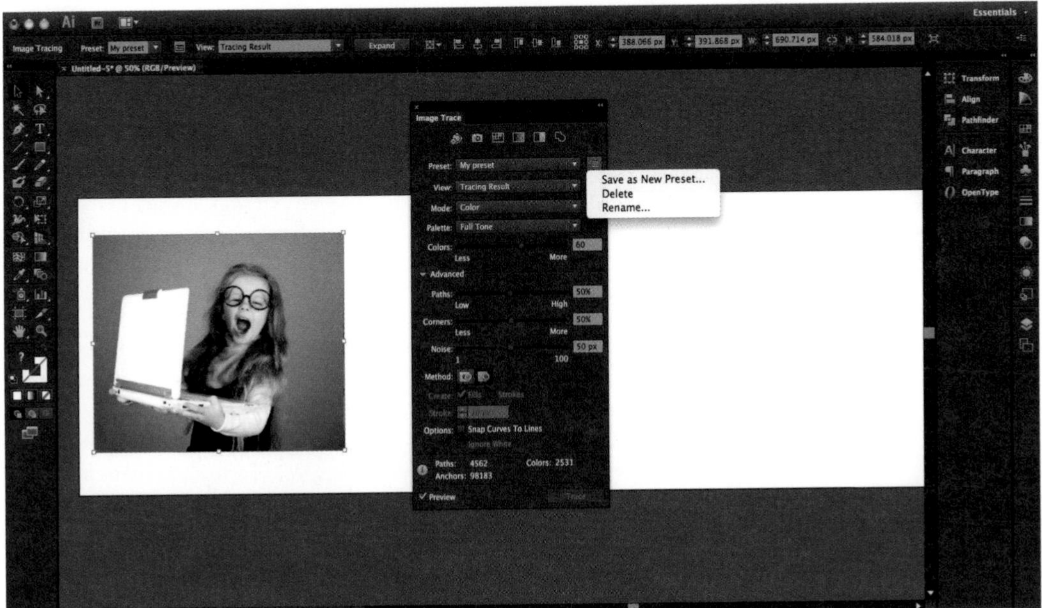

FIG 11-13 The Presets context menu

The View drop-down list is similar to the one that we discussed earlier in the top Control panel in the image trace section. Next to the View options, you can find a small eye, which is important because it lets you preview the original source image and see how the image changed based on the trace settings. Under the View list, you can find the Mode list, which allows you to choose the tracing to be in color, grayscale, or black and white.

The Color option means that the traced image will be in color. The number of colors is set based on another drop-down list number. The colors can be automatic, limited, full color, or document library. The Document Library option lets you choose the colors that will be used in the traced image based on the color groups or the colors in the Swatches panel. The Document Library option can produce very artistic effects, especially when you can use a variety of swatches groups by adding them through the Swatch Libraries icon in the Swatches panel, which was covered in Chapter 4.

FIG 11-14 The Image Trace set to color (document library), grayscale, and black and white

When you select any of these choices, you can set the number of colors and the level of black and white you would like to apply for the traced image. The more colors or gray levels you use, the more details appear in the image. Under the above section in the Image Trace panel, you can click the advanced arrow to expand the panel and display more tracing options that affect the final traced image:

- The paths value sets how tight the traced paths are from the original traced areas. A lower value creates paths that are tight to the traced areas, and a higher value creates less tight paths.
- The corners value sets how the corners of the traced areas will look. A high value means more curved corners, while a low value means sharp edges.
- The noise value tells the Trace option to ignore pixels with a minimum pixel size. For example, if the noise value is set to 10, areas that are 10 pixels or less will be ignored.
- Method sets how the paths of the traced areas interact with each other. They can be either cutout or stacked to each other.
- When you trace the image as an outline, you can use the Create Fill and Stroke and Stroke Size options to set the fill and stroke for the created areas.
- Snap Curves to Lines converts the little curved lines to straight lines.
- Ignore White Areas is a useful option, especially when you would like to ignore the white background for the object and replace the white with a transparent background. This option is not preferred for images that have objects with many white areas.

The End section of the Image Trace panel includes information about the created vector object, such as the number of paths, colors, and anchor points.

After we get familiar with different Image Trace and Image Trace panel options, let us follow this quick example, which shows how to use these different effects to convert a bitmap image to an artistic-style vector graphic:

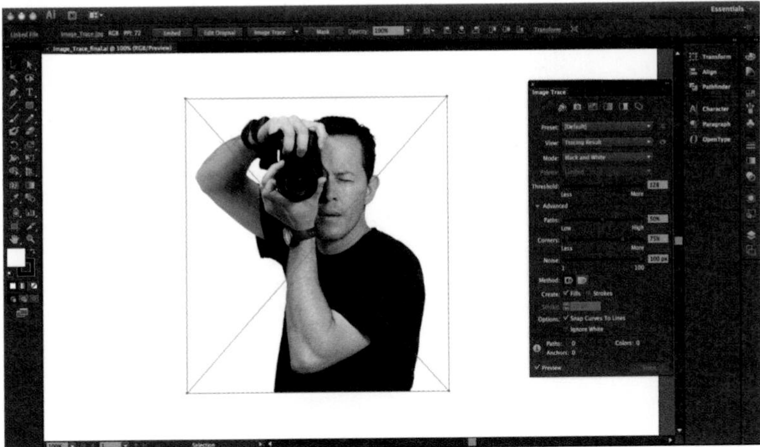

FIG 11-15 The bitmap image placed in the document

1. Open the document Image_Trace.ai. This file includes a placed photograph for a man taking a photo. The current photograph does not have a very artistic look. So, we will convert this image to a vector image and give it a more creative look.
2. While the image is selected, open the Image Trace panel from the Window menu.
3. In the panel, click the Low Color icon at the top. Notice that the image has converted to a vector image, but is still not as artistic as we want.

FIG 11-16 The image traced using the Low Color preset

4. In the Mode list, make sure that Color is selected.
5. From the Palette list, choose Document Library.
6. Open the Color list and check the current color groups. You will find there are few, and we need to add more of them to experience different effects through the Swatches panel.

7. Go to the Swatches panel; if it is closed, you can choose it from the Window menu.
8. Click the Swatch Libraries menu icon from the bottom left of the Swatches panel.
9. Navigate to the Kids Stuff library; it will open in a new panel.
10. Choose the Rainbow group and add it to the Swatches panel by dragging it to the panel or simply by clicking on it. It will appear in the panel as a new swatches group.

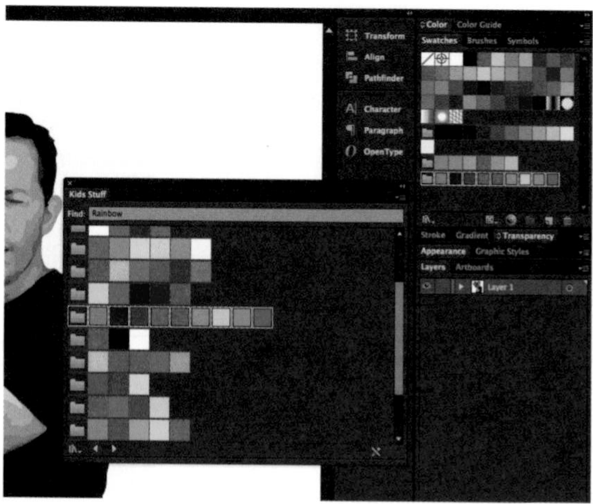

FIG 11-17 The rainbow swatches group

11. Now, go back to the Image Trace panel and make sure that the image is still selected.
12. Open the Color list again. Under it, notice that the new swatches group has been added to the list.
13. Choose the newly added swatch, Rainbow.
14. Expand the Advanced section by clicking on the advanced arrow.

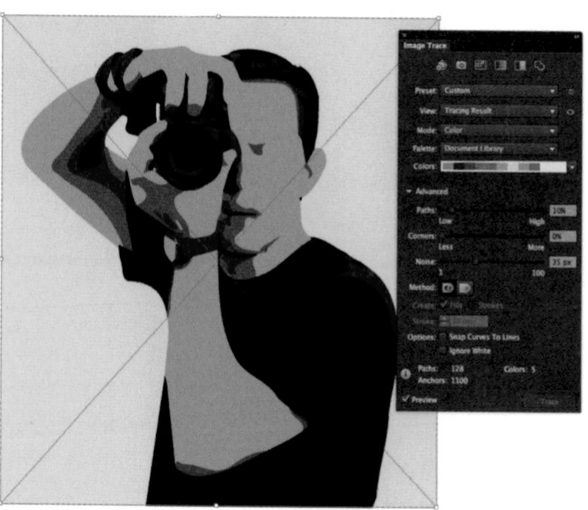

FIG 11-18 The traced image with applying the rainbow swatches group

15. Set the paths value to 10%; this will make the paths of the traced areas smoother.
16. Set the corners to 0%.
17. Set the noise to 35% to avoid the small areas being traced.
18. From the Control panel, click Expand to convert the image object to editable paths.
19. Repeat the above steps with different swatches group. The final results should look like the figure below.

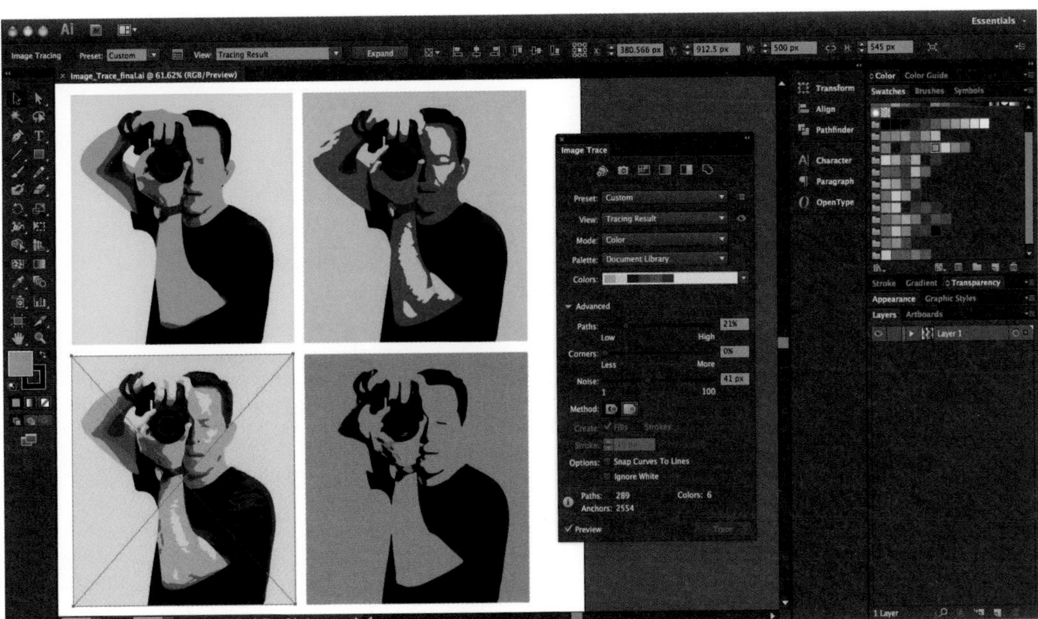

FIG 11-19 The final look for the traced image with different swatches groups

> **Note**
>
> If you want to remove the trace settings and return to the original image, you can do this from the Object menu by choosing Image Trace > Release.

Bitmap images are important elements in our design, and Adobe Illustrator allows us to import and work with images, as we have seen in this chapter. We also learned about the Image Trace option, which allows you to convert images into vector artwork with different settings and options. You can try using this feature with different images to explore the available vector results and artistic effects.

For examples pertaining to this chapter, visit www.illustratorfoundations.com.

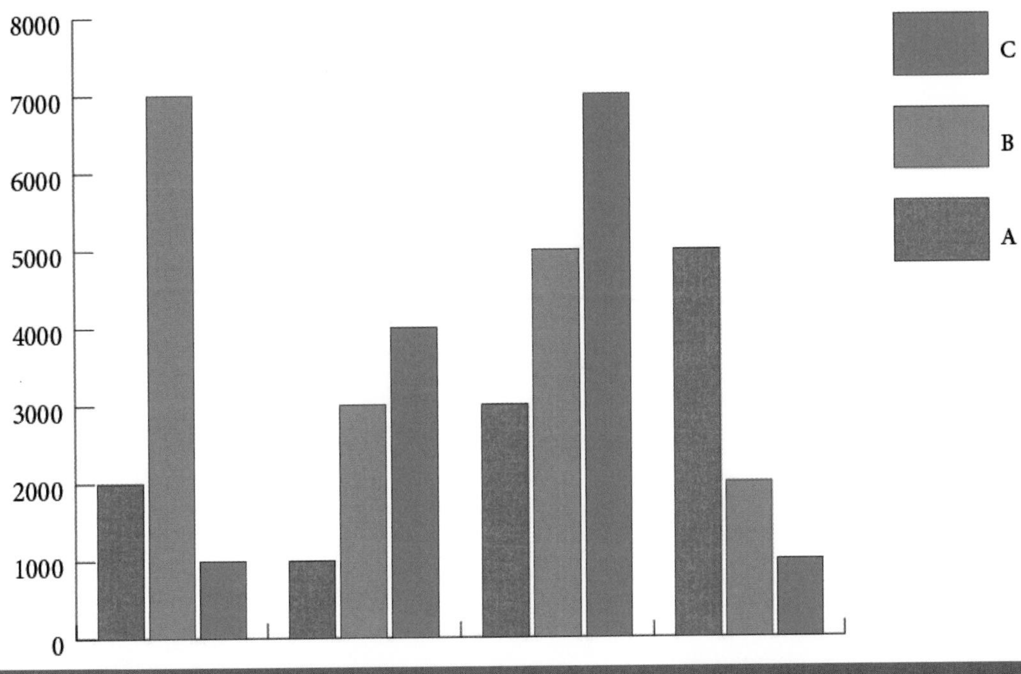

CHAPTER 12

Symbols and Graphs

As we have seen so far, Adobe Illustrator provides you with a comprehensive set of tools and features that help you build artwork from scratch or by using imported resources. However, the design process does not always depend on building elements from scratch. In some designs, such as web layouts, the designer can use elements such as buttons, banners, and separators again and again.

Creating these repeated elements from scratch consumes effort and time that can be allocated to more creative tasks. Thus, Illustrator provides symbols as reusable assets for repeated objects, as we will see later in the Working with Symbols section. Also, we will cover a useful element in Illustrator: graphs. Graphs allow you to create analytic graphs based on numerical values. They can be used as helpful tools to add diagrams to your design. In this chapter, we will cover these two object types and see how to work with them and adjust their settings.

Working with Symbols

Symbols are commonly used in different graphic applications, as the applications let you save your artwork in a library of artworks, and every time you need a specific artwork, all you need to do is to drag it onto the stage. When you drag a symbol onto the artboard, you are actually dragging an alias of it, which Illustrator calls an instance. So, the source is kept in the Symbols library, and every change or update done in the source symbol affects the symbol instances inside the document.

This concept does not save you the time and effort of creating the artwork, but it helps you to easily update and modify all the repeated elements in the document by editing the source symbol so that the changes are applied to the rest of the instances in the document. As we introduce the concept behind the symbols, let us move forward to see how to use the Symbols panel in Illustrator and achieve the aim of the symbol concept.

Converting Artwork to Symbols

In order to be able to benefit from the symbol's advantages, you need to convert your artwork into a symbol and add it to the Symbols panel. There are two methods to convert artwork into symbols. The first method is as easy as dragging the artwork to the Symbols panel. When you drag the artwork, a plus icon appears on the object while dragging to let you know that this object will be added to the panel.

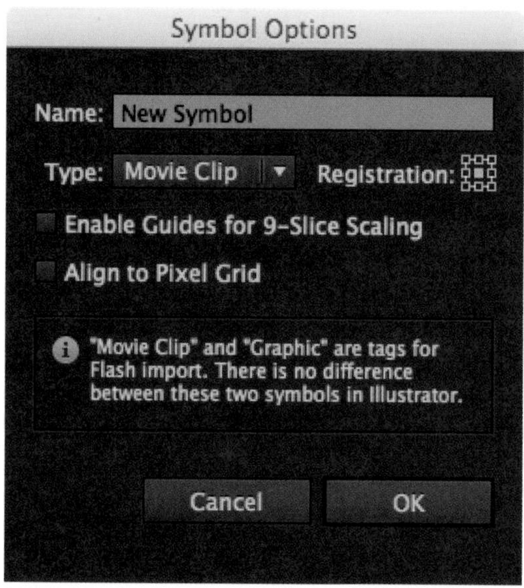

FIG 12-1 The Symbol Options dialog box

When you add the artwork to the Symbols panel, the Symbol Options dialog box appears to set up the symbol properties as follows:

- Name lets you add the name of the symbol; it is useful to add a proper name for better file arrangement.
- Using the Type option, you can choose the symbol to be either graphic or movie clip. This option is useful when you export the document to Flash. Adobe Flash can read the symbols imported from Illustrator as graphic or

movie clip symbols. These types do not affect your work in Illustrator; they are helpful only when exporting to Flash.

- Registration lets you set the center point for the symbol. You can click on any of the nine small boxes to set the center point to the selected point.
- Enable Guide for 9-Slice Scaling is useful when creating components that you need to scale proportionally. Each symbol is divided into nine parts. When you scale the object, it does not get distorted and preserves the artwork proportion.
- Align to Pixel Grid forces the symbol to be aligned to pixels. This option is useful when saving the layout as bitmap to make sure that there are any distortions in some lines as we covered in Chapter 7.

When you click the OK button, you will notice that the artwork turns to a symbol and appears in the Symbols panel preview thumbnails.

The other way to convert artwork to a symbol is through the Symbols panel as follows:

1. Create a new Illustrator document.
2. Select the Star tool from the Tools panel.
3. Draw a star object on the artboard, and change its fill and stroke color.
4. Open the Symbols panel.
5. From the panel bottom icons, click the New Symbol icon, the second icon from the right.
6. The Symbol Options dialog box appears; add a name for the symbol and click OK.

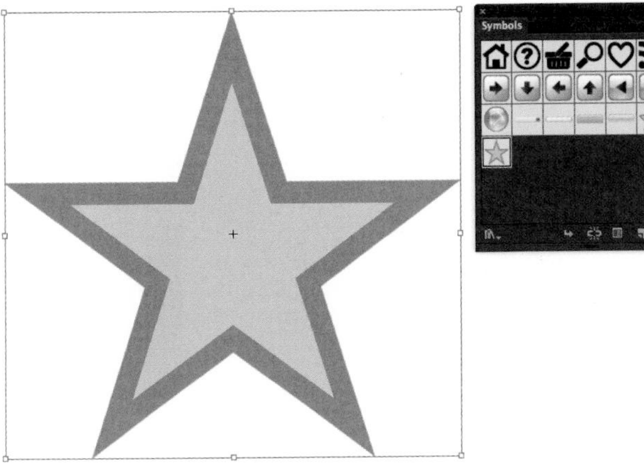

FIG 12-2 The new star symbol appears in the Symbols panel

In addition to the above New Symbol icon in the Symbols panel, the bottom icons let you do the following:

- Delete the symbol from the panel. When you click the Delete button, an alert box appears to let you choose to delete the symbol and its instances or delete the symbol and expand its instances to ordinary artwork.

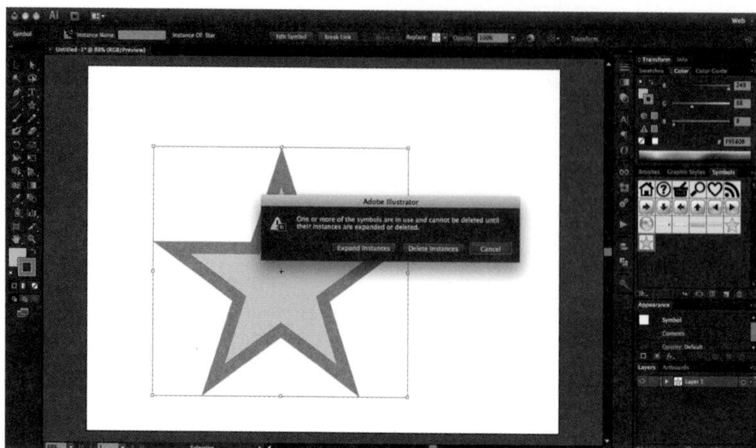

FIG 12-3 The alert message before deleting symbols

- The Symbol Option icon opens the Symbol dialog box that we covered earlier.
- In some cases, you would like to break the relation between the symbol and its instances on the stage. By clicking Break Link to Symbol, the stage copies of the symbol become unrelated to it and are not affected by any changes that happen to the symbol.
- Place Symbol Instance adds a new copy of the symbol on the stage.
- Illustrator comes with built-in symbols that you can use in your design and artwork. Click Symbol Library Menu to open the Symbols libraries and choose any library to open and use its symbols.

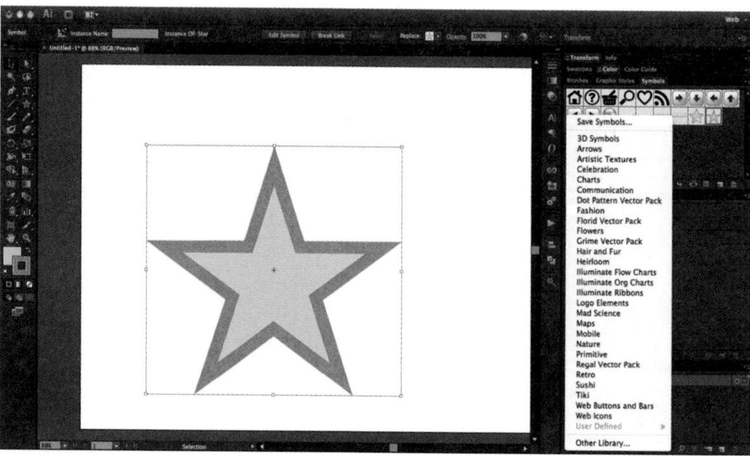

FIG 12-4 The Symbols libraries from the Symbols panel

Note

In the Libraries list, you can choose Save Symbols to save the current library as an Adobe Illustrator (AI) document, and you can choose Other Libraries to open external symbols libraries.

Modifying Symbols

Symbols artwork can be easily edited, and any modifications applied to the symbol are reflected in its instances in the Illustrator document. For example, if you have a symbol that is used five times in your design, the changes that you apply to the source symbol are applied to the five instances in the design.

To edit a symbol in the Symbols panel, you can double-click on it or choose Edit Symbol from the panel context menu. When you edit the symbol, Illustrator enters symbol isolate mode, similar to the rest of the artwork editing. When you finish the modifications and return to the main artboard, you will notice that the symbol changes are applied to the rest of the instances in the document.

In the following example, we will learn how to edit symbols in the Symbols panel:

1. Open the document Edit_symbol.ai. This document includes two custom symbols that are on the artboard.
2. Select one of the symbols in the library and double-click it.
3. In the symbol isolate mode, edit the symbol shape. You can change the color, for example.

> **Note**
>
> You can edit symbols directly from the artboard by double-clicking on them.

FIG 12-5 Editing symbols in the stage

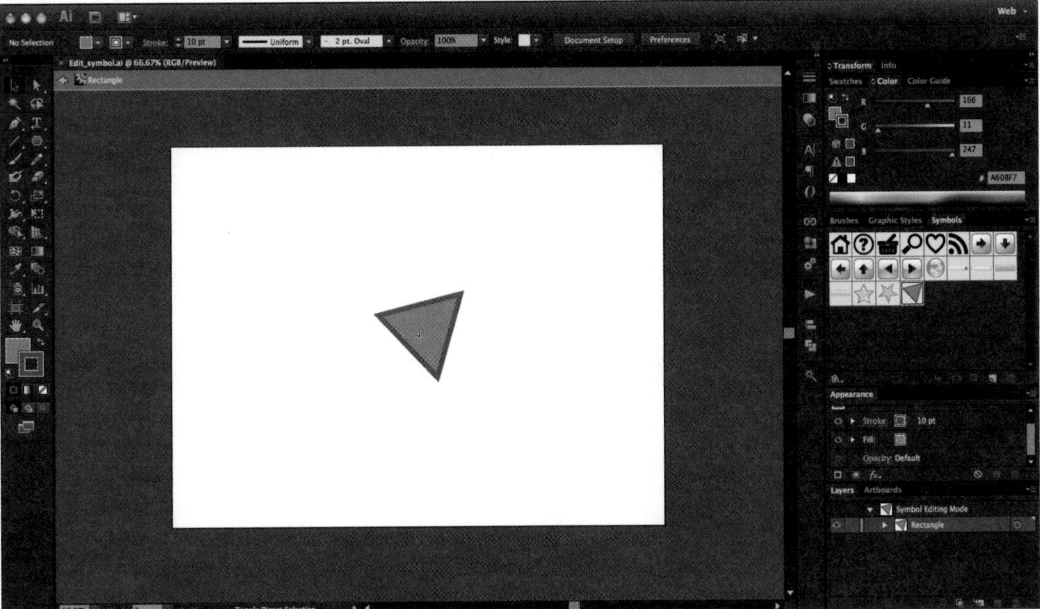

Notice that the rest of the symbols on the stage got the same color changes as the main symbol.

There is another method to edit symbols, through the Redefine Symbol command. This command allows you to replace the symbol from the library with another artwork selected on the artboard; we will continue with the above example:

4. Make sure the Edit_symbol.ai is open.
5. Create a new shape on the artboard and select it.
6. Select the symbol to which you would like to apply the changes.
7. From the Symbol panel context menu, choose Redefine Symbol.

Notice that the symbol on the artboard gets updated with the new modified shape of the symbol. Now, let us see a practical example of what we learned above to create a web layout menu that includes menu links with similar backgrounds:

1. Open the document Layout_symbols.ai. This document includes a web layout with one button at the menu. We will convert this button to a symbol and repeat and modify to create a web menu.
2. Select the first menu item background and drag it to the Symbols panel.
3. The Symbols Options dialog box appears. Write the name of the symbol as "menu background" and keep the rest of the settings the same. Click OK.
4. Drag the menu background to the stage to create the rest of the layout menu backgrounds as shown in the figure below.

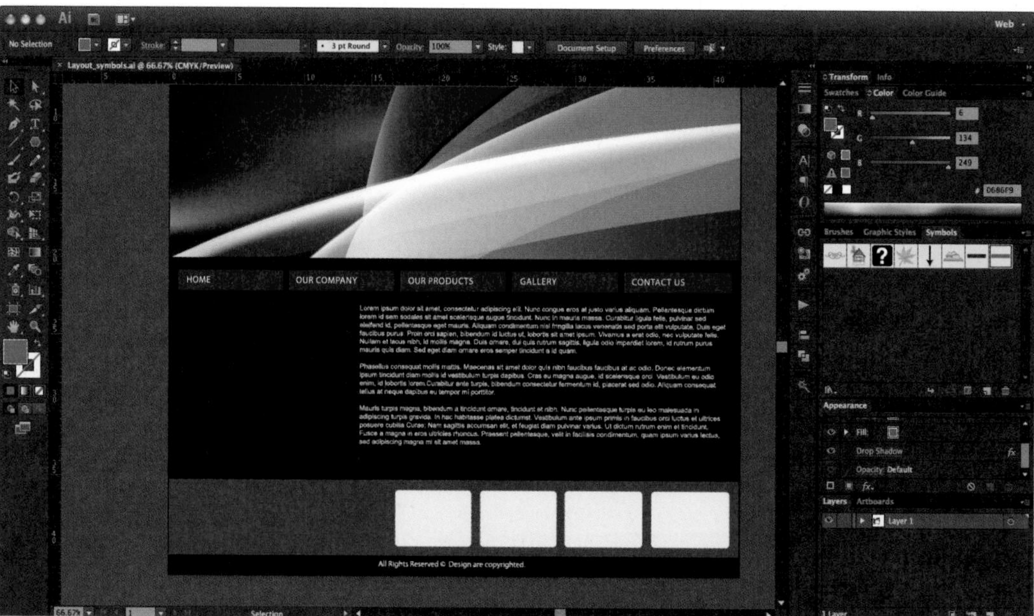

FIG 12-6 The layout with the horizontal menu

We have now created the horizontal menu, and will duplicate the menu background symbol to create the vertical menu, as follows:

5. Select the Menu Background symbol from the Symbols panel.
6. Open the panel context menu, choose Duplicate Symbol, and add a new name for the new symbol.
7. Double-click the symbol in the panel to enter its isolated mode.
8. Change the color of the menu background, and exit isolated mode.
9. From the Symbols menu, drag the new symbol into the layout and arrange it as shown in the figure below.

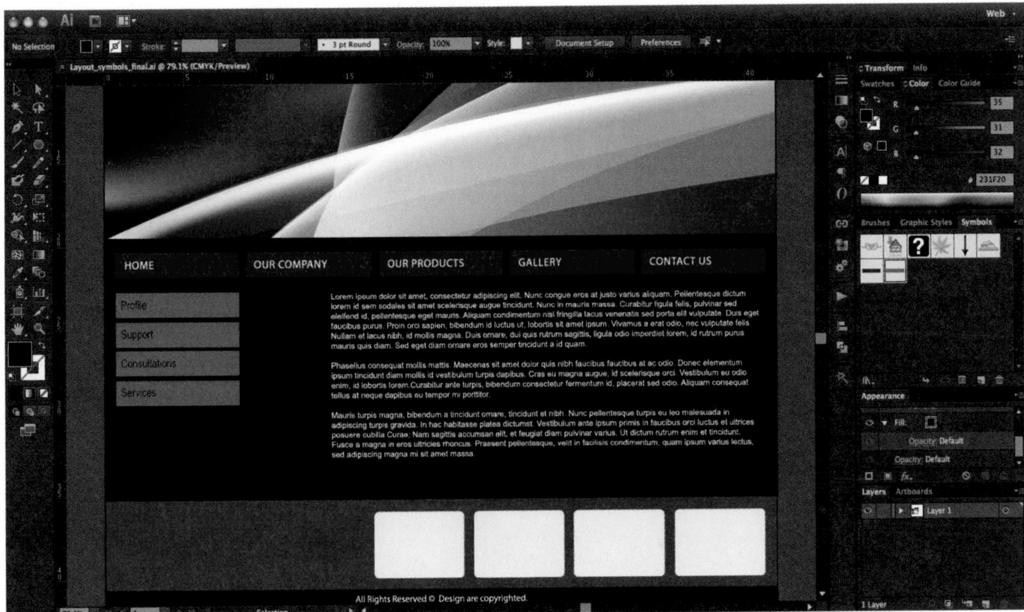

FIG 12-7 The layout with the vertical menu

Using symbols can help you to achieve your design faster than the ordinary way of repeating artwork. Try to use symbols in your design and practice how to implement different Symbols panel features.

Working with Graphs

One of the tasks that many designers face is to create informational graphs that are based on numerical values. When these graphs are done in applications such as Microsoft Excel, it does not provide a look or feel that satisfies the designer.

The Graphs tools and features in Illustrator are made to bridge the gap between creative artwork and the ability to modify the graph, and the numerical values of the graph. You can use the graphs feature in Illustrator to build infographic charts based on specific values that are used to calculate the values of these chart parts. In the next section, we will have an overview to the Graph tools and the important features associated with graphs.

You can access the Graph tools from the Tools panel. When you click and hold on the Graph icon, you will see that Illustrator provides a large variety of graph styles, such as

- Column Graph tool
- Stacked Column Graph tool
- Bar Graph tool
- Stacked Bar Graph tool
- Line Graph tool
- Area Graph tool
- Scatter Graph tool
- Pie Graph tool
- Radar Graph tool

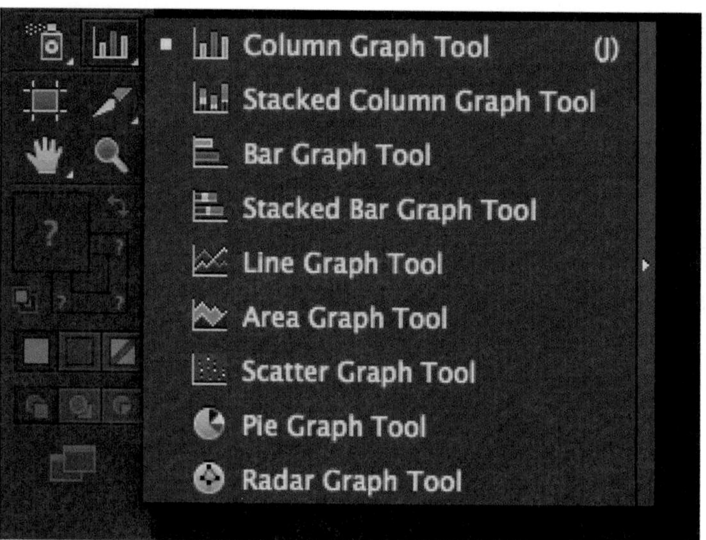

FIG 12-8 The different Graph tools in Illustrator

On the other hand, you can reach more settings for the graphs from the Object > Graph top menus.

While creating graphs requires you to know how to set the data for each graph, we will overview the different options and how to add values to create a graph and edit its style. So, let us start by following the steps below to build our first graph:

1. Create a new Illustrator document.
2. From the Tools panel, click and hold on the Graph tool and select the Column Graph tool.

3. Click and drag on the artboard to create your first graph.
   You will notice that the Data dialog box appears to allow you to add the values that should appear on the graph. Before continuing our example, let us have a look at the Data dialog box.

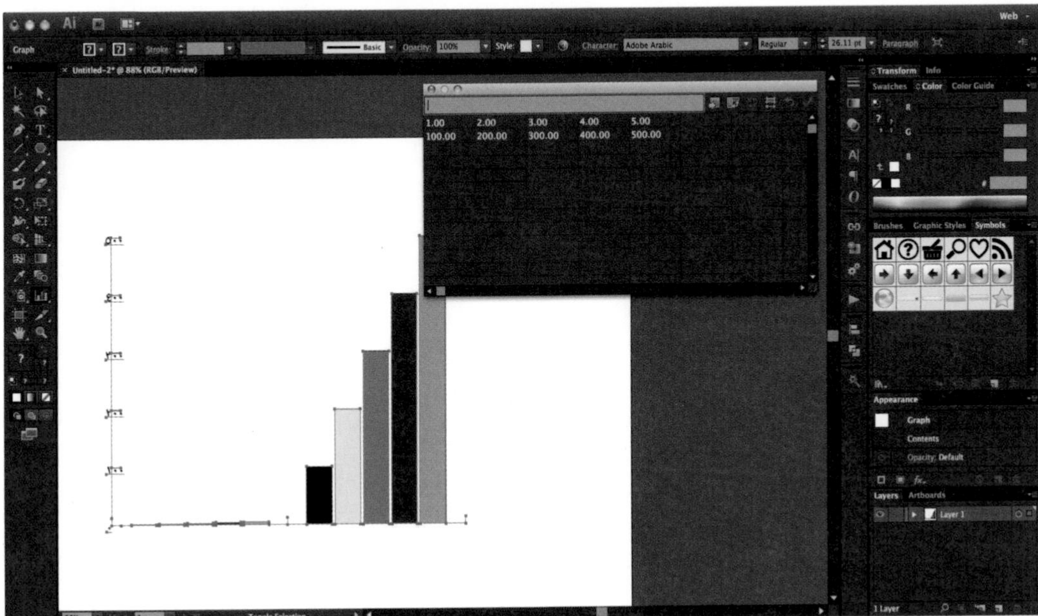

FIG 12-9 The Graph Data dialog box

The dialog box consists of cells of the graph values. The top functions include the following, from left to right:

- The Entry text box allows you to add each cell value by selecting the cell and adding the value to it.
- Import Data lets you import data from an external source such as an Excel file.
- Transpose Row/Column switches between the row and column positions.
- Switch X/Y switches the X and Y values.
- Cell Style lets you set the number of decimals and the cell width.
- Revert lets you undo your last step.
- The Apply button lets you generate the graph or update an existing graph based on the updated values.

Now, let us add the graph values as follows:

4. Select the first cell in the first row and add the value 1.
5. Repeat the last step and add other values in the next cells in the rows 2, 3, 4, and 5.
6. In the next row add the values 100, 200, 300, 400, and 500.
7. Press the Apply button.

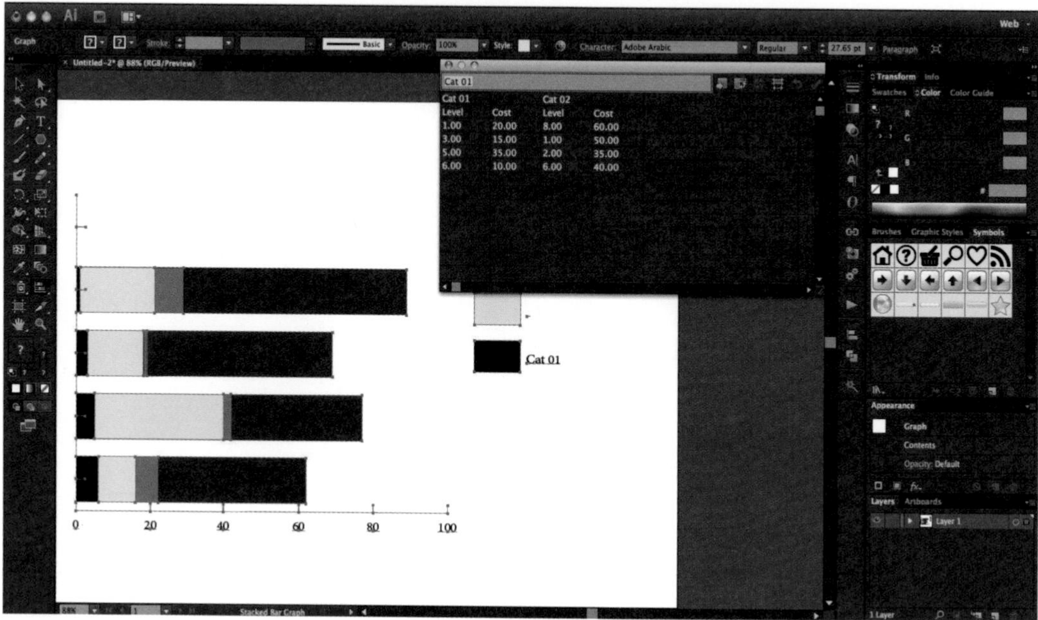

FIG 12-10 The column graph with the added values

Generally, the column values represent the values in the X axis in the graph and the row values represent the Y axis values. If there are other values in the row, each row value is represented with a column in the graph.

Let us apply this concept to a more complex graph, as follows:

1. Create a new Illustrator document.
2. From the Tools panel, choose Stacker Column Graph tool.
3. Click and drag on the stage.
4. The Data dialog box appears; set the rows and columns values as the figure below.
5. Click Apply to generate the graph based on the added data.

As you can see, the entered data appears as two groups with labels that we added in the data table.

> **Note**
>
> You can easily edit the graph values after you apply them. All you need to do is to select the graph, and from the Object menu, choose Graph > Data. This will open the Data dialog box to allow you to edit it.

Switching between Graph Types

You can use any of the tools in the Tools panel to create specific graphs, and you can easily switch between graphs type as follows:

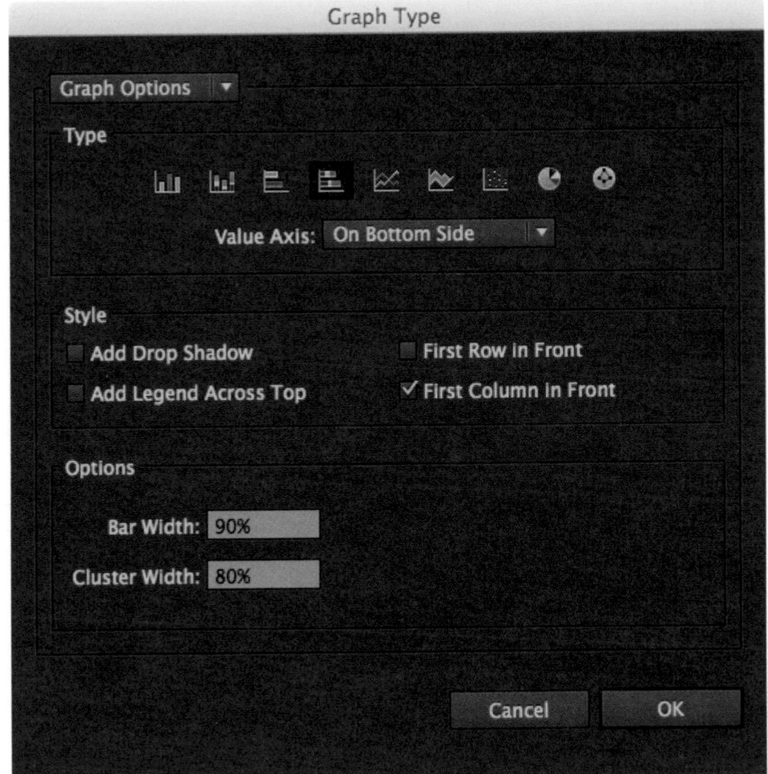

FIG 12-11 The Graph Type dialog box

1. Select the graph that you created on the stage.
2. From the Object menu, choose Graph > Type.
3. From the Graph Type dialog box, you can switch to any of the graphs by clicking the Graph icon from the top icons. You can also set each graph to have different properties.

Changing the Color of the Graph

While you are working with the graph, you will notice that the default graph colors are gray colors. This is not applicable when working with real graphs, because the colors of the graphs are essential to provide visual differences between values. Adobe Illustrator provides an easy method to change the colors of any of the graph elements while keeping the graph values editable through the Data dialog box, as we discussed earlier.

In the following example, we will create a graph and change the column colors:

1. Create a new document in Illustrator.
2. From the Tools panel, select the Column Graph tool.
3. Click and drag on the artboard to create the graph.

4. The Data dialog box will appear; set the information as shown in the figure below.

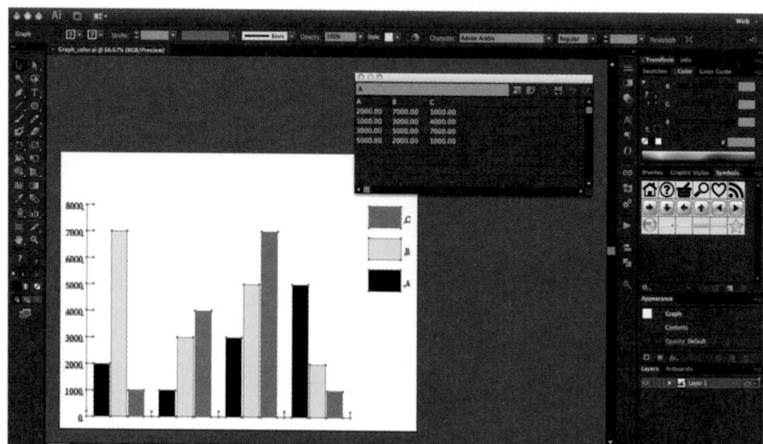

FIG 12-12 The Graph and Data dialog box

5. Select the Direct Selection tool from the Tools panel.
6. Select one of the columns.
7. Open the Appearance panel.
8. Click on the fill to expand it.
9. Click on the color swatch to open the Swatches panel.

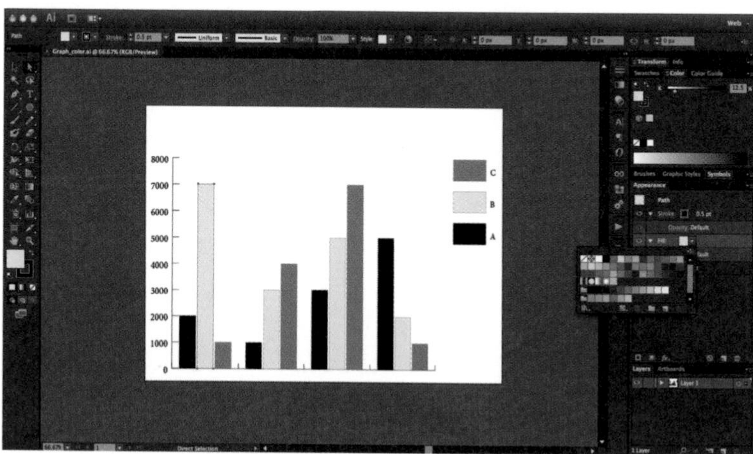

FIG 12-13 Changing the color from the appearance panel

10. Choose one color for this column.
11. Repeat the same steps with the rest of the columns.

Note

You can also change the graph text type and alignment. Select the graph and open of these panels to change the text size, font, and alignment options.

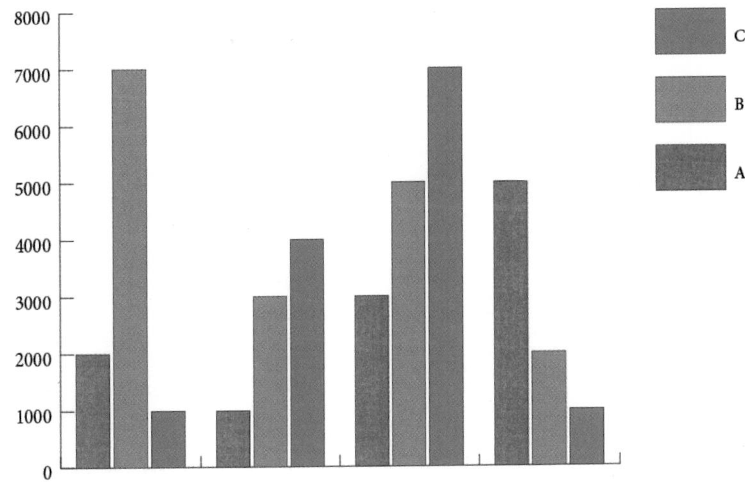

FIG 12-14 The final appearance of the graph

Add Artwork to Graph

Adobe Illustrator extends your ability to style graphs by adding symbols or artwork to graphs. In the following example, we will see how to apply artwork to a graph as a style:

1. Open the document Graph_style.ai. This document includes a graph and a piece of artwork next to it.
2. Select the artwork. From the Object menu, choose Graph > Design.
3. The Design dialog box appears; click the New Design button on the right. It will add the artwork as a new design in the Design list. Click OK to apply the changes.

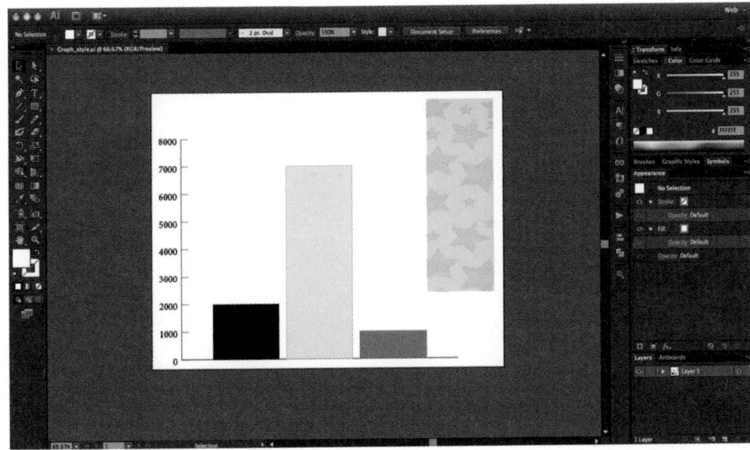

FIG 12-15 The adding the artwork to the Design dialog box

4. Select the graph on the stage.
5. From the Object menu, choose Graph > Columns.
6. In the Columns dialog box, select the newly created design and press OK to apply the design to the graph.

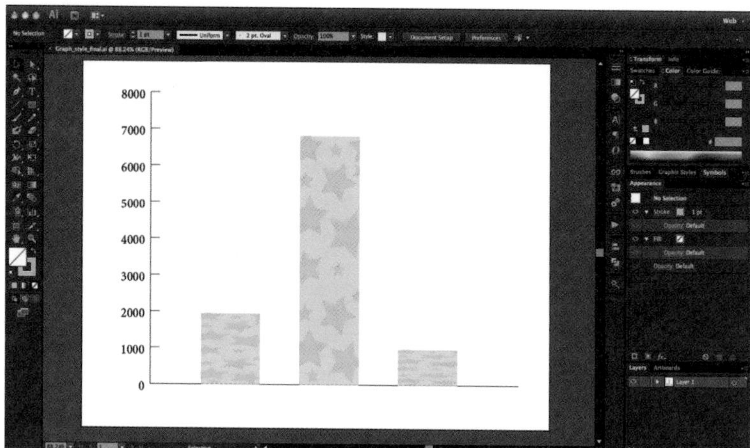

FIG 12-16 The graph with the artwork applied to it

You can expand your experience with graphs and graph styling by practicing the different options and features that we discussed in this chapter to create your own charts and ideas.

Both symbols and graphs are useful features to help you with your design. In this chapter we learned how to convert ordinary artwork into symbols and work with these symbols to achieve your design much faster, rather than creating the same artwork again and again.

We also covered the graphs in Illustrator and how to use the Graph tools to create graph charts based on numerical values that can be added to the graph and how to stylize the artwork using either color or objects. You can try these two features and use them in your projects.

For examples pertaining to this chapter, visit www.illustratorfoundations.com.

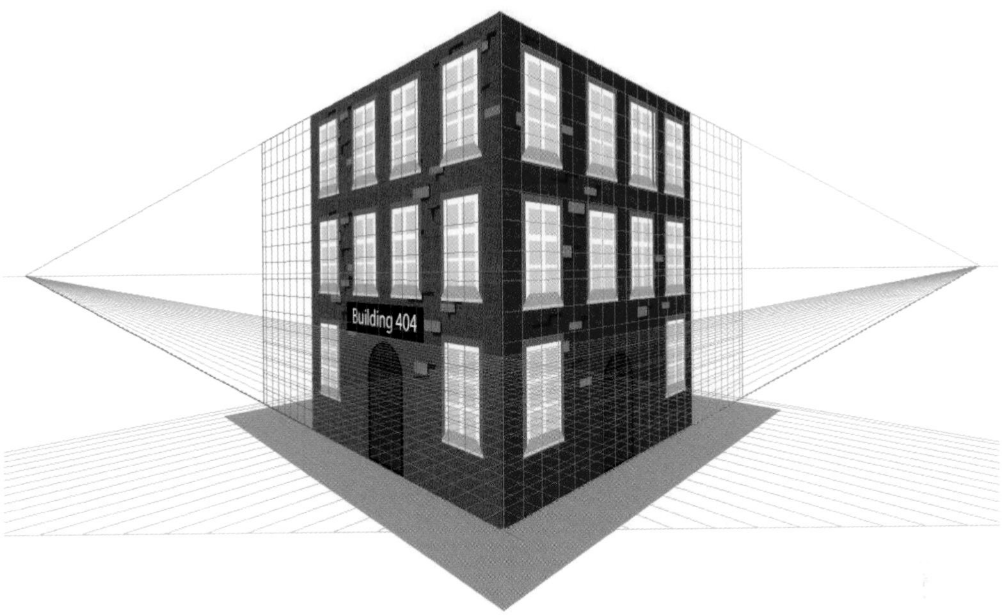

CHAPTER 13

3D and Drawing in Perspective

As a leading illustration application, Adobe Illustrator provides you with all the tools and features to help you to visualize your artwork ideas. Artwork in Illustrator can be created as 2D flat illustrations or in 3D with perspective depth. While drawing on paper, you can give your artwork "fake" depth using shades and perspective tricks. While this does not mean you turned your artwork 3D, it helps to give a 3D look and feel to your artwork. Adobe Illustrator can do the same. You can create your artwork using the 2D tools while applying some perspective using complex mathematical transformations and shade tricks, similar to what you do while you are drawing in the traditional way. This is one of the ways you can create a 3D look in Illustrator.

Using this method to create 3D-look artwork can give you creative results because it depends on an artistic look and feel, which gives the artists the freedom to control the shades and perspective in an unreal or artistic way. At the same time, it is a hard method unless you are very talented at drawing. It is also hard to edit after creating your effects, because this is done manually and involves many steps, especially when you are working with complex artwork.

Other methods include 3D effects and the new 3D Perspective Grid tool. Unlike the above method, these features allow you to create artwork and objects over the three dimensions X, Y, and Z. The 3D perspective grid is actually composed of grids that help you build objects in three dimensions with accuracy and much faster than with the normal guides. On the other hand, the 3D effects are based on converting 2D paths into 3D objects by using Extrude, Revolve, or Rotate options in the 3D space.

The 3D effects method is less creative than the manual way. I call it manual because artists used to create the 3D effect using traditional artwork tricks. At the same time, it is easy to edit and modify after creating the 3D effect because Adobe Illustrator keeps the original 2D path and allows you to edit the 3D options as one of the Illustrator effects applied to the path or the 2D object, as we will see later in the 3D Effects section. The first manual method actually depends on the Illustrator 2D tools that we covered in all the previous chapters; we will focus in this chapter on creating 3D content using the 3D perspective grid and the 3D effects from the Effects menu.

3D Perspective Grid

Before jumping to the 3D effects, we will start with the 3D perspective grid. This feature was added to Adobe Illustrator starting with CS5. It provides a middle ground between the manual method to create 3D content and 3D effects because it does not create the 3D objects for you. Instead, it gives you guides and a 3D grid that allow you to create accurate 3D objects.

The perspective grid helps you to create objects in perspective or in the third dimension. You can create the object directly on the grid, span the object to any of the grid sides, and transform the object applied to each of the grid sizes, as we will see in the practice example.

Before starting the example, let us understand the perspective grid and how to control it. To display the perspective grid, either select the Perspective tool in the Tools panel, or go to View > Perspective Grid > Show/Hide Grid. When you activate the perspective grid, it displays on the stage to allow you to draw an object on one of the three planes that are marked with three different colors: blue for the left planes, orange for the right planes, and green for the bottom planes. These colors are the default colors, which you can change from the View menu by choosing Perspective Grid > Define Grid Setup.

> **Shortcut**
>
> Use Ctrl+Shift+I (on Windows) or Cmd+Shift+I (on Mac) to show or hide the perspective grid.

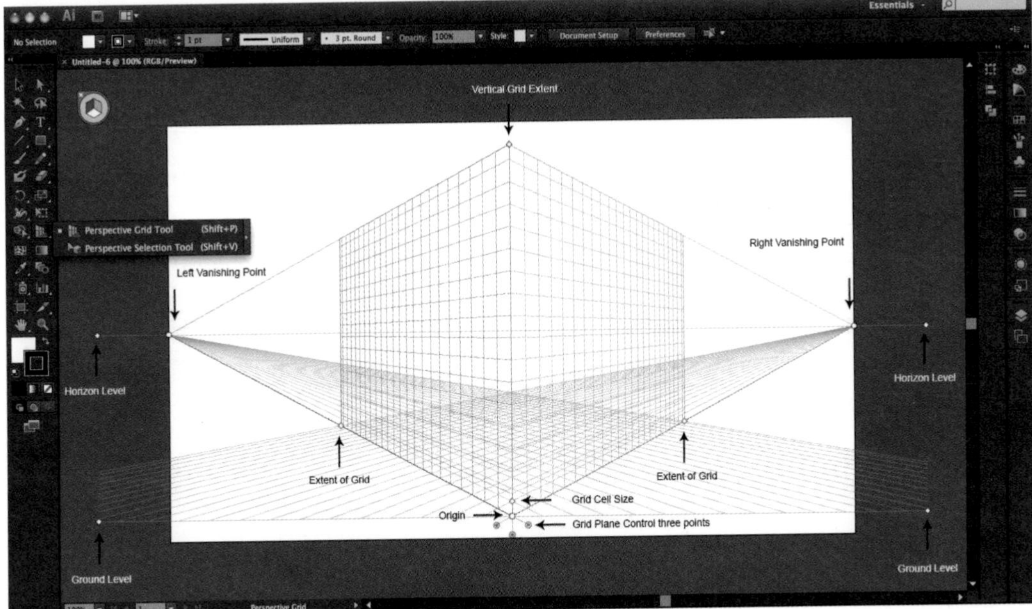

FIG 13-1 The perspective grid in Illustrator document

At the top left of the workspace, you will find the Active Plane widget that allows you to activate any of the three grids. The perspective grid is surrounded with points that allow you to edit the object's size and grids as follows. The far left and right circle points are the left and right vanishing points that allow you to change the right and left grid perspective. Each of these points moves independent of each other, which may lead to an inaccurate perspective.

> **Note**
>
> You can link both perspective points by choosing View > Perspective Grid > Lock Station Points.

Next to the vanishing points, there is a small diamond point that controls the horizontal perspective line level. Changing this line up and down affects the vertical view angle. At the top of the perspective grid, there is the Vertical Grid Extend option, which allows you to increase the height of the grid. Under this point, there is the Grid Cell Resize point, which allows you to resize the grid cells. On the right and the left are the Extend Grid Point points that extend the grid over each side.

At the bottom of the perspective grid, there are three gray points, and each point controls the position of each plane. For example, you can change the position of the planes to become more suitable for internal room planes than external building planes. In the middle of these points is the origin point.

While you can control the perspective grid from the working space, you can perform the same modifications using the Define Perspective Grid dialog box in View > Perspective Grid.

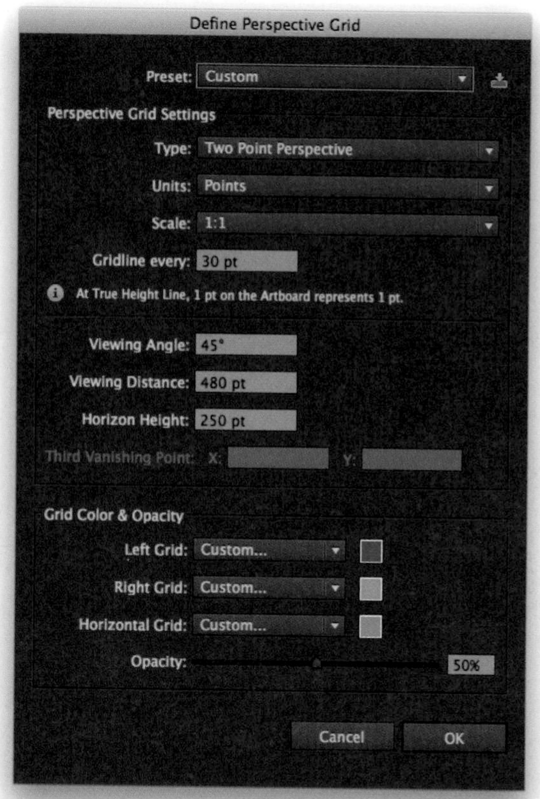

FIG 13-2 The Define Perspective Grid dialog box

Furthermore, the dialog box includes more options to control the perspective grid, such as creating a custom perspective grid view and changing between one-, two-, and three-point perspectives, as discussed next.

The Define Perspective Grid dialog box allows you to choose from one of the three view presets available in the Presets drop-down list. Each preset has a different view, based on the number of perspective points:

- One-point perspective view displays the grid as one-sided perspective.
- Two-point perspective view shows the default perspective appearance.
- Three-point perspective view looks similar to the default perspective but flipped down.

You can create your own setting for the perspective look, and you can save these settings as custom presets using the Save icon next to the Presets list. From the Edit menu, you can choose the Perspective Grid Presets command to edit, import, and export grid presets and define them.

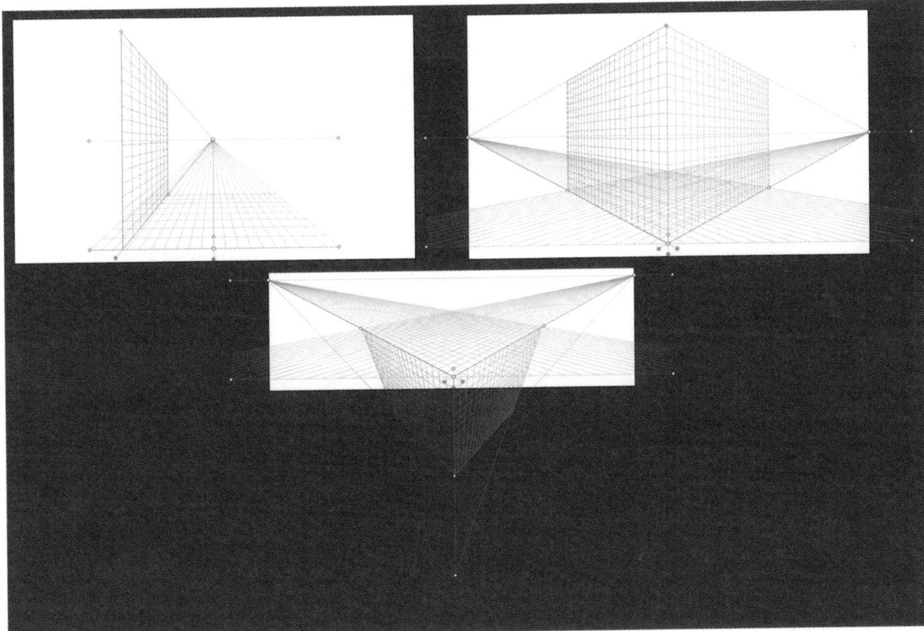

FIG 13-3 The different point perspective views, from top left: one-point perspective, two-point perspective, and three-point perspective

Next to the Preset section, the Perspective Grid Settings option allows you to change the perspective values as follows:

- Type lets you choose between the different three-point perspective values mentioned.
- Unites defines the measurement method, such as points, pixels, inches, and centimeters.
- Scale sets the scale aspect ratio between the artboard and the real-world measurements.
- Gridline lets you set the size of the grid cells.
- Viewing Angle allows you to set the horizontal view for the object and is related to the vanishing points. For example, a 45-degrees view means

that both right and left vanishing points stand at an equal distance from each other.

- Viewing Distance shows the distance between the viewer and the object.
- Horizontal Height shows the distance between the horizontal line and ground line.
- Third Vanishing Point becomes active when you select the three-point perspective, and it then lets you set the position of the third point.

The third section in the Define Perspective Grid dialog box lets you set the colors of each plane's grids and the opacity of the lines. In addition to the options in the Define Perspective Grid dialog box, the Perspective Grid menu allows you to show or hide the grid, show or hide rulers, enable Snap to Grid, lock the grid, and save custom perspective grids as presets.

In the example below we will learn how to use the perspective grid to create a building plan.

1. Open the file Perspective_grid_start.ai. In this document, you will find building architecture elements such as doors and windows. We will use these elements after we create the building walls in the next steps.
2. From the Active Plane widget, select the blue side to activate drawing on this side.
3. Use the Rectangle tool to create the first side of the building on the blue side. Notice that the created rectangle is attached and transformed according to the blue side.
4. Set this side's color to a dark red as shown in the figure below.

FIG 13-4 The first side of the building

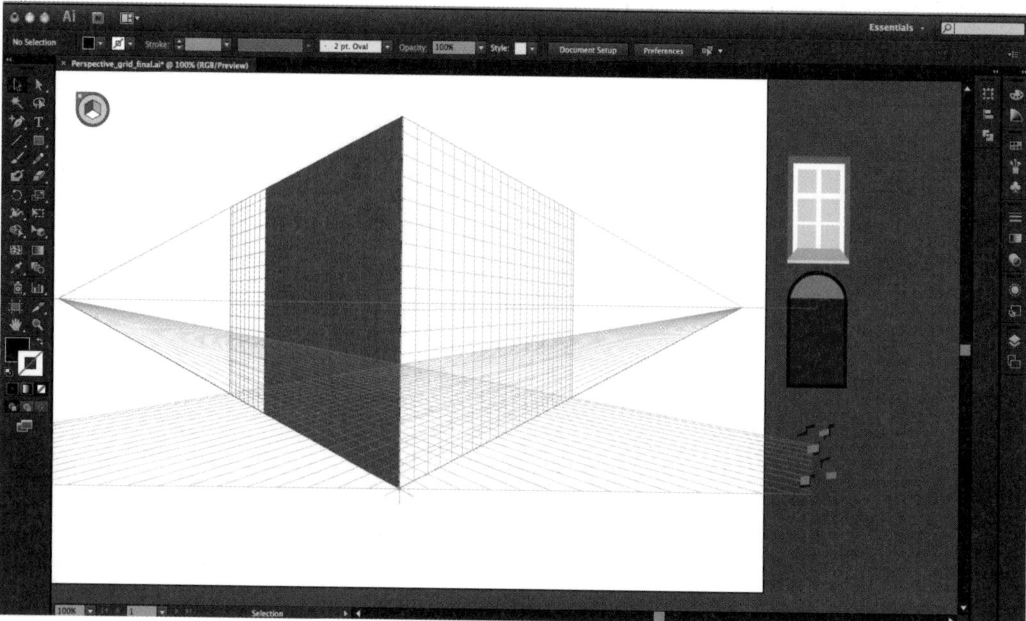

5. From the Active Plane widget, choose the orange side.
6. Using the Rectangle tool, draw the next side of the building and give it a darker red color.
7. Move to the green, bottom side by selecting it from the Active Plane widget.
8. Select the Rectangle tool and make the foreground color gray.
9. Click under the control points at the bottom center of the perspective grid, and drag to create the building ground. Also, try to extend it outside the building to form the sidewalk.
10. To send the rectangle behind the current walls, right-click on it, and choose Arrange > Send to Back.

> **Note**
>
> You can arrange objects in front of each other by right-clicking the object and choosing Arrange.

At this point we have created the building's main walls. In the next steps we will add the windows and doors to the building.

11. From the Active Plane widget, select the blue plane.
12. Select the Perspective Selection tool (Shift+V), select the window, and drag it to the blue plane.
13. Select the first window and press Option (Alt in Windows) while dragging to duplicate the window.
14. Repeat the duplication step to have the windows repeated over the building side.

FIG 13-5 The 3D building in the Perspective Grid setting

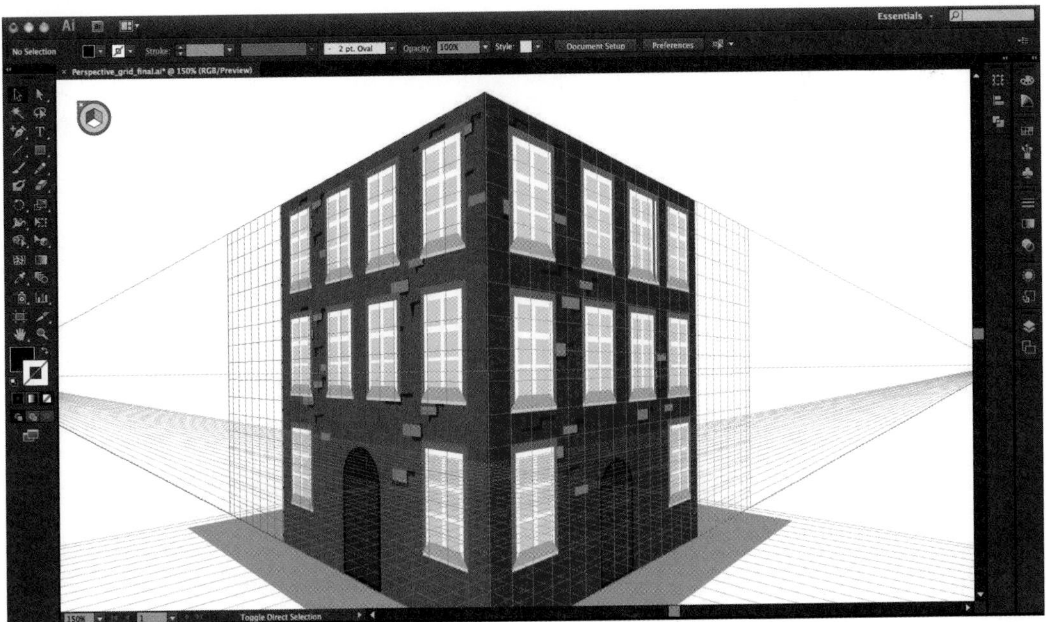

15. Repeat the above steps to add the door in the blue plane as shown in the figure below.
16. Move to the orange plane and repeat the above steps with the other side of the building.
17. Also repeat the same steps with the wall brackets, and make sure they appear under the windows.

Note

You can also click around the cube in the Active Plane widget to draw without any grid selected. In order to be able to select any side, you need to have the Perspective Grid tool selected.

Now that we have added the building details, we will learn about adding text into the perspective grid and editing it. You cannot directly write text in the 3D perspective, but you can write text outside the perspective sides and attach it to a specific side, as we will see from the steps below:

18. Make sure that the blue side is selected from the Active Plane widget.
19. Select the Rectangle tool and create a rectangle on the blue side. Make it in a dark color to be a background for the text that we will add.
20. Select the Text tool, click on the stage, and write the text "Building 404."

FIG 13-6 Adding the text to the 3D plane

21. Select the 3D Perspective tool, select the text, and drag it to the blue plane. Notice that the text follows the perspective of the rest of the objects in the plane.

Note

Notice that the text is converted into outline, as you can see the path points of the text letters. However, you can still edit the text by either double-clicking it to enter isolated mode or choosing Object > Perspective > Edit Text or by clicking the Edit Text button in the Control panel.

22. Double-click on the text to edit it.
23. Change the text to "Building 404."
24. Double-click outside the object to exit editing mode. You can also return to the document stage by clicking the back arrow on the document path at the top left of the document window.

FIG 13-7 Editing the text in the 3D plane

As we have seen from the above examples, the difference between the Perspective Grid tool and the Perspective Selection tool is that the first allows you to create and edit the perspective grid, while the second lets you select the plane side and the objects in each active plane. Also, there are number of tools that allow you to draw directly on the perspective plan: the Line Segment tool and the Rectangle groups of tools (Round Rectangle, Ellipse, Polygon, and Star), except the Flare tool.

Through this example, we have learned how to work with the 3D perspective grid and how to use it to build perspective-view architecture. You can use the same steps to create more buildings, experience different views, and see the results of each perspective view.

3D Effects

As we mentioned earlier, the 3D effects in Adobe Illustrator convert 2D paths into 3D objects using either the extrude, revolve, or 3D rotate features. This feature is applied to the path as a live effect, which allows you to edit or remove it without affecting the original path. The 3D effects in Illustrator are quite simple if you compare them with other 3D applications or Photoshop. Because it is not the core focus of the software, it is used to enhance and support you while doing your artwork or design such as logo designs, and so on.

While other 3D applications support multiple views for your object, Adobe Illustrator does not have this feature, because it does not support a camera view that allows you to navigate around the 3D object in the three dimensions X, Y, and Z. Illustrator doesn't have a concept like a 3D environment. Since the 3D effect is actually part of Illustrator's live effects, you can easily modify the object's 3D options and view angle through the 3D Effects dialog box, as we will see next.

The 3D effects in Illustrator include three main ways to convert your 2D path into a 3D object:

- 3D Extrude & Bevel
- 3D Revolve
- 3D Rotate

Each of these effects interacts with the 2D path in a totally different way, creating different 3D effects.

3D Extrude & Bevel

We mentioned that each of the 3D effects interacts with the 2D path and adds the third dimension information in a different way. The 3D Extrude & Bevel, as the name implies, extrudes the 2D path in the third dimension to create a 3D object effect.

When you create a 2D path object in Illustrator, you can reach the 3D Extrude & Bevel option from the Effects > 3D menu or the Fx button at the bottom of the Appearance panel. Before we learn how this effect works, let us explore its capabilities and options through the 3D Extrude & Bevel dialog box. The dialog box includes three main sections, discussed in the next sections.

Note

Make sure to enable the Preview option at the bottom of the 3D Effects dialog box to be able to see your changes directly on the Illustrator object.

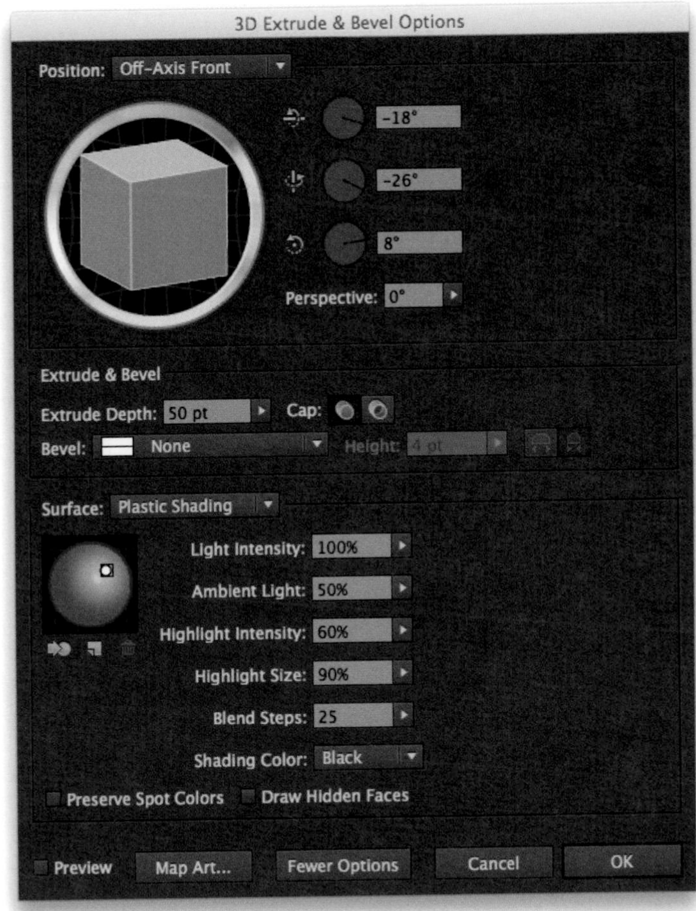

FIG 13-8 3D Extrude & Bevel Options dialog box

Position

Since Illustrator does not include a camera to allow you to navigate around the object in the 3D space, you can set the position of the 3D object through the position section. In this section you can choose a view from a preset position from the drop-down list or change the object through the X, Y, and Z axis values. You can also change the 3D perspective through the perspective slider.

Another method to control the view of the 3D object is through the cube preview to the left of the numerical values. The cube represents the 3D object, and when you roll over the cube edges, you will notice it is highlighted to let you know that you can rotate the 3D object around this axis. For example, to rotate the 3D object on the X axis, roll over the cube edges that show a red color and start dragging to rotate the 3D object on the stage in this direction.

> **Note**
>
> Notice how each axis is colored with a different color. The X axis colors is red, Y is green, and Z is blue.

When you click on the blue circle that surrounds the cube, you can rotate the object to the right or the left. Also, clicking and dragging in the black area around the cube, or in the cube inner part, rotates the 3D object in the three dimensions at the same time.

Extrude and Bevel

This section is responsible for giving the 2D object 3D depth and extrusion. Thus, it is the main part of the dialog box because it controls all the various extrusion settings of the object, like the depth and aspect of the bevel itself. This section is divided into two subsections. The Extrude section allows you to change the depth of the 3D object using the Extrude slider. Next to the Extrude slider are two icons: Turn Cap On for a solid appearance and Turn Cap Off for a hollow appearance. Clicking these two icons switches between hiding or revealing the original object from which the 3D object was created.

The other subsection is the Bevel option, which allows you to change the bevel shape of the extruded sides. You can control the bevel level from the height value and the shape of the level from the drop-down list. Also, you can control whether the bevel will extend out or in from the Bevel Extend Out and Bevel Extend In icons.

Surface

This part of the 3D Extrude & Bevel Options dialog box is responsible for controlling the shades and light applied to the 3D object. Next to the surface name, you can select the shading type for the 3D object. The available shading options are:

- Wireframe: displays the 3D object as wireframe without any colors applied to it.
- No Shading: uses the object's front colors as the default colors for the shades and extrudes.
- Diffusion Shading: reflects the light as if it were falling on a soft surface.
- Plastic Shading: reflects the light as if it were falling on a glossy surface.

You can also change the direction of the light source by dragging the point over the circle preview. You can add light sources and set them to be positioned on the back or front of the object. On the right side, the light options are:

- Light Intensity: controls the intensity of the light and its level.
- Ambient Light: affects the global light for all the surfaces.

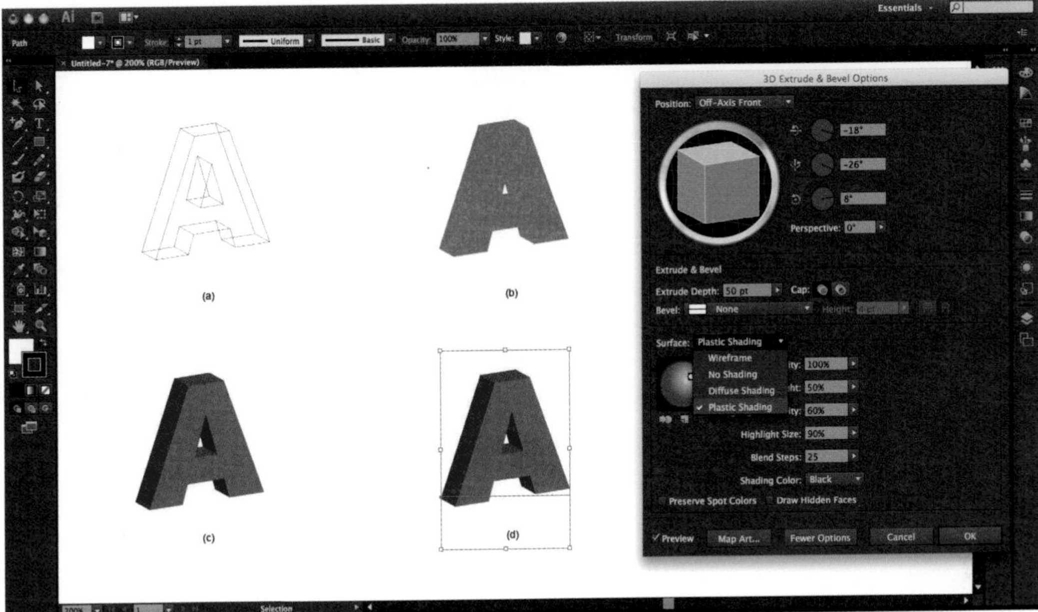

FIG 13-9 The different shading types, from right to left: Wireframe, No Shading, Diffuse Shading, and Plastic Shading

- Highlight Intensity: shows how much light the object should reflect.
- Highlight Size: controls the size of the highlight.
- Blend Steps: shows how smoothly the shades appear.
- Shading Color: shows the color of the shade.

At the end of the Surface section, there are two commands. The Preserve Spot Colors command is used to preserve a spot color on the object (you will need to view your document using Overprint Preview to be able to see the spot color accurately). The Draw Hidden Faces command draws 3D object faces that do not appear in the workspace.

Now, let us apply the above features in our next example. In this example we will convert the 2D text to a 3D object using the 3D Effects and Bevel feature.

Note

You will find guides in the section on Chapter 13 on the companion website, http://www.illustratorfoundations.com, to show the beginning and the final look of the next examples.

1. Create a new Illustrator document.
2. Use the Text tool to type the word "FUN" in the document.
3. Select the text using the Arrow tool.
4. From the Type menu, choose Create Outline.
5. Right-click on the text, and select Ungroup to have separated letters.
6. Select each letter insert and give each a different bright color.

FIG 13-10 The letters with different colors on the artboard

7. Select the first letter, and from the Effects menu, choose 3D > Extrude and Bevel.
8. Make sure that the Preview checkbox is selected.
9. Use the Position preview to change the letter's position as shown in the figure below.
10. Set the extrude value to 80.
11. Click on More option to expand the Extrude & Bevel Options dialog box.
12. Since we changed the perspective and position, the light may not suit the new position. So, we will move the light spot to the top right of the preview circle.
13. Click OK and repeat the above steps with the rest of the letters, giving each letter a different position. The final result should look like the figure on the next page.
14. Arrange the letters to intersect with each other as shown in the figure on the next page.

Solid colors are not the only option that can be added to the 3D extruded object; you can map objects and patterns to each of the 3D object sides using the Map Art dialog box from the 3D Extrude & Bevel option. This allows you to apply a graphic symbol on each side of the 3D object. This option allows you to apply objects, patterns, and other elements over the 3D object sides by simply converting them to a symbol by dragging them to the Symbols panel.

The Map Art dialog box includes the following options:

- The Symbol drop-down list lets you choose the symbol that you will apply on a specific side.

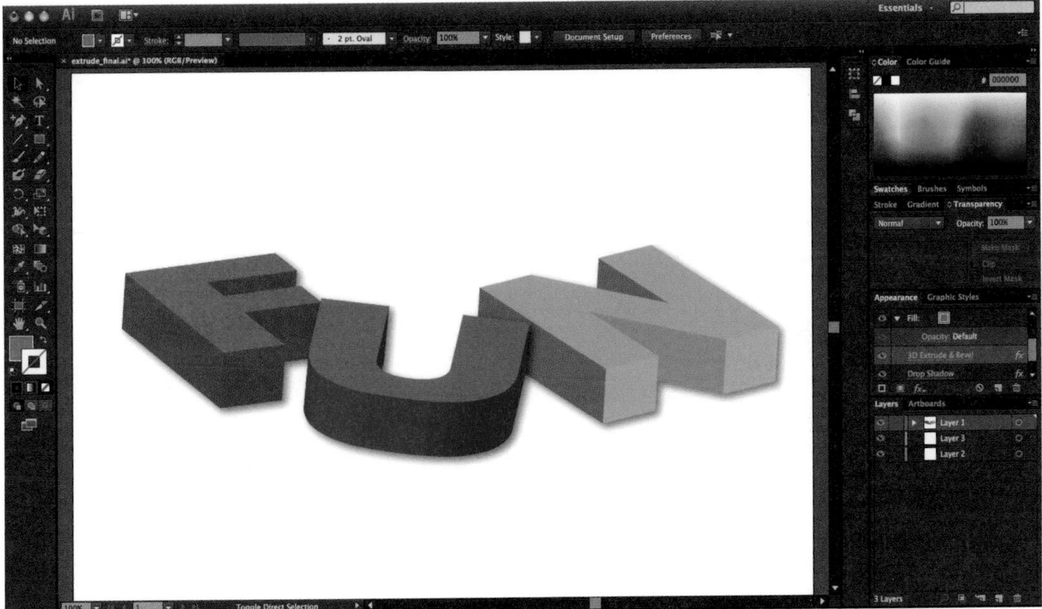

FIG 13-11 The letters with the 3D Extrude & Bevel applied to it

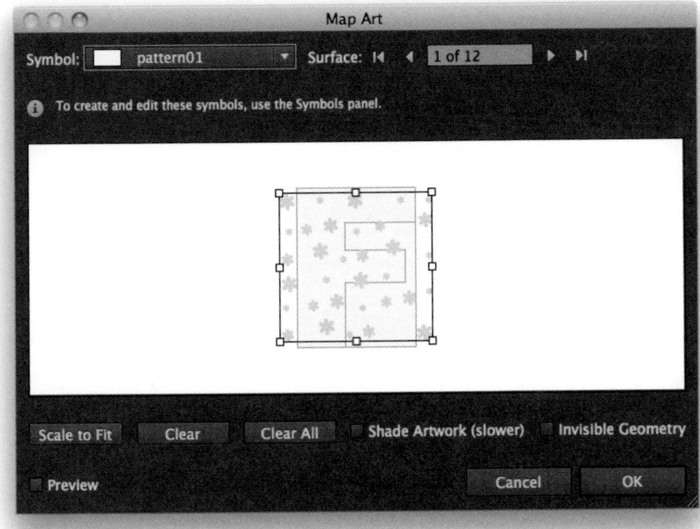

FIG 13-12 The Map Art dialog box

- The Surface navigator lets you choose the side that will have the symbol applied to it.
- The Preview area lets you control the symbol to scale, rotate, and reposition it.
- The Scale to Fit button resizes the symbol to fit on the current side.

- The Clear button removes the current symbol from the current side.
- The Clear All button removes all the symbols from all sides.
- Shade Artwork applies the object shades on the symbol and makes the file process slower than the normal view.
- Invisible Geometry removes the 3D object and keeps the symbols; this option is helpful if you would like to use a 3D object as a guide without displaying it and display only the symbols applied to it.

Let us continue our previous example by creating a pattern symbol and applying it to the 3D object:

15. Create three patterns as shown in the figure below.
16. Open the Symbols panel.
17. Select the first pattern, and click the New icon on the bottom of the Symbols panel.
18. Repeat the same procedure with the other patterns to have them listed in the Symbols panel. Name them pattern01, pattern02, and pattern03.

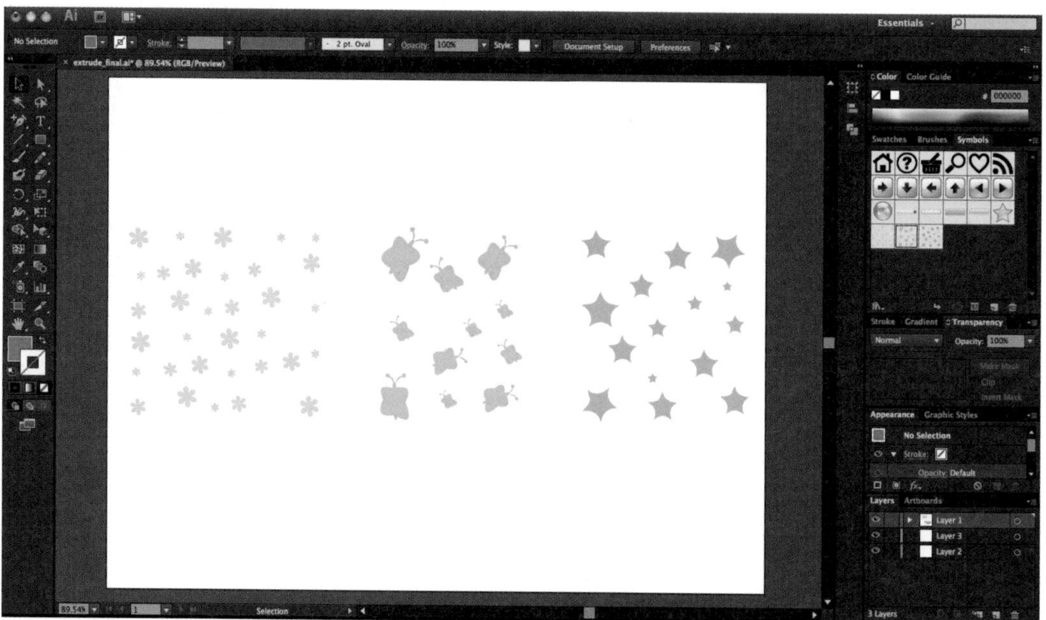

FIG 13-13 The three patterns symbols

19. Select the first letter, and from the Appearance panel, double-click the 3D Extrude & Bevel option.
20. Click on the Map Art button to display the dialog box.
21. Select the first pattern from the drop-down list.
22. Transform the pattern to fit with the side using the preview area.
23. Click the sides navigator to go to the next side of the 3D object.
24. Choose the same pattern from the drop-down list.
25. Repeat this step with the rest of the letter sides.

26. Select each of the rest of the letters, and apply to them different patterns to create the final figure shown below.
27. Select each letter, and from the Effects menu, choose Stylize > Drop Shadow. Set the drop shadow opacity to 50%, X and Y offset to 5 px, and blur to 5 px. Click OK. Add a background of your choice.

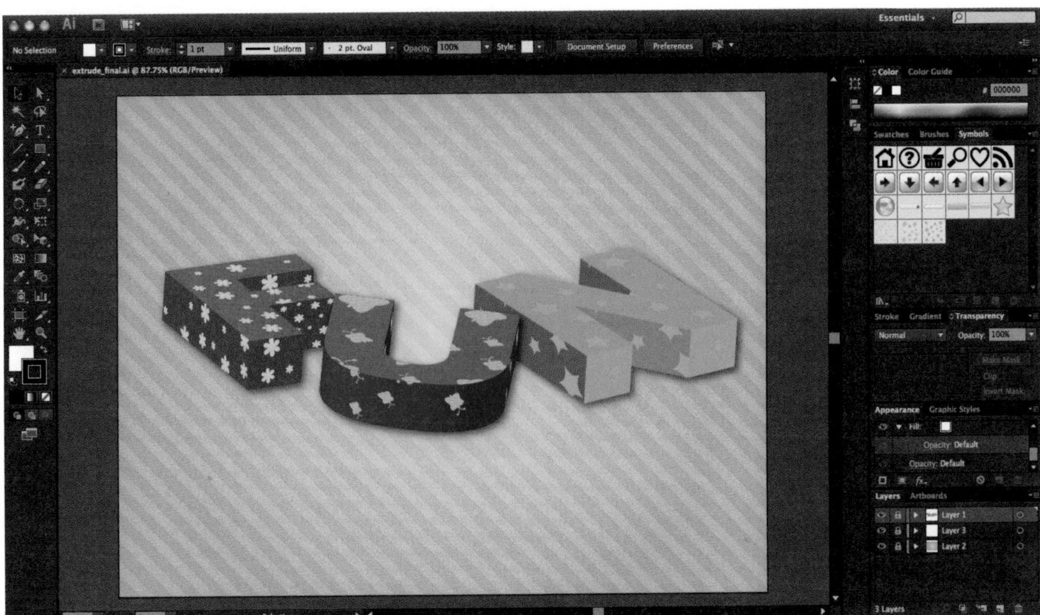

FIG 13-14 The letters with the patterns applied to them

3D Revolve

Each of the 3D effects options handles 2D paths in a specific way to create the 3D object based on the 2D path. The 3D Revolve option, as the name implies, revolves the 2D path 360 degrees to build a 3D object from it. The 2D path can be a closed or open path, and you can control the Revolve options through the 3D Revolve dialog box. The dialog box is similar to the 3D Extrude & Bevel dialog box; the only difference is in the Revolve section, which replaces the Extrude & Bevel section in the previous effect.

The Revolve section includes the following options:

- Angle shows the revolve rotation angle; 360-degree means that the revolve takes a full circle.
- The Cap icons switch the main surface of the object on and off, so the extruded object becomes opened from the two sides.
- The offset value increases the distance between the path and the revolve; you can set this shift to be from the right or left edge.

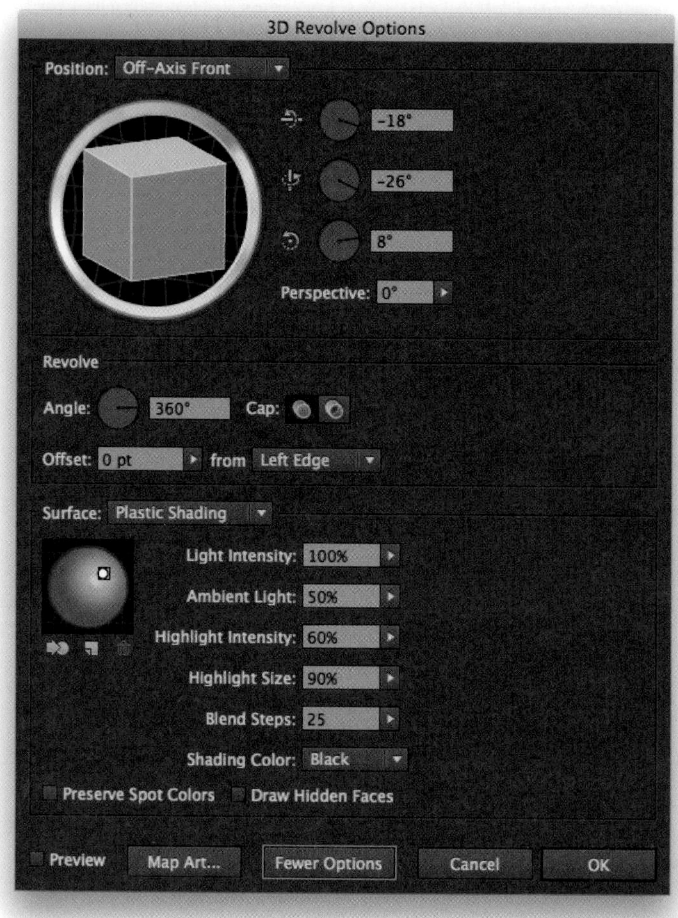

FIG 13-15 The 3D Revolve Options dialog box

Now let us move to an example that shows how to use the 3D Revolve feature to convert a 2D path into a 3D object. In the following example, we will create a 3D pushpin using the 3D Revolve effect. In the first steps, we will create the top part of the pushpin:

1. Create a new Illustrator document.
2. Use the Path tool to draw a path like the figure below, as we learned in Chapter 3. Apply a fill-only light cyan color. This path will be the base to which we will apply the 3D Revolve effect.
3. From the Effects menu, choose 3D > Revolve.
4. The 3D Revolve Options dialog box appears. Make sure to have the Preview checkbox selected to allow you to preview the effect updates.
5. Use the Position cube to change the position of the top of the pushpin, as shown in the figure below. You can do so by clicking and dragging over the cube edges.
6. Change the perspective value to 50 degrees.

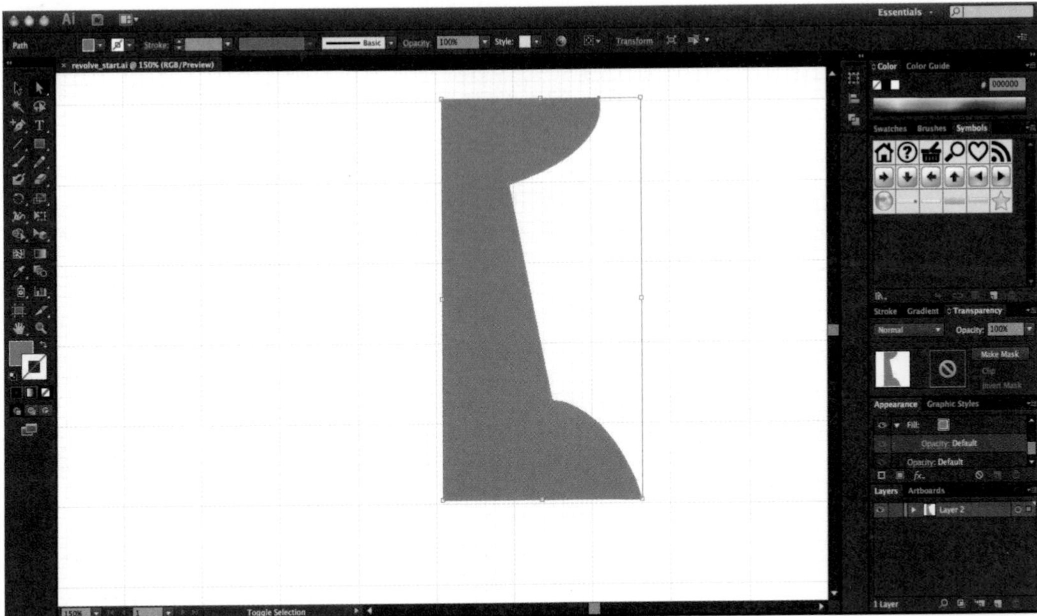

FIG 13-16 The pushpin path in Illustrator

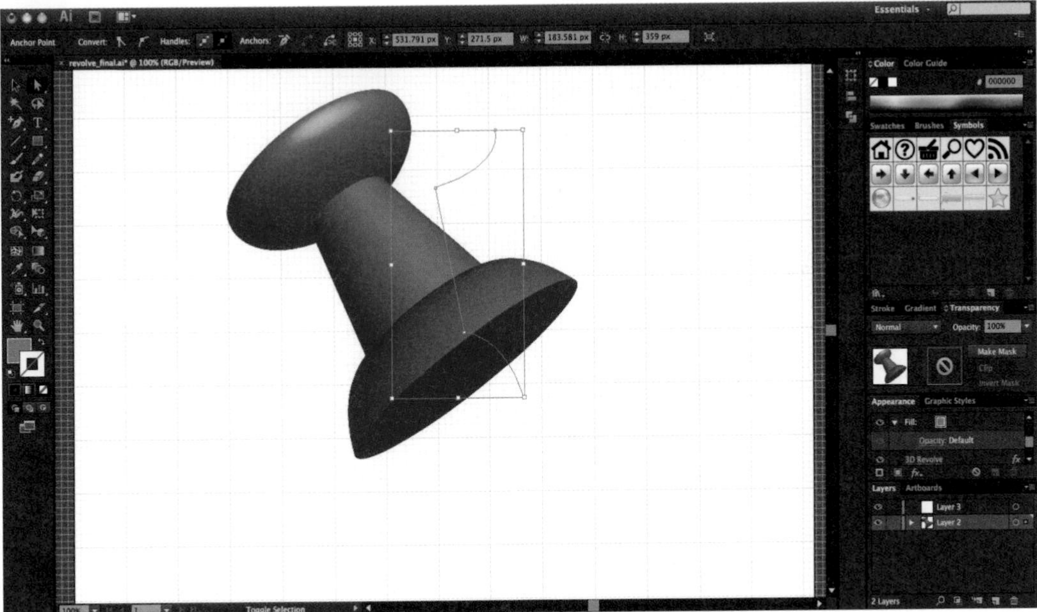

FIG 13-17 The 3D revolve effect applied to the path

7. In the Surface section, make sure to choose Plastic Shading from the drop-down list.
8. From the light preview circle, drag and move the light point to be similar to the figure below.

Now, we will use the extrude effect to create the pin metal end:

9. Create a path that will be revolved to create the pushpin end tip, as shown in the figure below.

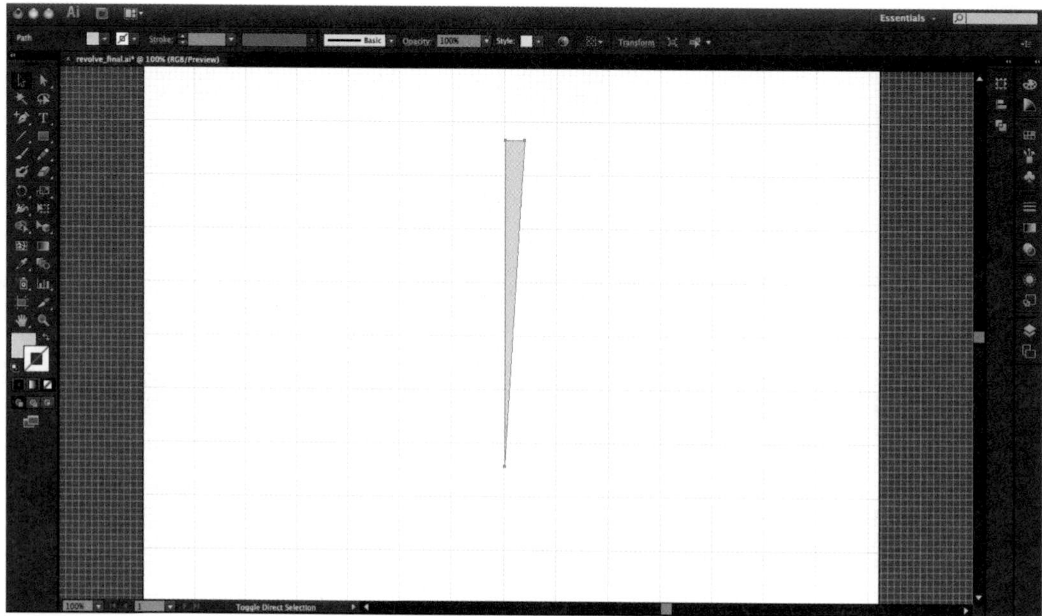

FIG 13-18 The pushpin bottom tip path

10. From the Effects menu, choose 3D > Revolve.
11. The 3D Revolve Options dialog box appears. Make sure to have the Preview checkbox selected to allow you to preview the effect updates.
12. Change the tip position to fit with the pushpin head, and click OK.
13. Use the Select tool to move the pushpin tip under the head, as shown in the final look below.

3D Rotation

Unlike the 3D Extrude and 3D Revolve effects, the 3D Rotate effect does not affect the object itself, but only allows you to rotate the object on the 3D space.

The 3D Rotate Options dialog box is much simpler than the previous 3D effects because it contains only the Position option, which is used to rotate the object, and the Surface option, which gives you the ability to add shades to the object and change the light direction and intensity.

In the next example, we will use the 3D Rotate effect to create a checkerboard in the 3D space:

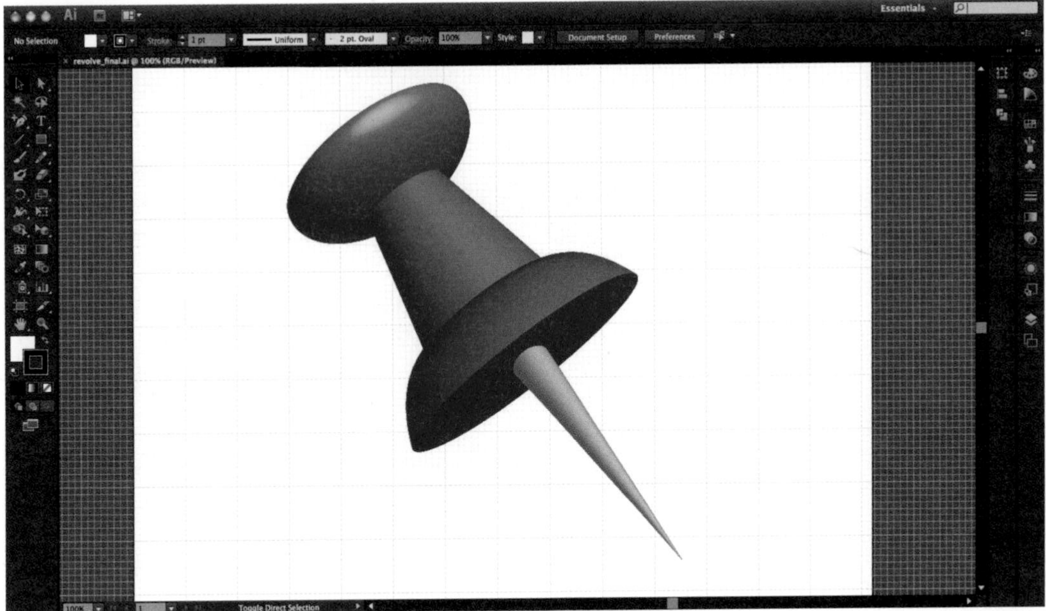

FIG 13-19 The final look for the pushpin illustration

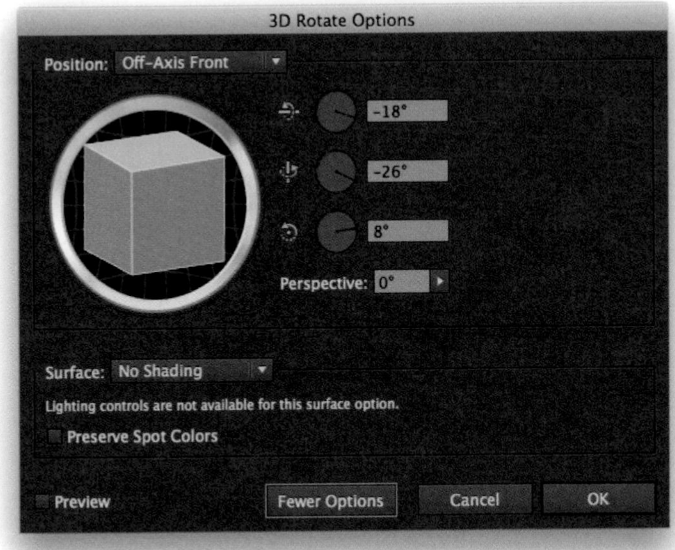

FIG 13-20 The 3D Rotate Options dialog box

1. Select the Rectangular Grid tool from the Tools panel. You can view it by clicking and holding over the Line tool.
2. Click on the artboard to bring up the Rectangular Grid Tool Options dialog box. Set the width and height to 800 pt.

3. Set the number of the cells to eight in the horizontal and vertical values, and click OK.

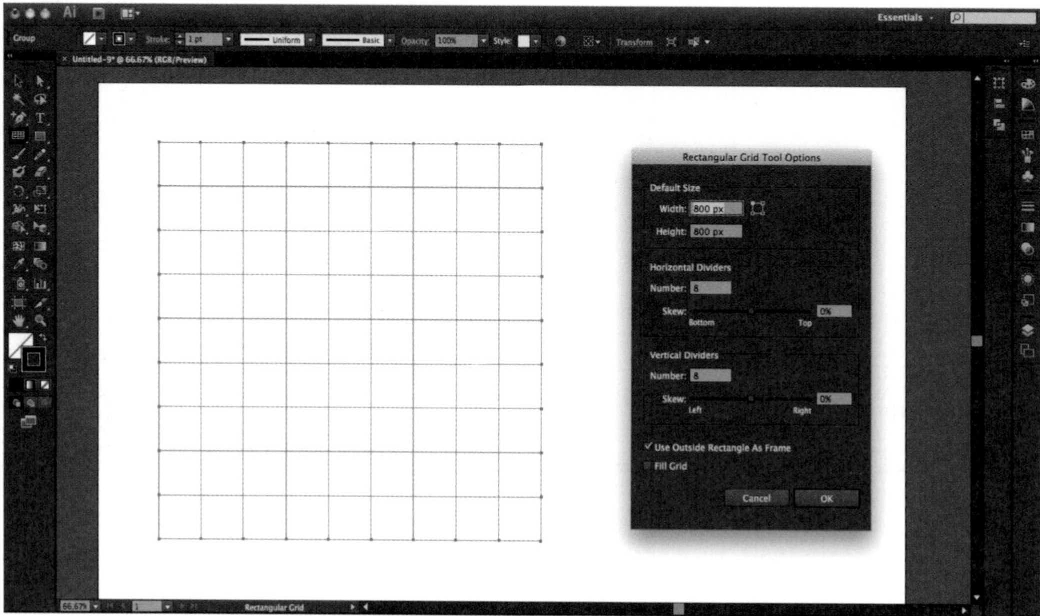

FIG 13-21 The table on the stage

4. The grid appears on the artboard. Select the Live Paint Bucket from the Tools panel, and set the front color to black.
5. Click on the cells to fill them with the black color to look like the checkerboard.
6. Switch to the white color, and fill the other cells.
7. Select the grid and from the Effects menu choose 3D Rotation.
8. In the 3D Rotate Options dialog box, make sure that the Preview checkbox is selected.
9. From the Position section, rotate the object 72 degrees around the X axis.
10. Change the perspective value to 50.

In this chapter we learned that Illustrator does not create 3D objects in a manner similar to 3D applications. However, you can use 3D Extrude, 3D Revolve, and 3D Rotate to convert a 2D path into a 3D look, with the ability to edit it through the 3D Effects dialog box. We also covered the Perspective Grid tool, which allows you to position content in the 3D space with accurate perspective. You can use this feature to create accurate 3D content using the

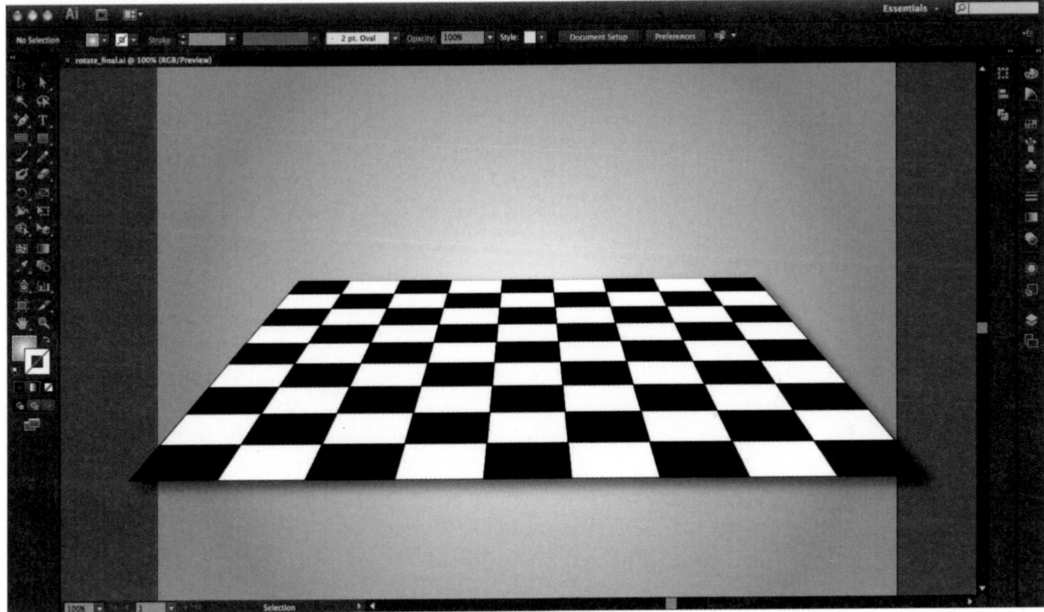

FIG 13-22 The checkerboard after 3D rotate effect

different options of the perspective grid. The examples mentioned in this chapter show how to use each feature and its options. Practicing the tools and merging these effects with the other effects we have covered can help you to create complex artwork.

For examples pertaining to this chapter, visit www.illustratorfoundations.com.

CHAPTER 14

Working with Effects

In addition to the drawing capabilities that Adobe Illustrator provides, it provides a number of effects that you can easily choose and apply directly to your artwork. If you have experience with Photoshop, you will notice that the effects work in a very similar way as the filters in that application; you can apply an effect on an object and edit its settings through each effect's dialog box.

The effects can provide great help in your project, because they are used frequently to create different outcomes that you cannot create using the drawing tools. Much of the Illustrator artwork that you can see in designs depends on Illustrator effects, as we will see later in the Illustrator Effects section. One of the advantages of using effects is that they are not permanent and do not alter your artwork. You can edit and modify them after applying them to the object.

In this chapter we will cover how to apply effects to artwork using the wide range of effects in Illustrator and the Appearance panel. Also, we will cover how to apply some effects using the tools from the Tools panel.

Appearance Panel

Before we jump to the interesting Illustrator examples, let us dig in to one of the most important panels in Illustrator, the Appearance panel. When it is essential to apply fills, strokes, transparency, and effects on artwork, the Appearance panel provides an easy way to preview the structure of the effects applied to the object and how the effects are organized.

The Appearance panel displays the object attributes, such as the fill, stroke, and opacity, in a stacking order. Thus, the top attribute displays first, then the next attribute. When you select an object, you can see that the object type appears in the top of the Appearance panel and under it the values such as the fill, stroke, and opacity.

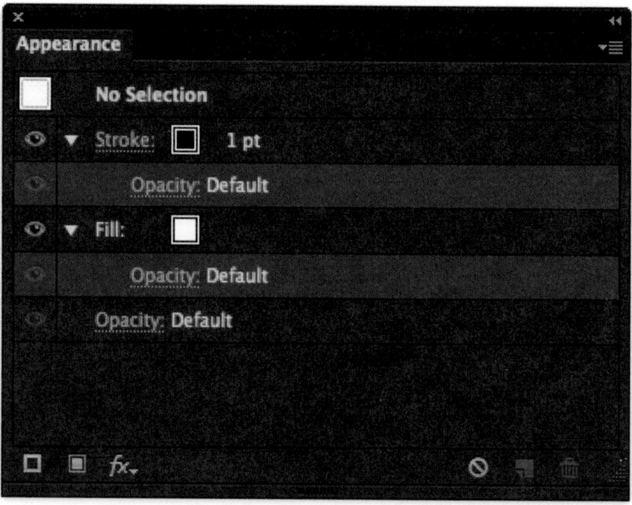

FIG 14-1 The Appearance panel in illustrator

Each of the stroke and fill attribute items are expandable. You can click the arrow next to the item to expand it to change the attribute's color and opacity, as in the example below:

1. Create a new Illustrator document.
2. Select the Rectangle tool from the Tools panel.
3. Draw a rectangle, and make sure it includes fill and stroke color.
4. Select the rectangle with the Selection tool.
5. Open the Appearance panel.
6. Select the fill item.
7. Click the fill color, and change the color of the rectangle to one of the swatches colors.
8. Click the arrow next to the fill to expand it.
9. Click in the opacity value, and change the fill color transparency from the Opacity slider.

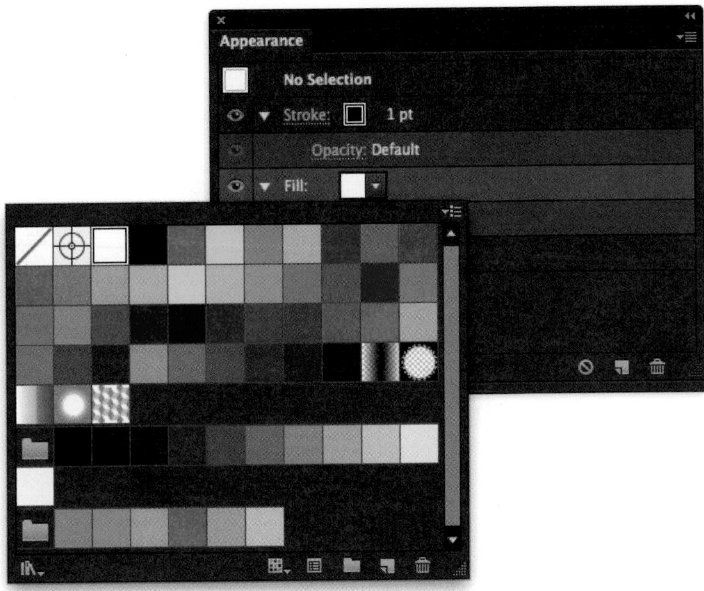

FIG 14-2 Changing the fill color properties from the Appearance panel

At the bottom of the panel, you can find more options to control this attribute:

- Delete Item lets you delete the currently selected item, such as stroke or fill.
- Duplicate Selected item lets you create a duplicate of the currently selected item in the panel.
- Clear Appearance clears both the fill and stroke to have no color applied to them.
- Add New Effect lets you apply effects to the object, as we will cover later in Illustrator Effects section.
- Add Fill lets you add one or more fill attributes to the object.
- Add Stroke lets you add one or more strokes to the object.

The attributes arrange in the Appearance panel in stacking order. The top item appears first on the object, and the next item appears behind the first one. In the example below, we will discover how to use the stacking order in the Appearance panel to create effects based on multiple stroke attributes applied to the object.

1. Create a new Illustrator document.
2. Select the Ellipse tool from the Tools panel.
3. Create a large circle using the Ellipse tool while pressing the Shift key to maintain the circle shape.
4. Open the Appearance panel.
5. Select the fill attribute. Click the color icon and from the swatches, set the fill color to orange.

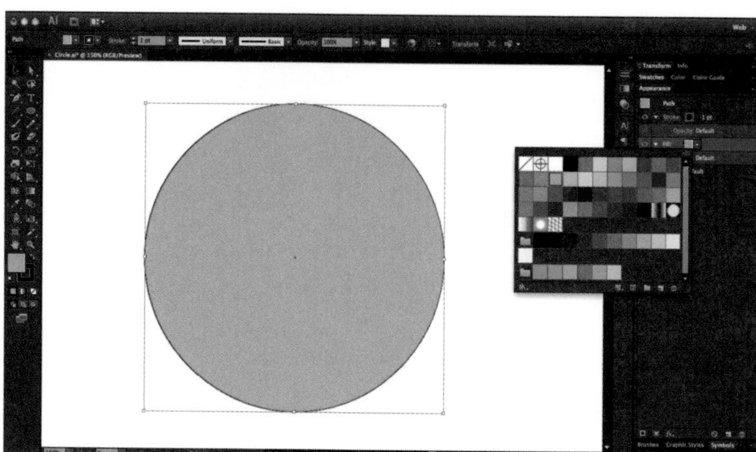

FIG 14-3 Set the fill color of the circle to orange

6. In the stroke attribute, set the stroke width to 100 px and the color to red.
7. Click Add New Stroke at the bottom of the panel.
8. In the new stroke, set its width to 80px and the color to orange.
9. Click Add New Stroke from the bottom of the panel.
10. In the new stroke, set its width to 60 px and the color to red.
11. Continue to create more strokes with decreasing width values, such as 40 px and 20 px.

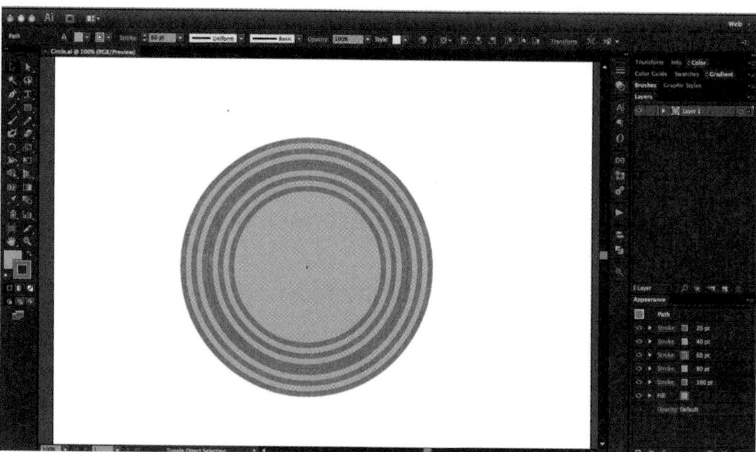

FIG 14-4 The final appearance of the multiple stroke effect

You will notice the stacking order in the above example. When you review the order of the items in the Appearance panel, you will notice that Adobe Illustrator applies the opacity attribute for the whole object, including the fill and stacked stroke attributes. Actually, using the multiple fills and strokes can help you to create many effects very easily, without the need to create multiple objects or paths. You can easily edit your effect by simply changing the color or width of the strokes or even by deleting the effect with a single mouse click.

Live Effect

Before we jump to the various effects in Adobe Illustrator, let us overview the concept of Live Effects. Unlike many other graphics applications, when you apply effects in Illustrator, you can still edit the object after applying the effects, even when you close the document; this is what we know in Illustrator as Live Effects.

When you apply an effect on artwork in Illustrator, it is saved in the Appearance panel as one of the attributes that can be applied to the object. The figure below shows the Appearance panel with the Live Effects.

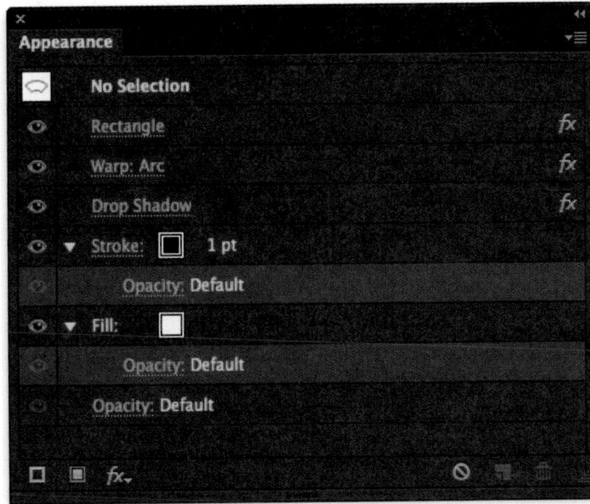

FIG 14-5 The Live Effects in the Appearance panel

You can apply the effect to either the whole object or select one item from the Appearance panel and apply the effect to that item. You can see if the effect has been applied to the whole artwork or a specific item or attribute from the panel as shown in the figure below.

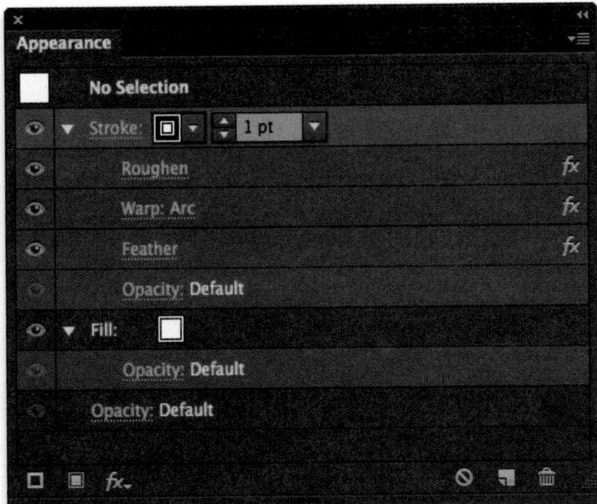

FIG 14-6 The effect applied to the stroke only in the Appearance panel

This part covers the general concept of Live Effects; we will be able to learn more about it in the next section, when we talk about the different effects in Illustrator. Adobe Illustrator provides a large number of effects that you can apply, preview, and modify using the Appearance panel. You can access the effects either from the Effects menu at the top of the Illustrator workspace or from the Effects menu in the Appearance panel.

Currently, Adobe Illustrator categorizes the effects into two main categories. The first is the Illustrator effects, which are located at the top of the Effects menu, and the second is Photoshop effects, which are similar to the effects you see in Adobe Photoshop and located in the bottom of the Effects menu.

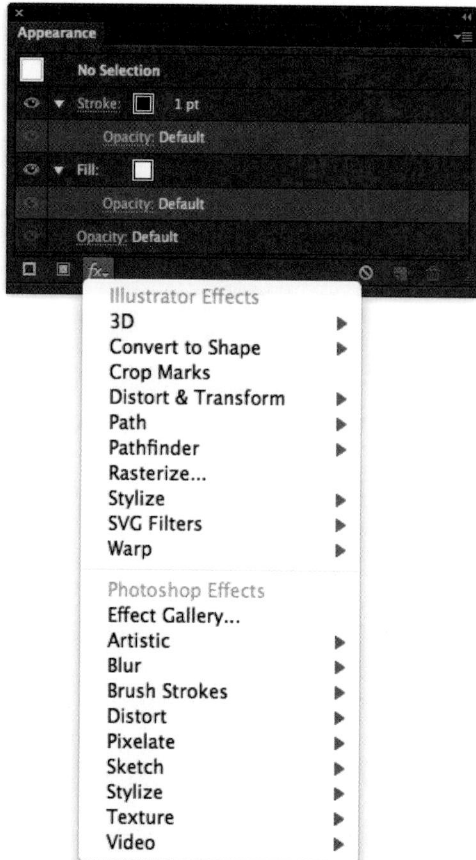

FIG 14-7 The effects in the Appearance panel

Let us move forward to see these different effects and how to use the different settings to produce creative effects on your artwork.

Illustrator Effects

When you apply an effect on an object, you can edit the settings before and after applying the effect. Each applied effect appears in the Appearance panel based on its stacking order. Illustrator effects in the Effect menu are categorized based on the function they perform, so related or similar effects appear in submenus of the basic categories. While success working with effects is based on experience, we will overview the commonly used effects and the functions of each category.

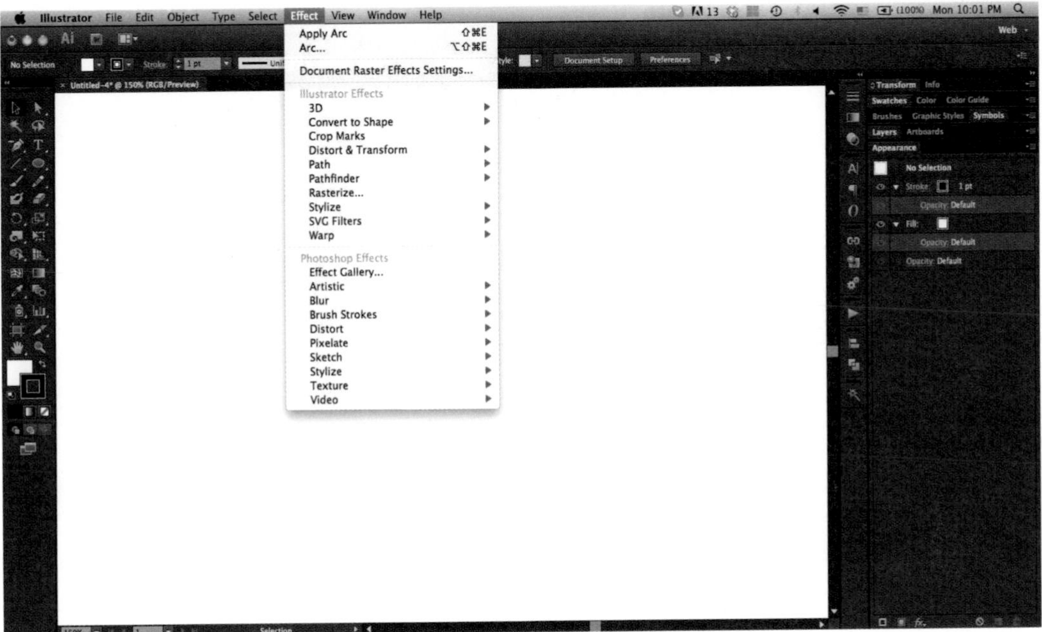

FIG 14-8 The Illustrator effects in the Effect menu

3D Effects

We have covered 3D effects in Chapter 13. These effects convert 2D paths into 3D objects through 3D Extrude, 3D Revolve, and 3D Rotate in the 3D space.

Convert to Shape

This effect changes the shape of an object to another shape, while the main shape is not replaced or modified with the new object. You can also still modify the effect properties in the Appearance panel. In this effect, you can convert the shape to a rectangle, rounded rectangle, or ellipse. The example below shows how to convert a star shape to a circle:

1. Open the document Star_shape.ai. This document includes a star shape with different strokes applied to it.
2. Select the star shape with the Selection tool.
3. From the Effects menu, choose Convert to Shape > Ellipse.
4. In the Shape Options dialog box, keep the values as default, and click OK.
5. From the Appearance panel, you can double-click the ellipse item to reopen the Shape options and edit the different values.

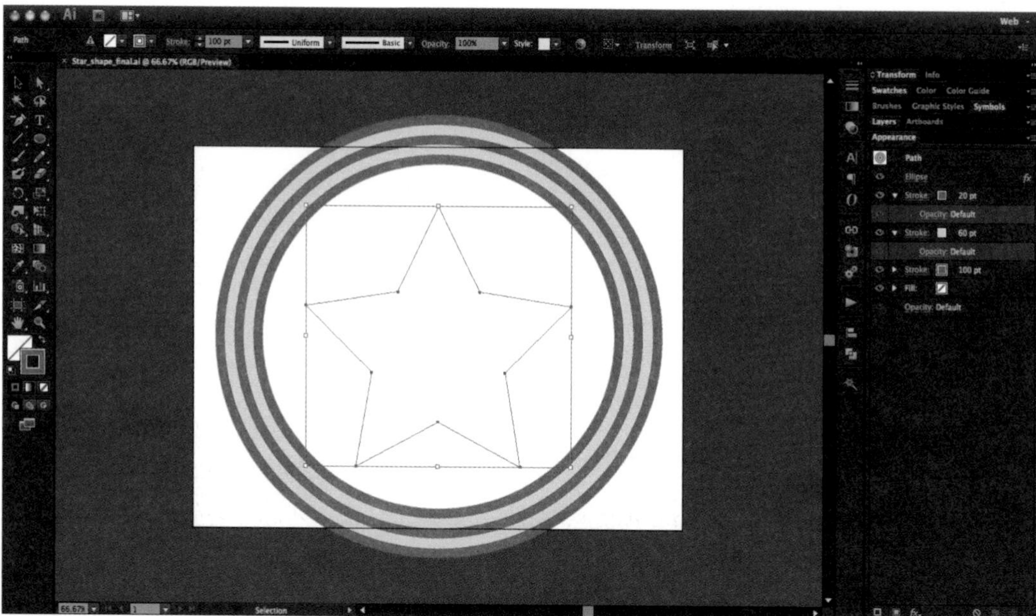

FIG 14-9 The star shape converted to a circle using the Convert to Shape effect

Crop Marks

The Crop Marks effect creates marks around the object to indicate its edges and where it can be cut on printed papers. For example, you can set the crop marks for a logo to indicate the outer edges of the logo. In printed materials, crop marks can be a guide to indicate the artwork boundaries so that you can crop or add the item into other printing media. Crop marks are printed with the registered color. You can activate the option by choosing Crop Marks from the Effects menu or the effects list in the Appearance panel.

Distort and Transform

As the name of these effects implies, they include the ability to transform artwork in a manner similar to the Transform tools that we covered in Chapter 7.

The advantage of using the Distort and Transform effects is that you can easily modify the object later through the Appearance panel.

In addition to the Transform options, the following effects distort the artwork:

- Free Distort allows you to freely distort the artwork through a dialog box. You can use Free Distort to create a perspective effect on the object.
- Pucker & Bloat pulls the anchor points out of the object while the segments go inside, or vice versa.
- Roughen turns the path into rough edges and angles. You can change its options from the Roughen dialog box.
- Tweak converts the path lines into random curves.
- Twist, as its name implies, twists the artwork path.
- Zig Zag turns the path into a zig-zag style with different setting options.

Now, let us see how to create a Milky Way galaxy shape in Illustrator using the Twist effect:

1. Open the document Galaxy_start.ai. This document includes a simple rectangle on the stage.
2. Select the white rectangle using the Selection tool.
3. From the Effects menu, choose Distort and Transform > Twist.
4. In the Twist dialog box, set the angle to 700 degrees and press OK.
5. Save this document as Galaxy_twist.ai to use in the next steps.

FIG 14-10 The galaxy shape after applying the Twist effect

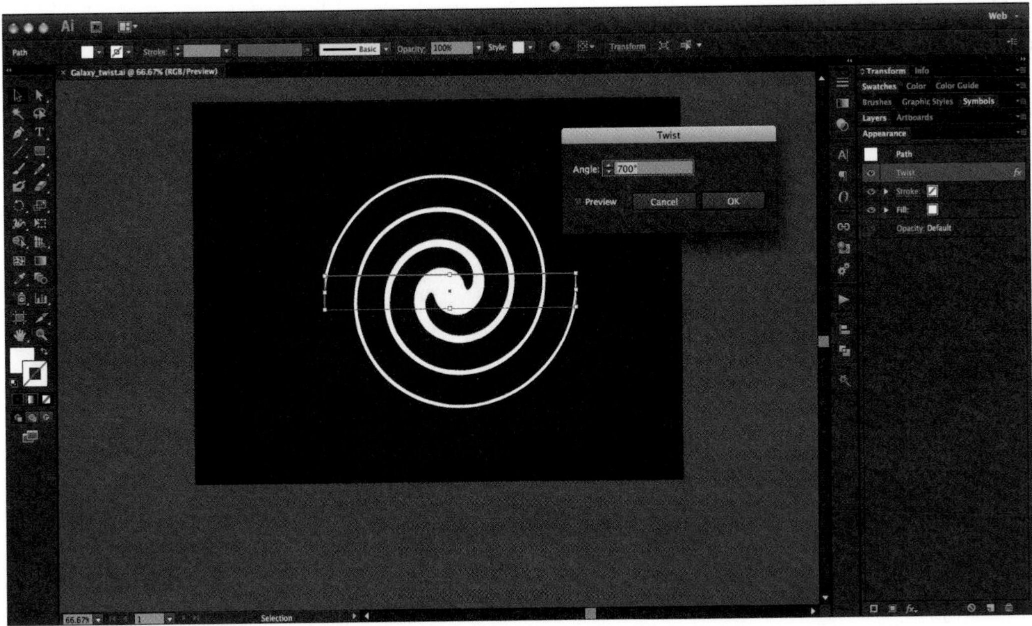

Path and Pathfinder Effects

The effects listed in these two categories are more concerned with the path itself and how to affect the path, such as the Offset Path option, which allows you to expand the outline of the object. The Pathfinder effects are very similar to the Pathfinder options that we covered in Chapter 7.

Rasterize

In some cases, we would like to convert vector artwork into bitmap. You can select an object and click on this effect to convert it into rasterized artwork.

Stylize

The Stylize effects are very commonly used because they let you add drop shadow, glow, feather, and scribble. Let us see how to add another effect to the last example by adding some feather to the galaxy shape:

1. Open the document Galaxy_twist.ai that we created earlier.
2. Select the galaxy shape with the Selection tool.
3. From the Effects menu, choose Stylize > Feather.
4. In the Feather dialog box, set the value to eight and click OK.

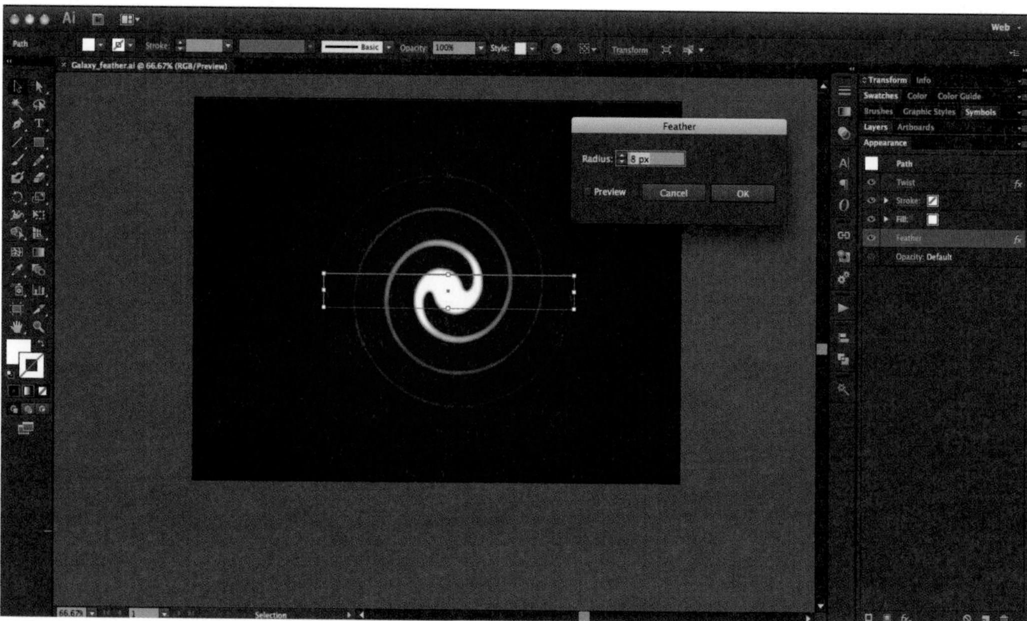

FIG 14-11 The galaxy shape with the feather applied to it

In our next example, we will learn how to use the Scribble effect to convert text in Illustrator into a handwriting style:

1. Create a new Illustrator document.
2. Select the Text tool from the Tools panel.
3. Click inside the artboard, and write the words "Adobe Illustrator."
4. Set the text size to 100, font type to Helvetica, and make it bold and the color light blue.
5. While the text is selected, from the Effects menu, choose Stylize > Scribble.
6. In the Scribble options, set the settings as follows:
   a. Set the angle to 30 degrees.
   b. Set the path overlap to 0 px and variation to 5 px.
   c. Set the stroke width to 1 px.
   d. Set the curviness to 0% and variation to 0%.
   e. Set the spacing to 1.5 px and its variation to 0.5 px.

FIG 14-12 The text with the Scribble effect applied to it

SVG Filters

The filters in this category are raster filters. Raster filters and effects generate a pixilated look. When you apply any of the SVG filters to the artwork, you can click the filter item in the Appearance panel to switch between different filters.

Warp

These effects are very similar to the Warp effects that you can find when editing text or envelopes in Illustrator. We covered these different effects in

Chapter 9. The Warp effects include arc, arch, fish, fish eye, rise, squeeze, twist, and so on.

Photoshop Effects

The second type of effect in the Effects menu is the Photoshop effects. If you have artwork or an image in Illustrator that you would like to apply to any of the commonly used filters in Photoshop, you do not need to export your artwork into Photoshop in order to apply the any of the Photoshop filters to the artwork.

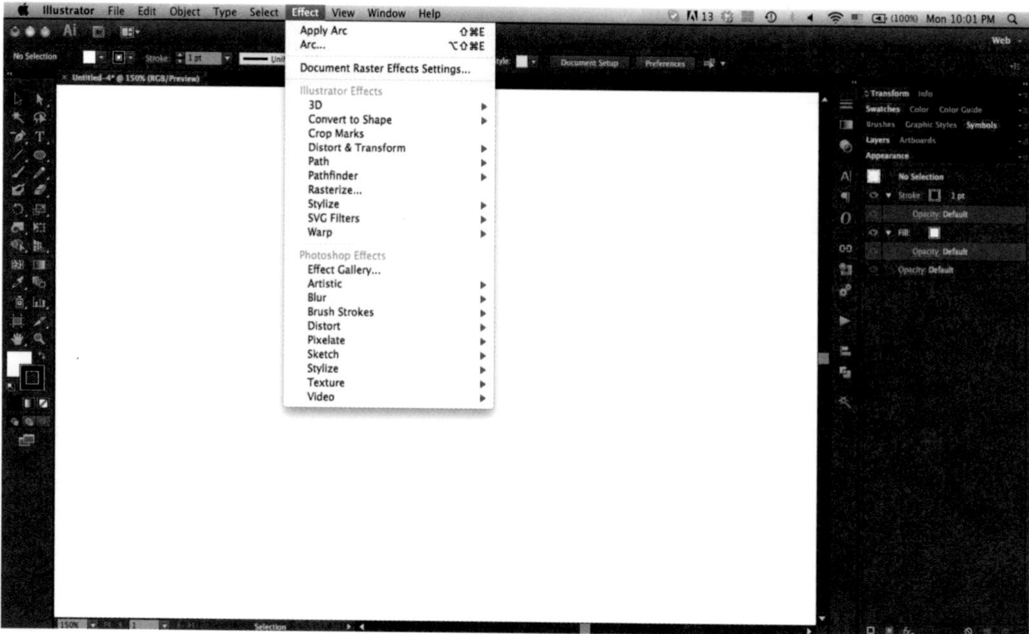

FIG 14-13 The photoshop effects in the effect menu

The Photoshop Effects section includes the same filters that you can find in Adobe Photoshop. Furthermore, these effects act very similar to the Illustrator effects you can see in the Appearance panel and that you can click to edit from each Effect Options dialog box.

There are many settings for each effect that can help you to create various styles. You can practice and explore each different effect. Effects and filters depend on practical experience.

Object Distortion Tools

In addition to the effects, Adobe Illustrator provides some tools in the Tools panel that let you distort artwork and paths. These tools include the following:

FIG 14-14 The Object Distortion tools

- Width increases the width of the artwork paths or part of the path.
- Warp deforms the artwork by warping its outline.
- Twirl creates twirling distortion for the object by clicking in the place where you would like to apply the distortion.
- Pucker distorts the artwork by moving the object anchor points toward the curser.
- Bloat distorts the artwork by moving the object anchor point away from the curser.
- Scallop moves the anchor points to the center of the mouse curser.
- Crystallize moves the anchor points away from the center of the mouse curser.
- Wrinkle changes the artwork outline to be a wrinkle-like line instead of straight or covered lines.

Now, let us see how to use these tools through the below example. In the below steps we will make a sweet piece more natural by distorting its edges:

1. Open the document Distort_start.ai. This file includes a sweet shape that we will distort using the tools we mentioned above.
2. Select the Warp tool and double-click on it to display the Warp options. Set the width and the height of the warp to 100 px.
3. Click and drag from the outside toward the center to distort the sweet's right and left edge as shown in the figure below.

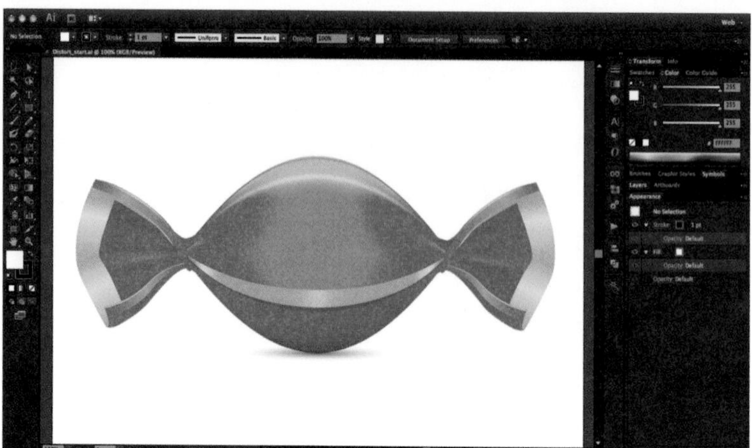

FIG 14-15 Applying the warp distortion to the artwork

4. Now select the Twirl tool.
5. Double-click the Twirl tool to open the Option dialog box. Set the width and height to 75%, and set the intensity to 25% from the global brush dimensions.
6. Start by clicking to distort the inner orange lines of the sweet. The final image should look like the figure below.

FIG 14-16 The final look for the artwork after applying the twirl distortion

As we have seen, you can implement the distortion tools to add more effects to your artwork by a simple click of the mouse. You do not need to create these distortion effects manually, and doing so will consume time and effort.

Blending Modes

If you have experience with Adobe Photoshop, you will find the blending modes in that application are very similar to the ones in Illustrator. Generally, the blending modes let Adobe Illustrator determine how the colors of the overlapped objects interact with the others below. There are many blending modes that affect overlapped objects in Illustrator; each mode provides different results for how the colors appear in the intersected area between the two objects.

You can select from blending modes from the Transparency panel. The best method to understand the difference between each mode is to try it and see how it affects the different objects, images, and colors. For example, the darken, multiple, and color burn modes turn the overlapped area to a darker color. The lighten, screen, and color dodge modes turn the overlapped area to be more bright than the original colors.

Let us follow these steps to try the blending modes in Illustrator:

1. Create a new Illustrator document.
2. Select the Ellipse tool.
3. Create two overlapped circles on the stage.
4. Set different colors for each circle.
5. Select both circles.
6. From the Transparency panel, open the Blending Modes drop-down list and try each option to see how it affects the overlapped area.

FIG 14-17 The blending modes options in the drop-down list

While the blending modes in Illustrator are not used as often as those in Photoshop, you can use them to generate different color combinations and create artistic effects, such as pop-art posters and vintage style designs.

At this point, we have learned how to use masks, blends, and blending modes in Adobe Illustrator and how to implement them to create different effects. Masks can be used to crop artwork and hide unwanted parts of the artwork or image. You can also use the opacity mask to create reflections, faded effects, and more. Both the effects and the distortion tools in Adobe Illustrator are practical tools whose effective use depends on your own experimentation. Try different effects and combinations of effects to reach more creative styles.

For examples pertaining to this chapter, visit www.illustratorfoundations.com.

Arranging and Saving Artwork

In previous chapters, we learned how to create documents and build artwork in Adobe Illustrator; we went in depth with each feature to discover its capabilities and discussed practical examples for how to work with the important tools and features in Illustrator. We also covered different effects and how to easily edit and modify artwork.

One of the common issues that beginner illustrators and designers face is that they usually start learning with a focus on the tools and how to create artwork. While this is important, arranging your artwork and building a professional-looking document can help you to make the design workflow easier and help other designers or developers who work within your team to better understand the artwork and document that is built. It is also important, when you work with complex Illustrator artwork that includes a lot of shapes and objects, to maintain an easy way to understand your document structures, especially when you are working in various projects and may return to your archived documents a long time after you save them.

In addition to arranging your work file, it is important to understand the different saving options and formats that you can use to export your Illustrator artwork. A good understanding of these formats and their different settings can help you to create the proper files for web, printing, and digital media. For example, if you are exporting your artwork for the web, you have to consider having a low file size along with a good-quality image in order for it to load quickly and smoothly on web browsers. Saving artwork for printing requires high resolution and quality without concern for the image size, since the final product with be printed on paper; for example, brochures and posters. In this chapter, we will review how to arrange documents and artwork inside Illustrator, and we will learn how to save artwork and export it to different formats.

Working with Groups

Working with groups involves gathering shapes or pieces of artwork into one composition or unit that allows you to handle these elements as if they were one object. Although the groups feature is very common in many design applications, it is especially important when working in Adobe Illustrator because it helps you to create complex artwork.

Groups are the first method to organize your artwork in Illustrator, so you can gather the parts of the artwork and apply and interact with them as one object. Groups also prevent your or other designers from accidently moving or changing pieces of the artwork design. The steps below show how to create a group of objects in Illustrator:

1. Create a new Illustrator document, and use the Rectangle tool to draw two rectangles on the stage.
2. With the Selection tool, drag over the objects on the artboard to select them. You can also click while pressing the Shift key to select multiple objects.
3. From the Object menu, choose Group. You can right-click on the selected objects and choose Group from the context menu.

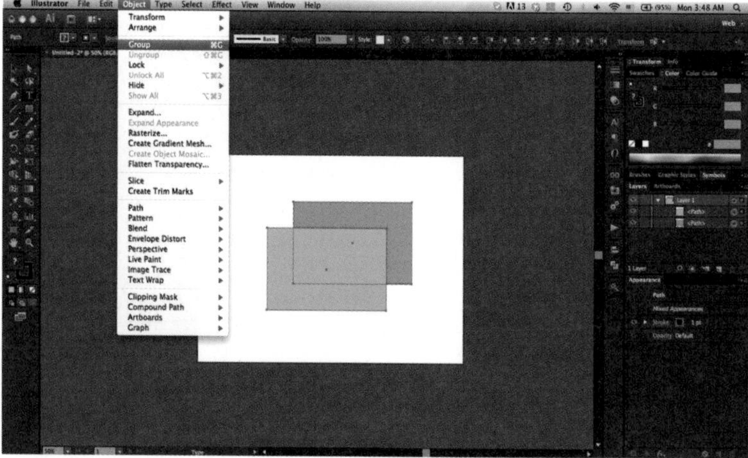

FIG 15-1 Selecting the Group command from the top menu

> **Shortcut**
>
> While selecting multiple objects, you can click Cmd+G (Ctrl+G in Windows) to directly create a group of the selected shapes.

Now, try to move the group object and apply different effects to it to get an idea of how Illustrator interacts with a group as if it were one object on the stage. After creating the group, you can ungroup it as follows:

4. Select the group that we created in the above steps.
5. From the Object menu, choose the Ungroup command. You can right-click and choose Ungroup from the context menu.

Working with groups is the first step to arranging your artwork and one of the most common steps, especially when working with complex artwork.

Lock Artwork

In some cases, complex artwork includes intersected paths and objects, which makes it hard to edit or modify the overlapped paths and shapes. Therefore, you need to lock the objects that you do not want to accidently select or change. There are three locking options that you can reach from Object > Lock in the top menu:

1. Selection lets you lock only the selected object or objects.
2. All Artwork Above lets you lock all the objects located above the currently selected object.
3. Other Layers lets you lock all the objects that are located in the other layers in the Illustrator document. We will cover this later in the Working with Layers section.

> **Shortcut**
>
> You can lock selected objects by pressing the Cmd+2 (Ctrl+2 in Windows).

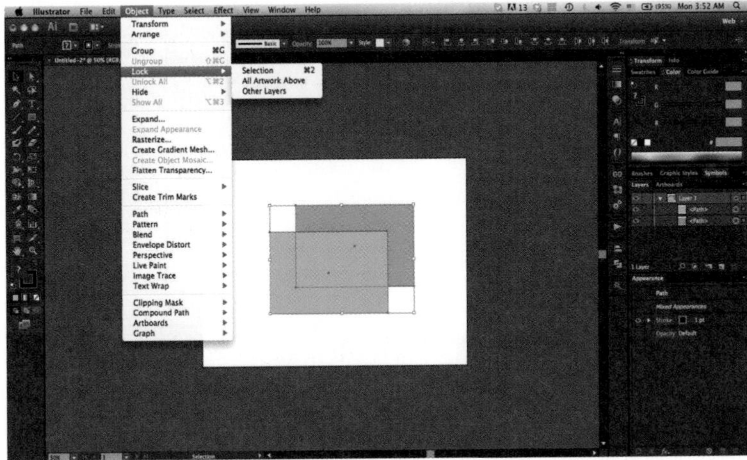

FIG 15-2 The Lock command in the Object menu

Using the example document Arrange_artwork.ai, you can experience the difference between each of the above locking options. You can unlock the locked shapes by selecting Unlock All from the Object menu.

> **Shortcut**
>
> To unlock all objects, press Cmd+Options+2 (Ctrl+Alt+2 in Windows).

Hide Artwork

Another method to handle complex artwork shapes and elements is to hide the objects that you do not need to show or for which you would like to reveal the parts underneath. The Hide command is one of the useful features that gives you more capability to control your artwork.

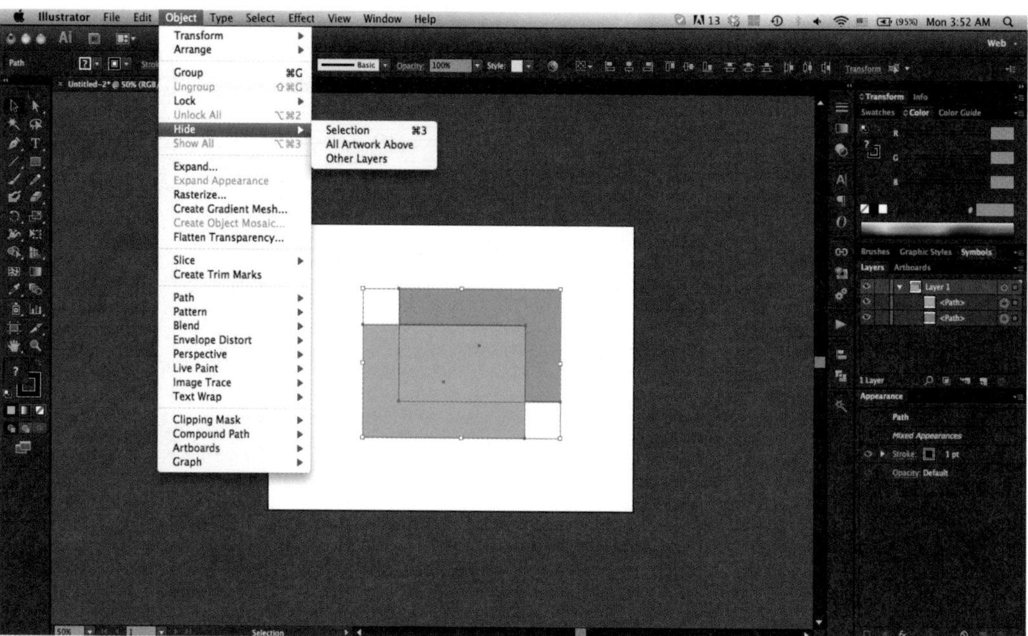

FIG 15-3 The Hide command in the Object menu

Similar to the locking options, you can hide either the selected object, the artwork above the selected object, or objects in layers other than the selected one. The Lock and Hide commands are actually associated with the Layer panel in Adobe Illustrator, as we will cover later in the Working with Layers section.

> **Shortcut**
>
> You can hide the selected object or object or objects by pressing Cmd+3 (Ctrl+3 in Windows).

Arranging Objects

One of the most important and commonly used methods to arrange objects within your document and the shapes in your complex artwork is to arrange the paths and shapes in comparison with each other. For example, you may want to send one object behind another one, or vice versa. However, you will notice that you are arranging objects frequently while you build your artwork.

You can change the order of the objects in the same layer from the Object > Arrange top menu. You can also right-click the object to reveal the Arrange options from the context menu. The Arrange options are as follows:

- Bring to Front sends the object to the top of all the objects in the same layer.
- Bring Forward sends the object above the current object in the same layer.
- Bring Backward sends the object behind the current object in the same layer.
- Bring to Back sends the object behind all the objects in the current layer.

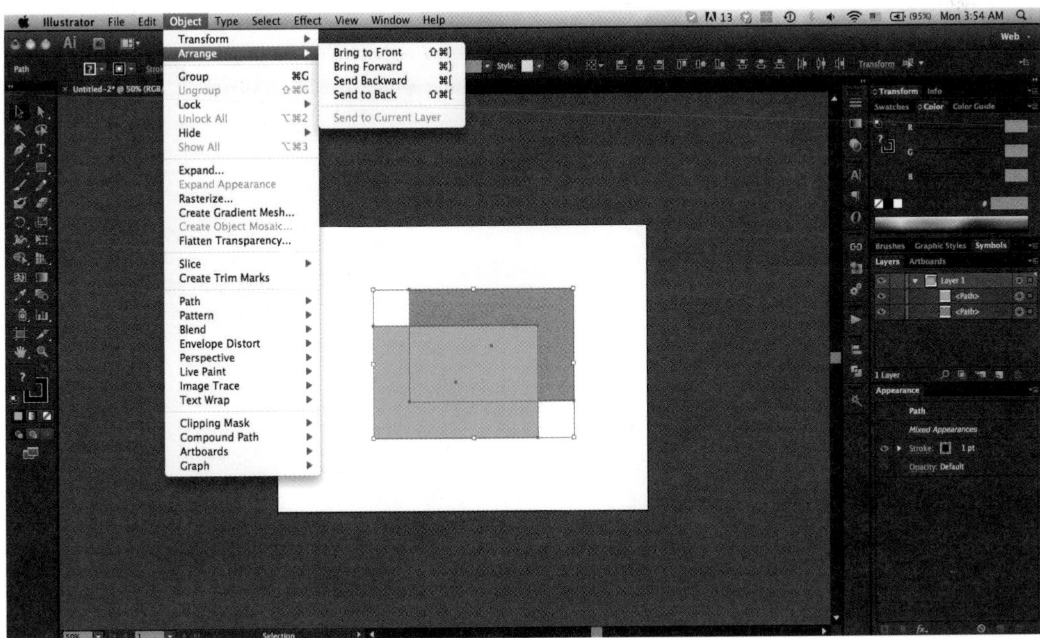

FIG 15-4 The Arrange commands from the Object menu

> **Shortcut**
>
> You can bring an object to front of back by pressing Cmd+] or Cmd+[(Ctrl+] and Ctrl+[in Windows). You can bring an object forward or backward by pressing Shift+Cmd+] or Shift+Cmd+[(Shift+Ctrl+] and Shift+Ctrl+[in Windows).

In the following steps, we will practice the different arrangement options:

1. Open the document Arrange_artwork.ai.
2. Select the top object using the Selection tool from the Tools panel.
3. From the Object menu, choose Arrange > Send to Back.

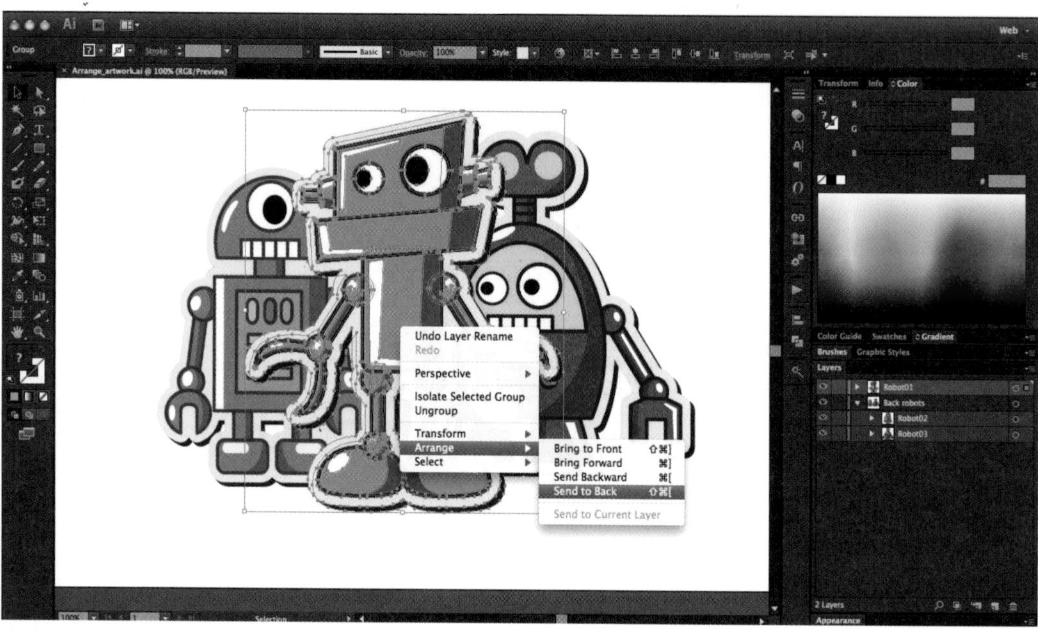

FIG 15-5 The Arrange command in the Context menu

Working with Layers

The layer concept is very common in graphic design applications. It is based on an old style for creating cartoons, when the artist needed to add scene objects on different transparent paper drawings to animate each object separately from the others. This concept has moved to digital applications such as Photoshop and Illustrator. While you can move each piece of artwork or shape individually, you can also select the layer to select and interact with all its content, including resizing, moving, and so on.

While many designers and artists, especially beginners, focus on creating artwork in Illustrator, they do not give much focus to how to work with layers. Layers in Illustrator help you to arrange artwork and build a professional file structure. For example, you can add the related parts of a piece of artwork to one layer.

You can manage layers in the Layer panel. If you cannot see it, you can select it from the Window menu. Each layer includes sublayers, which include the paths that construct the artwork, as you can see from the layer structure in the figure below.

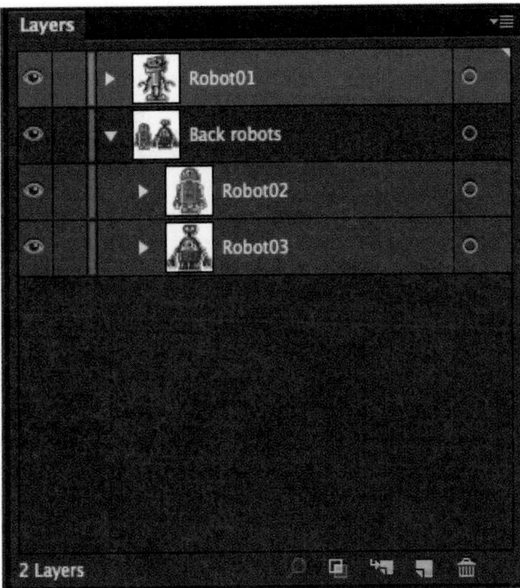

FIG 15-6 The layers structure in the Layer panel

Each layer allows you to do the following:

- You can click on the Eye icon next to the layer or its sublayers to hide or show a specific layer and its associated objects.
- To the right of the Eye icon, you can click to show or hide the Lock icon, which indicates whether this layer or sublayer is editable.
- To the right of each layer you will find a small circle. Clicking this circle selects all the objects in the layer. If you click the circle next to a sublayer, it selects only the path included in the sublayer.
- You can double-click on a layer to rename it. You should have a unique representative name for each layer in order to create a better arrangement for your work in the Illustrator file.

At the bottom of the Layer panel, you will find the following icons, from right to left:

- The Delete icon will delete the selected layer. You can drag the icon to the layer that you would like to delete or drag the layer that you would like to delete to the icon.
- The Create New Layer icon lets you create a new layer in the Layer panel. You can also drag a layer to this icon to create a duplicated copy of the layer.
- Create New Sublayer lets you create a new sublayer inside the selected layer.
- Make/Release Clipping Mask converts the selected layer to a clipping mask or releases an existing clipping mask, as we discussed in Chapter 10.

- The Locate Object icons make visible in the Layer panel the selected object in the layers hierarchy.
- To the left of the icons, you can find the numbers of layers.

Note

You can also see that the active layer in the Layer panel has a small triangle that appears at the top right corner of the layer.

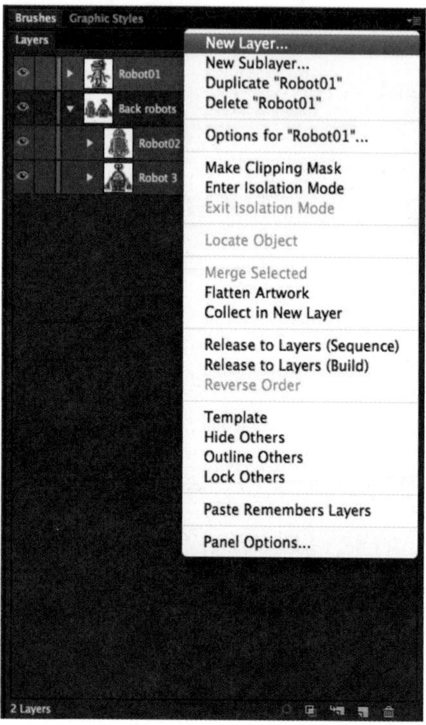

FIG 15-7 The Layer Panel Options menu

In addition to the above options, you can find more options in the Layer Panel Options menu:

- Duplicate Layer lets you create a copy from the selected layer.
- The Options command displays the settings for the selected layer.
- Flatten Artwork collects the artwork in one layer.
- Collect in New Layer converts the current layer to a sublayer of a new layer.
- Release to Layer Sequence releases each item to a new layer.
- Release to Layer Build releases each item to a new layer, and the bottom item appears in each new layer.
- Template converts the layer into a template layer.
- Panel Options displays the Layer panel options.

Saving an Illustrator Document

After creating and arranging your artwork, Adobe Illustrator provides support to save documents in a large range of formats, including documents such as Microsoft Word and PDF, vector formats such as AI and EPS, and bitmap formats such as JPG, PNG, TIFF, PSD, and so on. Choosing the best format to save your Illustrator artwork depends on the target media and the type of project that will use the artwork. For example, if you are working on a printing project, you need to save the document in a printer-friendly format such as AI and PDF that does not affect image colors due to image compression. Web projects require you to save artwork in web-friendly formats such as JPG and PNG for transparent content.

Save Document as Template

The first saving method is to save the artwork or design as a template. Templates are reusable designs that you can save as references for further design or upcoming projects. For example, you can save a design for a DVD template or a brochure design that you can use in future projects.

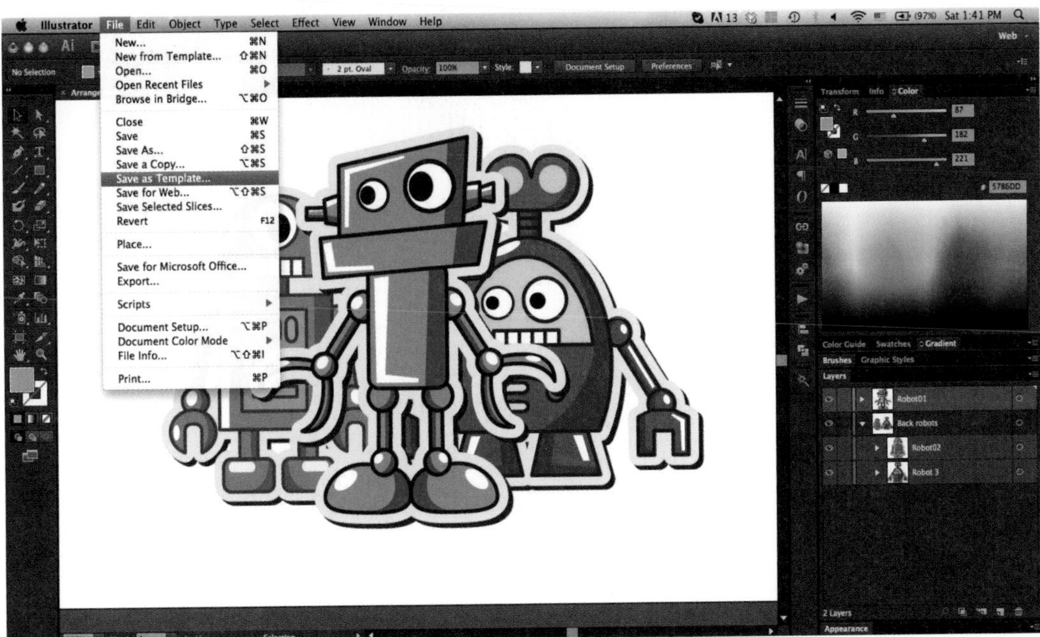

FIG 15-8 The Save as Template from the File menu

You can open a new Adobe Illustrator document from a template. The newly created document will have the template design, and you can continue your work based on this template. You can save the design as a template from File > Save as Template. The saved files are in AIT format.

Save Document as PDF

PDF is one of the commonly used formats for creating documents and printing projects and is a useful format to transfer artwork for project reviews with the team and through emails. Saving your artwork in PDF format is one of the more powerful features in Adobe Illustrator and includes different options, such as saving artboards as PDF pages and more.

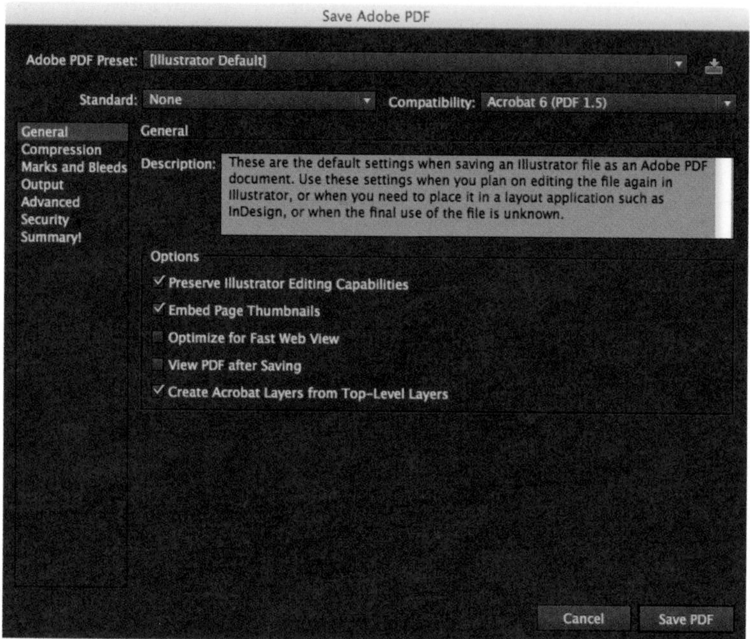

FIG 15-9 The Save Adobe PDF dialog box

To save a document as PDF, choose Save or Save As from the File menu. The Save Adobe PDF dialog box appears to let you set up the PDF options:

- You can choose from different PDF options using the Adobe PDF presets.
- You can control the image format and compression quality and method.
- You can set the marks and bleeds for the document.
- You can set up the security options and add passwords.

Save Document as JPG

JPG is a common format to create small-size and good-quality artwork, especially for the web. Adobe Illustrator allows you to export artwork in JPG format with different options. To export artwork as JPG, follow the below steps:

1. From the File menu, choose Export.
2. Choose the JPG format from the formats list.

3. Click Use Artboard to select the artboard that you would like to export, if your document includes more than one artboard.
4. Click OK (Save in Windows).

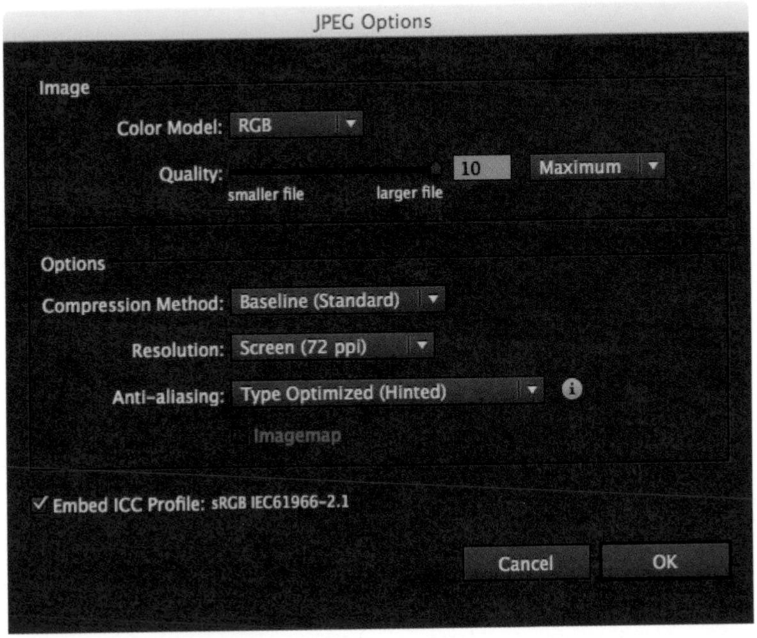

FIG 15-10 The JPG Options dialog box

The JPG Options dialog box appears with the different JPG options, including:

- Color mode options: RGB, CMYK, and grayscale.
- The quality of the image: higher quality means larger size, and vice versa.
- The compression method: baseline (standard), baseline optimized, and progressive. Keep the standard method, as most browsers recognize it.
- The resolution of the exported image: higher resolution means larger size and higher quality.
- Anti-aliasing methods: removes distorted edges in the artwork and keeps them smooth.
- The option to embed or not embed current color profiles.

Save Document as PNG

PNG is another important and commonly used format because it supports transparency and produces small-sized and high-quality images, which makes it more suitable to create transparent web images.

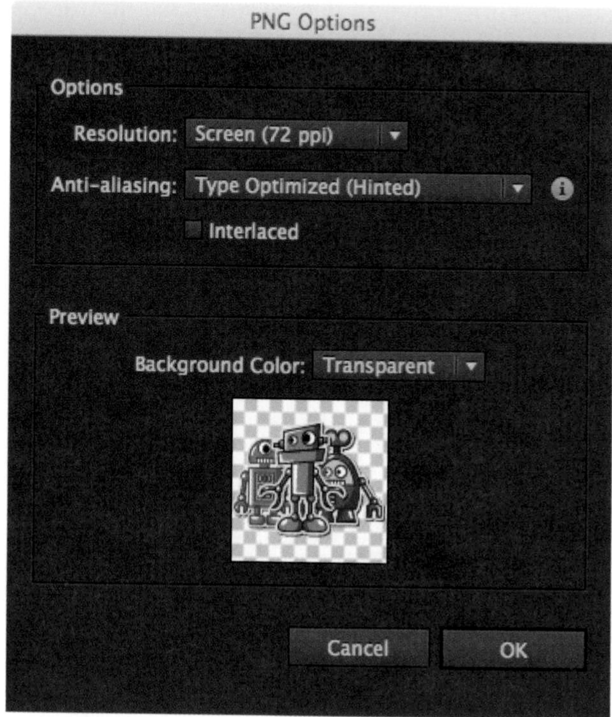

FIG 15-11 The PNG Options dialog box

You can save artwork as PNG from the Export command, similar to what we did for the JPG format. When you choose the PNG format, the PNG Options dialog box appears and includes the below options:

- Resolution sets the quality of the exported PNG image. For the web, the commonly used resolution is 72 ppi.
- Anti-aliasing options are similar to those in the JPG format.
- Background lets you choose the background for the image, and you can set it to transparent background.

Save Documents as Photoshop PSD

Many designers who use Adobe Illustrator use Adobe Photoshop as part of their design workflow. There are many ways to share artwork between Illustrator and Adobe Photoshop. You can simply export the artwork as an image and open it in Photoshop. Or, you can copy the artwork and paste it into Photoshop, as we will discuss in Chapter 18. The only disadvantage of these two methods is that they do not support exporting Adobe Illustrator artwork as layers. However, exporting a document as a Photoshop PSD file preserves the layer structure.

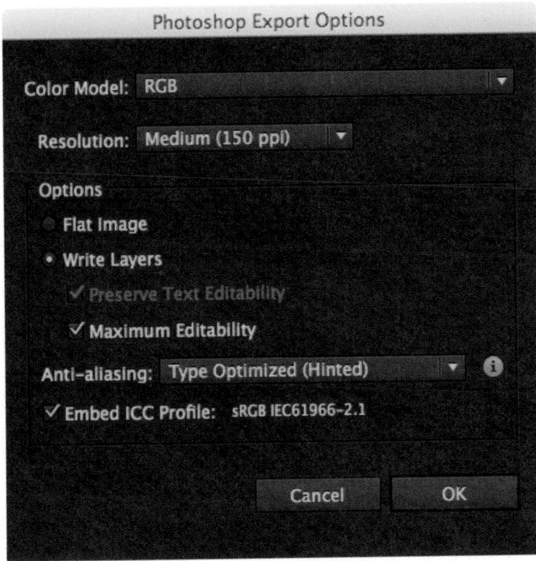

FIG 15-12 The Photoshop Export Options dialog box

When you choose the Photoshop PSD format from the Export dialog box, the Photoshop Export Options dialog box appears and includes the following:

- Color mode lets you choose from RGB, CMYK, and grayscale.
- Resolution sets the exported PSD file resolution and quality.
- Flat Image exports the artwork as one flattened layer.
- Write Layers preserves the artwork layers in the Photoshop PSD exported file.
- Anti-aliasing options are similar to those in the JPG format.

In addition to the above formats, Adobe Illustrator supports exporting artwork to various types of formats Such as PNG, TIFF, SWF, TGA and more. As mentioned at the beginning of the chapter, choosing the correct format depends on many factors, such as the target project and the media in which you will use the images. Thus, you need to set the image quality and resolution based on the project's size and quality requirements. For example, creating a website requires the images to be of a good quality and small size. You need to consider this when you set each format's options from the Photoshop Export Options dialog box.

In this chapter, we learned how to arrange and organize an Illustrator project to look more professional and readable by other designers. We also learned how to export artwork as different image formats and the options associated with each format. You can practice the features in this chapter by starting to organize the examples you have already completed and trying to export them in different formats. You will see the differences in quality and size between these formats.

For examples pertaining to this chapter, visit www.illustratorfoundations.com.

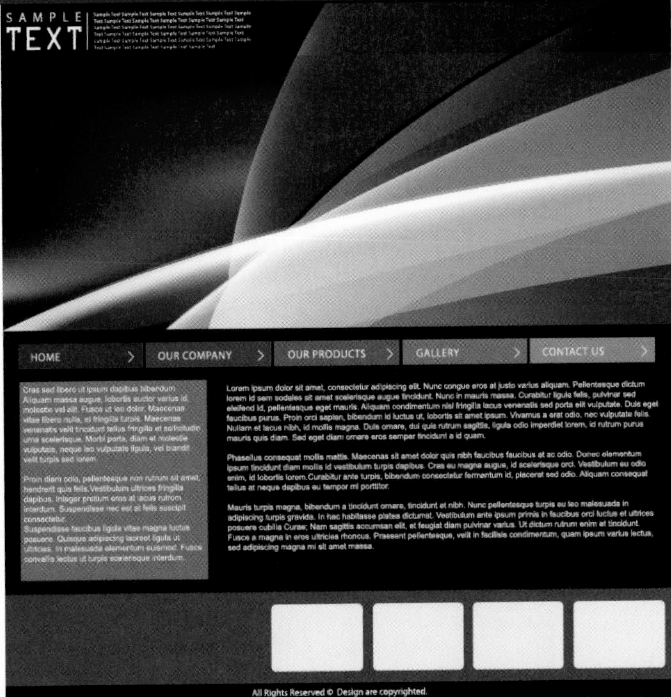

CHAPTER 16

Illustrator for Web

We have learned about Adobe Illustrator as an application to create artwork and printing designs. But what about web designs? Can Illustrator be used to create web page layouts? The answer is yes. Adobe Illustrator can be an essential part of your web design projects, not only because of its extended design features and tools, but also because it can provide scalable layout elements for your design as you are building the web design using vector elements. Furthermore, Adobe Illustrator can help you take your web project design to the next stage by allowing you to slice it and save it as separated images to implement in your Web design.

Illustrator integrates perfectly with other web and interactive applications such as Adobe Fireworks, Adobe Photoshop, and Adobe Flash. You can easily export Illustrator content to these applications and import different resources from different applications and formats into Illustrator. These reasons make Adobe Illustrator a useful tool in creating web layout. The features we will cover in this chapter will take your artwork to the next stage of web design production by preparing, optimizing, and exporting artwork for web usage.

Preparing Illustrator Documents for Web

The first step to initiate your web layout project is to prepare your document to fit with the web size and color standards. As you learned in Chapter 2, you can create a new document in Illustrator from several presets. One of these presets is the Web Profile, which lets you set your document to meet web standards regarding the size, colors, and so on.

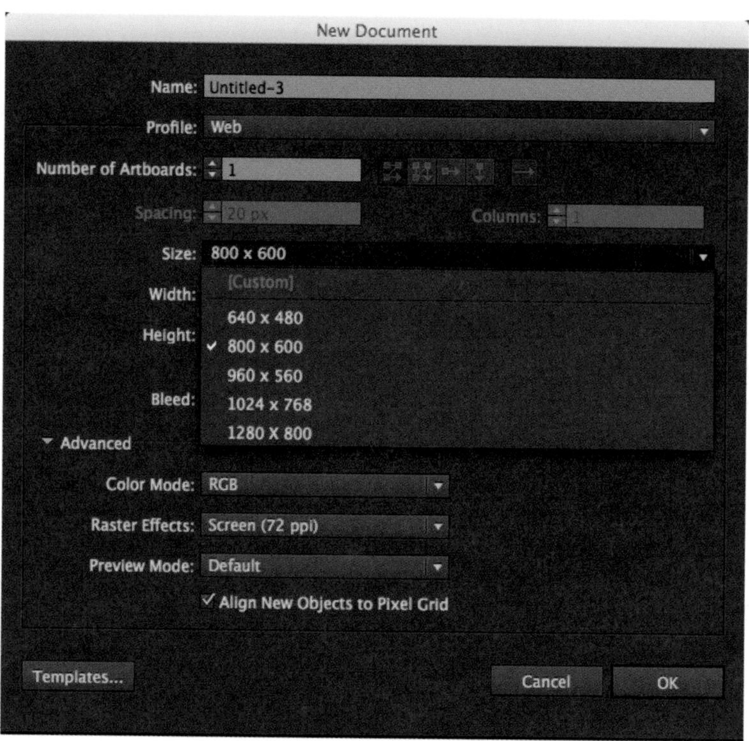

FIG 16-1 The Web presets options

When you choose Web from the Profile drop-down list in the New Document dialog box, the document options change to reflect the web standards. The Size drop-down list lets you choose from different web-standard sizes such as 640 x 480 px, 800 x 600 px, 960 x 560 px, 1024 x 768 px, and 1280 x 800 px. Although low resolutions are rarely used in current display technologies, they are still included as part of the standard sizes, as some users may need to develop low-resolution websites or html email templates. The measurement unit is set to pixels because this is the standard measurement unit for the web and digital media. The bleeds are also set to zero because these are no bleeds in web page layouts, unlike printing layouts.

In the Advanced section of the New Document dialog box, you will find more options, such as the color mode, that will be used in the document. You will notice it is set to RGB, because this is the standard color mode for web and digital media projects.

When you create a graphics element for the web, size is one of the important factors you should consider, as we will discuss in the section "Optimizing Web Graphics." However, lower resolution produces smaller-size graphic elements and images; therefore, the standard resolution for web graphic elements is 72 ppi. As we mentioned in Chapter 1, the resolution is the number of pixels in each inch or point in the design. A higher number means the image is a higher quality and larger size.

Why this specific resolution for the web? In the days of the old computer and slow Internet connections, there was a rule that keeping your graphic elements in as low a resolution as possible helped web pages to load quickly, and the user did not have to wait for a long time for all the graphic elements in the image to load. Thus, 72 ppi was chosen as the standard for web graphics resolution.

Nowadays, we have very fast Internet connections, computers, and devices that can display a higher resolution without the loading problems that we had to face a long time ago. However, in some situations related to websites that have a large number of visitors and search engine considerations, this rule still exists. It is always good to optimize your work and lower the size of your artwork while also considering the quality of the content. Later in this chapter, in the Optimizing Web Graphics section we will cover optimizing artwork in more detail as well as how to work with different image formats in web design.

In addition to the above presets, the Preview Mode options are very helpful and allow you to preview your artwork in different ways:

- Default preview is the standard preview and lets you see the artwork on the stage exactly as it is, without any changes.
- Pixel preview lets you preview the artwork to see how it looks in the exported pixel images. This preview does not change the vector nature of the artwork into pixilated.
- Overprint preview gives an ink preview for the layout and is useful in the color-separation print preview, which is not our main focus in this chapter.

The default preview is the standard choice for the web preset and is recommended because it avoids the confusion of the pixel preview, which does not give you idea of the type and the quality of the elements within your document.

Under the Preview Mode option you can find a checkbox called Align New Object to Pixel Grid. This is a useful option because it will snap the outline to the pixels to avoid a bad anti-aliased look for the artwork edges. Next, we will learn more about anti-aliasing and how to work with the preview modes when you are in the Illustrator workspace.

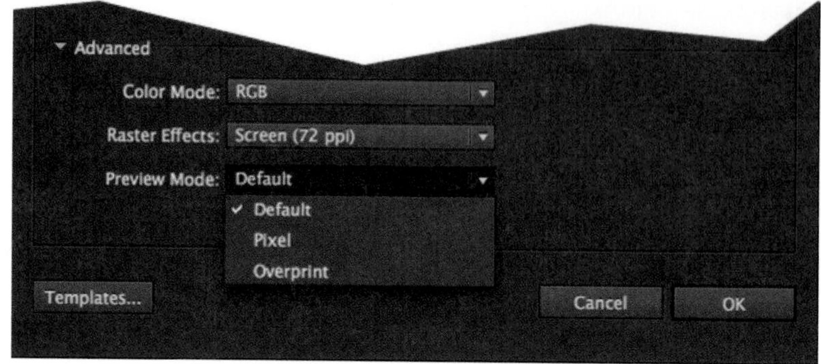

FIG 16-2 The preview mode in the New Document dialog box

Anti-aliasing

While vector images maintain the quality and smooth lines even when zoomed, bitmap images consist of pixels that are arranged next to each other. Thus, the outline and color edges of the bitmap image do not appear smooth and appear jagged, as shown in the figure below.

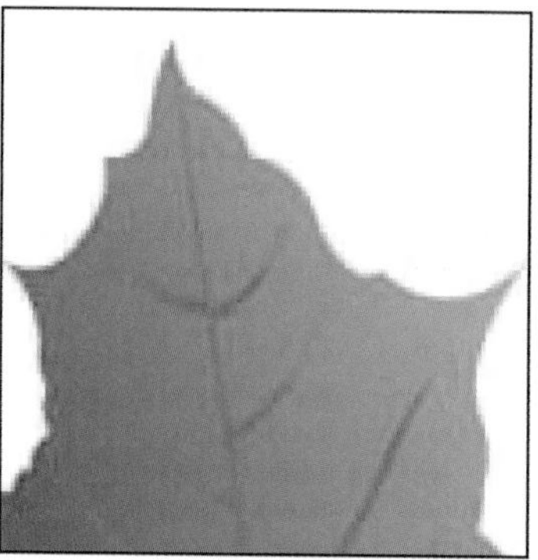

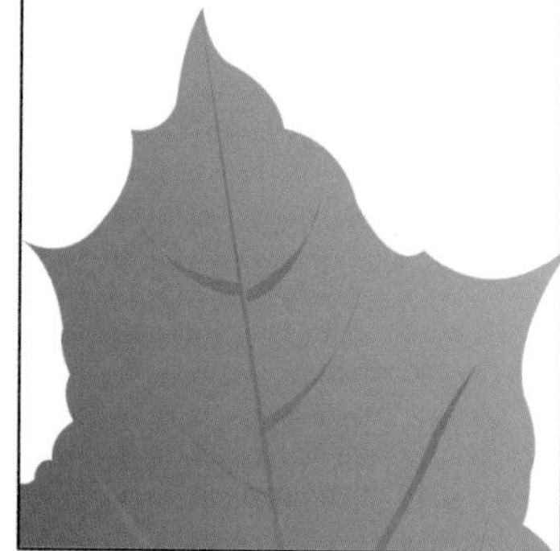

FIG 16-3 The bitmap vs the vector image

Anti-aliasing creates intermediate pixels to make the bitmap graphics look smooth in the normal size display. When you zoom into any bitmap image, you will find that the anti-aliased pixels appear in the image edges, as shown in the figure below. When you zoom in to the pixilated outline, you will notice that the anti-aliases do not appear, because it is meant to have the best results in 100% preview. This concept is very important in web design because the layout that is exported from Illustrator actually converts to bitmap images; therefore, its quality after exporting should be considered while you are working in the layout.

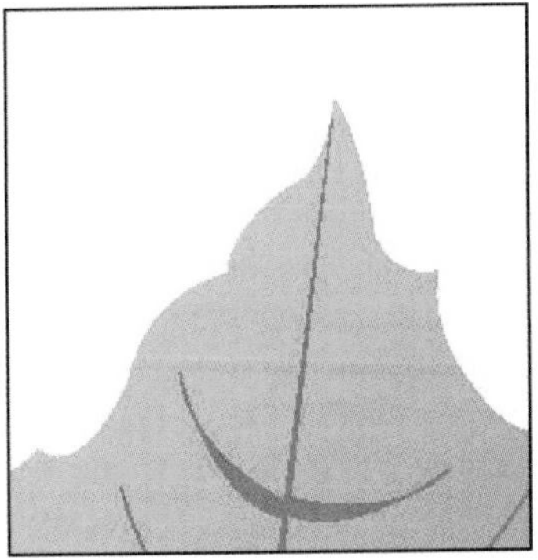

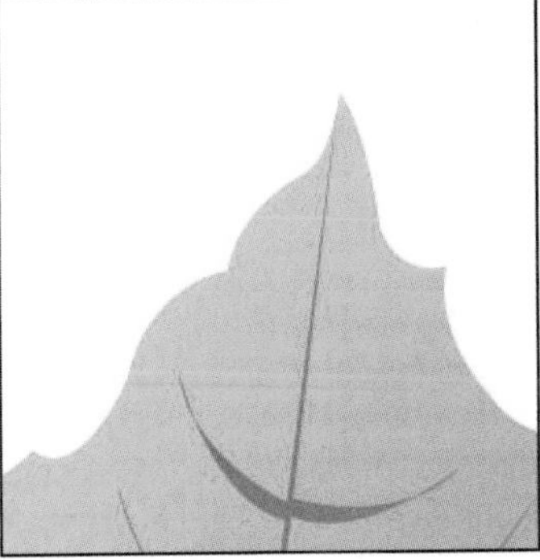

FIG 16-4 The aliased vs the anti-aliased images

> **Note**
>
> The anti-aliased quality is determined based on the normal size view for the bitmap image. If you zoom in to the image, the quality of the image may appear less than the normal view. Most web designs are set to display at the best quality at a normal size view of 100%.

The preview options in the New Document dialog box let you choose to display your work in Illustrator as if it were bitmap and not vector graphics. If you choose the Default View option, you can still switch between different

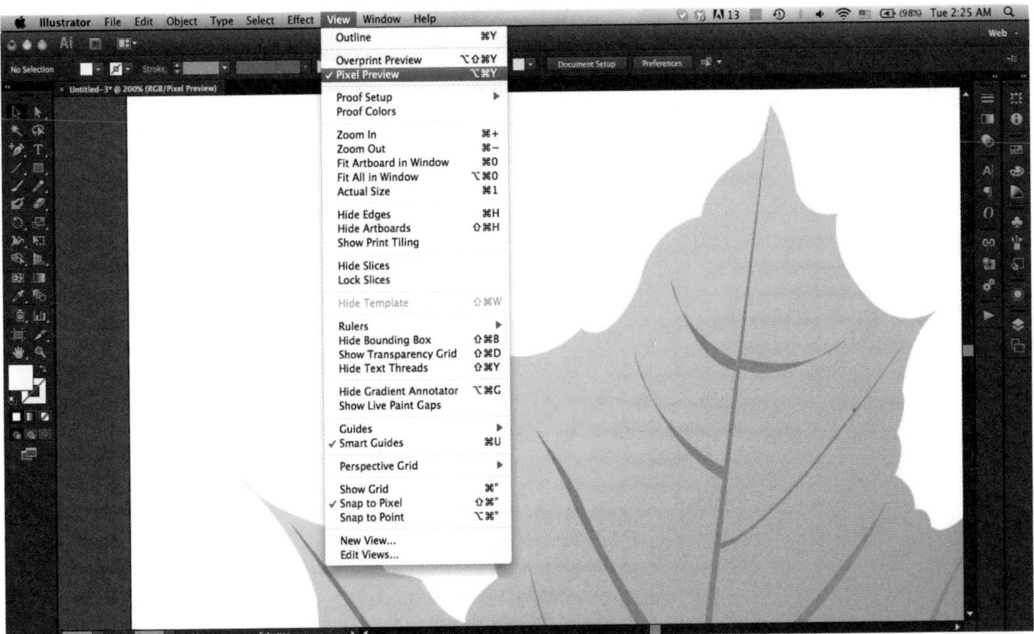

FIG 16-5 The pixel preview mode for vector graphics in Illustrator

preview options while you are working to preview how your layout will appear in the bitmap view. From the View menu in the top menus, you can choose Pixel Preview. This command does not convert the artwork to vector; it is just for preview purposes. You can still return back to the vector layout look by deactivating this preview mode by checking it again from the View menu.

When you design for web, one of the best practices is to preview your layout using the pixel preview mode to make sure that the quality of the exported graphics is good and meets your needs. Another point that is closely related to anti-aliasing is the alignment of the objects to the to document pixels. To understand more about this issue, see the figure below: the left rectangle is set to Align to Pixel Grid, and you can see that the rectangle lines appear sharp. The right rectangle is placed within a range of pixels and is not aligned with the pixels. The anti-alias fills the uncompleted pixels.

FIG 16-6 The line aligned to pixels in the right and not aligned to pixels in the left

The Align New Object to Pixel Grid option in the New Document dialog box forces the new objects to align with the pixels. Thus, the edges appear more smooth without the need for anti-aliasing extra pixels to be created. You can also choose Align to Pixel Grid from the Transform panel.

Optimizing Web Graphics

Now, let us move on to one very important concept before learning how to create and prepare a web layout in Illustrator: how to optimize artwork for the web. As we mentioned at the beginning of the chapter, size plays a critical role in web graphics, even with the rapidly increasing Internet speeds and computer specifications. When you export an image for web use, you need to optimize the image and choose the best format for web use and compatibility with different browsers and viewers. The artwork in Illustrator is saved for web through the Save for Web dialog box from the File menu.

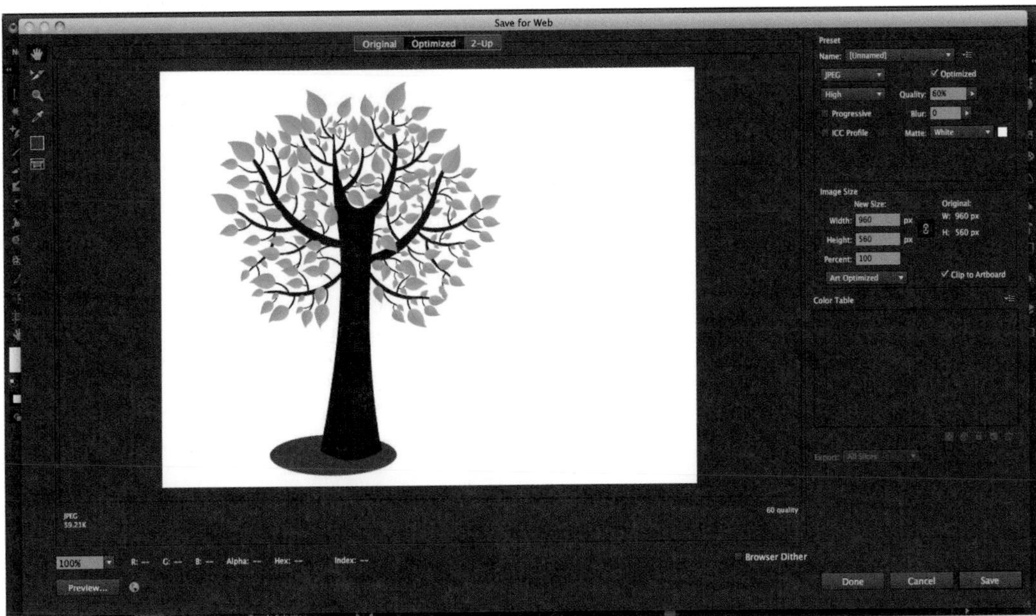

FIG 16-7 The Save for Web dialog box

> **Shortcut**
>
> You can open the Save for Web dialog box by pressing the shortcut Cmd+Shift+Option+S (Ctrl+Shift+Alt+S in Windows).

Through the Save for Web dialog box, you can choose the file format for the saved artwork and set the different settings for this format, as well as other features that can help you to choose the best format. Before we learn about different web formats and how to optimize the image for the best quality and lowest size, let us understand the anatomy of the Save for Web dialog box.

The tools on the left side include some that you can use to control the preview of the artwork:

- The Hand tool allows you to navigate, drag, and move around the layout in the Preview section.
- The Slice Select tool lets you select the slices in the layout; we will talk about slices in the section "Using Web Slices."
- The Zoom tool allows you to zoom inside the Preview section to view more details about the image. This tool is useful to check how

optimization has affected the image quality by zooming and checking the image details.

- The Eyedropper tool lets you select specific colors in the image.
- The Eyedropper Color tool indicates the currently selected color in the Eyedropper tool. You can also specify any color from the color picker.
- The Toggle Slice Visibility tool lets you display or hide the slices.

The Preview section lets you preview the final result of the artwork after optimization. The preview section is very important, because it gives you a good indication how the final optimized image will appear in the browser. Thus, you can change the settings to maintain the best quality and lowest size possible. The Preview section has three types of views: original, optimized, and 2-up, which can be changed from the tabs on the top of the Preview section. The first is original, which displays the original artwork regardless of the changes you make in it.

The second view option is optimized, which shows only the artwork after optimization. Thus, when you change the image setting from the right side of the Save for Web dialog box, you can only see the changes. This option is useful when you would like to display the optimized image in the whole space to give you a better preview of the output.

The third view is 2-Up, which splits the preview area into two sections, one for the original artwork on the left and the optimized artwork on the right. This view is very helpful when you want to compare the original and optimized images regarding the quality and size.

FIG 16-8 The 2-Up preview in the Save for Web dialog box

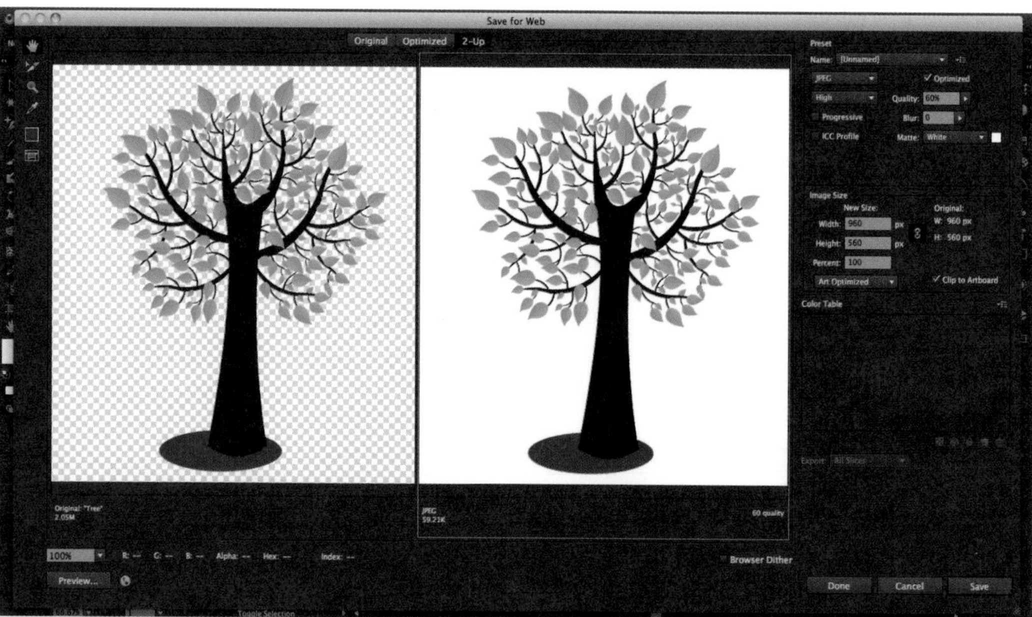

Under each side of the 2-Up preview, you can find information about the size and settings of the artwork. This information is useful to compare between the size and quality of the artwork before and after the optimization. At the bottom of the Preview area, you can find the zoom value and the preview button, which allows you to preview the artwork in the browser. You can click the icon next to the preview button to select the browser you would like to use in the test.

The right side of the Save for Web dialog box is the most important part, because it lets you choose the format in which you want to save your artwork and optimize the images based on specific settings related to each format. The right side of the dialog box includes three main parts: Preset, where you can change the artwork save settings; Image Size, where you can change the size of the output image; and Color Table, which includes the color swatches that are included in the image.

Let us briefly review the different saving formats and see which format is the best for web projects. While the Preset section in the Save for Web dialog box includes a number of predefined saving formats, you can set a custom setting using the values associated with each format. When you open the Formats drop-down list under the Presets list, you will see the available saving formats in the Save for Web dialog box: GIF, JPG, PNG-8, and PNG-24.

Saving for Web as GIF

GIF format is one of the old formats that was used widely in web images because of its significant compression of the images, which was suitable for the slow Internet connections of the past. The main disadvantage of GIF images is that they allow the image to have only 256 colors. These colors are the web colors that used to be the standard colors for the old web browsers. Thus, saving an image in GIF format can make it lose much of its quality. Another disadvantage is that GIF compression is that it is not very efficient in large images. However, GIF format is preferred for small images such as icons and small images with fewer colors.

Note

Old web browsers had a limit to the number of image colors they could display, which was set to 256 colors (web-safe colors). Thus, GIF images can display only these 256 colors. If the image has colors that are not in the range of these 256 web-safe colors, the browser will try to simulate the unavailable colors, which is known as dithering.

Let us jump to a practical example that shows how to save artwork for web in GIF format and explore some of the commonly used settings in the Save for Web dialog box.

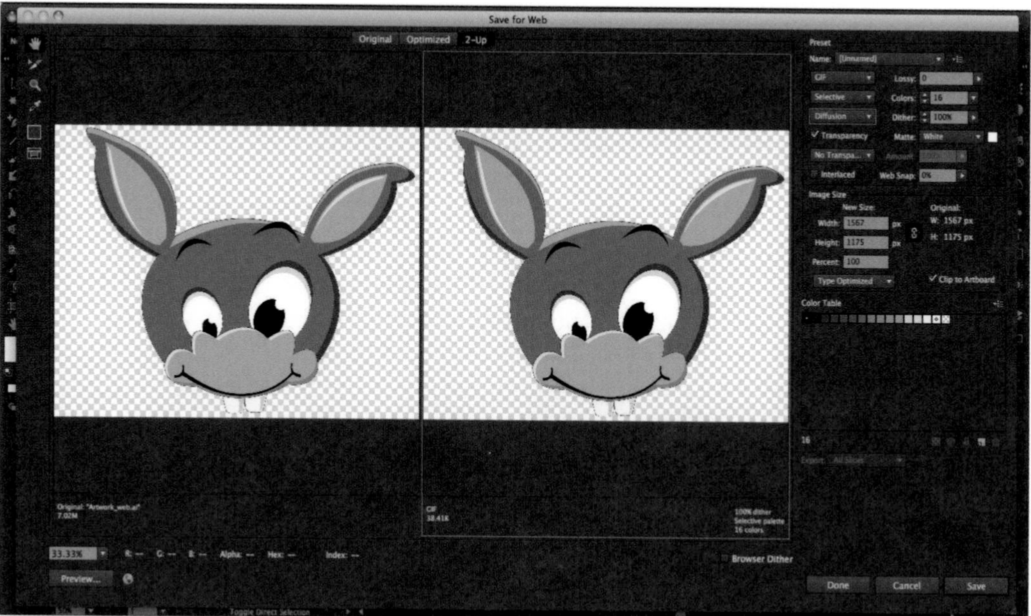

FIG 16-9 Saving artwork for web in GIF format using the Save for Web dialog box

1. Open the file Artwork_web.ai. This document includes artwork that we would like to save for web.
2. From the File menu, choose Save for Web, or press the shortcut Cmd+Shift+Option+S (Ctrl+Shift+Alt+S in Windows).
3. From the Save for Web dialog box, you can select any of the GIF presets from the Name drop-down list in the Preset section to see different GIF setting presets. In this example, we will choose our own setting. Choose GIF format from the Format drop-down list.
4. Keep the lossy value zero; this value sets the amount of lossiness allowed in the GIF compression.
5. Keep the color reduction algorithm selective.
6. In the Colors drop-down list, you can specify the limit of colors that the image should include. This limit can range from 8 to 256. A lower number of colors means a lower size, but affects the image quality. In our example, we will reduce the number of colors to only the colors available in the image. For example, choosing 16 colors gives us a good result and does not affect the quality of the images, and at the same time it avoids adding unwanted colors to the image file.
7. Choose Diffusion from the Dither Algorithm drop-down list. This value sets how the unavailable colors in the web-safe 256 colors will be simulated.
8. Set the dither value to 100%.
9. Check the Transparency checkbox; this allows you to make the artwork background transparent. Transparency in GIF format may result in distorted image edges because the GIF does not have a variety of color limits to apply the transparency on the edges. Thus, the matte value next

to the transparency value directs the GIF to set edge colors to the nearest preferable colors; this is known as the matte color. You can set the matte color to none, eyedropper, white, black, or other. The eyedropper value lets you set the matte color to be similar to a specific color in the image. Also, you can set the matte color to any other color by choosing the other value. The image below shows the difference between the artwork set to white matte and another matte color. In our example, let us set the matte value to white.

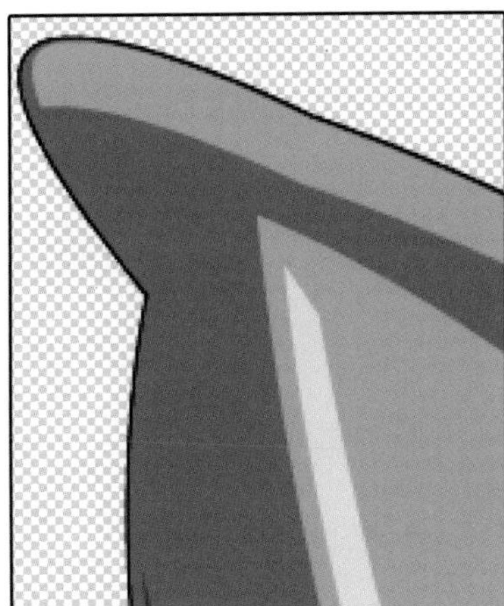

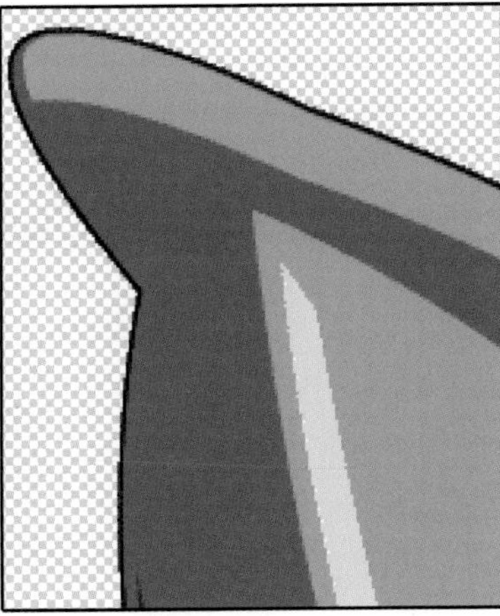

FIG 16-10 The left GIF artwork matte is set to white, and the right artwork matte is set to another color (red)

Note

When you create transparent web images in GIF format, it is important to make sure that the image's transparent edges blend well with the background color. The matte value lets you choose the color that matches the image background or the background color that you plan to use in the web design. This is one of the options that allows you to avoid the problem of distorted edges in GIF images.

10. In the Image Size option, keep the image size the same as the original.
11. When the Preview section is set to 2-Up, you will notice the decrease in size between the original image and the optimized image in the bottom part under each preview.
12. Click Save, and save the image as Artwork_web.gif.

From the color table, you can preview the colors included in the image. The icons at the bottom of the table let you modify the color table. For example, you can choose a specific color and convert to transparency, lock a specific color, delete, and add eyedropper color to the palette. You can also use the context menu of the color table to save a palette for future use, replace the current colors from a previously saved palette, and more.

Saving for Web as JPG

JPG is one of the commonly used formats to save images for web because it provides good compression along with high-quality image output compared to GIF format. The only disadvantage of the saved JPG from the Save for Web dialog box is that it does not support transparency. However, the JPG setting is very easy compared to the many settings in GIF format. When you select JPG from the Format drop-down list in the Save for Web dialog box, you can use the following values to control the quality and size of the output JPG:

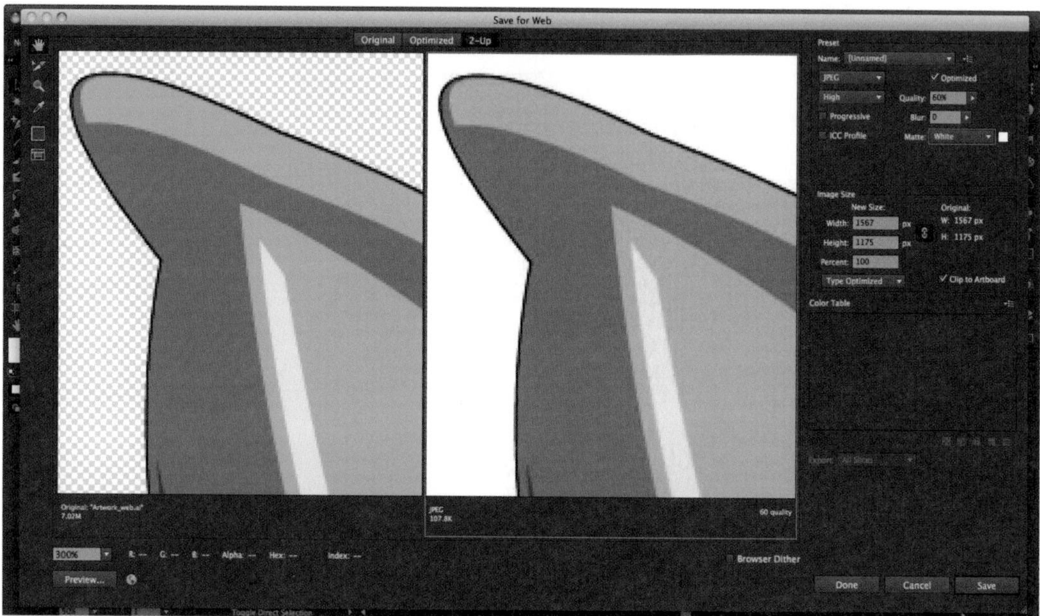

FIG 16-11 The JPG format setting in the Save for Web dialog box

- The Optimized checkbox gives you the option to increase the compression, but results in a less-compatible JPG file.
- Compression quality lets you choose the level of compression; maximum means higher quality, and low means lower quality. You can also set the quality percentage from the Quality slider on the right of the Compression Quality drop-down list. This option is commonly used when saving files as JPG; usually the rest of the values are kept as default.
- The Progressive checkbox allows the image to be downloaded into the browser in multiple passes.
- ICC profile attaches a color profile to the image based on the file color profile.

- The Matte option is similar to the one we discussed with GIF format; the only difference is that this value sets the background of the artwork in the JPG file, since transparency is not supported.

Saving for Web as PNG

PNG is another format that is used widely in web graphics, especially when it can produce a better-quality image than the other formats, including the JPG. The results can be higher in size, but many websites uses this format in banners and images that must be in the highest quality possible.

The Save for Web dialog box allows you to save the output image in two different PNG formats: PNG-8 and PNG-24. PNG-8 is very similar to GIF in the available options, but the results are much better than GIF. When you save images as PNG-8, you will notice that the edges are aliased compared to the GIF output.

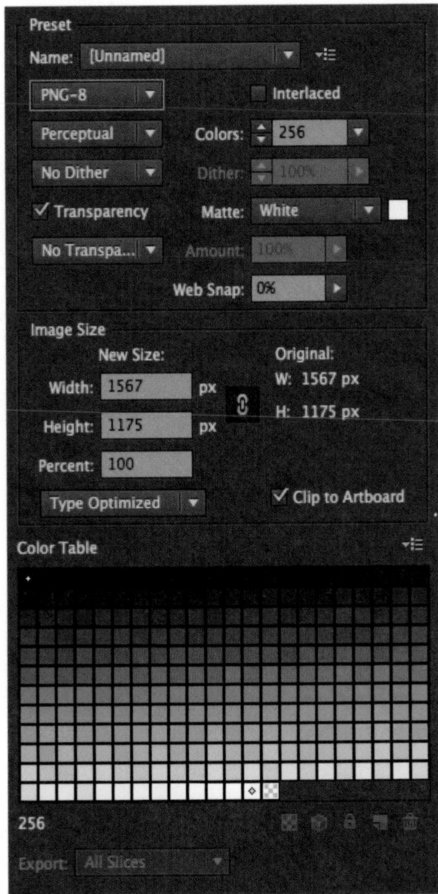

FIG 16-12 The PNG-8 settings in the Save for Web dialog box

The other PNG option is the PNG-24 format, which produces the highest quality and size. It is preferred for creating banners and areas of focus in web layouts because of the sharp quality of the results; also, it does not limit you to 256 colors as the GIF format does. PNG-24 does not have many settings. You can only allow or disallow transparency and the Interlaced options. When the transparency is disabled, you can set matte background color from the Matte drop-down list.

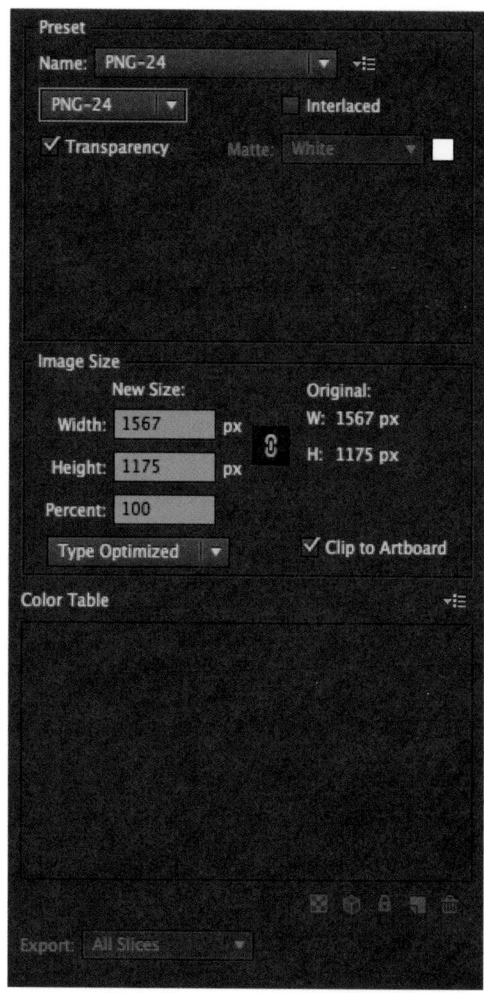

FIG 16-13 The PNG-24 settings in the Save for Web dialog box

Using Web Slices

When you create a website design or a layout that will appear in a web browser, it appears to be one graphic element, but it is not. The web page that you see and navigate in your browser is actually made of more than just a design layout. The layout that the design creates is actually split into several images. These images are linked to each other through web developing codes such as HTML and CSS. This is because not all the parts of your design are images. Some of the content is added as text inside the coding language or retrieved from the database. Other areas, especially the solid colors, are converted to code-based colors to save site space and make the website load much faster with fewer images.

Adobe Illustrator lets you not only design your web layout, but also slice it to make it ready for the web developing stage in applications such as Adobe Dreamweaver, Adobe Fireworks, or Adobe Photoshop. You can slice your web layout using the Slice tool in the Tools panel. Let us learn more about it through the following example, in which we will slice a web layout and save it as images that can be used in web development:

1. Open the document Web_layout_start.ai. This document includes a layout for a web page design.
2. Select the Slice tool from the Tools panel.
3. Start to divide the layout into parts, as shown in the figure below.

FIG 16-14 The layout with the web slices applied to it

> **Note**
>
> You can use the Slice Select tool to drag and resize the created slices. All you need to do is select the slice and drag it to change its position. Also, you can roll over and click any of the slice sides to be able to change its size.

4. From the File menu, choose Save for Web.
5. Use the Slice Select tool to drag and select all the slices in the layout.
6. From the Format drop-down list, choose JPG and set the quality to high.
7. Make sure to choose All Slices from the Export drop-down list under the color table section.
8. Click Save to save the slices as separate images.

FIG 16-15 Saving the layout using the Save for Web dialog box

The next step after converting your layout into separated images is to take it into any web developing tool, such as Dreamweaver, to construct the layout again, but this time using both images and codes like HTML and CSS.

In this chapter, we learned how to take our Illustrator artwork to a new level and utilize it in creating web projects. We also learned how to create optimized artwork that is suitable for web usage, and we learned about the different available formats to create artwork. The information in this chapter is used frequently in web projects. Practicing it can give you more control and balance between quality and size, which is a very important factor in creating web graphics.

For examples pertaining to this chapter, visit www.illustratorfoundations.com.

CHAPTER 17

Printing

Although digital media has expanded to provide information in multiple formats and on different devices, printing is still a dominant method in many fields, such as advertising, publishing, and delivering content. The printing process is challenging due to two main reasons. The first is that you cannot edit the final result of the design once it is printed, unlike the digital media, in which you can edit the artwork and republish it to the website or the application files. The only way to edit after printing is to reprint the design after fixing or modifying it. This can be a big problem if you are printing a large number of copies. The printing process requires a good testing and review process to make sure that the printed design does not includes any errors.

The second reason is that the colors and resolution for the printed design need to be exactly the same as those on your design screen. This requires good calibration between the screen and printer as well as good calibration of the software used in the design and printing process. Adobe Illustrator is one application that has been in use since printing was the only available media in the advertising, book, and magazine industries.

This chapter begins with basic tips that you should consider when you are preparing an Illustrator document for printing; then we will move to setting up pages and printing them. Before jumping to the printing options in Illustrator, we will review some of the general tips that designers should consider when building their printing projects to ensure a better printing project experience.

New Document Settings

When you start building your print artwork in Adobe Illustrator, you start by creating a new document that meets the printing sizes and specifications. In Chapter 2 we covered how to create new documents and how to start with the new document presets. While you can add you own custom presents, the print presets provide a large variety of printing sizes and options. The standard sizes make it easy for you to create printings that fit within printer papers' standard sizes. In some cases, you may want to create custom sizes. However, there are some issues that you should consider when creating a new printing document.

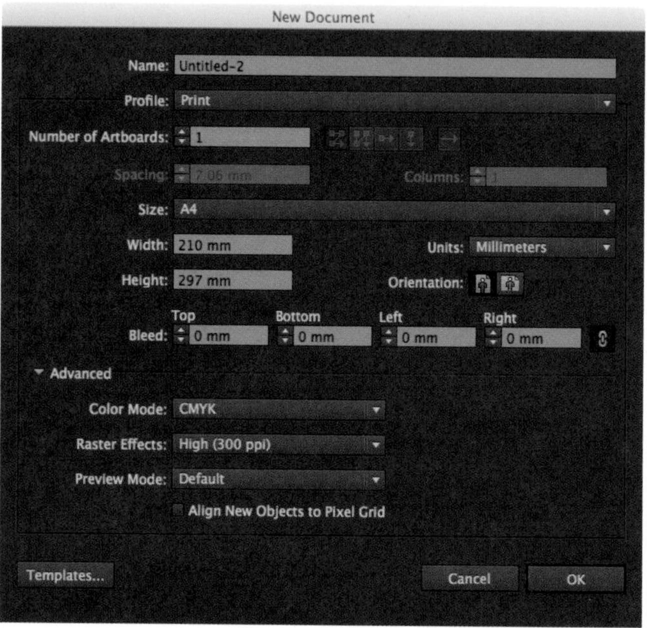

FIG 17-1 The New Document dialog box

Set the document dimensions to printing-friendly measurements. While pixels are a more suitable measurement unit for web and digital media, printing projects use inches, millimeters, or pica. Set the color mode to CMYK. In professional printing houses and companies, they use the color separation technique to print the image colors on four transparent films. The CMYK printing process lets you separate the image's colors into four colors, and the rest of the colors are mixed and created using these four colors. The four colors are cyan, magenta, yellow, and black.

Set the raster effects resolution to printing-friendly resolution. This value sets the resolution that will be used to export your artwork as raster images for printing. For example, for brochures, flyers, and printouts, it is advisable to use a high resolution of 300 ppi. If you are going to print large images such as billboards, where high resolution is not required, you can use a lower resolution such as 150 ppi or 72 ppi. These large files are printed in low resolution because they are hung a long distance from the viewer, so the viewer will not be able to see the fine details.

Converting Text to Outline

One of the common problems that appears when sharing Illustrator documents with other designers in the team or through different computers is missing fonts. In some situations, your design or the design you receive may include a font that is not installed on your computer. In such a case, Adobe Illustrator displays an alert message when it opens the document with the missing font. In this alert message, you can either choose a substitution for the missing font or search for it on your local drive.

This problem puts your design at risk, because this replacement may change the format of the text in your design. Even if you attached the font inside the design folder, it is still risky because the other team member may not notice it, the font may not work properly with the new system, or the font may be lost while transferring the fonts. Designers should convert the fonts in their artwork into outline paths to make sure that the design will not run into missing font issues.

In the figure below, you will notice that the nature of the font characters is editable and you can easily modify the font by double-clicking it and editing it as normal text.

FIG 17-2 The editable text layout in the design

When you convert the text to outline paths, it loses its form as an editable text, and Adobe Illustrator interacts with it as a path. Thus, you do not have to have the fonts installed on your computer to view them in the document.

FIG 17-3 The text converted to outline path

You can convert any text to outline paths through the following steps:

1. Select the text in the artboard.
2. From the Type menu, choose Create Outlines.

Also, you can right-click on the selected text and choose Create Outline from the context menu.

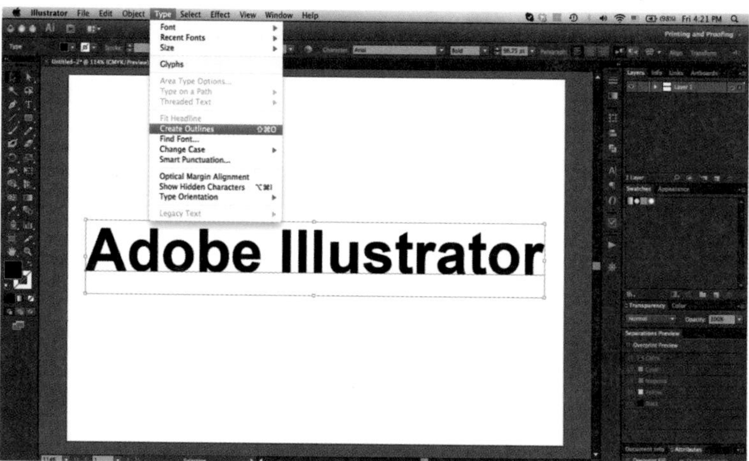

FIG 17-4 The Create Outline command

> **Shortcut**
>
> You can press Shift+Cmd+O (Shift+Ctrl+O in Windows) to convert text to outline.

Working with Bleeds

Bleeds are defined as artwork that extends outside the document edges. Bleeds are important because they avoid trim work in printing, which is especially important when the print sheet includes multiple copies of a design or you are printing a multiple-page design. With bleeds, you do not have any extra white areas or margins in the printed artwork.

You can set the bleeds for your document from the New Document dialog box. You can set the bleeds for the top, bottom, left, and right. You can also click the icon to the right of the bleed values to link all the values and have similar values for all the document sides.

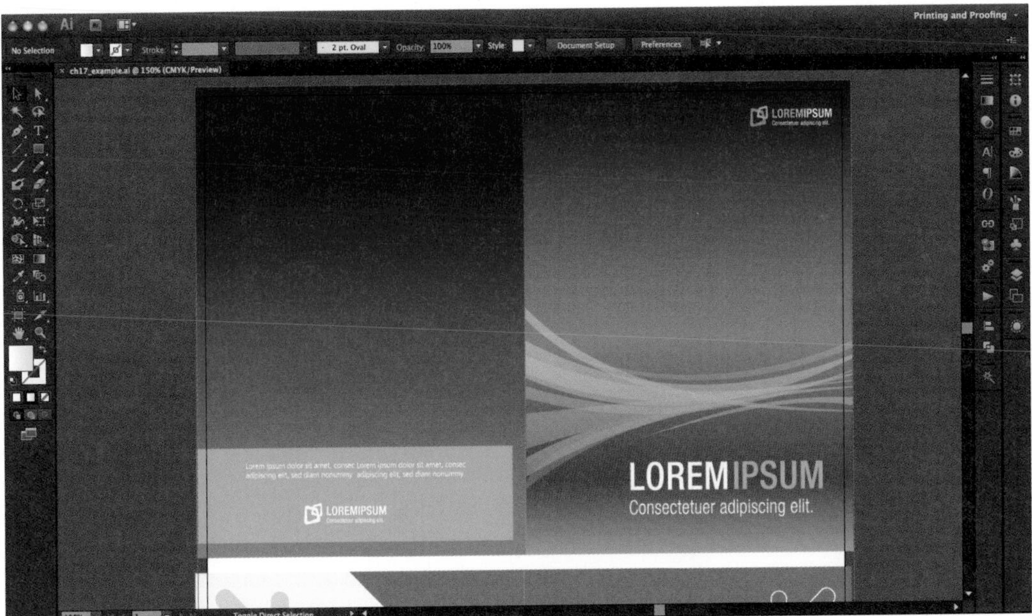

FIG 17-5 The artwork with the bleeds applied to it

You can edit the bleeds for an existing document by choosing File > Document Setup or by clicking the Document Setup button from the top control bar when nothing is selected. Under the Bleeds and View options you can change the bleeds of the document.

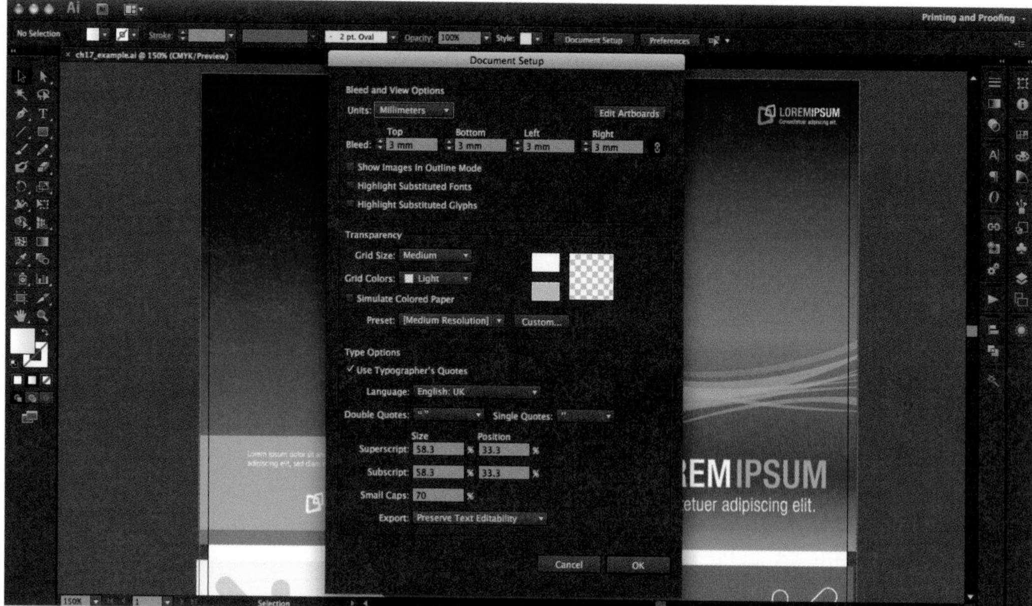

FIG 17-6 The Document Setup dialog box

As we will see later in the Marks and Bleeds section, you can also handle the bleeds for the document from the Print dialog box.

Note

Increasing the bleeds makes Illustrator print more parts of the artwork beyond the trim marks. We will cover the trim marks later in the Marks and Bleeds section.

In the following example, we will set the bleed values for an existing brochure design before printing it:

1. Open the document Print_brochure.ai from the section for Chapter 17 on the companion website, http://www.illustratorfoundations.com.
2. Make sure that nothing is selected. From the top Control panel, select the Document Setup button.
3. Make sure the icon to the right of the bleed values is active by clicking on it. This will ensure that you add the same values to all the document edges.
4. In the bleed values, add the value 3 MM to create a bleed around the document.
5. Press OK to apply and preview the bleeds.

FIG 17-7 The brochure design with the bleed applied to it

Setting Up Trim Marks

In some cases your artwork may include white areas around it, which makes it hard to identify its edges when printing it. It can be even harder when you have multiple artwork printed on the same sheet or paper. Trim marks are thin lines that identify the edges of your artwork and make it easy for you to cut or separate them from the printing sheet. You can create trim or crop marks as a command by selecting the object and choosing Object > Create Trim Marks or as an effect from Effect > Crop Marks.

In the following example, we will see how to identify the artwork edges on the printed sheet:

1. Open the document Frog_sheet.ai from the section for Chapter 17 on the companion website. This document includes shapes of a frog arranged on the print sheet.
2. Select the first frog shape. From the Effects menu, choose Crop Marks.
3. Repeat the same with the rest of the frogs in the sheet.

FIG 17-8 Apply the crop marks effect to the artwork

As you can see from the results of the example, you can easily cut the frogs from the print sheet using the trim mark guides.

Working with Colors

As we mentioned in the section "New Document Settings," the printing process uses the CMYK color mode, where each color is represented with a combination of cyan, magenta, yellow, and black. However, you may need to add to your design special colors if the client requires that the design be based on one of the Pantone colors.

The Pantone colors are standard sheets that include the different colors with their associated codes. The aim of using Pantone colors is so the requested colors will look exactly as the client expects, so the names of these colors are very important when working in the Swatches panel.

To add one of the Pantone colors to the document Swatches panel and use it in the design, follow these steps:

1. Open the Swatches panel.
2. From the Swatches Libraries menu, navigate to the color books. The swatches libraries in this category represent the different Pantone colors.
3. Select Pantone Solid Coated to open it.
4. Click on any color to add it to the current document swatch.

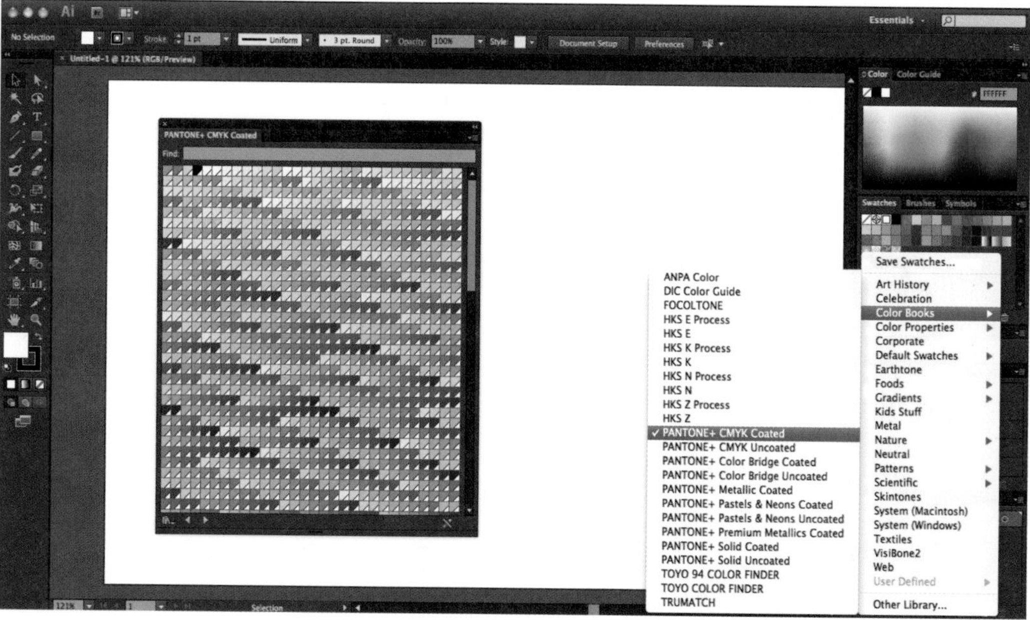

FIG 17-9 The Pantone Color Swatch Options dialog box

When you double-click the chosen spot color to open its Options dialog box, you will notice that the color mode is set to book color. The rest of the options are not active because book color is associated with standard Pantone color.

Separations Preview

When the artwork color is set to the CMYK color mode, based on the cyan, magenta, yellow, and black colors, you can preview the amount of these four colors that is required to represent the artwork colors using the Separations Preview panel.

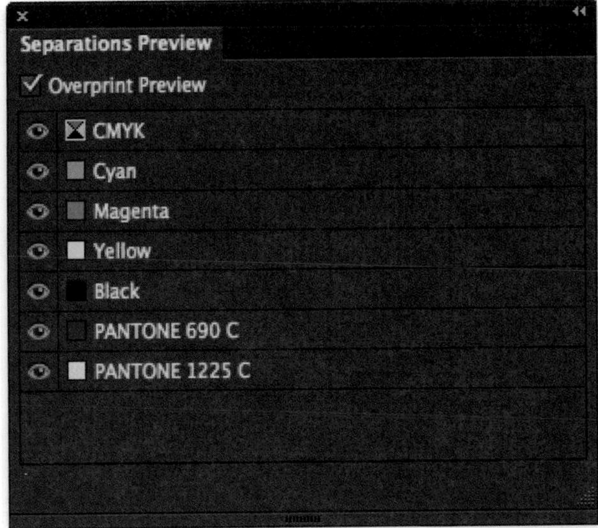

FIG 17-10 The Separations Preview panel

The Separations Preview panel includes layers that represent each of the CMYK colors plus the Pantone colors added to the document, as we saw in the above figure. You can click the Eye icon to show or hide any of the color channels. Also, you need to check the Overprint Preview box in the Separation Preview panel, as Adobe Illustrator applies an overprint to avoid errors that may appear on the overlapped colors.

In the brochure example below, let us see how to preview the black color for the text in the Separations Preview panel:

1. Open the document Print_brochure.ai.
2. From the Window panel, choose Separations Preview panel.
3. Click the Overprint Preview checkbox.
4. Click the Eye icon next to the black channel while pressing the Alt key to hide all the channels and display only the black channel. Notice how the black text appears.

5. Now, show all the layers, hide the black channel, and notice how the black text is represented only in the black channel and does not appear in any other color channels. This means that the black text values are cyan = 0%, magenta = 0%, yellow = 0%, and black = 100%.

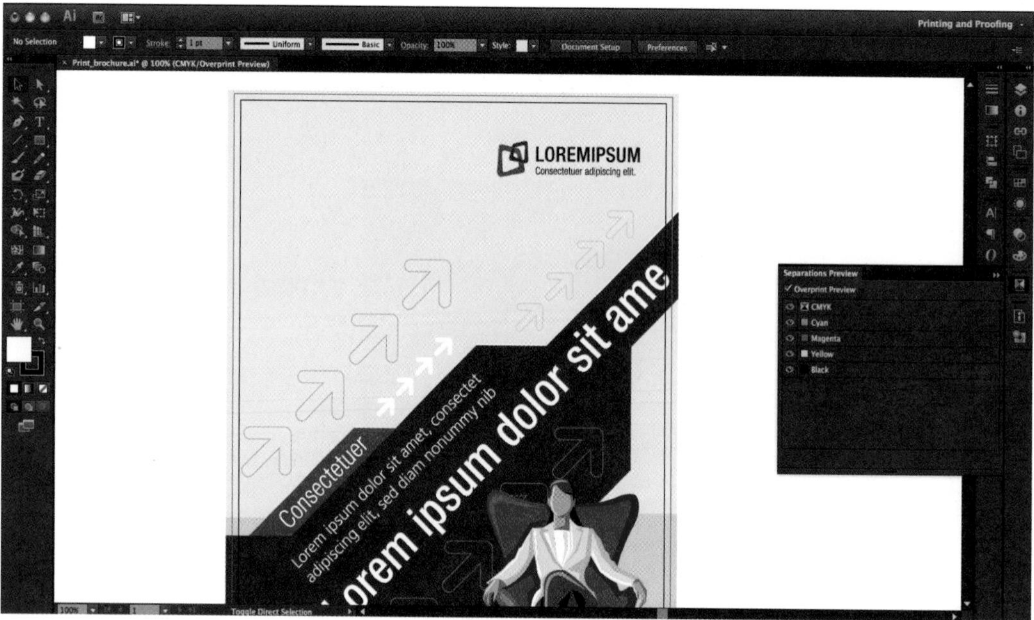

FIG 17-11 The black channel hidden from the Separations Preview panel

Printing Options

In the first part of this chapter, we shed light on some of the important topics and issues that you should consider when working in a printing project. After setting up your document and preparing it for the printing stage, you can choose Print from the File menu to open the Print dialog box. In this dialog box you will find the settings required to print your document. In the next sections, we will cover the necessary settings in the Print dialog box and how they affect the final results of the artwork.

The Print dialog box consists of four main parts. The top part includes the printer type and presets, the left top side includes the different print setup categories, the left bottom includes a preview for the document, and the right side includes the detailed settings for each category you choose from the left-side category navigator. At the bottom of the dialog box, you can find buttons that let you set up the Page, Printer, and Print commands. Let us see these parts in more detail in the figure below.

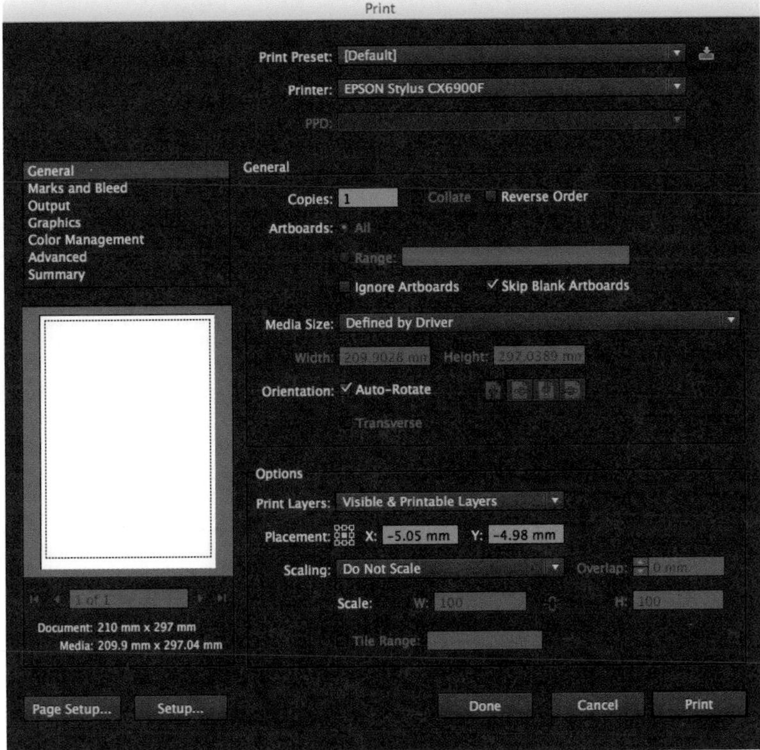

FIG 17-12 The Print dialog box

Print Preset lets you choose one of the current printing setting presets or save your custom settings as a new preset for further use. The Printer option lets you choose the printer that you would like to use to print the artwork. You can also choose PostScript printing and use the PPD setting. The PPD file includes information about the output printer, printer, fonts, and available media sizes.

General Settings

You can click the General option on the left side to open the General settings, which include the settings discussed next. The Copies option sets the number of the copies you need to print. For more than one copy, you can set the Collate option to on or off. Using the Collate option, the application prints all the document artboards before creating a new copy. For example, if the document includes five artboards, this option will make the application print from pages 1 to 5 and then start printing the second copy. If this selection is not active, Illustrator will print copies of each page before moving to the next page.

Reverse Order reverses the order of artboard printing, so the printer prints the last artboard and then moves to the beginning. Artboards lets you, if you would like, set to print all the artboards or specific artboard numbers. The Media Size list displays a number of standard sizes from which you can choose for your printing design, or you can set a custom size by adding values to the width and height values.

Orientation lets you set the orientation of the artwork, or you can set it to Auto-orientation. Print Layers lets you choose to print only the visible layers, the printable layers, or all the layers. Placement and Scaling lets you specify the position of the artwork and the resizing options for the printed copy.

Marks and Bleeds

Printing marks are not that different from the crop marks and bleeds that we applied to the artwork in the sections "Working with Bleeds" and "Setting Up Trim Marks" at the beginning of the chapter. Printing marks are signs that appear on the edges of the printed artwork to mark the edges.

In the Marks section, you can add the following marks:

- Trim marks
- Registration marks
- Color bars
- Page information

You can also set the font type and size used to create these marks. In the Bleeds section, you can either use the bleeds that you applied to the document in the working environment, or you can set the bleeds directly from the values in this dialog box.

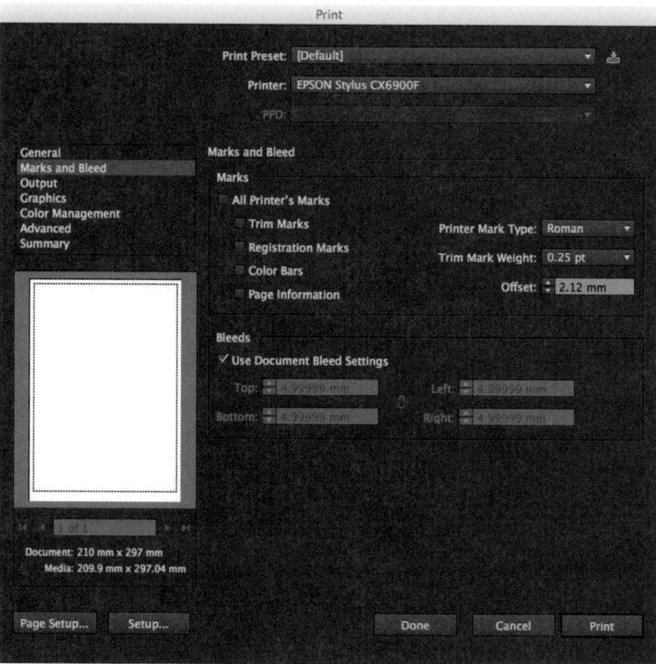

FIG 17-13 The marks and bleed in the Print dialog box

Output

The options in this section are more related to the printer options and document ink. For example, you can specify the printer resolution, printing mode, and positive or negative color image. You can also choose to convert the sport colors in the design to process colors and overprint the black color.

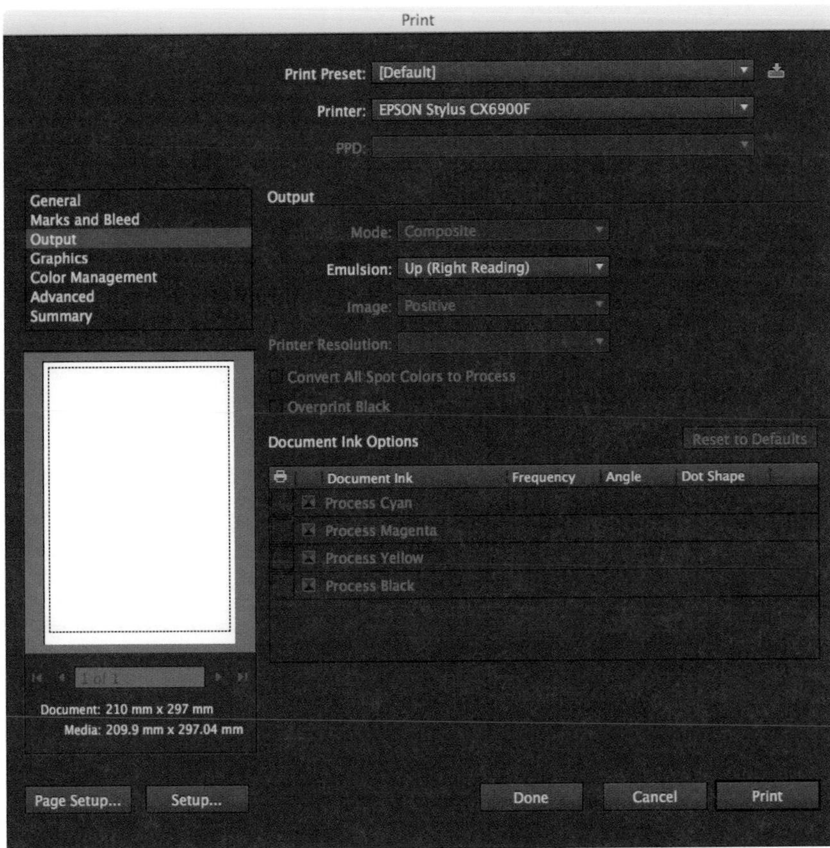

FIG 17-14 The output options in the print dialog box

Graphics

In this section you can set the quality of the printed paths. A high quality means a slower printing speed, while a low quality means a faster printing speed. You can also set the version of the PostScript printing and the type of the data format to be either binary or ASCII.

The Paths section allows you to set the accuracy of the curves using the Flatten Slider. You can also check the Automatic checkbox to allow auto flatten for the curves.

Color Management

In this section, you can set the color management settings between Illustrator and the printer. With color handling, you can set how the color profiles of the document will be handled between Illustrator and the printer. You can either let Illustrator determine the colors, which is recommended, or let the PostScript printer handle the colors. You can also set a printer color profile that you choose from a list of the printer color profiles. The default choice is U.S. Web Coated (SWOP) v2.

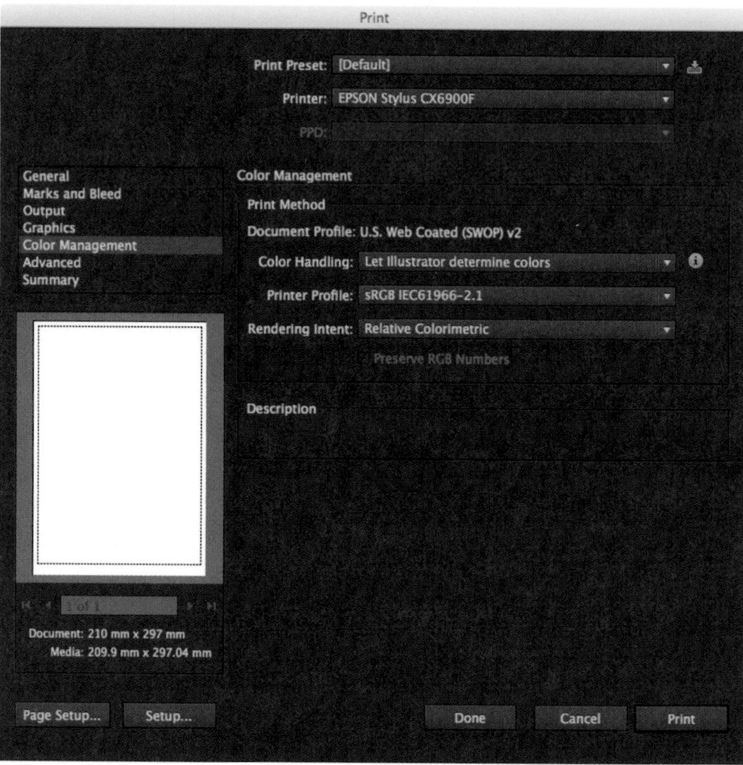

FIG 17-15 The Color Management options in the Print dialog box

The Rendering Intent option sets how the document colors will be handled with the printer colors. There are four options:

1. Perceptual preserves a natural look for the colors, even when the color values change.
2. Saturation creates more vivid and saturated colors, such as for graphs and business charts.
3. Relative Colorimetric compares the white color with the white in the source color and shifts the colors accordingly.
4. Absolute Colorimetric leaves the colors that are under the gamut unchanged, while it changes the out-of-gamut colors to the closest reproducible colors.

Advanced and Summary

The Advanced section includes settings for the overprinting options, and the Summary section gives a brief overview of all of the settings.

Understanding the printing process in Adobe Illustrator is very important, as you need to be aware of all the tips and options to avoid errors in the printed materials. Any error that may occur while printing can be expensive, compared to digital projects. In this chapter we covered some of these tips you should consider when creating printing artwork and the printing options in the Print dialog box.

When you have a printing project, you need to have the required information from the client or your manager to make sure that you have a clear vision about the settings that you will apply to your artwork. One of the best practices is to create a checklist with the requirements to apply to your project to make sure that you do not miss anything. You can practice the different options and see the results and quality in a print house or on your home printer to get a better idea of the concepts and different options we covered in this chapter.

For examples pertaining to this chapter, visit www.illustratorfoundations.com.

CHAPTER 18

Integration with Adobe CS6 Applications

When you review the applications included in Adobe Creative Suite, with its different focuses, you will notice that Adobe Illustrator is part of all of these Creative Suites. This is because Adobe Illustrator is an essential application for different graphic, web, and video projects. As the most powerful vector tool in the Creative Suite, it is a center point and a powerful application that many designers and video experts depend on to create vector artwork, which they use in their projects and as part of their workflow in other applications in the Creative Suite package, such as Adobe Photoshop, After Effects, and Flash.

Before the release of Creative Suite, exchanging resources and files between applications was a difficult process that required many steps and conversions from one file format to another. Now, with the amazing integration between the Adobe products in the Creative Suite release, exchanging files has become much easier and faster. You can easily move your file between applications, as we will see in this chapter. Here we will extend our knowledge with Illustrator to go beyond the amazing application itself. We will learn how easy it is to share Illustrator files with other Adobe applications, especially Photoshop, After Effects, and Flash.

Integration with Photoshop

Adobe Illustrator and Photoshop are close products that many designers use frequently to build designs based on both vector and bitmap images. Generally there are three methods to share artwork with Adobe Photoshop.

Export Artwork as Flattened Image

The first method is simply to export Illustrator artwork as one of the available image formats, such as JPG, PNG, and TIFF. While this method seems easy and does not require extra knowledge as do the next methods, it does not support any options or advantages. For example, you can export your artwork as JPG and open it in Photoshop, but you will eventually need to go back to the Illustrator source to modify the artwork and then export it again and replace it in Photoshop when required.

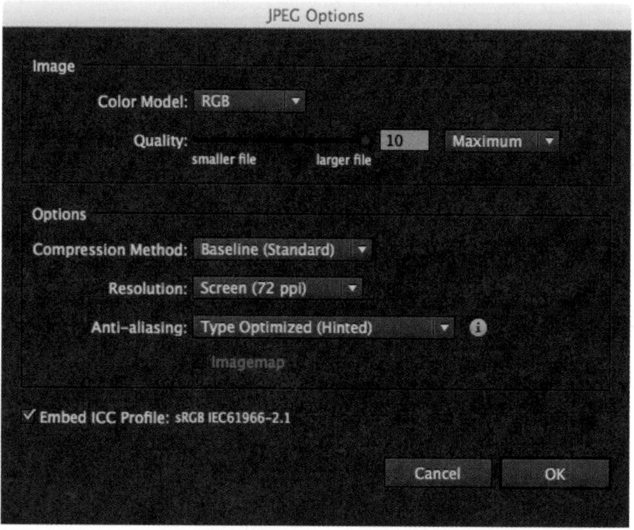

FIG 18-1 Exporting JPG dialog box

In Chapter 15, we covered how to prepare and export artwork in different formats and the options associated with each of these formats. You need to think about issues such as the best format to use and the options available in each format. For example, you need to save the artwork in PNG or GIF format in order to have artwork that supports transparency.

Export Artwork as Photoshop PSD Format

One of the available formats in the Export options in Adobe Illustrator is the Photoshop PSD format. Through this format, you can export the artwork while preserving the Illustrator layers. When you open the document in Photoshop, you will notice that the Illustrator layers are preserved and you can display them in the Layer panel in Photoshop. The biggest advantage of this method is that it preserves the layers. Thus, you can easily edit and modify your artwork through the Layer panel, as shown in the following example:

1. Open the document Export.ai. This file includes a number of objects that are arranged in different layers.
2. From the File menu, choose Export, and select Photoshop PSD format from the extension list.
3. Enable Use Artboards and enter 1 in the range field.
4. The Export PSD dialog box appears. Set the resolution to 300 ppi in the Options section, and check the Write Layers checkbox to make sure that the Illustrator layers will be exported into the PSD document.

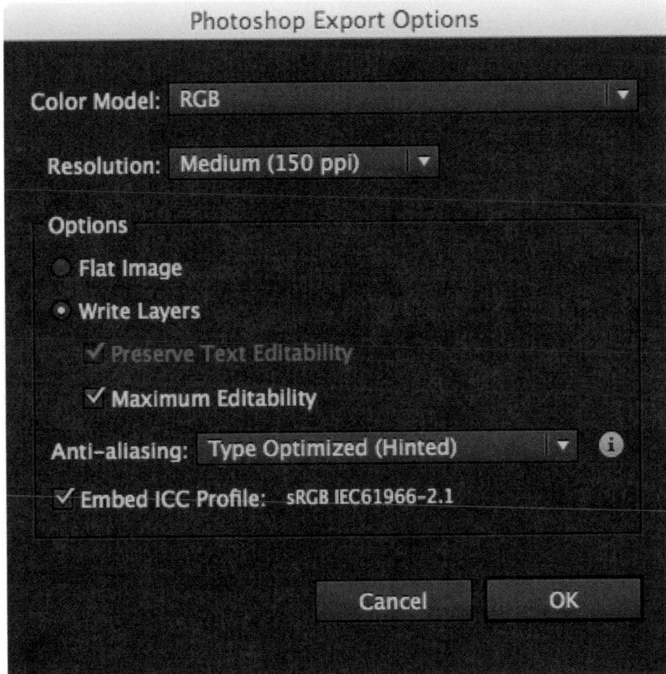

FIG 18-2 Exporting artwork as photoshop PSD

5. Open the saved document in Photoshop.
6. Check the Layer panel. If you cannot see the panel, you can open it from the Window menu.
7. Notice how the layers are preserved and available in Photoshop.

The only disadvantage of this method is that it converts the Illustrator artwork into bitmap raster images, so it will be distorted if you resize it to a larger size. Therefore, it is advisable to export the images in a high resolution to make it easier for you to edit later in Photoshop.

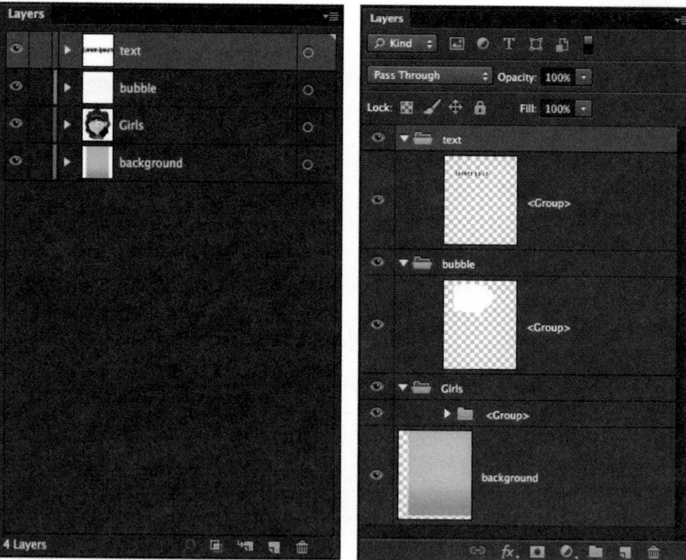

FIG 18-3 The document layers in Illustrator on the right and in Photoshop on the left

Copy and Paste

The easiest way to share elements from Adobe Illustrator and Photoshop is to copy the artwork and paste it into Photoshop. When you paste the artwork into Photoshop, a dialog box appears to let you choose between four different pasting methods: smart object, pixel, path, and shape layer. In the next sections, we will overview these four choices and the results associated with each one.

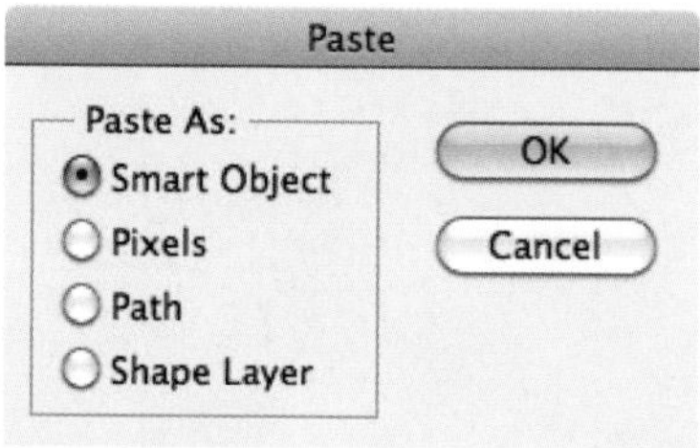

FIG 18-4 The Paste options in Adobe Photoshop

Smart Objects

The concept of smart objects was added to Adobe Photoshop as a new feature in version CS2 and is one of the revolutionary features that allows users to modify artwork without losing quality. The idea behind the smart object is that when you convert an object to be a smart object, Adobe Photoshop keeps an internal copy of the original object. Thus, resizing the object or modifying it does not affect the object quality.

The following figure shows a normal object in Photoshop. Using the Free Transform tool, we have increased and decreased the size of the object, trying to distort it. Notice that the quality of the object edges has been decreased due to the multiple edits in the objects.

FIG 18-5 The normal object edges distortion

The next figure shows the same shape, but this time it is copied from Adobe Illustrator and pasted in Photoshop as a smart object. We have repeated the same size increases and decreases to distort the edges as we did in the first figure. Notice how the edges and object quality are much better than the first one. Adobe Photoshop saves the original object information, thus its quality does not get distorted with the multiple modifications.

FIG 18-6 The smart objects edges quality

In the following example, we will see how to copy artwork from Illustrator to Photoshop using the Smart Objects option:

1. In Illustrator, open the document Smart_object.ai.
2. Select the artwork in the document.

3. Choose Copy from the Edit menu or simply press Cmd+C (Ctrl+C in Windows).
4. Move Adobe Photoshop and create a new document by pressing Cmd+N (Ctrl+N in Windows).
5. Press Cmd+V (Ctrl+V in Windows) to paste the artwork in the screen.
6. The Paste dialog box appears; choose Smart Object from the current choices, and click OK.
7. Resize the object using the resize handlers.
8. Double-click on the canvas or press Enter to apply the Smart Object changes.

FIG 18-7 The smart object in Adobe Photoshop

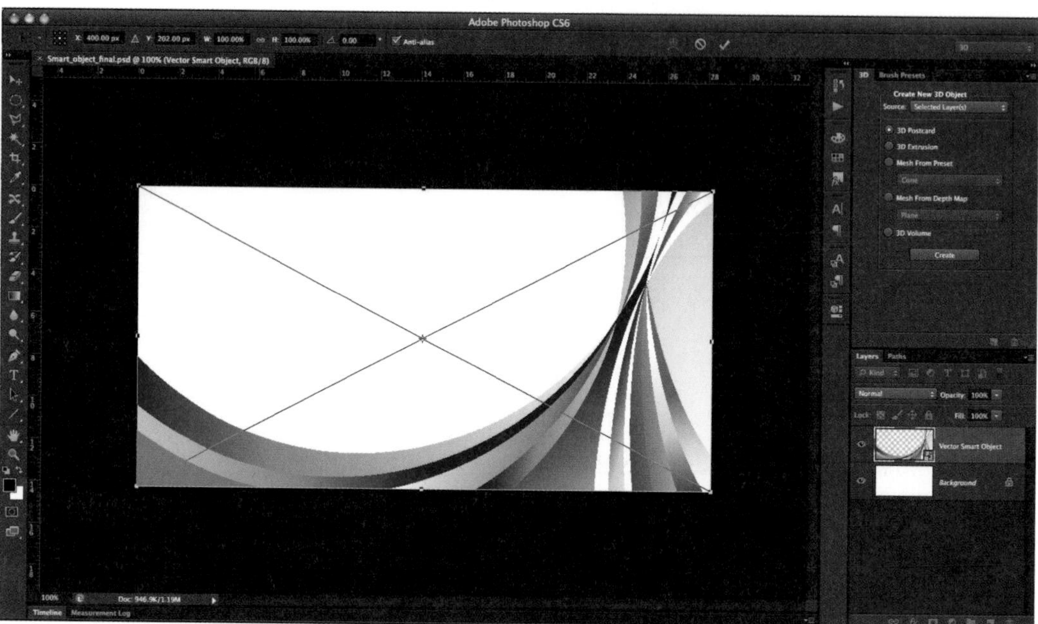

Note

In Photoshop, you can choose the Edit > Free Transform command or press Cmd+T (Ctrl+T in Windows) to resize or edit the smart object size.

One of the big advantages of using smart objects is that you can edit the artwork in its original application. For example, you can double-click the smart object in the Layer panel, and you will notice it opens in Adobe Illustrator, where you can modify and edit it. When you finish editing the artwork and save it, you will notice it is automatically updated in the Photoshop file. Thus, smart objects can save much time and effort when sharing and updating artwork between applications.

Pixel

When you choose the Pixel option from the Paste dialog box, the artwork is pasted in pixel format, even if it was created in vector format in Adobe Illustrator. While the pasted artwork becomes harder to edit than with the previous smart object method, pixel method is useful for large, complex artwork, because pasting these pieces of artwork as vector smart objects takes longer and consumes more CPU processing.

Path

This option pastes the artwork copied from Illustrator as a path. You actually do not transfer the artwork itself; instead, you copy the artwork's outline path. Although this option is not useful in copying the artwork itself, you can use it to copy the outline path for the artwork.

One useful practical example of using this method would be when you create a package design, and you would like to identify its outline in Photoshop. This option allows you to create outline for the package as a path and then you can use or modify this path in Photoshop. The created path appears as a layer in the Paths panel, so you do not see it in the Layer panel unless you select it from the Paths panel first.

In the below steps, we will see how the Path option pastes the artwork as a path in Photoshop:

1. In Illustrator, open the document Smart_object.ai from the section for Chapter 18 on the companion website, http://www.illustratorfoundations.com.
2. Select the artwork in the document.
3. Choose Copy from the Edit menu or simply press Cmd+C (Ctrl+C in Windows).
4. Move to Adobe Photoshop and create a new document by pressing Cmd+N (Ctrl+N in Windows)
5. Press Cmd+V (Ctrl+V in Windows) to paste the artwork in the screen.
6. The Paste dialog box appears; choose Path from the current choices, and click OK.
7. Open the Paths panel from the Window menu.
8. Notice that the artwork outline has been added into this panel as a new path. Select the path layer.

Shape Layer

Pasting the artwork as a shape layer is very similar to the Path option; the only difference is that the shape layer fills the path area with a solid color. By default, it fills the artwork area with the foreground color. You can change the shape color by double-clicking the layer thumbnail.

Smart object, pixel, path, and shape layer give you a variety of options to transfer artwork. Choosing any of these methods to transfer artwork from Adobe Illustrator to Photoshop depends on your project and how you would like to transfer the artwork.

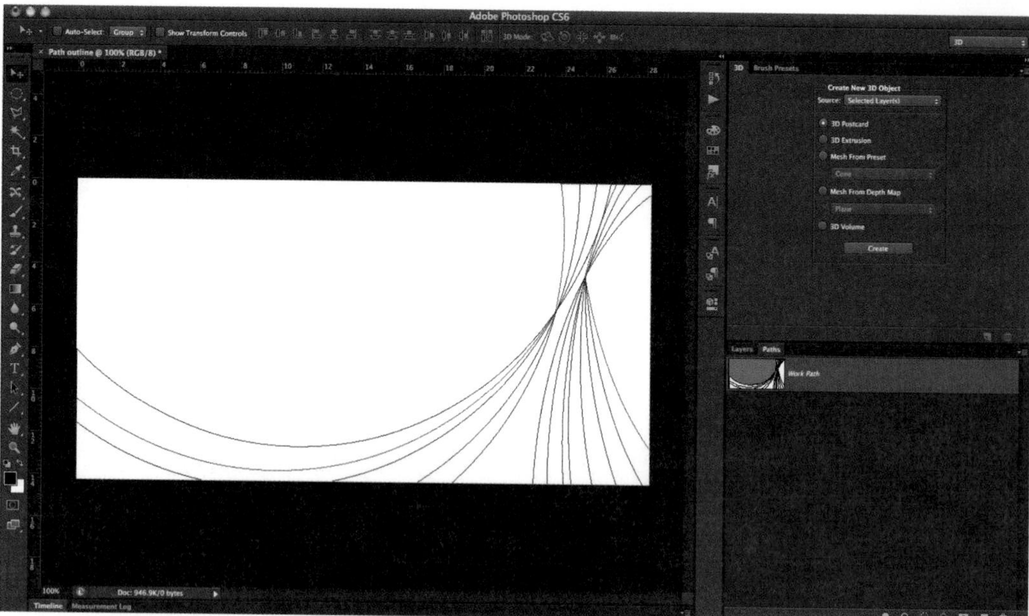

FIG 18-8 The pasted artwork outline path in the Paths panel

Integration with Flash

Adobe Flash is one of the most well-known applications that can create animation and interactive content for web, desktop, and DVD presentations. While Flash includes vector-based sophisticated drawing tools, Adobe Illustrator provides more tools and options to create artwork. Therefore, many Flash designers and animators depend on Adobe Illustrator to create artwork, or part of it, to use in their Flash projects. This requires clever integration between Flash and Illustrator, as we will see in this section.

To transfer artwork from Illustrator to Flash, you can export the Adobe Illustrator file as an image and import it into Flash, similar to the method we discussed for Photoshop; however, this method converts the artwork into bitmaps, which make it distort easily when resized, and hard to edit. The second method lets you copy the artwork from Illustrator and paste it into Flash, or import it into Flash using the Import command from the File menu.

Note

In order to import Adobe Illustrator (AI) or EPS files into Flash, the file must be in the same CS version or a lower version. For example, AI or EPS files need to be CS6 or lower in order to open them in Adobe Flash CS6.

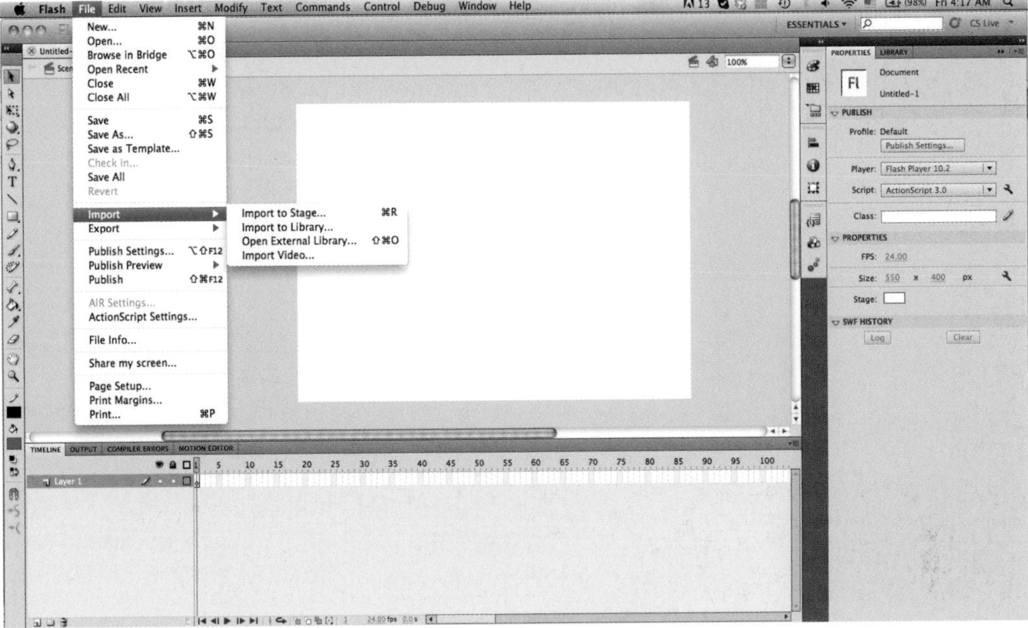

FIG 18-9 The Import commands in Adobe Flash

When importing artwork into Flash, you can either import it to the stage through the Import to Stage command or import it into the Flash library using the Import to Library command. The following example introduces how to import Illustrator artwork into Flash using the Import to Stage command. (In this tutorial, I am using Flash CS5.5, so the document is saved as an Illustrator CS5 document. The versions do not matter here since the import concept is the same.)

1. Open Adobe Flash and create a new document by choosing New Document from the File menu or pressing Cmd+N (Ctrl+N in Windows).
2. Choose ActionScript 3.0 from the New Document dialog box, and click OK.
3. From the File menu, choose Import > Import to Stage.
4. Navigate to the section for **Chapter 18** on the companion website for the document Export.ai, and click Open.

Shortcut

You can click Cmd+R (Ctrl+R in Windows) to import the artwork to the stage.

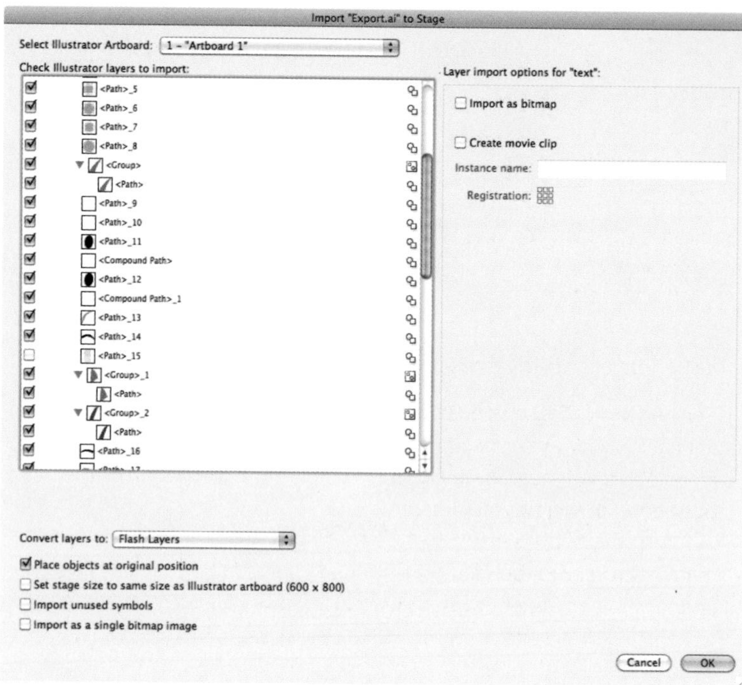

FIG 18-10 The Import to Stage dialog box in Flash

The Import dialog box appears to let you set up the artwork before importing it. The dialog box includes the options discussed next. Artboard List lets you choose the Illustrator document artboard that you would like to import.

The left side includes a preview of the imported document's layer structure. This structure is the same as the file structure in Illustrator. To the left of each layer is a checkbox that lets you choose the layers you would like to import. Also, on the right side of the layer, you can find an icon that identifies the artwork in the layer as bitmap, vector, or symbol.

Note

The symbols are objects that are saved in the Flash library. When you use them on the stage, you are actually using an instance from them, and the source object is kept in the library. These symbols improve your work in Flash and help you add ActionScript code and interact with it.

On the right side of the preview area, you can find the options available for each layer:

- Import As lets you choose either to import the artwork as an editable path, or bitmap.
- Create Movie Clip lets you convert the object in the selected layer to a movie clip symbol and is one of the symbol types to which you can

add interactions. You will see under it a text area where you can add the instance name for coding purposes and set the registration point for the symbol.

Shortcut

You can click Cmd or Shift (Ctrl or Shift in Windows) to select multiple layers to import.

At the bottom of the dialog box, you can find the following options:

- Convert Layers To lets you choose to convert the layers to Flash layers, animation keyframes, or single Flash layers.
- Place Objects in the Original Positions imports the object in its exact position as the original document.
- Set the stage size to same size as Illustrator artboard.
- Import Unused Symbols lets you import the Illustrator symbols that are added in the document but do not appears in the artwork.
- Import as a Single Bitmap Layer flattens the artwork and converts it to a bitmap.

Note

When you have text in the imported Illustrator file, you will have the option to keep the text editable.

Now, let us complete the above example to see how the artwork appears in Flash:

5. In the Import dialog box, select all the layers.
6. Choose Flash Layers from Convert Layers To list.
7. Check Place Objects in the Original Positions.
8. Uncheck the options below it and click OK to preview the artwork on the Flash stage.

You can also try different options and see how they affect the artwork when you import them onto the Flash stage.

Integration with After Effects

Adobe After Effects is a powerful application in the Creative Suite that can create and modify video and animation. Video producers build their animation in it based on different resources, known as footage. These resources can be video, audio, images, or vector objects. The advantage

FIG 18-11 The imported artwork on the Flash stage

of using Adobe Illustrator vector files is that it preserves the layers after importing the file into After Effects and keeps its vector status and quality. You add the Illustrator file to the Adobe After Effects projects as flattened footage that does not support the layers or as a composition with the layers similar to the structure in Adobe Illustrator.

> **Note**
>
> After Effect compositions are similar to scenes that include layers and footage. Each After Effects project can include one or more compositions.

In the following example, we will learn more about exchanging Illustrator files between Illustrator and After Effects:

1. Open Adobe After Effects.
2. From the File menu, choose New > New Project.
3. From the Projects panel on the left, right-click and choose Import > File. If you do not see this panel, you can open it from the Window menu.
4. Navigate to the document Export.ai, and click Open.

The Import dialog box appears to let you set how After Effects imports the file. The Import Kind options let you choose to import the artwork as footage or a composition. If you choose footage, you will need to choose either to flatten

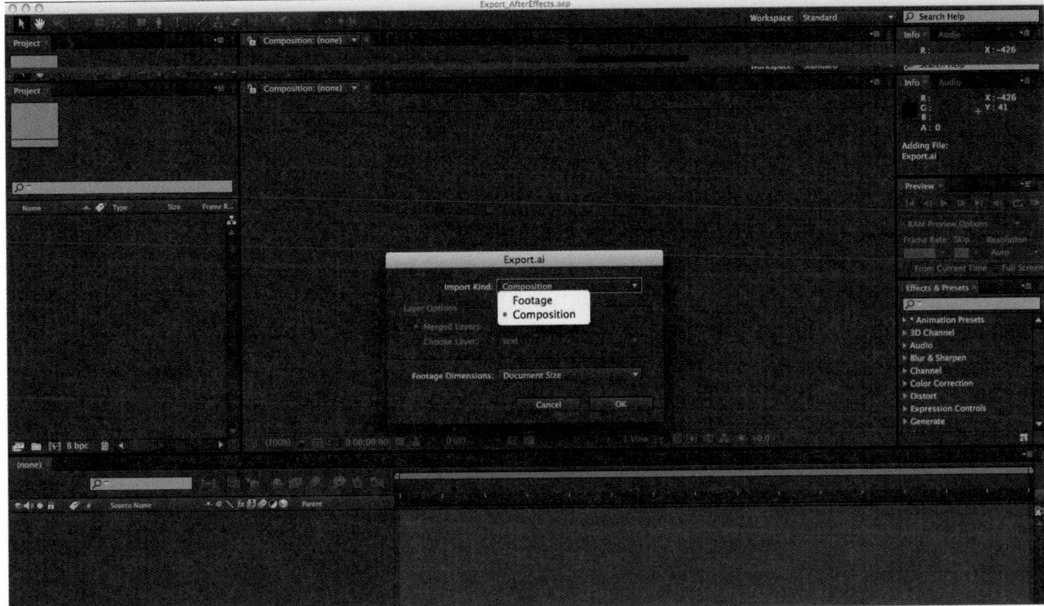

FIG 18-12 The Import dialog box in After Effects

the layers or choose the specific layer from the file to import. If you choose composition, the Illustrator layers will be added to the composition, and you will have the option to set the size of the composition to be the same as the layer size or the original document size.

> **Note**
>
> Unlike importing Illustrator files to Flash, After Effects supports only layers in AI files and imports EPS files as vector image footage.

Let us complete the above steps:

5. Choose composition from the Import Kind list.
6. Set the footage dimensions to the document size, and click OK.
7. From the Project panel, double-click the added composition to open it.
8. Open the Timeline panel to see the layers structure. If you do not see the panel, you can open it from the Window panel.

Taking your Illustrator artwork into the powerful After Effects application helps you to add creative animation and effects easily to your artwork. You can also take your artwork to a new level of animation capabilities.

At this point, we come to the end of the book. We have covered the most important features and tools and how to work with different Adobe Illustrator

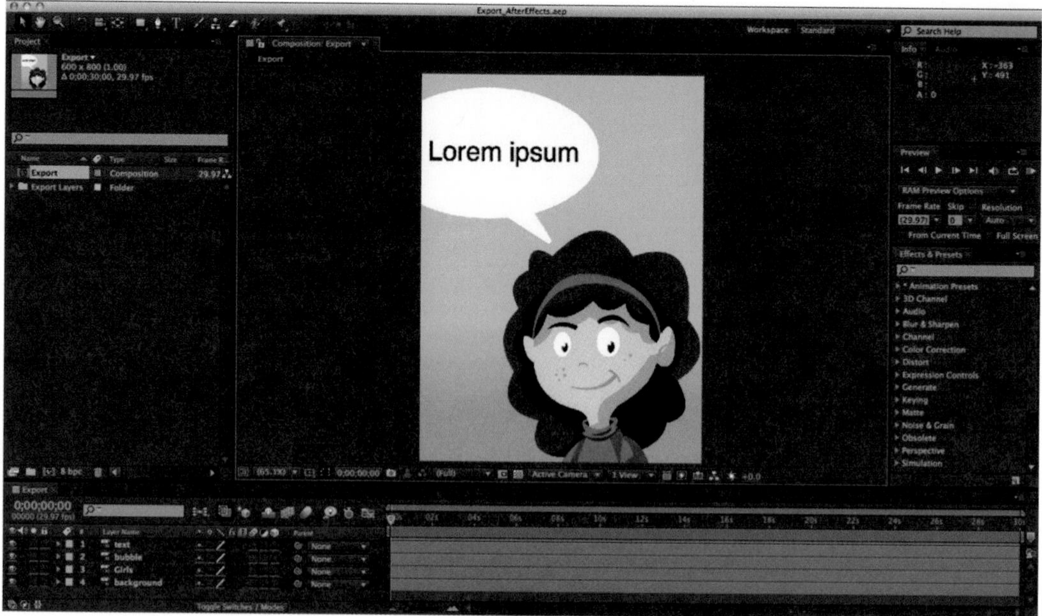

FIG 18-13 The imported artwork composition

options. We learned how to use Illustrator through practical step-by-step examples that cover each tool and its usage in real projects. We also covered the effects, working with text, and working with the different options associated with each tool. At the end of the book, we covered how to integrate Illustrator with other applications in the Adobe Creative Suite: Photoshop, Flash, and After Effects.

The book flows from one tool to another and one feature to another. I recommend it for both self-learning and classes, because it provides students with a useful syllabus based on practical experience. Finally, I hope you find this book useful. You can visit the book's website at http://www.illustratorfoundations.com to follow news and get in touch with me if you have any questions.

For examples pertaining to this chapter, visit www.illustratorfoundations.com.

Index

Boldface page numbers refer figures or tables

A

Adobe Bridge, 9; basic icons and features, 17–18; Batch Rename feature, 21, **21**; Collections panel, 18; Compact mode, 20, **20**; Content panel, 19–20; Export panel, 19, **19**; Favorites panel, 18; Filter panel, 18; folders, 18; interface, **17**; metadata and keywords panel, 20; Output panel, 21
Adobe Creative Suite 6, 5
Adobe Flash, **194,** 261, 300–3, **301–2, 304**
Adobe Illustrator CS, *see also* Adobe Bridge: Auto-Collapse Iconic Panels option, 14; Brightness Level option, 14
Adobe Illustrator CS6: 64-bit support, 6; Canvas Color option, 14; Clear button, 16; customizing workspace, 11–12; Edit menu, 15; Go To Conflict button, 16; gradient to strokes feature, 7, **7**; image tracer feature, 7–8, **8**; keyboard shortcuts, **15**; main sections of workspace, 9–10; Open Documents As Tabs option, 14; panel's size and position, handling of, 10–11, **11**; pattern creation, 6; plug-ins, 13–14, **14**; preferences dialog box, 13–14; scratch disks, 13–14, **14**; Set drop-down list, 15; shortcuts, 13–16; Undo button, 16; user interface, **5,** 5–6; user Interface options, 14; workspace, 8–12, **9**
Adobe Photoshop, 2–3, 69, 242, **242,** 258–9, **259, 294–8,** 294–9, **300**
Adobe Swatches Exchange (ASE), 69
AI format, 3
AI swatches, 69
appearance panel, 232–4, **232–4**
application designs, 2
arc tool, 51–2, **52**
art brush dialog box, 133–4, **133–4**
artboards, 26, 28–32; artboard options icons, 30; artboard panel, 31, **31**; dialog box, **30**; edit artboard option, 29, **29**; modification steps, 29; move/copy artwork with, 30; presets dropdown list, 30; reference point icon, 30; saving, 31–2; show central mark option, 30; show cross hairs option, 30; show video safe area option, 30; steps to choose, 28; width and height options, 31
artwork editing, *see also* effects to artwork; saving artworks: applying transform effects, 116–22; arranging objects, 251–2, **252**; circle compound path, **103**; compound paths, 101–3, **103,** 110; create an old camera film shape, 112–13, **112–13**; creating a gear shape, 106–8, **106–8**; crop icon, 110, **110**; divide icon, 109, **109**; effects menu, 110; exclude icon, 105, **105–6**; Free Transform tool, 121–2; highlight stroke, 114; intersection icon, 105, **105**; merge icon, 110; minus front icon, 105, **105**; moving objects, 116–17, **117**; open-path shapes option, 114; outline icon, 110; panel context menu, 110–11; pathfinder, 103–12; reflection option, 118–19; releasing a shape and expanding a shape, 111; rotating objects, 117–18, **118**; scale dialog box, 119–20, **120**; shape builder tool, 112–14, **114**; Shear Options dialog box, 120–1, **121**; simple compound path, **102**; splitting objects into grids, **115,** 115–16; unite icon, 104, **104**; using shape modes icons, 104

B

bitmap images, 2, 177, 179, **189,** 191; formats, 2; *vs* vector graphics, 3, **264**
blends, 171–5; gear with blend effect, 171–2, **171–2**; intermediate transition between first and last shapes, 174–5; modes in Illustrator, **245,** 245–6; object top menu, 175; rainbow blending effect, 174, **174**
blob brush dialog box, 140–2, **141**
BMP format, 2–3, 177
bristle brush dialog box, 134–8, **135–8**
brushes: art, 133–4, **133–4**; blob, 140–2, **141**; bristle, 134–8, **135–8**; Brushes panel, 124–6; calligraphy, 127–30, **128–30**; global Brush Options, 126; new brush dialog box, **127,** 128; Paintbrush tool, 123; pattern, 138–40, **139–40**; scatter, 131–2, **131–2**; stylus pen, 129–30; tolerances section, 142; types of, 126–42

C

calligraphy brush dialog box, 127–30, **128–30**
CDR format, 3
clean up command, 59, **59**
closed path primitives, 47
CMYK color mode, 63, 71
color features: adding the cartoon character, 68, **68**; for artwork, 64, **64**; CMYK color mode, 63,

71; color guide panel, 72–4; color modes, 63; color panel, 64–5, **65**; color picker dialog box, **63**; color swatches, 63, **66–8,** 66–71, **70**; control panel, 65, **66**; creating new swatches, 71; Edit Color dialog box, 74; file and stroke indicator, **62**; global process color changes, 70, **70**; process colors, 69–71, **70**; RGB colors, 65; spot colors, 71
CorelDraw, 3
corner anchor point, 42, **43**
crop icon, 110, **110**

D

digital graphic designs, 2
divide icon, 109, **109**
3D-look artwork: active plane widget, 209–10, 213–14; checkerboard after 3D rotate effect, **229**; convert 2D text to a 3D object, 219–20, **220**; creating a pattern symbol to 3D object, 221–2, **222**; 3D extrude and bevel, 216–22, **217**; 3D revolve, 223–6, **224–5**; 3D rotation, 226–9, **227**; define grid dialog box, **210,** 211–12; draw hidden faces command, 219; editing the text, **215**; effects, 216; grid, 208–15, **209**; light options, 218–19; Map Art dialog box, 220–1, **221**; perspective grid settings option, **211,** 211–12, **214**; position of the 3D object, 217–18; preserve spot colors command, 219; pushpin bottom tip path, **226**; shading options, 218; turn cap on/off, 218
document management: align new object to pixel grid option, 27; artboards, 26, 28–32; bleeds list, 26; CMYK color system, 26–7; Document Profile, 24, **25**; drop-down menu, 25–6; Flash Catalyst, 26; grids, 37–8; guides, 35–7; icons to change flow of artboard, 26; naming the document, 24; New Document dialog box, 26–7; new documents, 24–7; preferences dialog box, 37–8, **38**; preview mode, 27; raster effect option, 27; RGB, 26–7; rulers, 33–5; saving documents, 32–3; saving illustrator option dialog box, **32**; size drop-down list, 25–6; templates, 27–8, **28**; units drop-down list, 26; XMP metadata, 38–9
drawing in Illustrator: arc tool, 51–2, **52**; clean up command, 59, **59**; closed path primitives, 47; creating an outline for an image, 43, **44**; creating compound paths, 54; ellipse tool, 49, **49**; eraser tool, 55; fidelity controls, 46; flare tool, 50; identifying the path of the object, 42; join and average points, **56,** 56–7; line segment tool, 51, **51**; modifying paths, 55–9; modifying selected path, 46; open paths primitives, 51–5; path eraser tool, 55; polar gird tool, 54–5, **55**; polygon tool, **49,** 49–50; rectangle dialog box, **47,** 47–8; rectangular gird tool, 53–4, **54**; rounded rectangle tool, 48, **48**; selecting anchor points, 42–3; simplify path command, 57–9, **58**; smoothness controls, 46; spiral tool, 52–3, **53**; star tool, 50, **50**; using Pen tool, 41–4; using Pencil tool, 44–6, **45–6**

E

effects to artwork: appearance panel, 232–4, **232–4**; applying feather to the galaxy shape, **240**; changing shape of an object, 237–8, **238**; crop mark, 238; 3D effects, *see* 3D-look artwork; distort and transform effects, 238–9; illustrator effects, 237, **237**; live effects, 235–6, **235–6**; path and pathfinder effects, 240; Photoshop effects, 242, **242**; rasterized artwork, 240; scribble effect, **241**; stylize effects, 240–1; twist effect, **239**; using SVG filters, 241; warp effects, 241–2, **244**
EPS format, 3
eraser tool, 55
exclude icon, 105, **105–6**

F

fidelity controls in drawing, 46
file extensions for Photoshop files, 2
flare tool, 50

G

GIF format, 2–3
Gradient Annotator, 75, 84
gradient tool: appearance drop-down list, 89–90; Apply Gradient to Stroke icon, 77; applying gradient to stroke, 79–81, **80–1**; Aspect Ratio icon, 77; creating gradient, **78,** 78–9; creating of shape of water drops, **87–9**; fill and stroke color indicator, 76; gradient fill list, 77; gradient panel, **76,** 76–7; Gradient Slider, 77; linear gradient, 82–3, **83**; Location value, 77; Opacity value, 77; radial gradient, 83–6, **84**; Rectangle tool, 79, **79**; Reverse Gradient icon, 77; in tools panel, 81–6; Type list, 77; working with meshes, 86–90, **90**
graphs, 199–206; apply artwork to, 205–6, **205–6**; changing color of, 203–5, **204**; column, 202, **202**; data dialog box, 201, **201**; graph properties dialog box, **203–4**; switching between types of, 202–3; tools, 200, **200**
grids, 37; preferences dialog box, 37–8, **38**
guides, 35–7; convert paths into, 36; preferences dialog box, 37–8, **38**; smart, **36,** 36–7; view menu, **35**

H

hiding artwork, 250, **250**

I

illustrator effects, 237, **237**
image to illustrator, adding, **178**
image trace feature, 184–6; color option, 187; document library option, 187; end section of the image trace panel, 188; final look for traced image, **191**; Image Trace panel, 186–91; image traced using low color prebset, **189**; presets context menu, **187**; presets drop-down list, **184,** 184–6; rainbow swatches group, **190**; tracing options that affect final traced image, 188; view drop-down list, 187
InDesign, 69
integration of Illustrator: with After Effects, 303–6, **305–6**; with Flash, 300–3, **301–2, 304**; with Photoshop, **294–8,** 294–9, **300**
intersection icon, 105, **105**

J

join and average command, **56,** 56–7
JPG format, 2–3, 177

L

layer panel, 252–4, **253–4**
line segment tool, 51, **51**
links panel, 179–84; bounding box, 183; context menu, **181**; Embed Image command, 183, **183**; placement options dialog box, 182, **182**; preserve drop-down list, 183; reserve drop-down list, 182, **182**; show section in the context menu, 183; sort section, 183
live effects, 235–6, **235–6**
local artworks, 249–50

M

mask function in Illustrator: applying to artwork, 162–5, **163**; applying to images, 165–7, **166**; creating reflected image, 168, **168**; editing mask, 164, **165**; gaussion blur effect, 169, **170**; gradient panel, 168, **168**; idea behind, 162; layer panel, 164, **164**; make/release clipping mask icon, **167**; opacity, 167–71, **169**; rectangle tool, 170, **170**; transparency panel, 169
merge icon, 110
mesh point, 86
mesh tool, 86–9
minus front icon, 105, **105**
move dialog box options, 116–17, **117**

O

object distortion tools, 242–4, **243**
open paths primitives, 51–5
outline icon, 110

P

PaintShop, 3
Pantone Matching System, 67
path eraser tool, 55
pattern brush dialog box, 138–40, **139–40**
pattern options panel: brick offset options, 97; brick tile options, 97; choosing tile edge color, 98, **98**; converting artwork into pattern, **93–5,** 93–6; copies option, 97; editing mode, 96; H and V spacing value, 97; overlap icon controls, 97; patterns tile tool, 97; rectangle tool, 99, **99**; swatches panel, 96, 99; understanding pattern design, 91–2; width and height options, 97
Pen tool, 41–4; steps to create a path, 42, **42**
place command, 178, **178**
PNG format, 2–3, 177
polar gird tool, 54–5, **55**
polygon tool, **49,** 49–50
printing: advanced section, 291; converting text to outline, 279–81; document setup dialog box, **282**; editable text layout, **279**; general settings, 287–8; graphics, 289; marks and bleeds, 288; new document settings, **278,** 278–9; outline command, **280**; output, 289, **289**; pantone color swatch options dialog box, **284**; print dialog box, 286–7, **287–8**; separations preview panel, 285–6, **285–6**; setting bleeds, **281,** 281–2; setting colors, 284–5, 290, **290,** 290–1; setting raster effects resolution, 278–9; setting up trim marks, **283,** 283–4; text converted to outline path, **280**
PSD format, 177

R

raster images, *see* bitmap images
rasterized artwork, 240
rectangle dialog box, **47,** 47–8
rectangular gird tool, 53–4, **54**
reflect tool, 118–19, **119**
rounded rectangle tool, 48, **48**
rulers: measurements, 34, **34**; shortcuts, 33; video, 35

S

saving artworks, *see also* artwork editing; effects to artwork: anti-aliasing options, 259; document as JPG, 256–7, **257**; document as PDF, 256, **256**; document as Photoshop PSD, 258–9; document as PNG, 257–8, **258**; document as template, 255, **255**; Photoshop export options dialog box, 259, **259**; working with groups, 248–9
saving for web dialog box, 267, **267,** 269; as GIF, 269–72, **270–1**; as

JPG, **272,** 272–3; layout, **276**; as PNG, 273–4, **274**
scatter brush dialog box, 131–2, **131–2**
shape builder tool, 112–14, **114**
Shear Options dialog box, 120–1, **121**
shortcuts: activating Free Transform tool, 121; creating a compound shape, 108; creating a path, 44; hiding the selected object, 250; join and average command, 57; mask, 164; to move object to front of back, 251; opening New Document dialog box, 24, **24**; pattern editing mode, 98; Pen tool, 43; Rotate tool, 118; save for web dialog box, 267; Scale tool, 120; to show or hide rulers, 33; to show or hide the perspective grid, 208; smart guides, 37; to switch between add anchor point and delete anchor point tools, 44; to switch between artboard rulers and global rulers, 33; to switch between the active fill or stroke color, 62; toggle between available measurement units, 35; to transform the perspective for the shape, 122; to unlock all objects, 250
simplify path command, 57–9, **58**
smooth anchor point, 42–3, **43**
smoothness controls in drawing, 46
spiral tool, 52–3, **53**
Split into Grids dialog box, **115,** 115–16
star tool, 50, **50**
swatch panel to color, 63, **66–8,** 66–71, **70**
Swatches Library icon, 67
symbols: alert message before deleting symbols, **196**; aligning to pixel grid, 195; converting artwork to, 194–6; editing, **197,** 197–8; libraries, **196**; modifying, 197–9; new symbol icon, **195**; option icon, 196; panel, **195**; redefine symbol command, 198; 9-slice scaling, 195; symbol properties dialog box, **194**

T

templates, 27–8, **28**
TIFF format, 177
typeface and fonts in Illustrator: adding text inside a path, 157–9; align panel, 149; area text options, 152–4, **153**; character menu, 149; color icon, 148; convert any text into a path, 160; envelope icon, 149, **151**; mesh options, 150–1; paragraph direction icons, 149; paragraph panel, 152, **152**; place command dialog box, **144, 146**; placing text into Illustrator file, 144–7, **145**; recolor artwork icon, 149; stroke size drop-down list, 149; text editing, 148; text on a path applied to brochure design, **159**; text properties, 148–9, **151**; threading the text area, **154,** 154–7; transform panel, 149; type tool, 146; warp options, 149–50, **150, 155, 157**

U

unite icon, 104, **104**

vector graphics, 2–3, 177; edges of, 3; formats, 3; *vs* bitmap format, 3; *vs* bitmap images, **264**
video sequence images, 2

W

Wacom Intous, 45
web and interactive applications, Illustrator for: advanced section of new document dialog box, 262; align new object to pixel grid option, 266; anti-aliasing images, **264–5,** 264–6; creating graphics elements, 263; optimizing graphics, 266–74; preparing documents for, 262–4; presets options, **262**; previewing artwork, 263–8, **264–5, 268**; resolution choices, 263; save for web dialog box, 267, 269–74; slicing web layout, 274–6, **275**
web design, 2

X

XMP metadata, 38–9